HELEN SHAW is known as one of the great fly-tyers of all time. She is a member of the fishing Hall of Fame and has been honored as one of the world's greatest fly-tyers by the Sportsmen's Club of America. An experienced teacher of the art, Miss Shaw has also contributed to numerous magazines and newspapers. *Esquire* refers to her as a legendary figure in the world of fly fishermen.

Fly-Tying

By HELEN SHAW

MATERIALS

TOOLS

TECHNIQUE

[THE] RONALD PRESS COMPANY

NEW YORK

10MP

Library of Congress Catalog Card Number: 63–14904

PRINTED IN THE UNITED STATES OF AMERICA

Preface

Basically, fly-tying is a simple process of binding various materials to a hook with thread. It appears difficult only to one who has never really tried it, for the "secrets" of fly-tying are just individual ways of accomplishing a particular step in the making of a fly.

Although flies are tied of fragile materials, they must be made as durable as possible. All flies are vulnerable to the teeth of fish they will encounter, to the sunken rocks of stream or lake, and to the branches into which they may be inadvertently cast. None are indestructible, but a carefully tied fly will long outlast a carelessly tied one.

In order to fasten the materials to the hook quickly and securely, the tyer must learn how to handle them well. He must know how they will behave in his hands and the effects he can achieve with them. Since each material has its own characteristics, the tyer must know what to expect and how to cope with them in order to use them to their best advantage and to his own satisfaction.

Practice materials for the fly-tyer are always at hand, once he has acquired the necessary tools and a few hooks. For example, a nymph can be made with a strand of yarn, a small, soft feather, and a length of sewing silk. It will probably be no orthodox pattern, but what of this? Many a fish has been caught on a nameless fly! The fact that the fly may resemble no insect ever seen is unimportant. The relationship of some very successful fly patterns to real insects is purely imaginary, anyway.

With the sewing silk, the piece of yarn, and the little feather, a great deal of valuable practice-tying can be done and the unfamiliar procedure of binding them to a hook will gradually lose its mystery as the tyer becomes adept at handling them.

I have been very fortunate to have had the indispensable help of Hermann Kessler, who took all the photographs in this book.

Helen Shaw

January, 1963

Contents

Photograph Sequences

Fly-Tying

Tools

A minimum selection of tools and materials is all that is necessary for the beginner. Even for a professional tyer, it is preferable to have a small, useful collection of equipment, carefully chosen. The initial cost is moderate and one is not burdened with materials or equipment for which there is little or no real need. The addition of special materials or extra pieces of equipment can always be made.

VISE. The vise must be adjustable for height and have a clamp base that will provide a firm grip on the edge of the tying table. Its jaws should be tapered, of excellent-quality steel, and adjustable for either large or small hooks. A lever control is comfortable to use; it is quickly and easily raised with an upward movement of the left hand to open the jaws, while downward pressure on it securely tightens them against a hook.

SCISSORS. One good pair of scissors will suffice. It should be of good steel with straight, sturdy blades not over 4 inches in length including the finger grips. The blades should taper to a fine, sharp point.

PLIERS. Several good fly-tying pliers are available, and all are made to remain closed without pressure and to open when pressed. Select whichever style you prefer, but make sure that the jaws have a firm grip.

STYLET. A serviceable one can be made by embedding a needle in a wooden dowel. The needle point is necessary for removing varnish from the hook eyes of finished flies, for releasing hackle barbs that have been bound down in tying, and for "picking out"

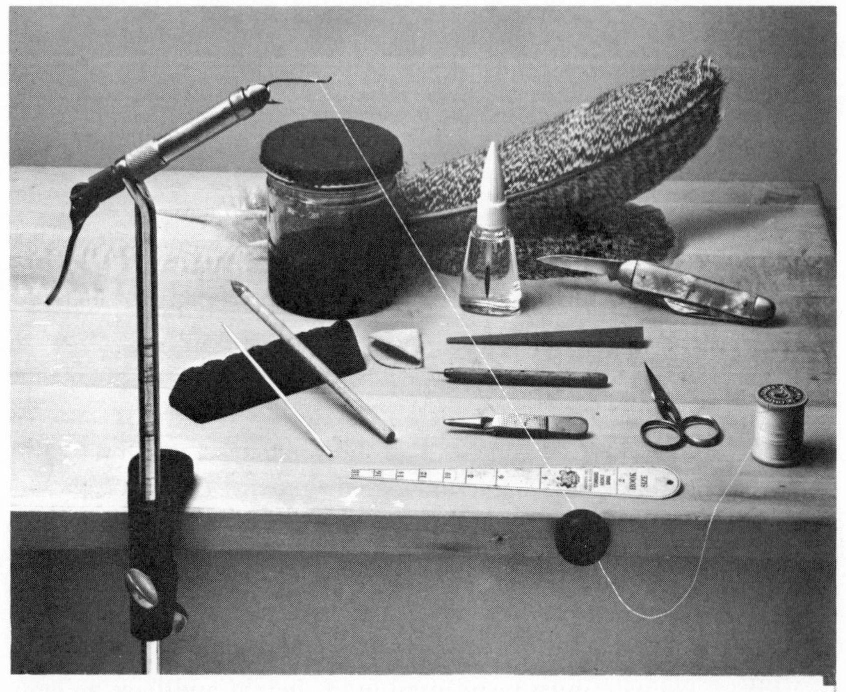

dubbing bodies. A small hatpin can be substituted for this useful tool.

RUBBER BUTTON. Attached to the front edge of the tying table approximately 8 inches to the right of the vise base, the rubber button becomes a grip to hold the tying thread and to maintain tension on it while the tyer's hands are busy elsewhere. It is called a rubber bumper and has a screw center. It is inexpensive and can be purchased at any hardware store.

WOODEN DOWELS. A few dowels the length and diameter of a pencil will be useful, as a wax stick, for a stylet handle.

HOOK HONE. A good hone is always necessary to insure needle-sharp points on all hooks. There are several available shapes from which to choose, all of which are approximately 4 inches in length.

HACKLE GAUGE. For use in determining the size of hackles to use for various hook sizes, which is roughly 1½ times the distance between the point and the hook shank.

The following, although technically not tools, are necessities basic to the craft of fly-tying.

WAX. The wax I use on tying thread is made according to a very old recipe with powdered or crystal rosin and turpentine. A wide-topped glass jar (approximately 2¾ inches wide by 3¼ inches high) is filled to a depth of 1 inch with rosin. Just enough turpentine to saturate the rosin is added. The jar is set uncovered in a pan of hot water over a very low flame and allowed to remain until the rosin and turpentine become a clear amber substance about the consistency of honey. Removed from the heat, the jar may be covered and allowed to cool. The wax will thicken as it cools until semi-firm. This wax, insoluble in water, will eventually set or harden, acting as a binder to the materials it touches.

WAX PAD. A small piece of oilcloth, about 2 inches square, makes a good holder for a little of the wax. A few inches of tying thread is pulled gently through the wax when the tyer is ready to begin work. A fresh pad can be made whenever needed. I have found this method of waxing thread to be desirable because it permits the tyer to regulate the amount of wax he wants anywhere throughout the construction of a fly.

LACQUER. The head of a fly and any other exposed windings of thread should be covered with a penetrating waterproof varnish or lacquer to give them a permanent finish. A bottle of colorless nail polish can be used, since it comes in a small, convenient quantity, is colorless, has its own applicator, and is inexpensive. The little brush, however, should be trimmed to a fine point.

TYING TABLE. The tying table should be large enough to hold all necessary tools and materials required at the moment without crowding. A drawing board 20 by 26 inches makes an excellent tying surface which can be placed wherever the tyer finds it most convenient to work. It has a smooth finish and can be easily stored when not in use.

With the vise attached firmly to the front edge, the lever at the left, the hook in the vise should be centered and at a height comfortable for viewing while tying is in progress. Adjust the jaws to grip the hook firmly but not overtightly, so that you may also release the hook quickly. Attach the rubber button to the front edge also, approximately 8 inches to the right of the vise base. A small finishing nail driven into the top surface a few inches to the right of the rubber button becomes a spindle to hold your spool of tying thread. This arrangement gives you the maximum free area for manual movement around your vise.

Lay the scissors, pliers, stylet, and prepared wax pad within convenient reach of your hand. Always replace each in the same spot so that reaching for them will become automatic, an economy of movement that will be valuable to you later. Establish this good habit from the very beginning, and once you have mastered handling your materials, you will find that your speed in tying will increase easily because of it.

Tying Thread

The technique I use may be called the continuous-thread technique. When employing this method, the most important thing to remember is to keep the tying thread taut. The thread is the binding medium, anchoring all materials to the hook. It must be kept taut from the beginning until the finishing knot secures the entire fly. After you have learned to manipulate the materials easily and to secure them properly to the hook, you will begin to combine a tail and body, a body with wing and hackle, and so on. The thread will be the continuous, uninterrupted binder for all the parts or sections of which the fly is composed.

The following photographs show each part of a fly being tied onto a hook with the remainder of the hook bare. Thus, a wing is shown being tied on alone in order to emphasize its position on the hook and the manner in which it is bound there. Tying each part of a fly should be practiced this way repeatedly so that you will concentrate solely on one part at a time, thus acquiring the ability to tie each part quickly and well.

A black salmon-fly hook was selected for demonstration. A hook of this size is preferable for all practice-tying. The turned-up eye prevents the tying thread from slipping forward off the hook. The thread used is an ordinary spool of white nylon thread found wherever sewing supplies are sold.

If some of the instructions seem to be repetitious, this is because fly-tying itself is repetitive. Until the motions necessary to tying each part of the fly become automatic, reiteration is necessary here but will be held to a minimum.

The first step in fly-tying is to wax the tying thread.

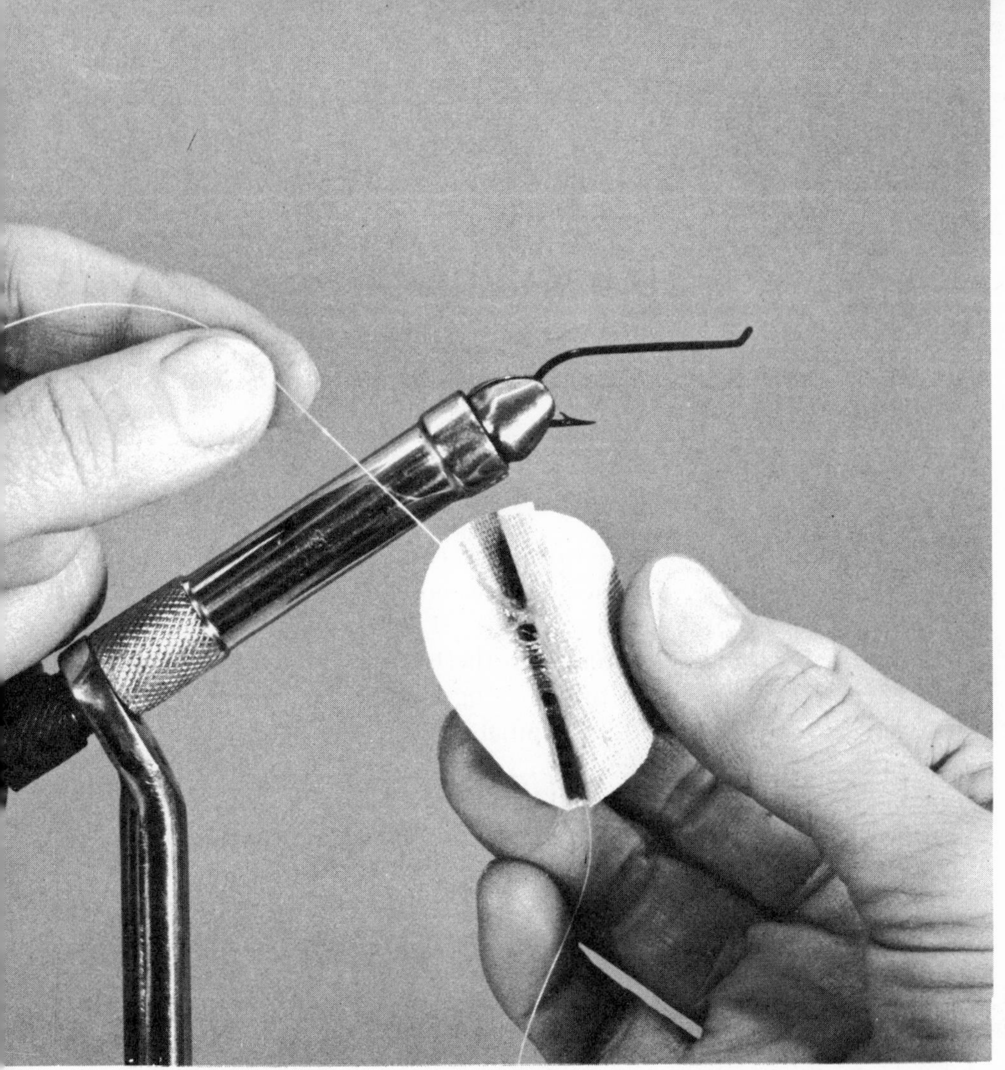

1a. Draw the thread directly from the spool on its spindle. Wax about 6 inches of it at a time. Lay the thread across the wax on the open wax pad.

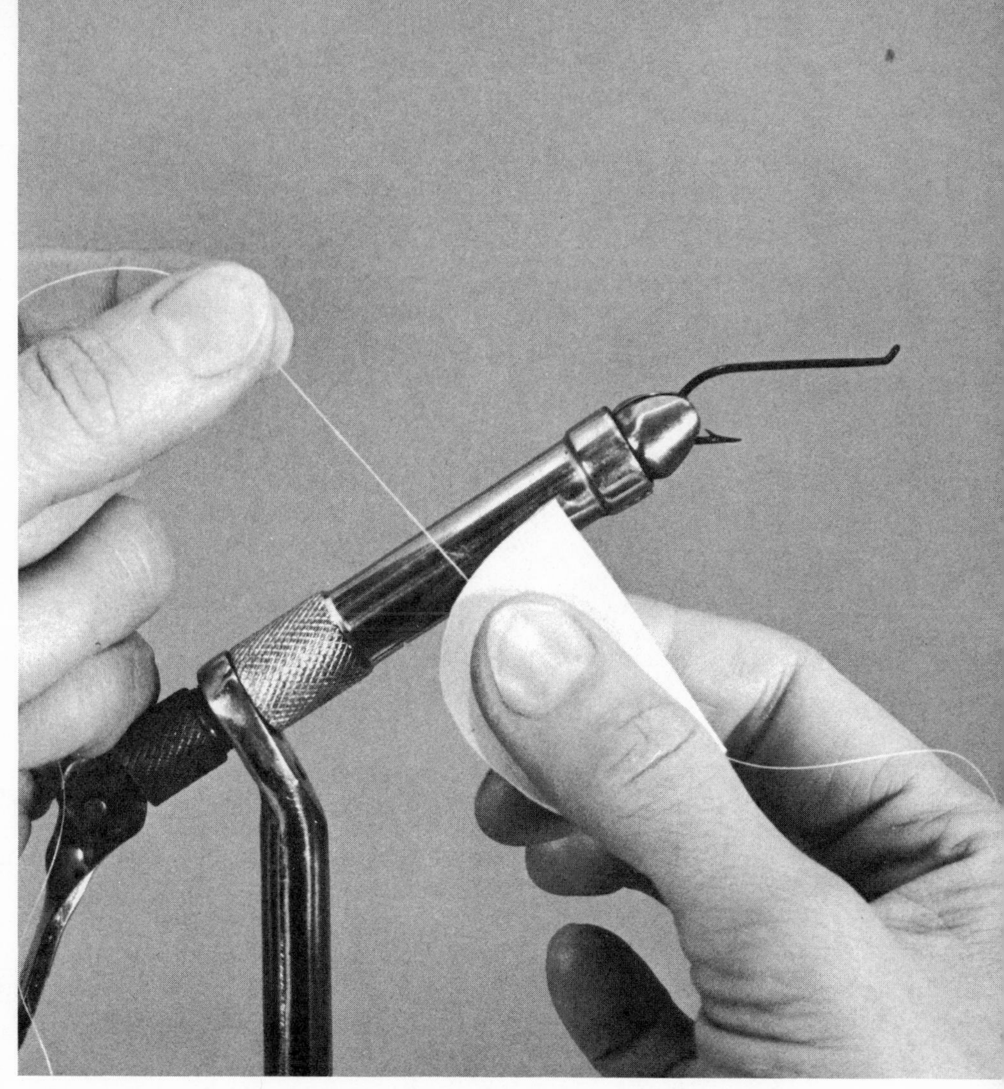

1b. Fold the wax pad over the thread. Hold it firmly enough to force the thread into the wax. Pull the end of the thread through the wax. Any excess wax will be removed by the unwaxed edge of the pad. The waxed thread should be "tacky," not sticky. If too much wax clings to the thread, draw it through the pad again close to the edge away from the waxed center.

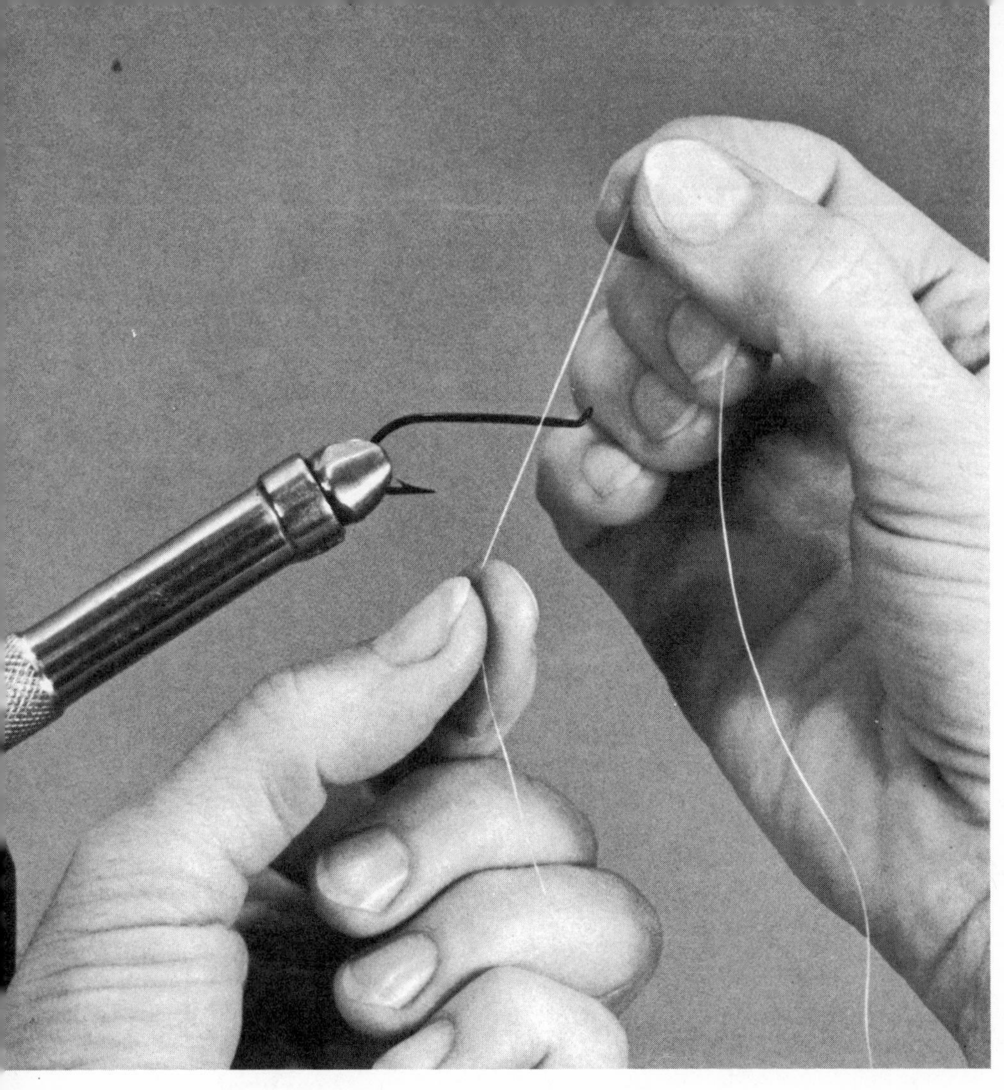

2a. Hold the end of the waxed thread in the left hand and place the thread against the hook at "wing position" as shown.

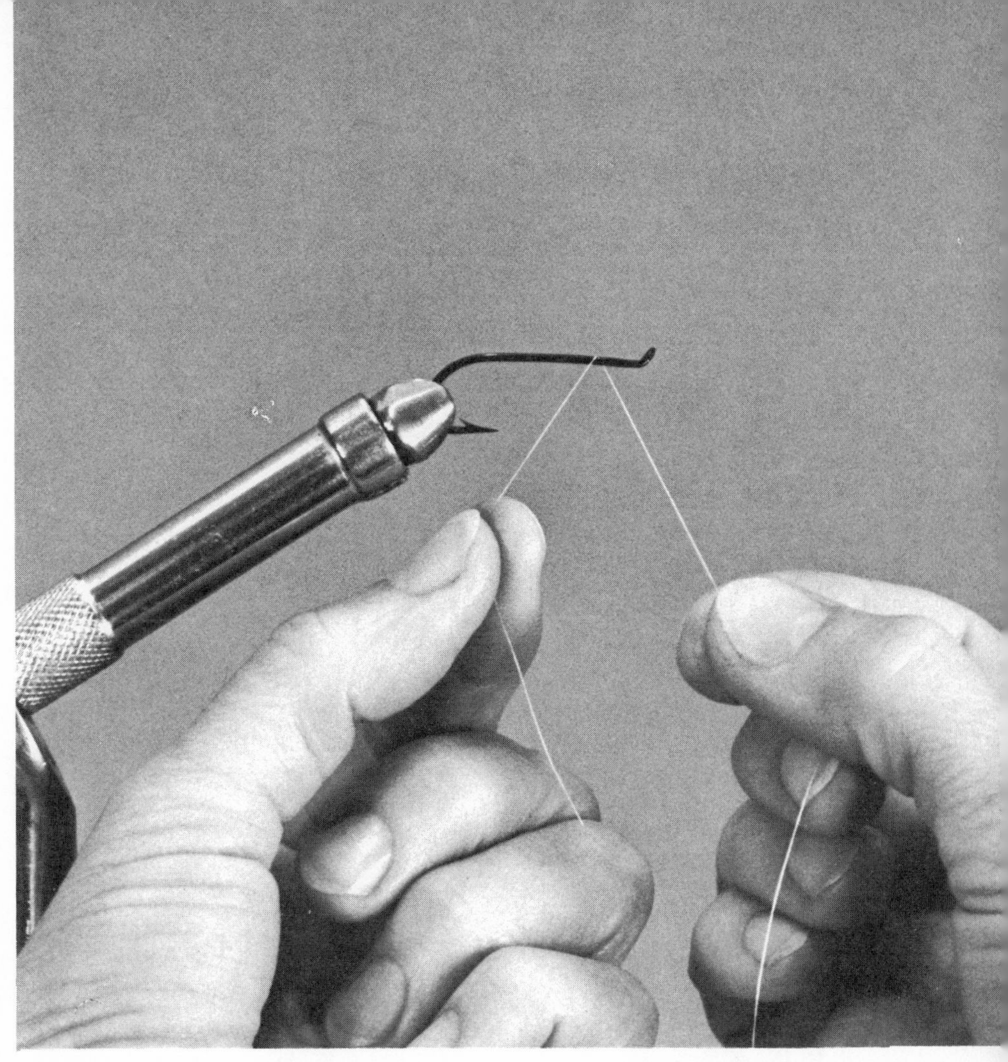

2b. With the right hand, carry the thread down behind the hook. Notice that the thread is held taut against the hook, the fingers gripping it a short distance from the hook.

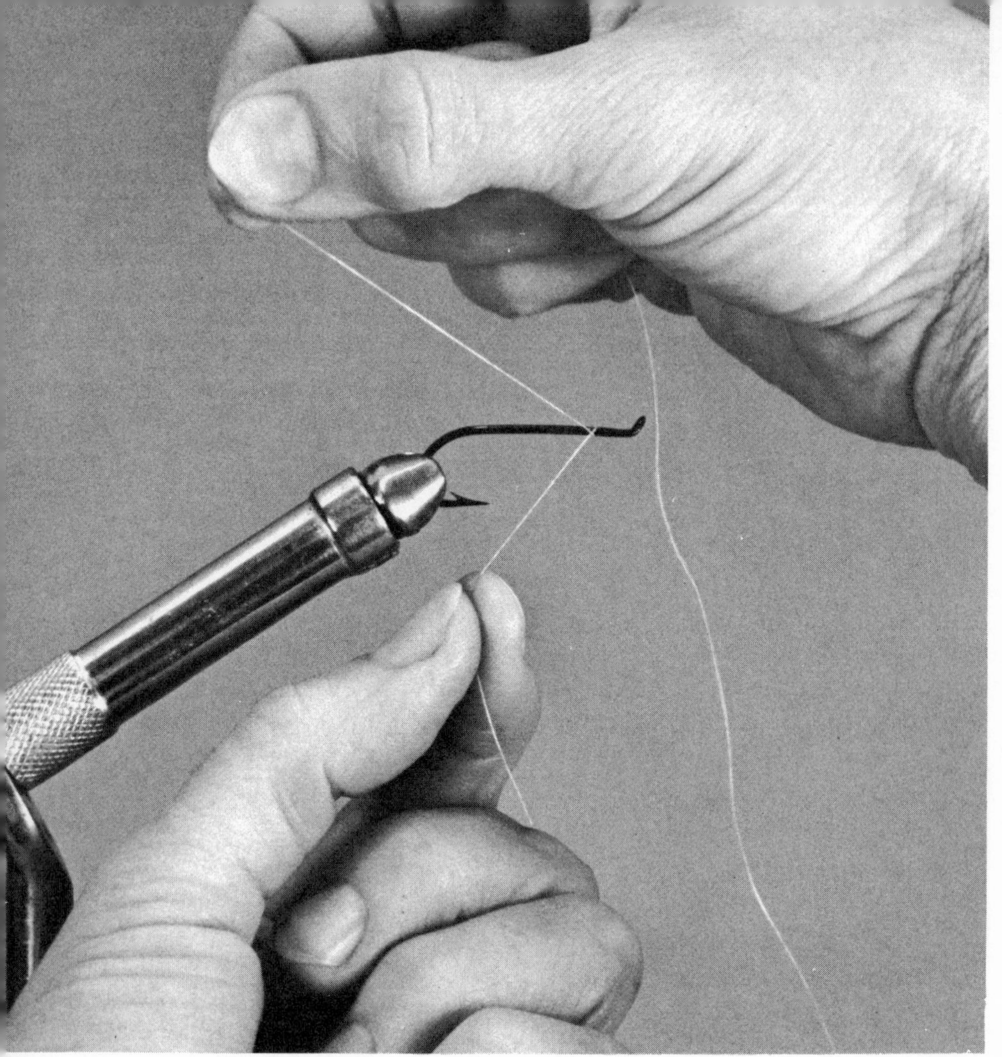

2c. Continuing with the right hand, bring the thread up in front of the hook and across the thread held against the hook with the left hand.

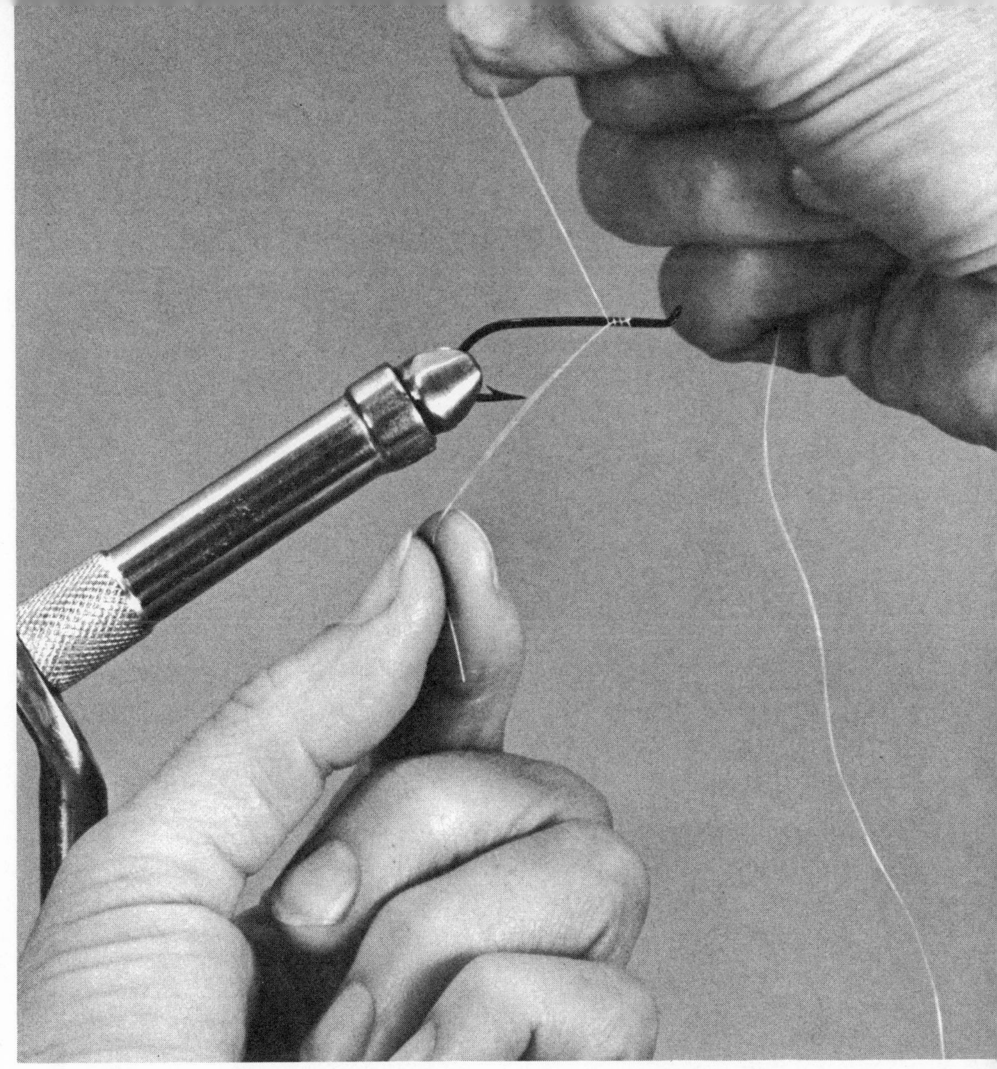

2d. Carry the thread down behind the hook and up in front three times, creating a spiral winding, each turn of thread close to the preceding one but farther away from the hook eye, binding the thread held by the left hand securely against the hook.

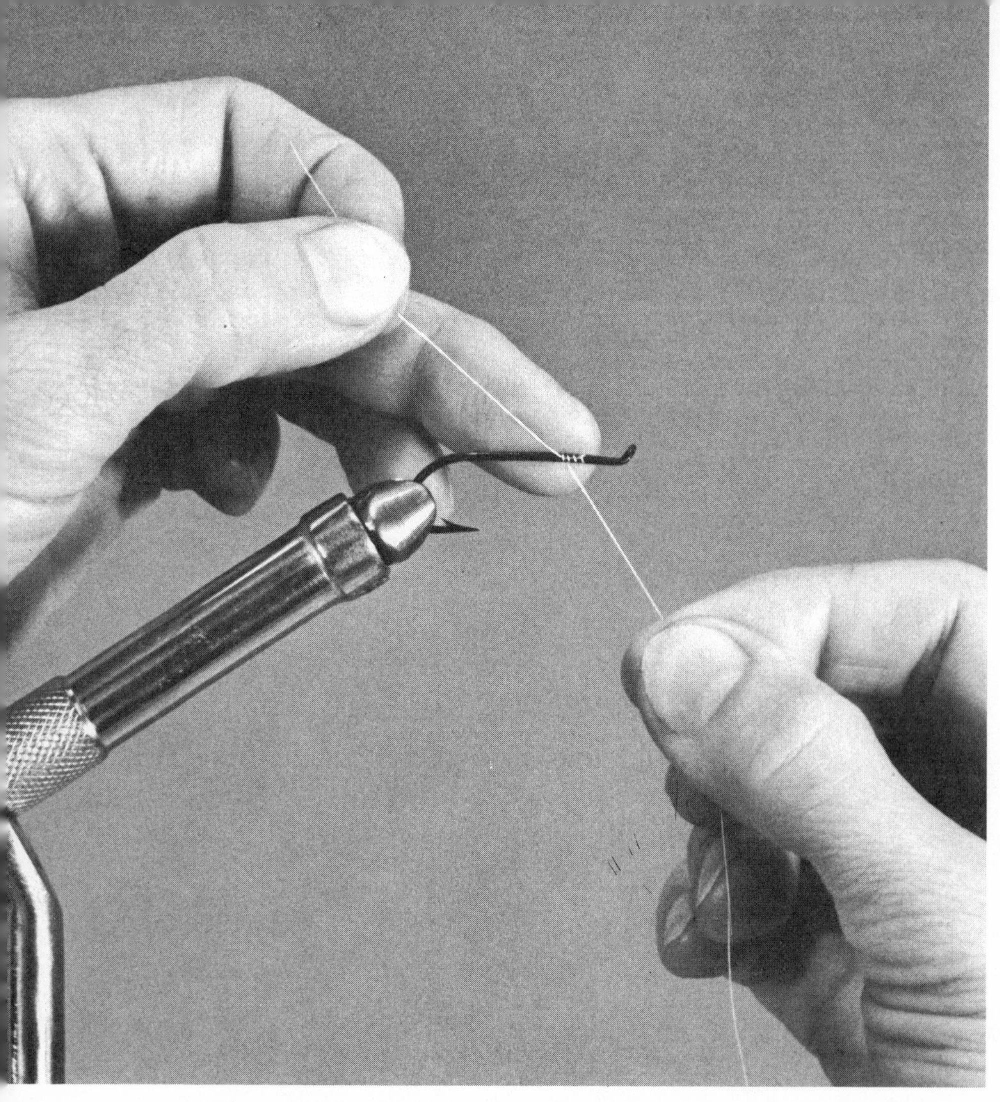

2e. Keep a grip on the end of the thread with the left thumb and forefinger and extend the middle finger to press against the thread winding, to prevent it from loosening while the right hand slides down the thread and catches it snugly behind the rubber button.

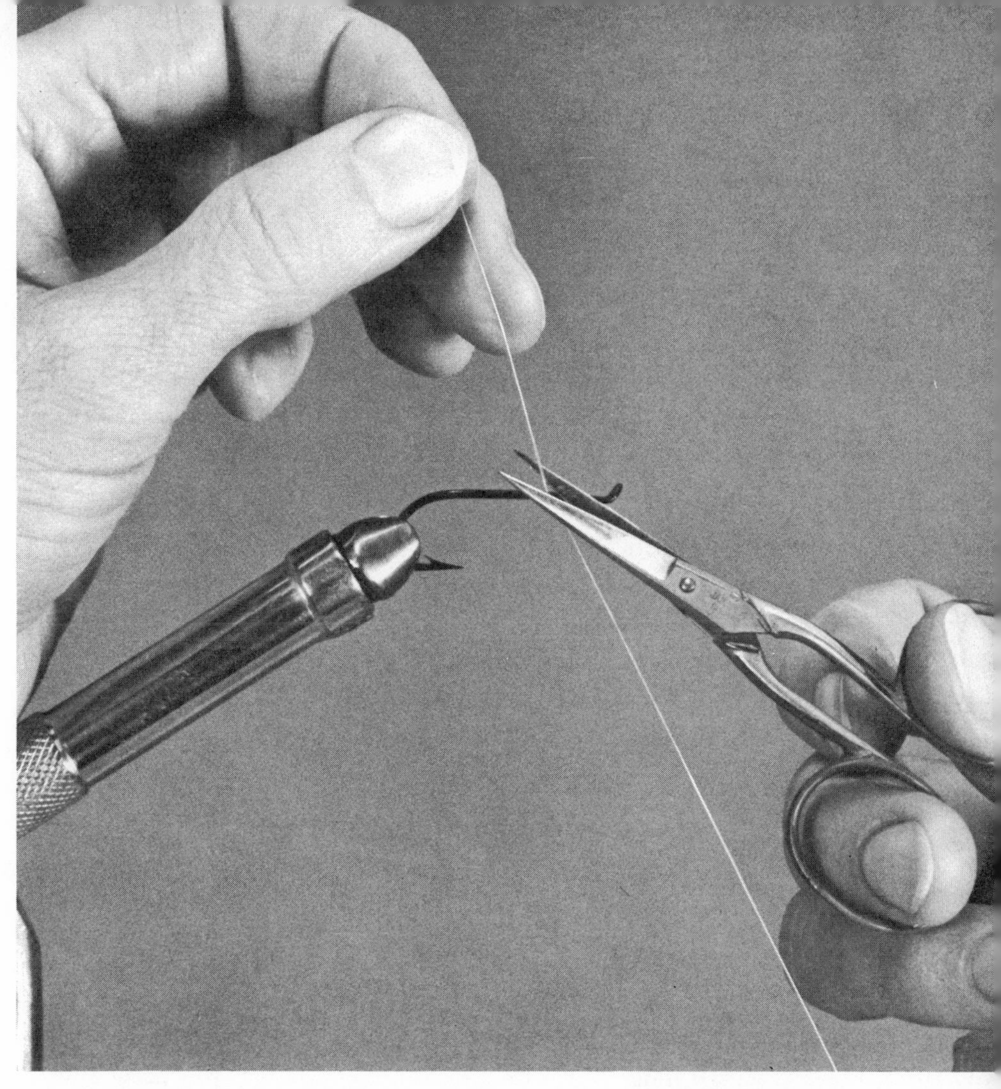

2f. The rubber button will maintain tension on the thread, freeing the right hand to pick up the scissors and cut off the short end of the thread close to the windings on the hook. The thread is attached to the hook at "wing position." Now! *Unwind* the thread from the hook and follow the instructions once more from the beginning. Practice attaching the thread until you can do it quickly and with assurance.

Tinsel

Tinsel is the sparkle and flash that is added to many an otherwise drab fly, providing the glitter which will help attract attention to the fly under water. Light in weight and quite tough because of its tensile strength, tinsel adds protection to fly bodies when it is wrapped over other materials in an open spiral. Used alone on a hook, it makes a smooth and shiny body.

The thin, flat strips of this bright tarnish-proof metal come in three general widths: fine, medium, and wide. Of the widths available, the fine and medium are the easiest to handle, the medium being adaptable to the most frequently used sizes of hooks. Fine tinsel is necessary only for very small flies, the wide tinsel for very large ones.

Flat tinsels may be plain or embossed with a pattern which breaks the shiny surface into many facets.

Oval and round tinsels are made of the flat metal wrapped over a central core of threads. These tinsels are used for added texture on a fly, giving a corded appearance when used alone as a body or making a raised rib when wound over a body of flat tinsel or other material. All tinsels come in colors of gold and silver; the fine flat tinsel is available in other colors as well.

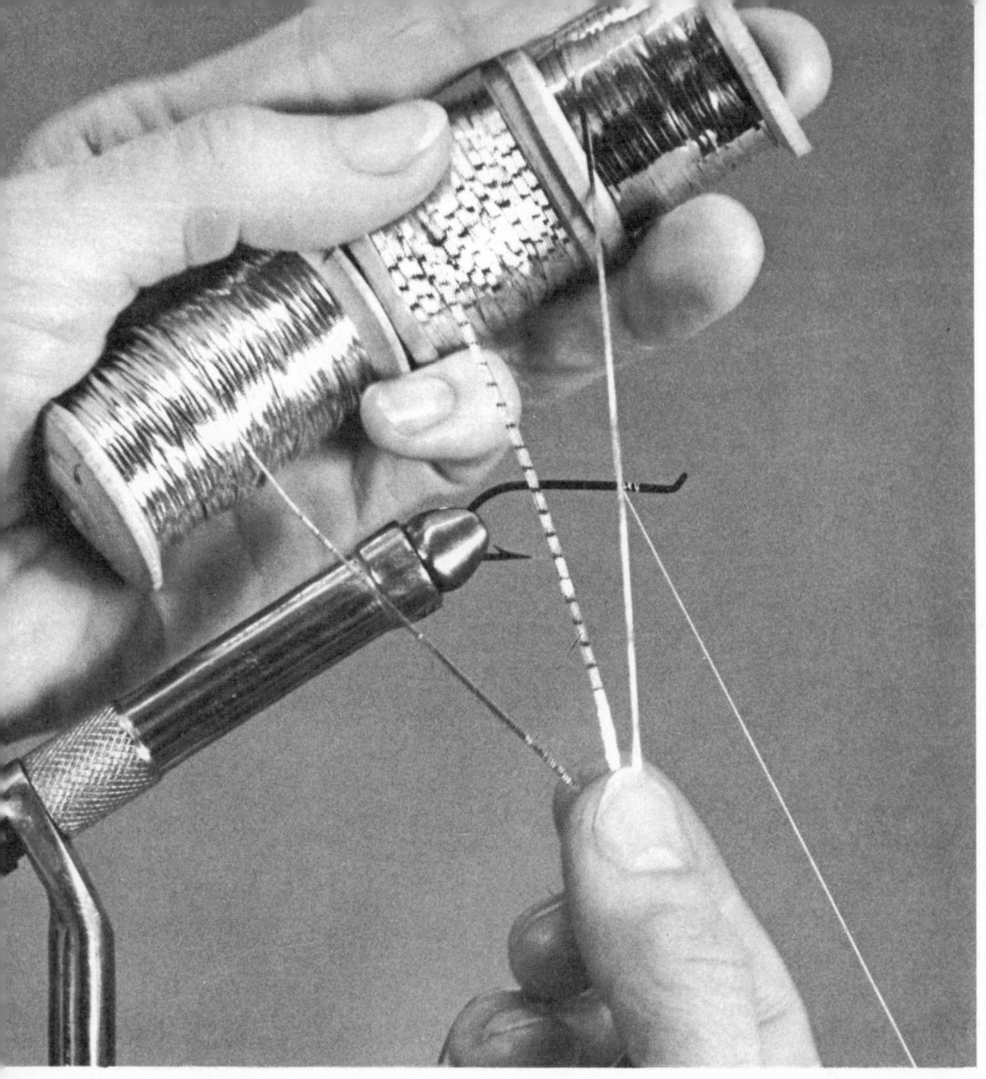

3a. *Left to right:* oval tinsel, embossed flat tinsel, plain flat tinsel. The embossed and plain tinsels are handled alike. The simplest tinsel body is made of plain flat tinsel wound directly onto the hook. Cut off a piece approximately 1 foot in length, making the cut a diagonal one. The thread is attached to the hook at "wing position."

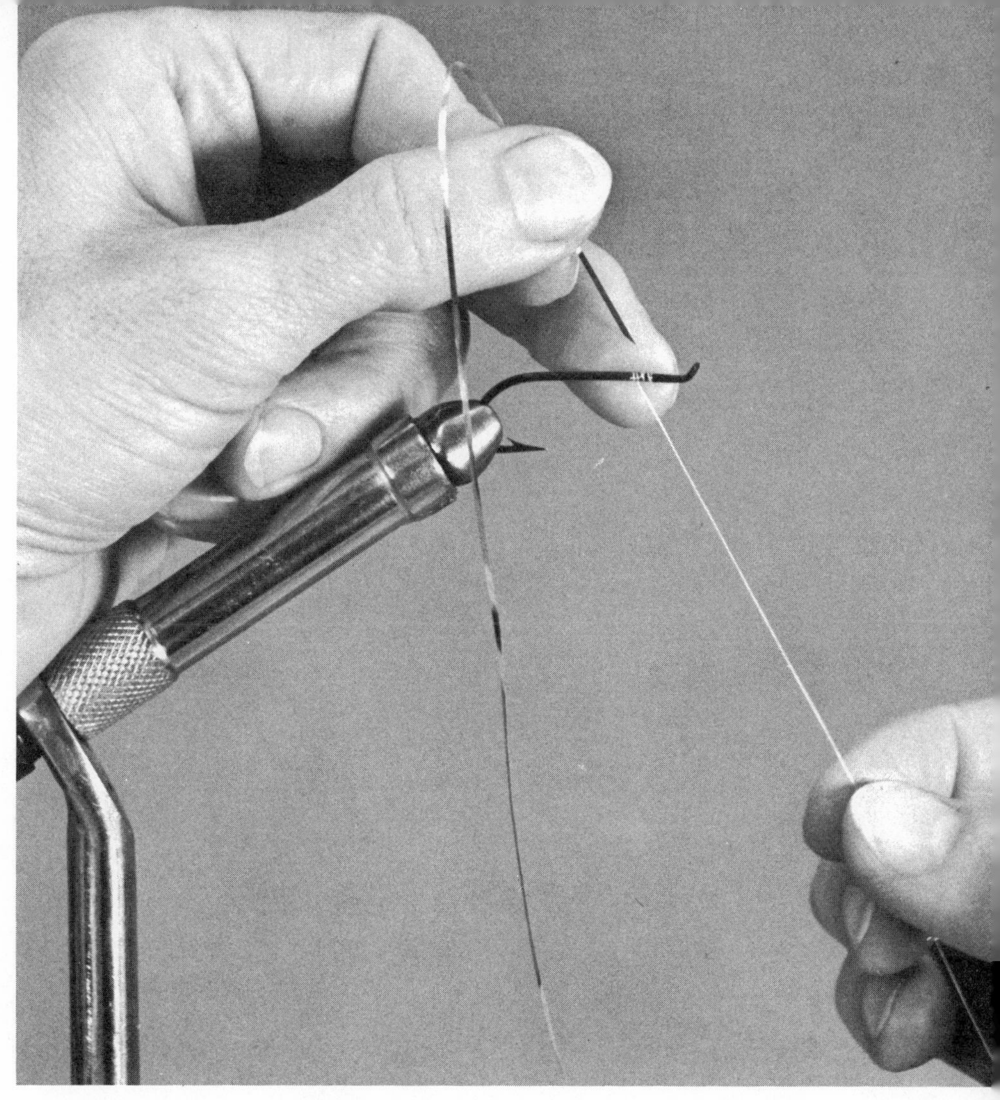

3b. Hold the tinsel between the left thumb and forefinger and extend the middle finger to press the tying thread against the hook while releasing it with the right hand from the rubber button. This use of the left hand should be repeated whenever it is necessary to release the thread.

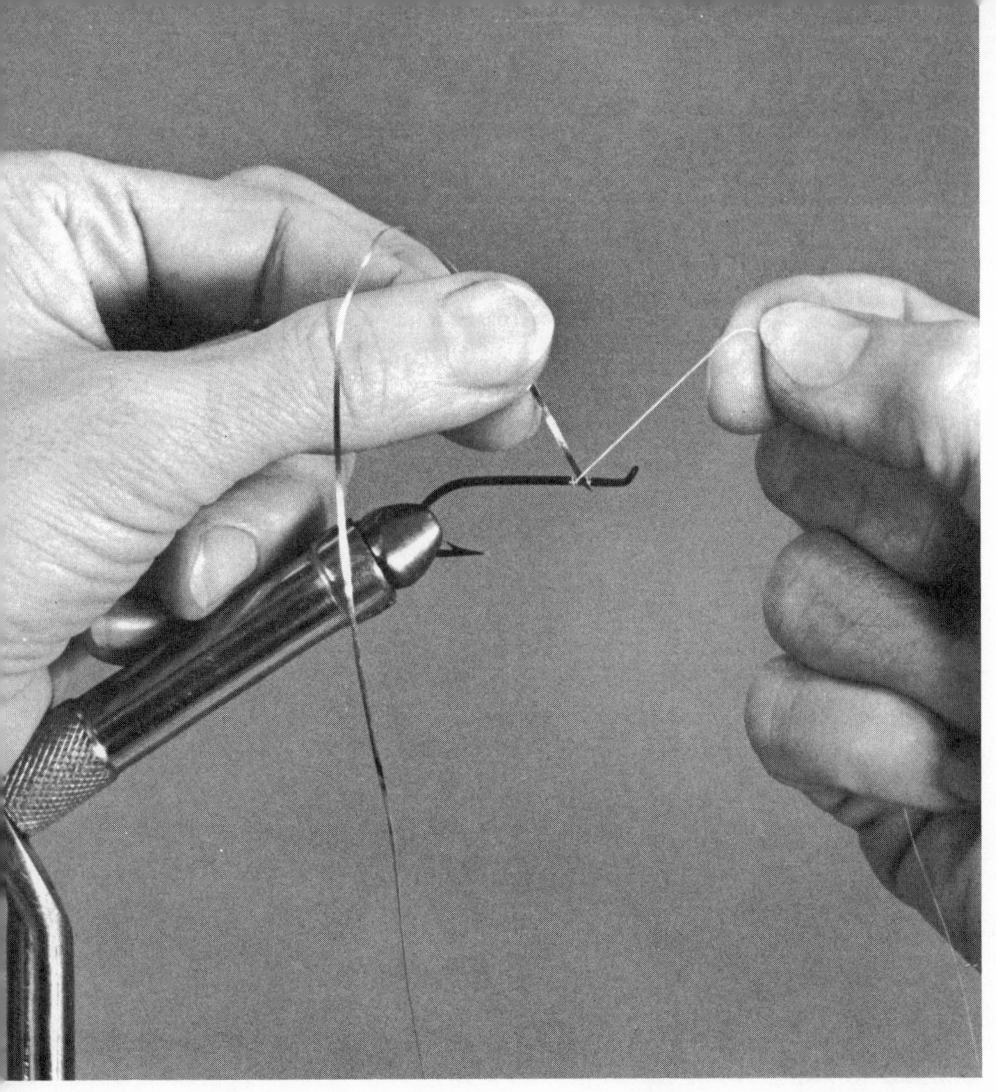

3c. Lay the cut end of the tinsel against the side of the hook at "wing position" and bring the tying thread up and across it. Carry the taut thread down behind the hook, up in front, and across the tinsel once more. Place the second turn of thread to the right of the first one. As you carry the thread down in back of the hook this time, slide the fingers down the thread and secure it behind the rubber button.

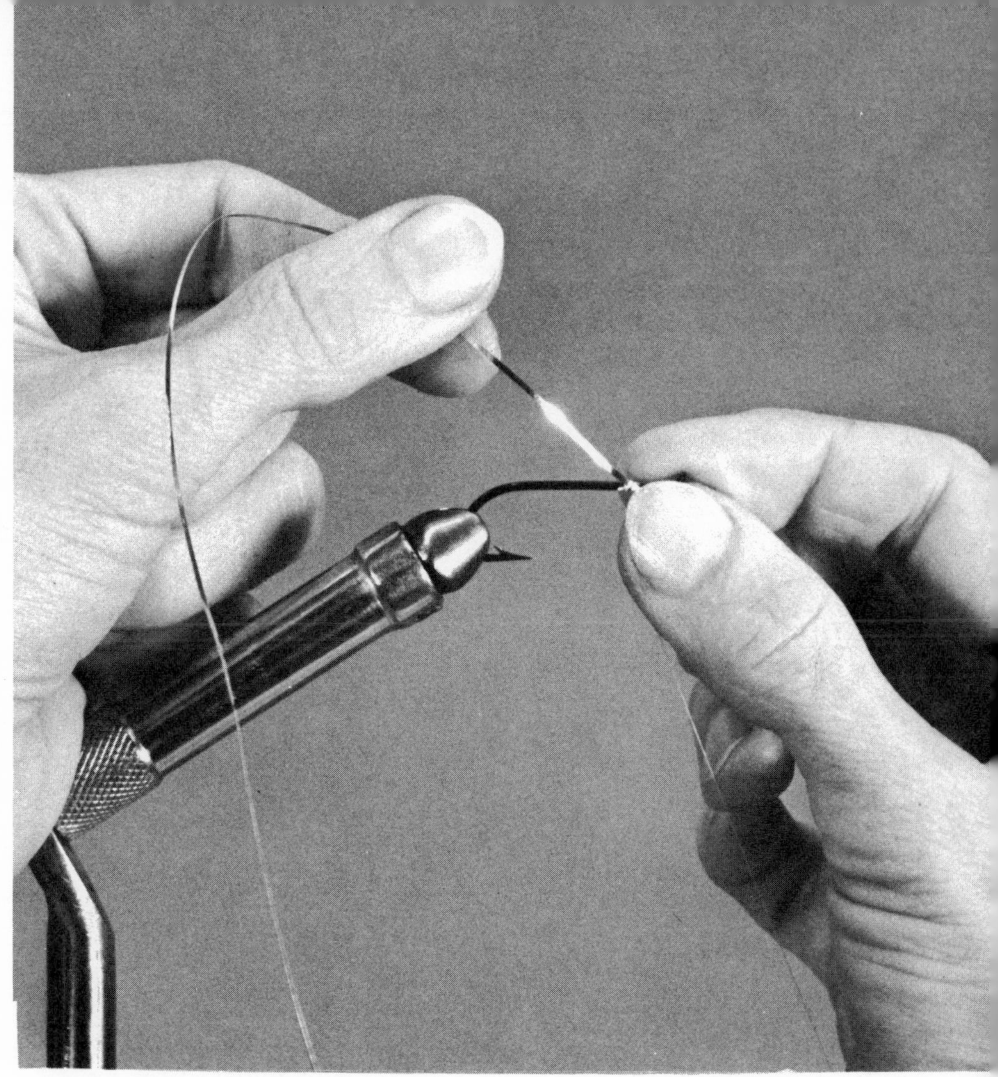

3d. With the right thumbnail, turn the point of the tinsel back over the thread windings. Release the thread (place the middle finger of left hand extended against the windings as before) and wind one more turn of thread across the folded tinsel. This creates a lock for the tinsel and will prevent its being pulled out from under the thread windings while the tinsel is being wound on. Secure the thread behind the button.

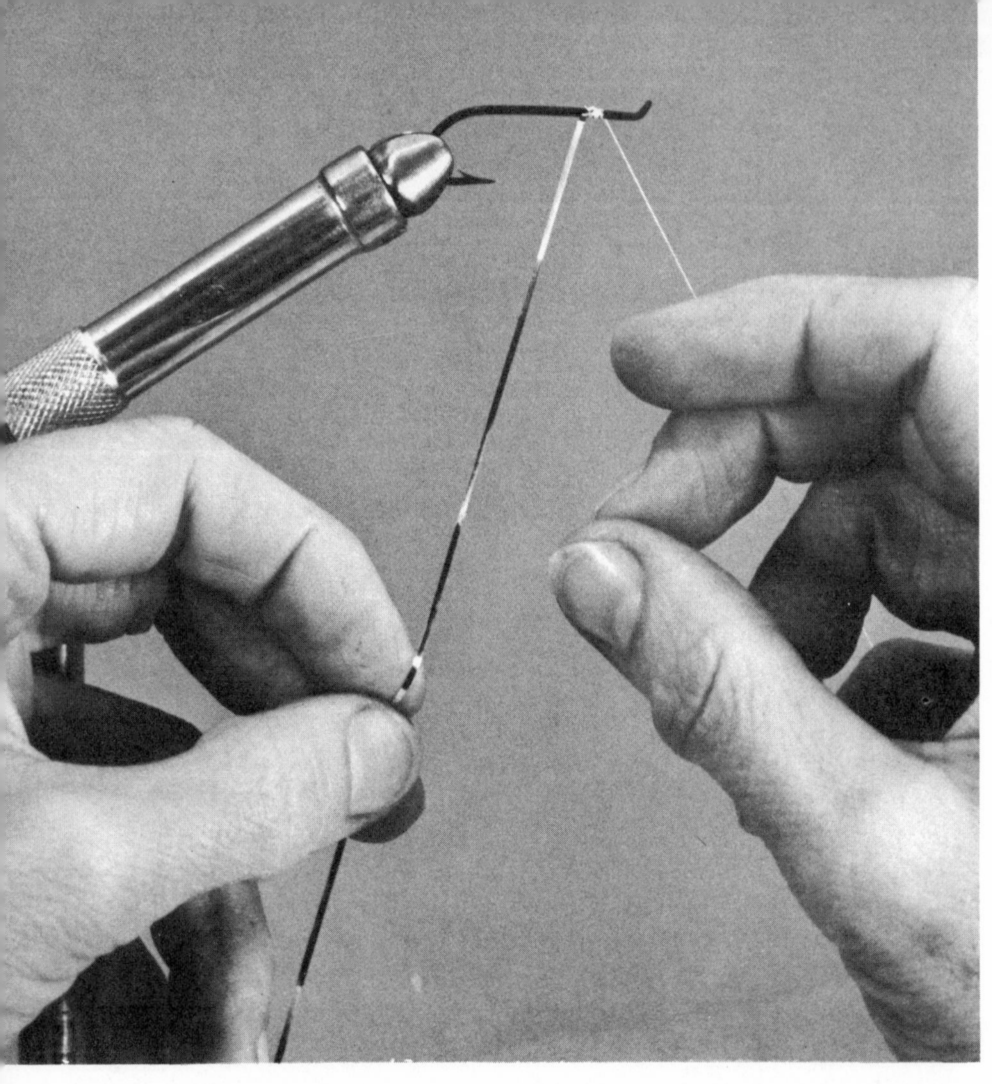

3e. Bring the tinsel forward underneath the hook, keeping it flat. Hold it slanting in the direction in which it is being wound—in this instance, toward the bend of the hook.

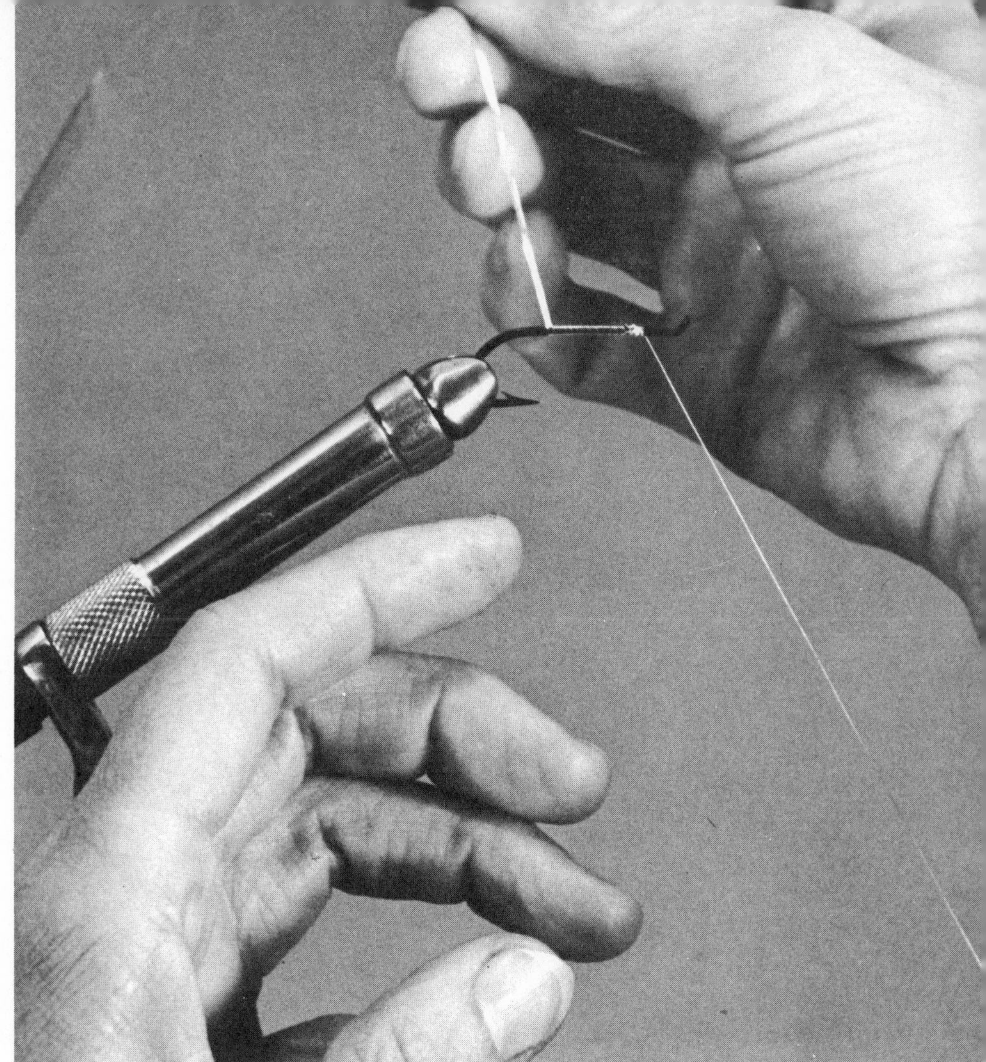

3f. Transfer the tinsel to the right hand and carry it up in front of the hook, over, and down behind the hook, transferring it to the left hand when the right is about to encounter the tying thread. Wrap each successive turn of tinsel next to the preceding one, edge to edge without overlapping. Keep the tinsel snug between hand and hook, alternating the hands when necessary.

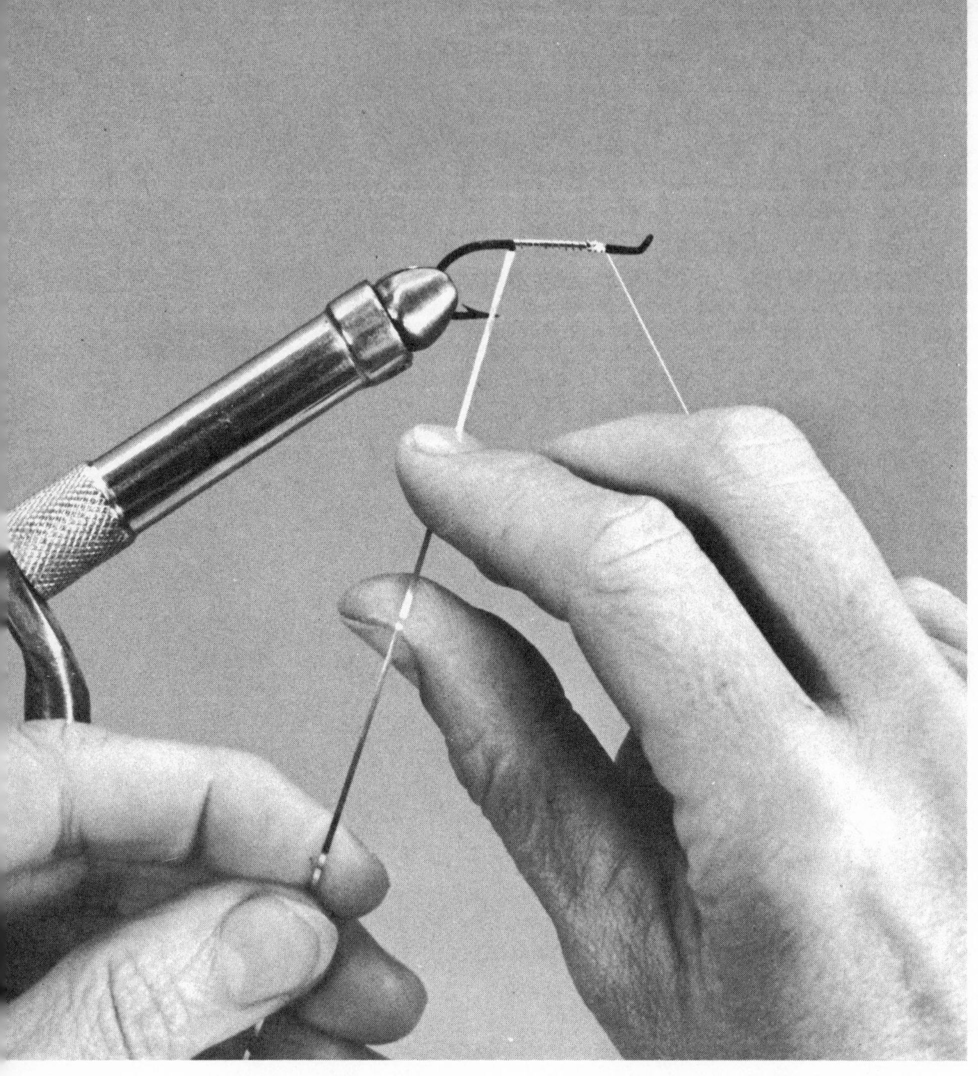

3g. Continue winding the tinsel on until it is above the barb. As the tinsel approaches the bend of the hook, avoid catching it on the hook point.

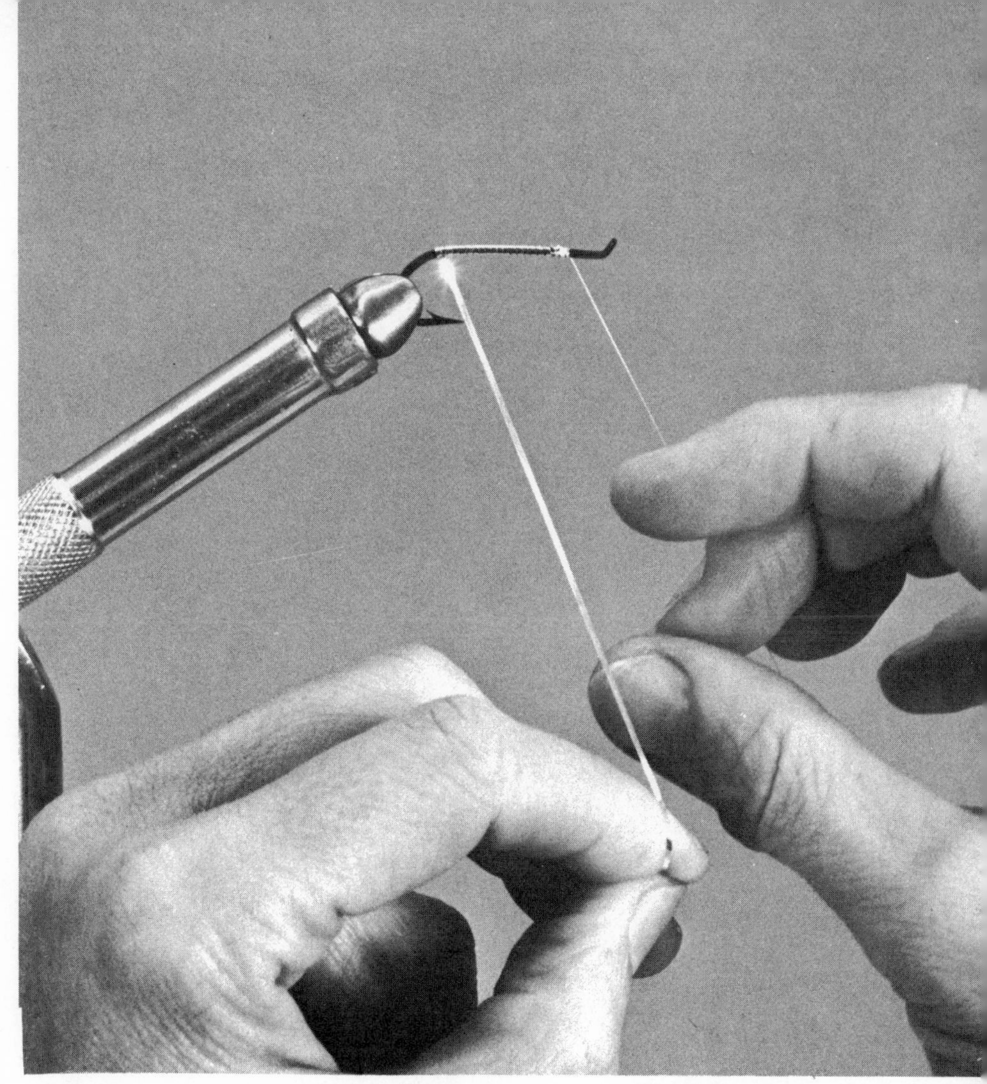

3h. The barb will mark the end of the fly body. The straight part of the hook shank directly above it ends approximately here and the downward curve which forms the bend of the hook begins. The direction in which the tinsel is held changes here, directly above the barb. The tinsel will be wound over itself now, forward, toward the hook eye.

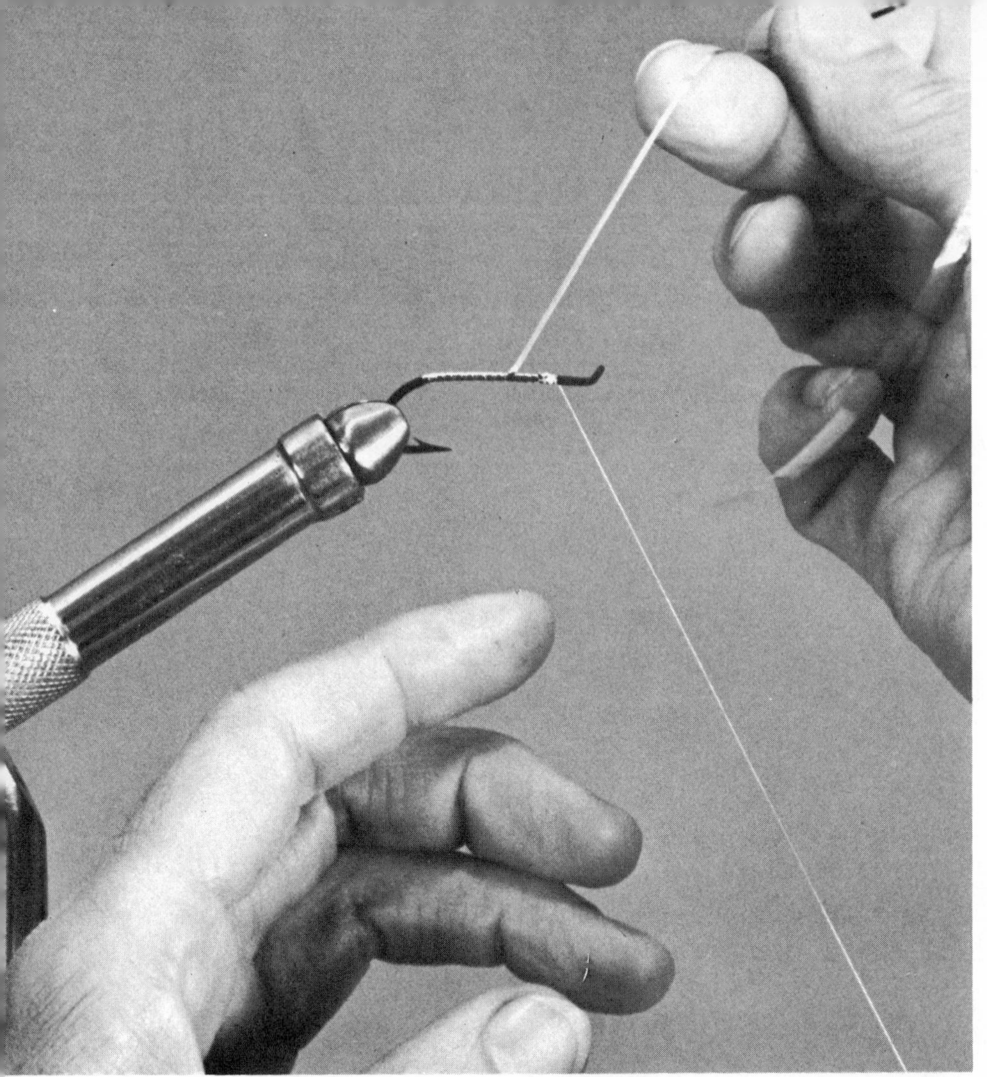

3i. Continue winding as before, each turn of tinsel flat and edge to edge with the preceding turn. Do not allow edges to overlap. Alternate the hands during the winding, and return the tinsel toward the hook eye.

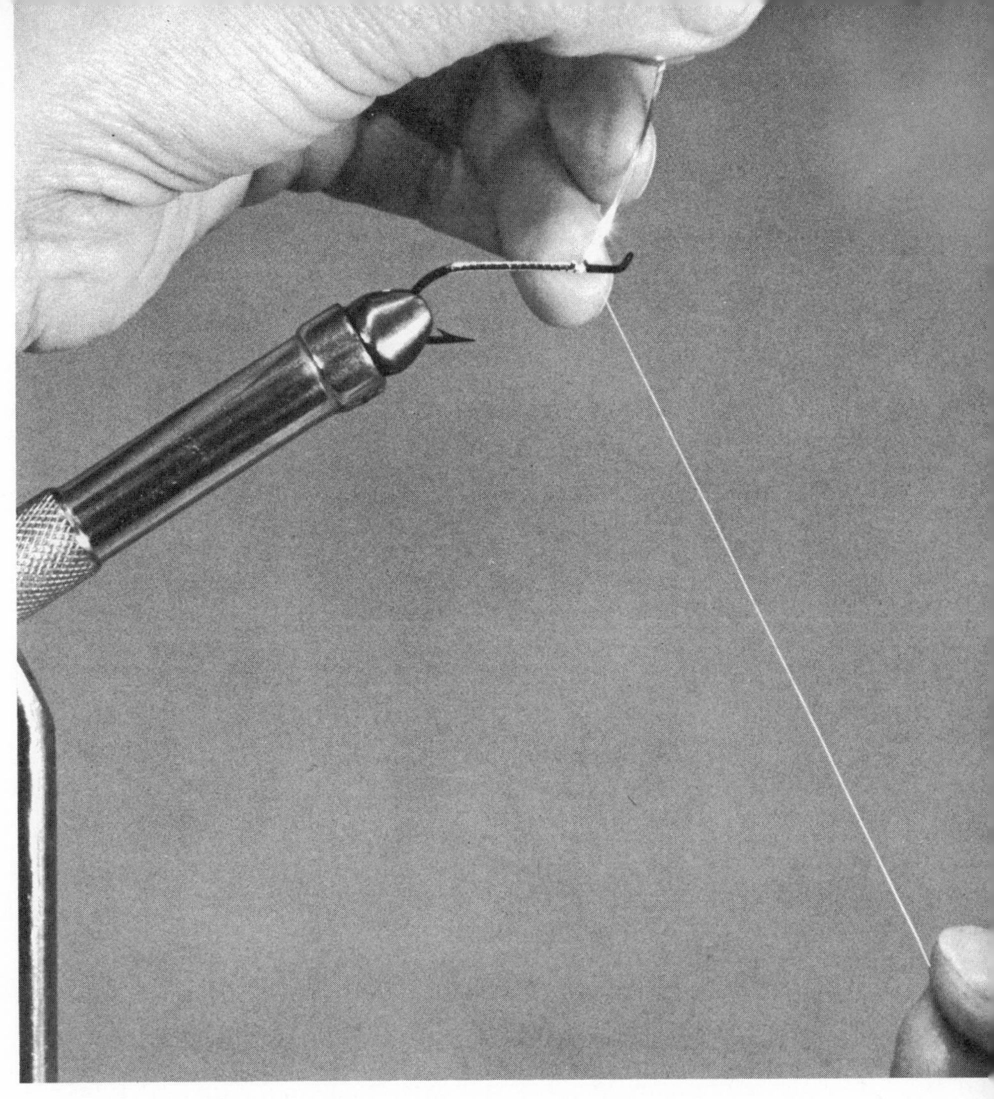

3j. Wind the tinsel until it covers the place where it was tied on. Then, with a finger of the left hand against the tying thread, release the thread with the right hand.

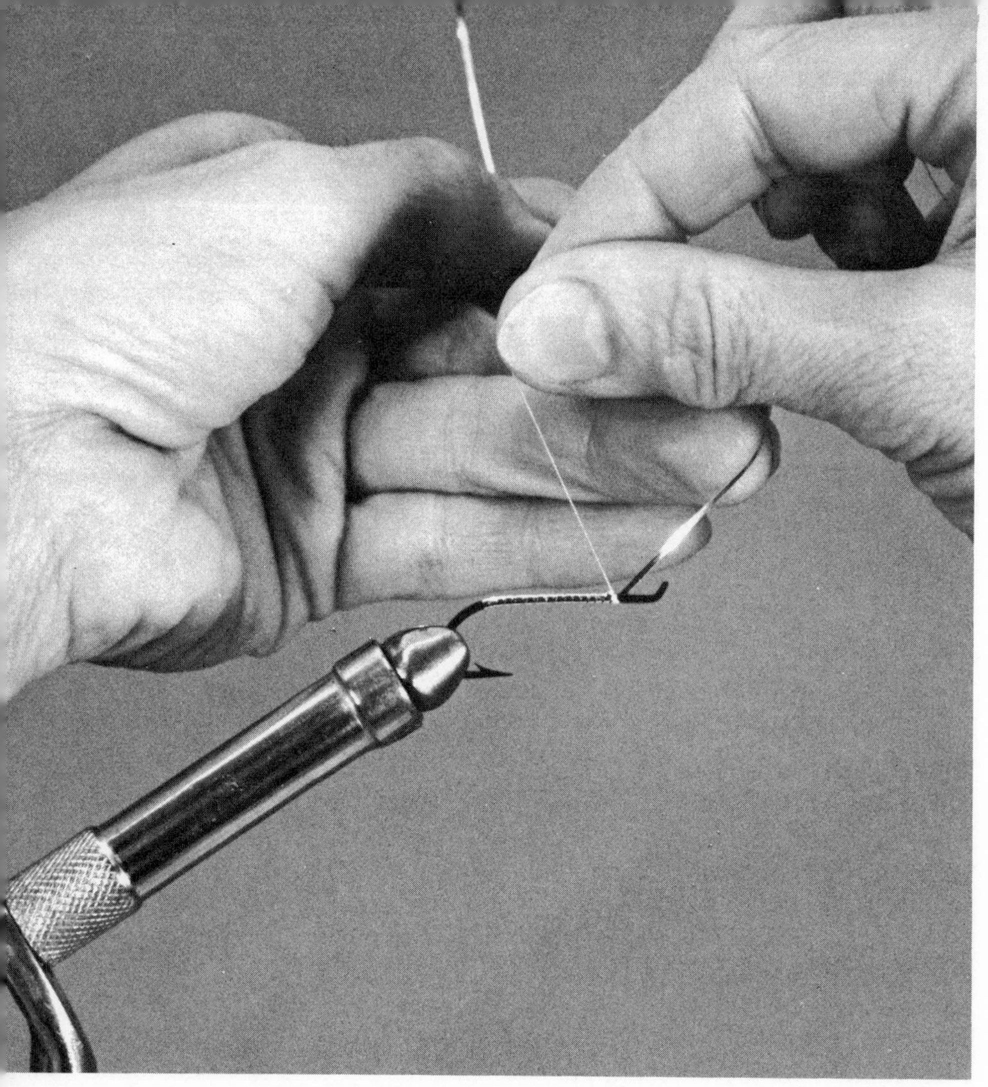

3k. Bring the thread up and across the tinsel. Two turns of thread close together and spiraling toward the hook eye will catch the tinsel.

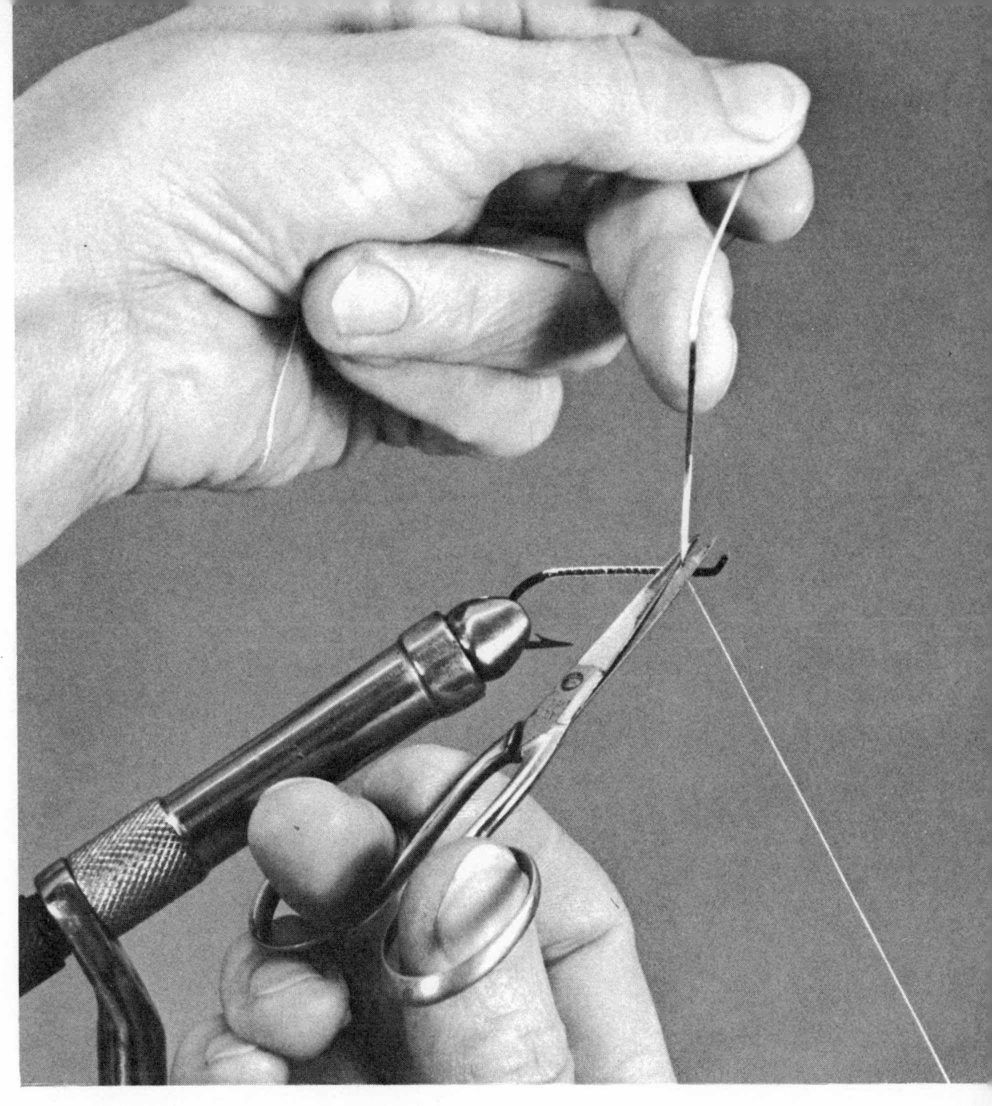

31. Secure the thread behind the button. Cut off excess tinsel on a diagonal.

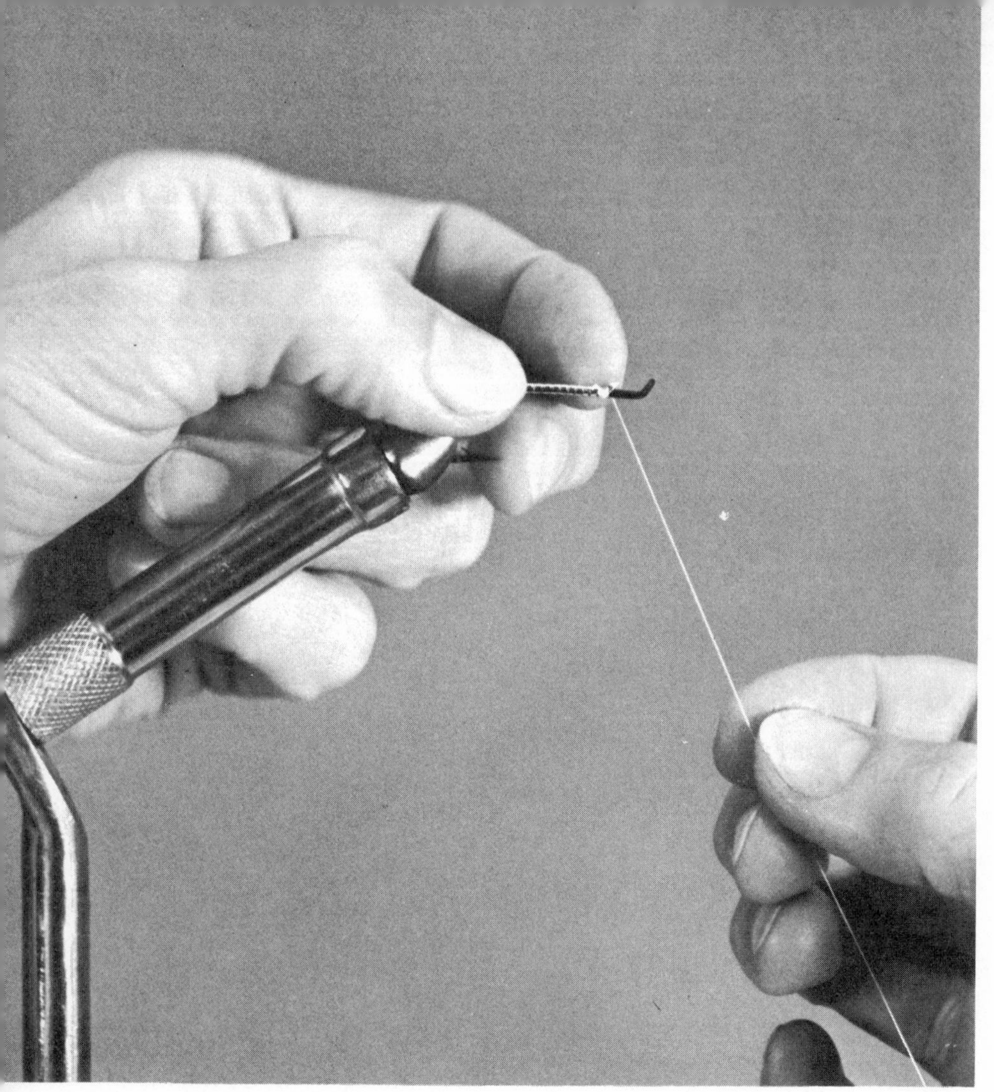

3m. Turn the point of the tinsel back over the thread to lock it. Release the thread, keep it taut, and wind one more turn of thread over the folded tinsel.

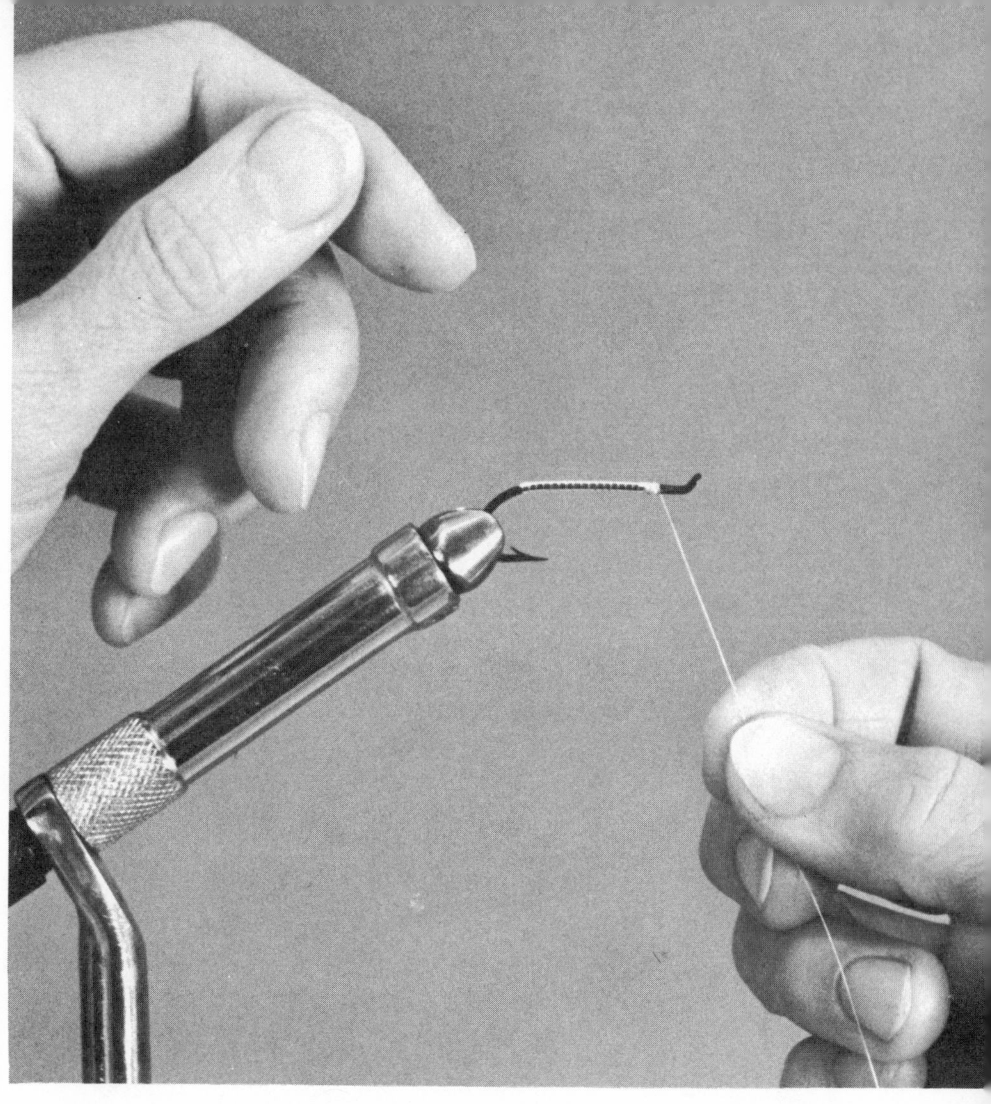

3n. The simple tinsel body is now complete and should be smooth, almost as though the hook were plated. Practice tying this body several times until you can wind it quickly and smoothly every time. The body at this stage is ready for a wing or hackle, but until you have practiced tying each separate part of a fly several times, do not try to combine them. The next step will be to learn to tie the wrap knot, with which all flies are finished. Then, when you have learned how to make this tinsel body and have one you would like to keep until you are able to handle other materials as well, secure it with the wrap knot and put it aside to use later.

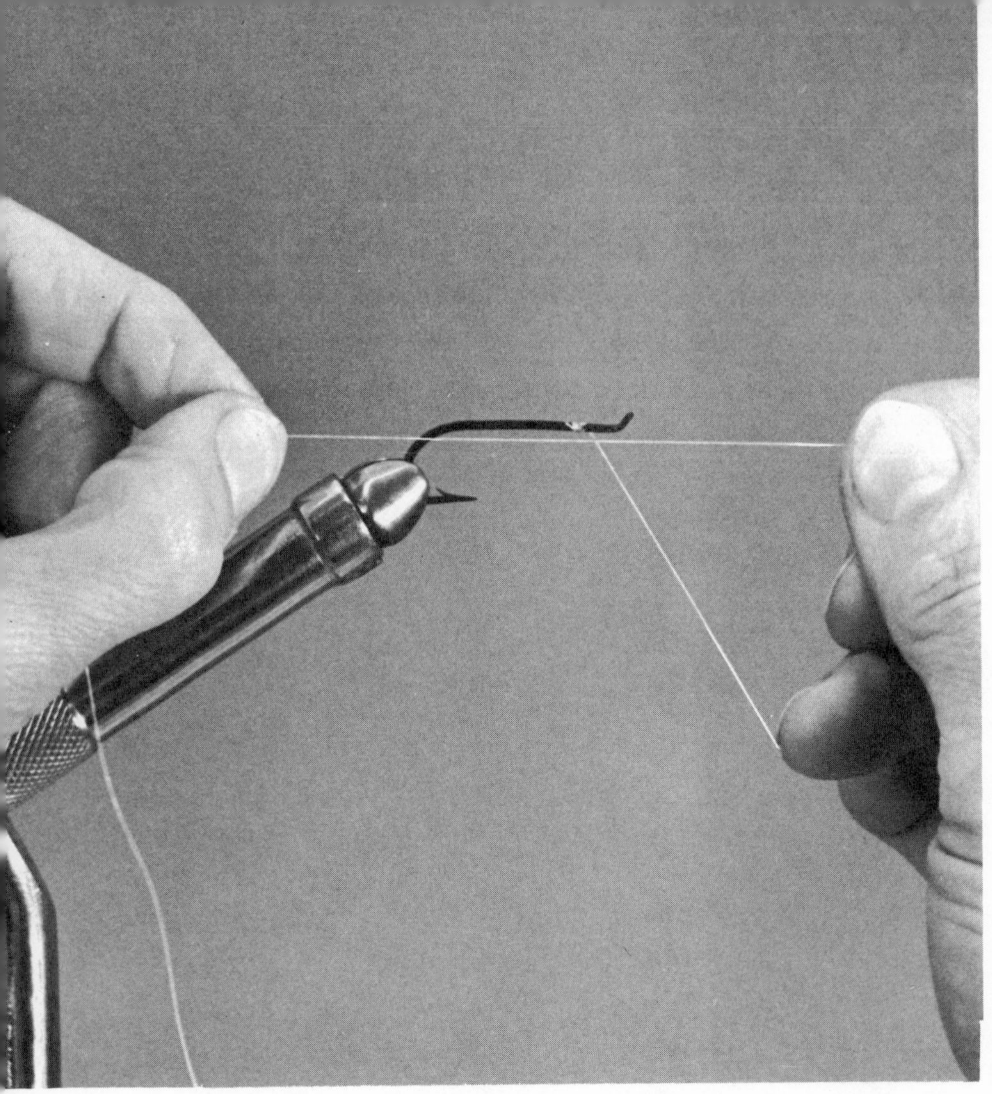

4a. This is the beginning of a wrap knot. The thread is attached at "wing position." It is coming from the hook to the right hand, under the fourth finger, up across the inside of the fingertips, and is gripped by the right index finger and thumb. Hold a length of it in front of and against the hook, as shown here.

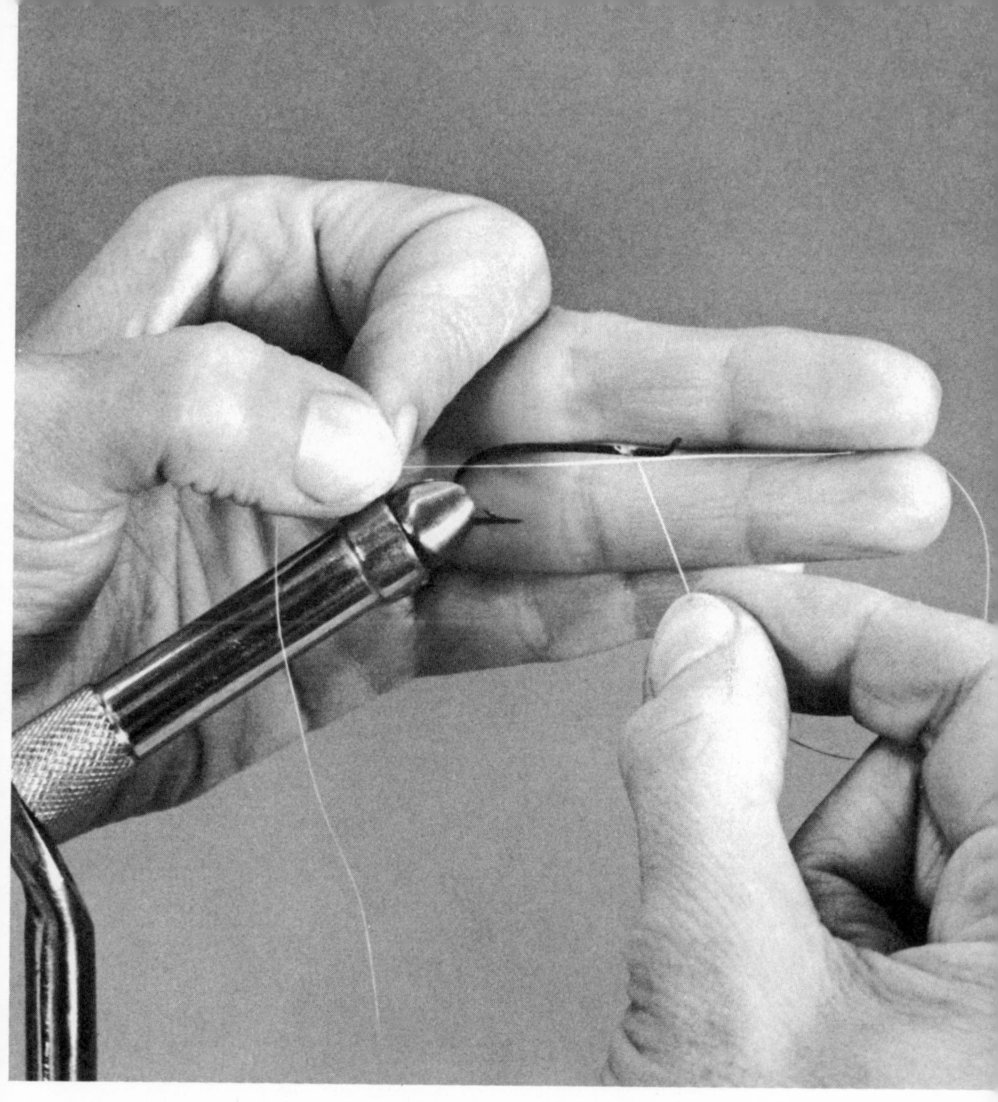

4b. By extending the middle and fourth fingers of the left hand, catch the thread between them, keeping it between yourself and the hook shank and parallel to the hook. You will notice that the thread now makes a rough circle from the fingers to the hook. With the first finger and thumb of the right hand, grip the taut thread coming down from the hook.

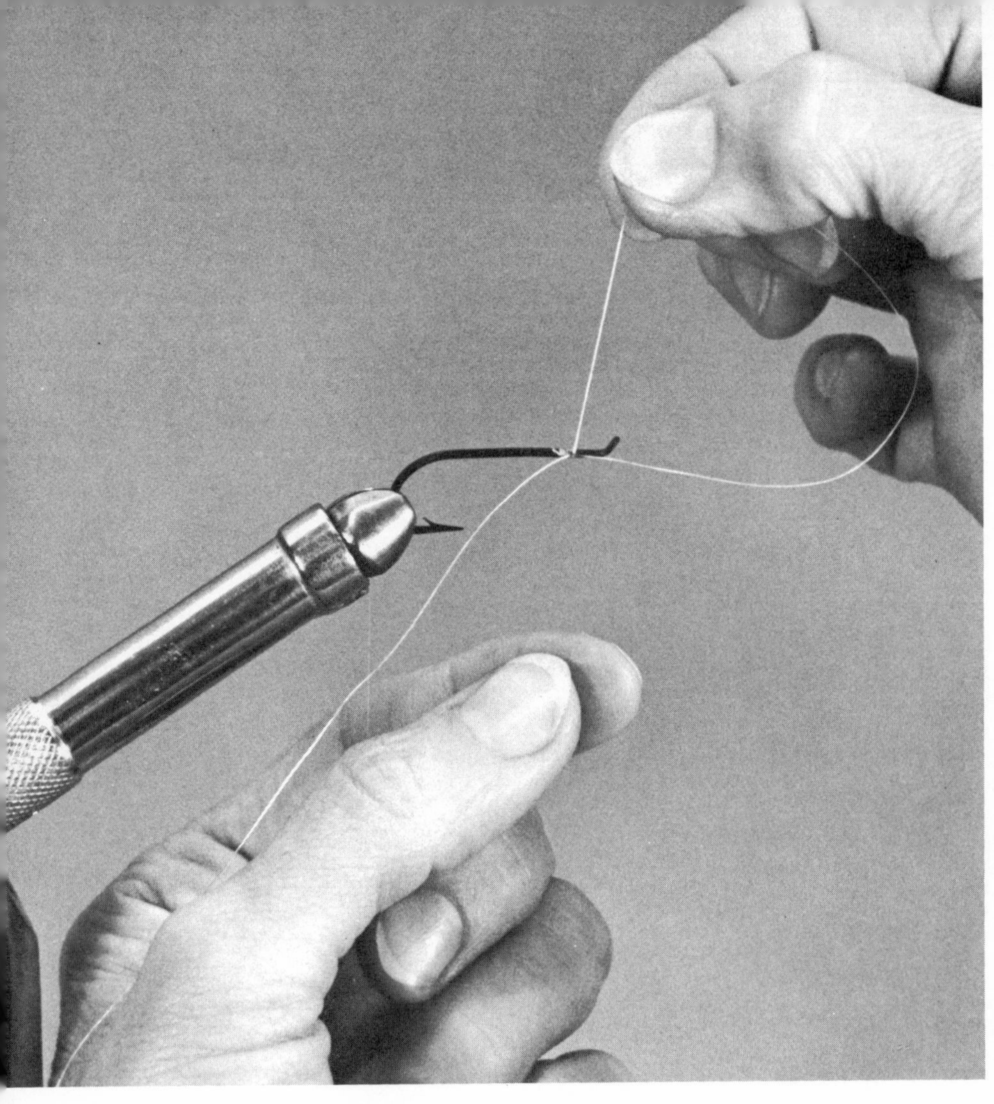

4c. Lift the taut thread up and across the parallel thread in front of the hook.

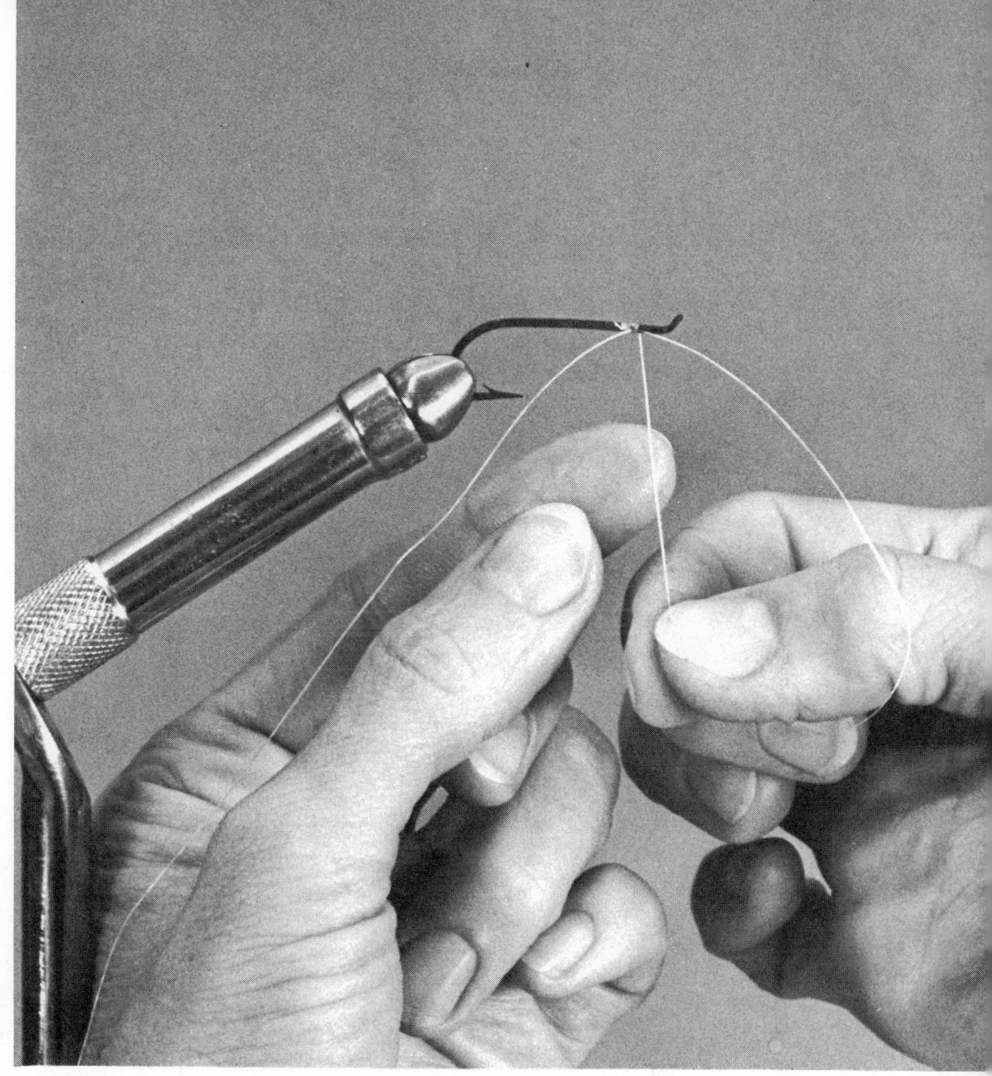

4d. When the parallel thread is held against the hook by the taut thread, the left hand is released to help wrap it around the hook, which will bind the parallel thread to it.

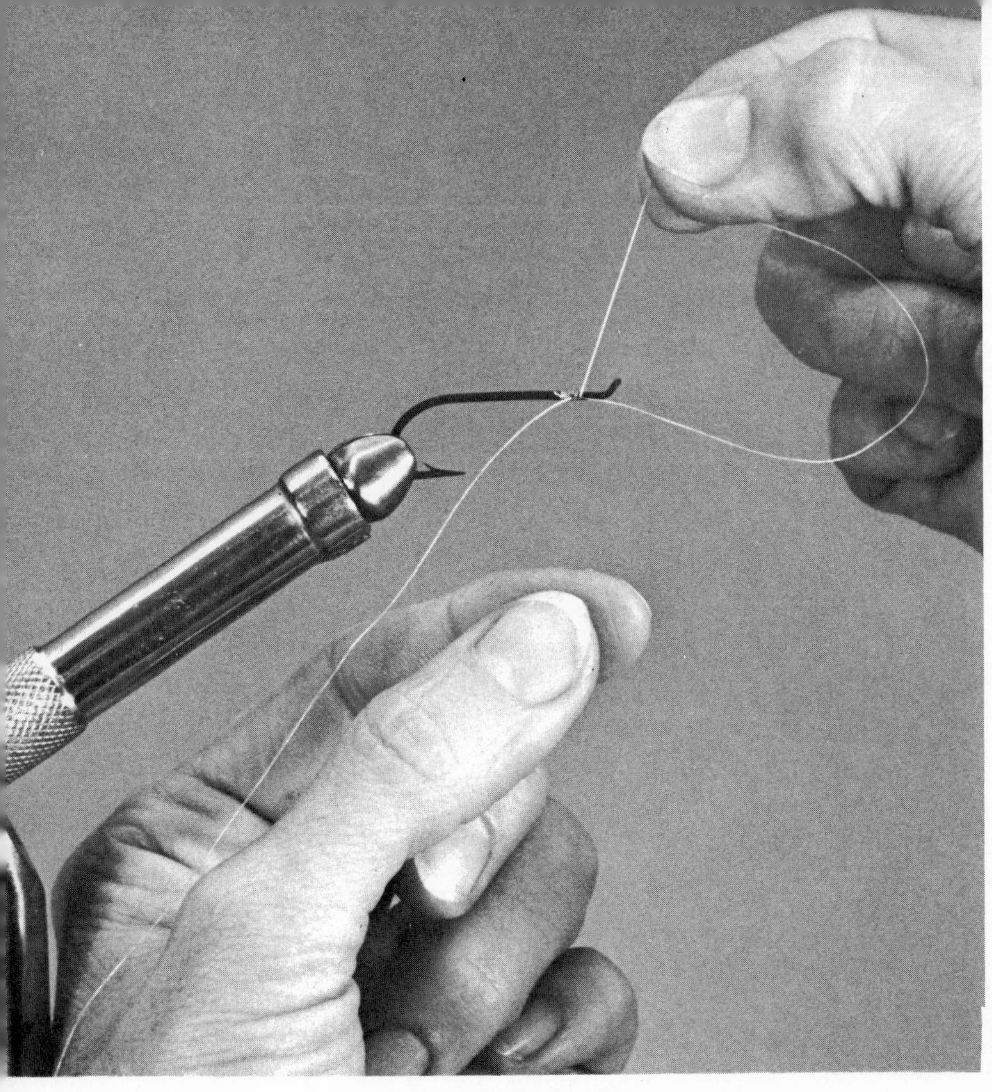

4e. Wrap the taut thread up and over the parallel thread and hook four times, in a close spiral toward the hook eye.

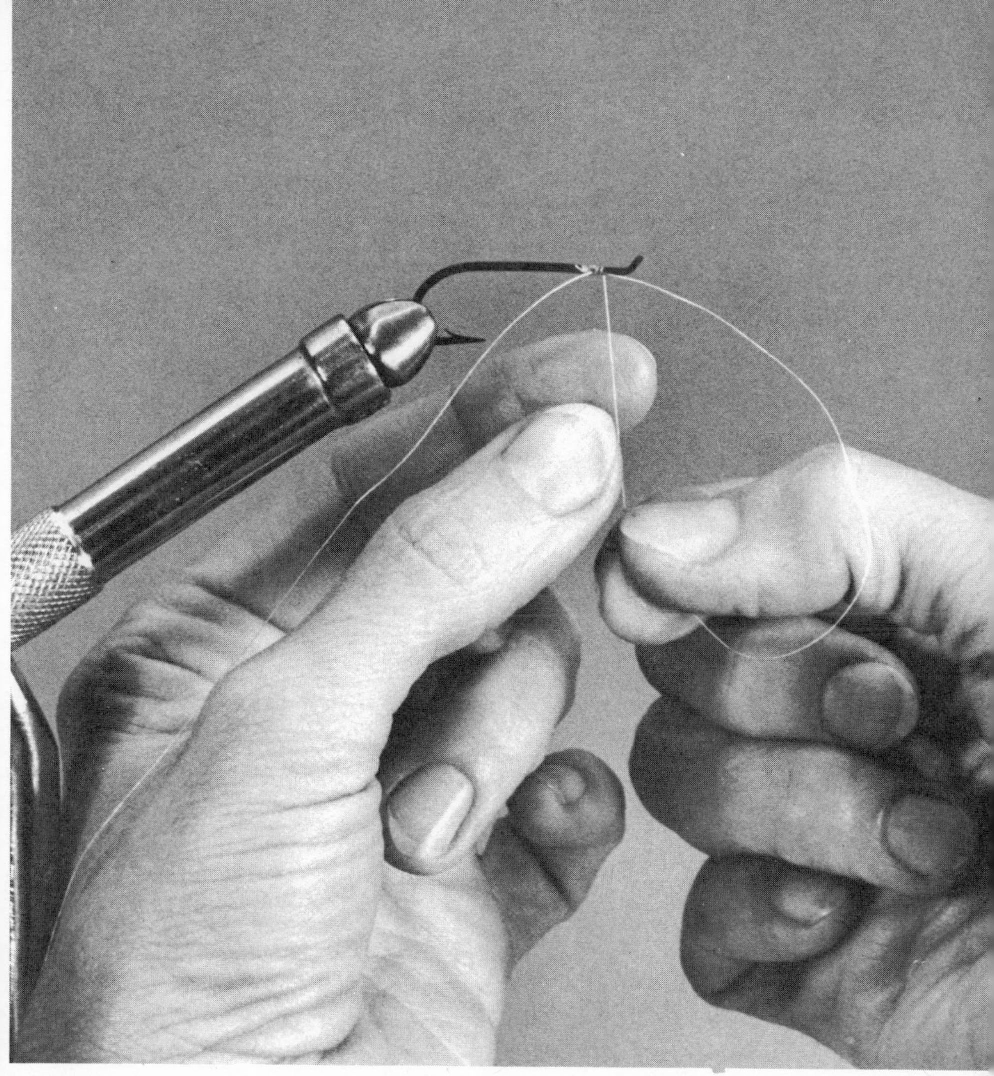

4f. Use the left hand to assist in wrapping the four turns of thread. Hold the taut thread with the left hand and regrip it after each turn with the right fingers so that the index finger is inside the loop when you carry the taut thread up and over.

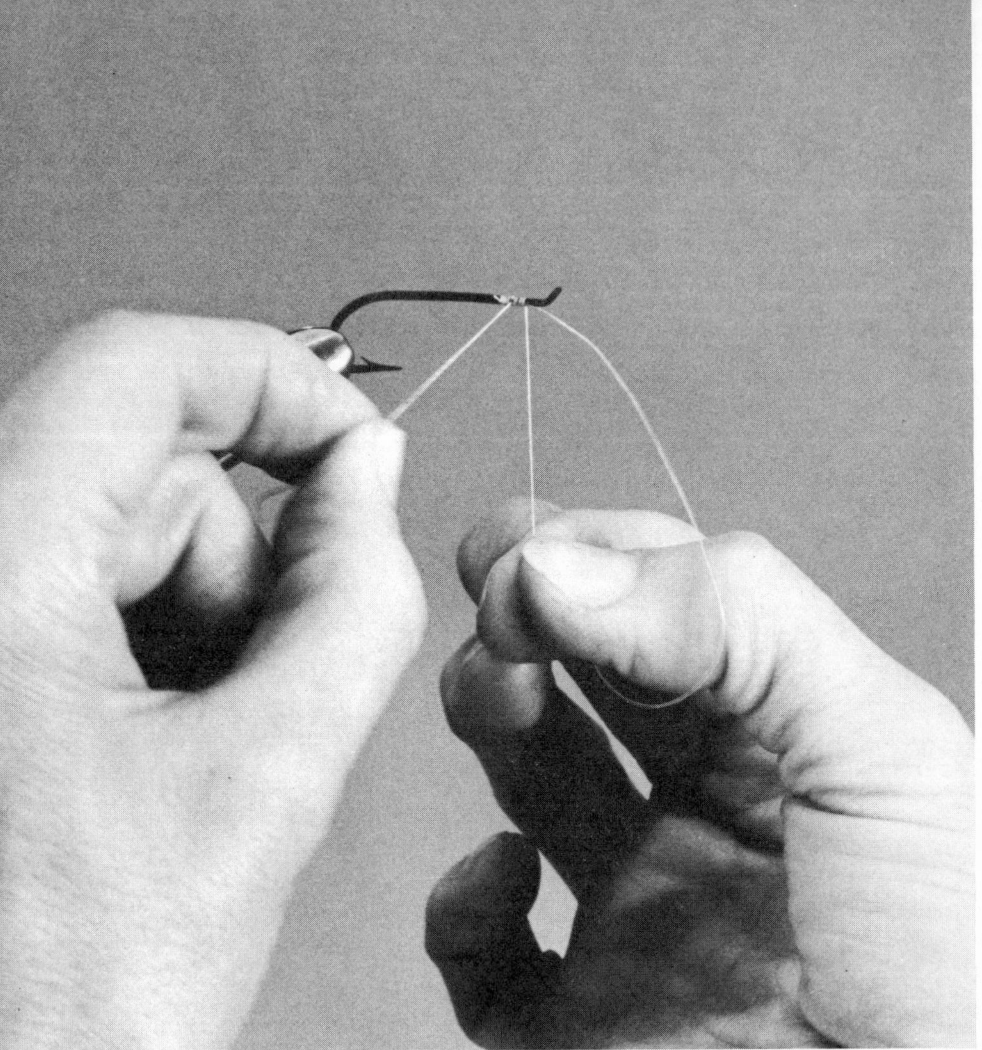

4g. While holding the taut thread with the right hand, take hold of the long end of the parallel thread with the left and begin to pull.

4h. The rough circle of thread at the right will begin to grow smaller. As it diminishes, reach up with the middle finger of the right hand and press it against the turns of thread on the hook from in back. The loop will continue to grow smaller as you continue to pull.

Let go of the thread with the right thumb and forefinger, but keep a protective finger pressed against the threads until the loop has *disappeared entirely*. The thread is now securely bound against the hook and the long end may be cut off. Never break the thread off—always cut it—for breaking i. may result in its parting under the loops of thread and weakening the knot. Practice tying the wrap knot until you can do it quickly and surely. Eventually, you will be able to tie it with one hand, sliding the fingers around inside the "rough circle," using other only to pull thread tight at the finish.

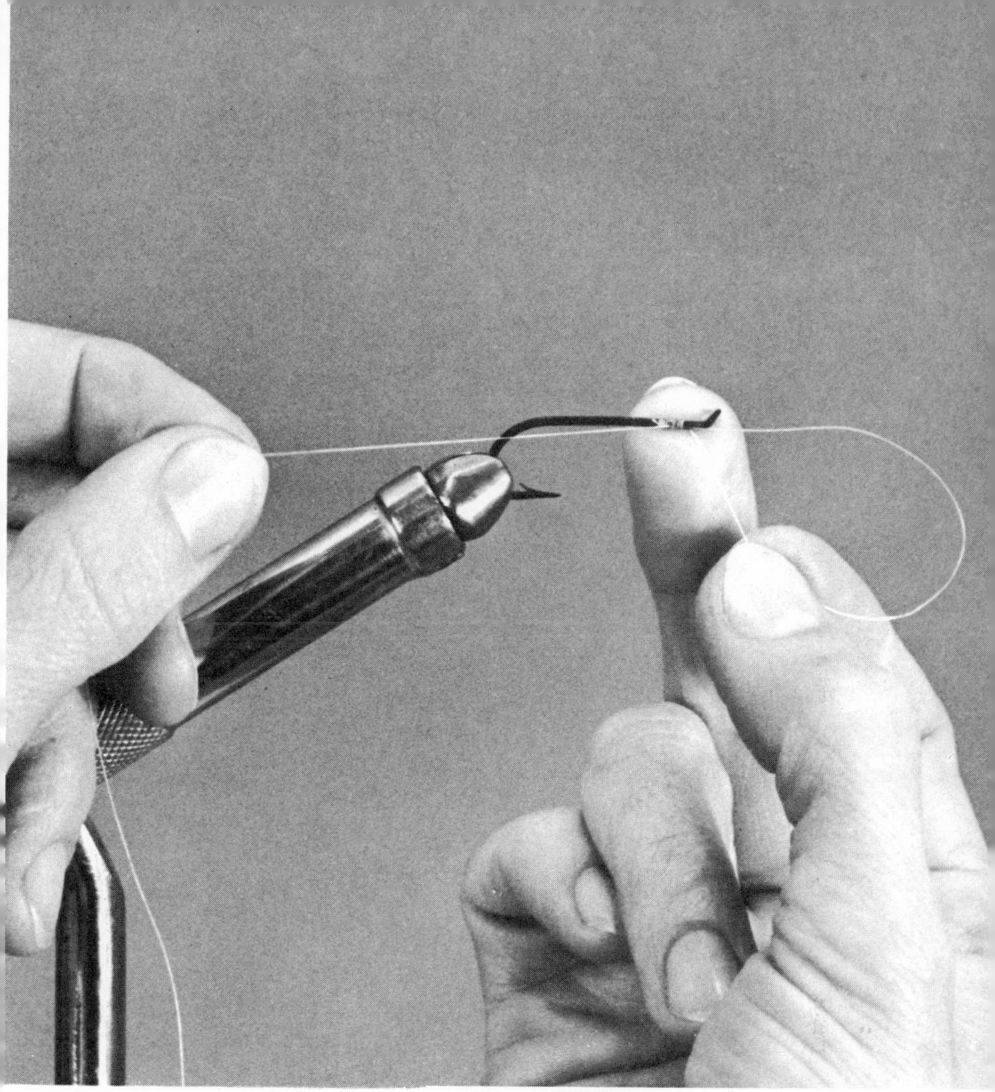

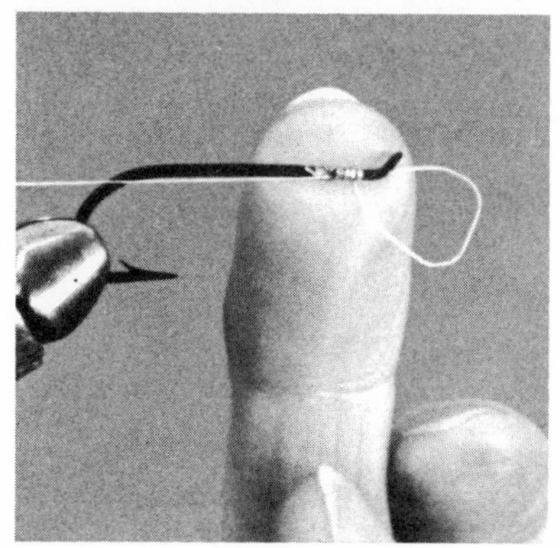

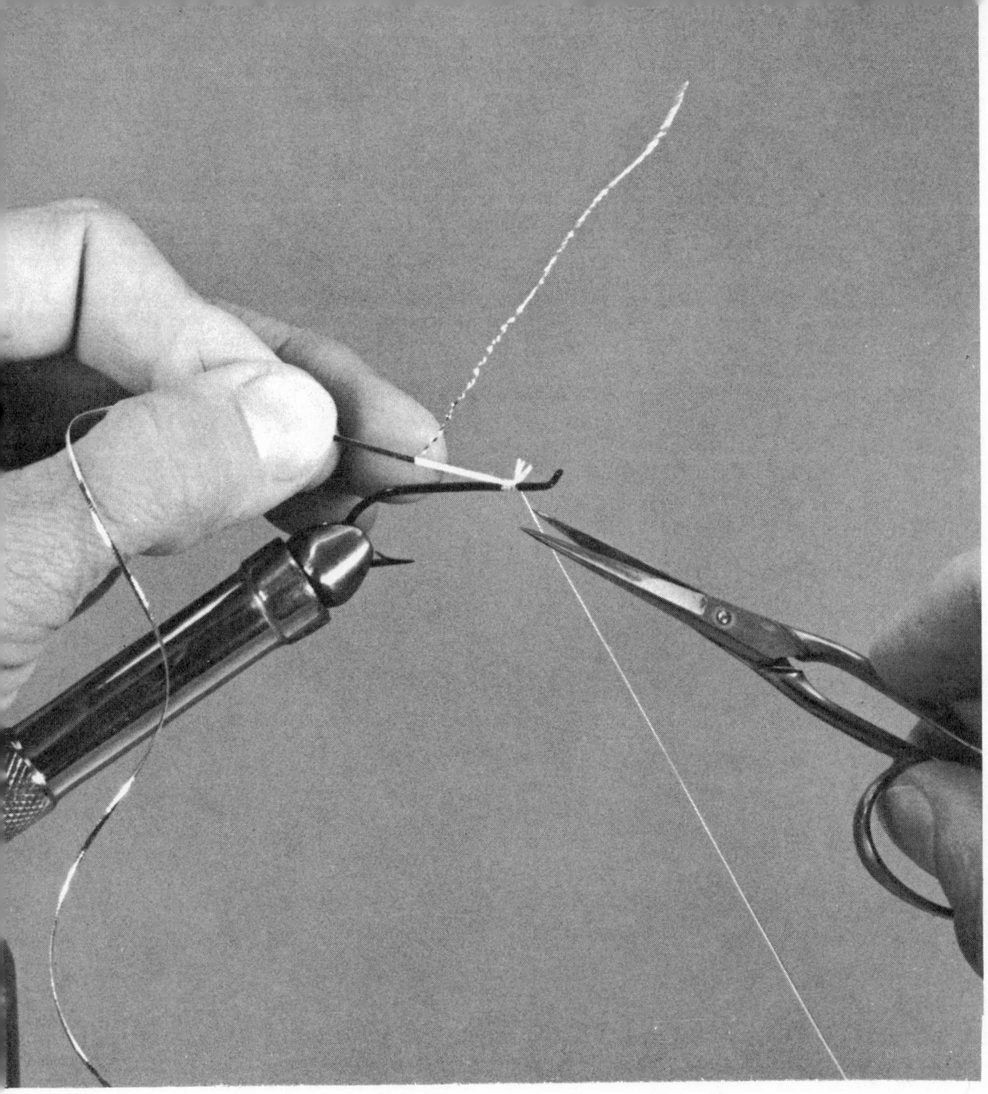

5a. Take a piece of oval tinsel, approximately 6 inches in length, gently strip the fine tinsel covering away from the thread core until about ½ inch of the core is exposed. Fasten the thread core to the hook. Secure the tying thread at the button. Clip away the stub end of core at an angle, release the tying thread, and bind down the clipped end with another turn of thread. Secure the thread.

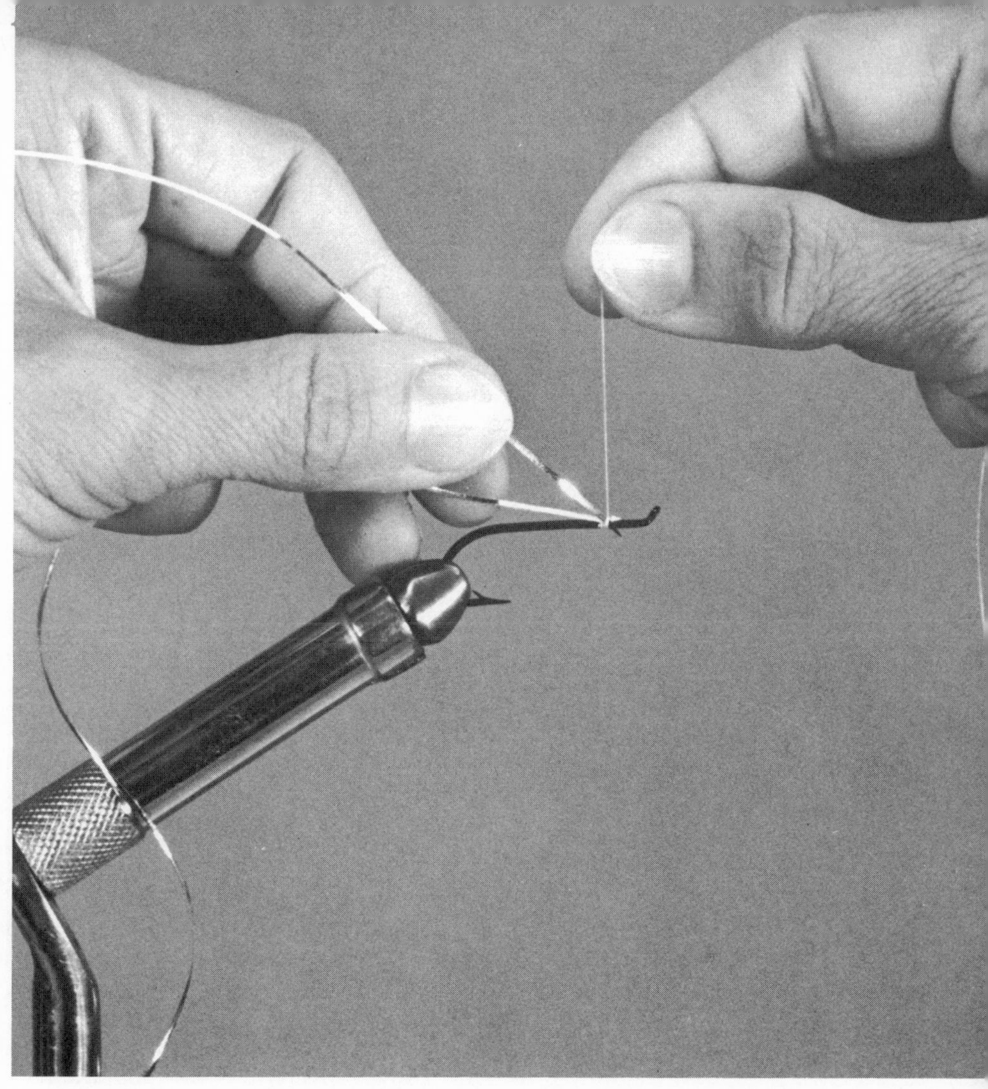

5b. Hold the thread core along the top of the hook. Carefully clip away the stripped tinsel from the thread core at a place midway between the point and barb of the hook. Now, attach a length of flat tinsel to the hook on top of the thread core at "wing position." Remember to taper the end of the tinsel before attaching it, and to turn back the pointed end as you did for the plain tinsel body, to lock it. Secure the thread.

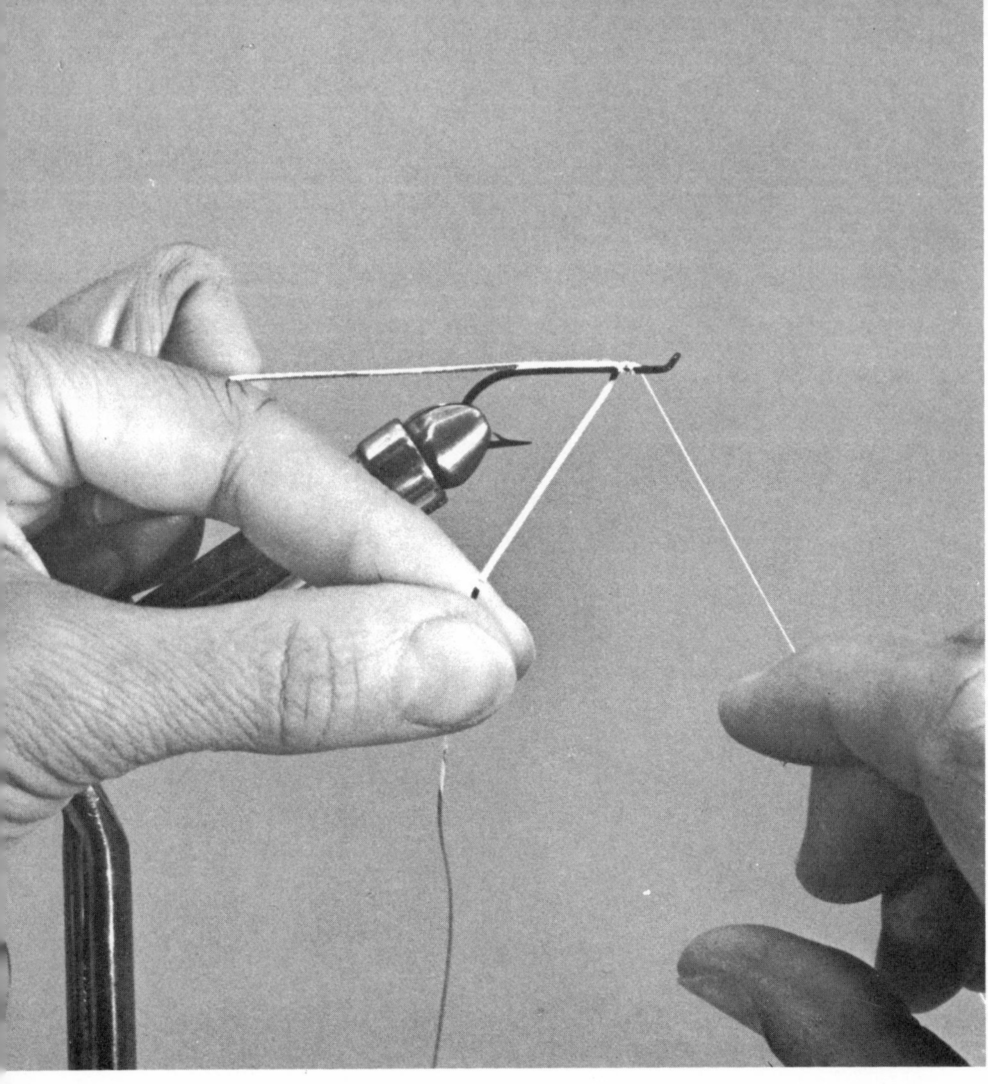

5c. Hold the oval tinsel along the top of the hook with the third and fourth fingers of the left hand and begin to wind the flat tinsel over it, each turn edge to edge with no overlapping. Keep the thread core on top of the hook, for if it slides to one side the finished body will not be smooth.

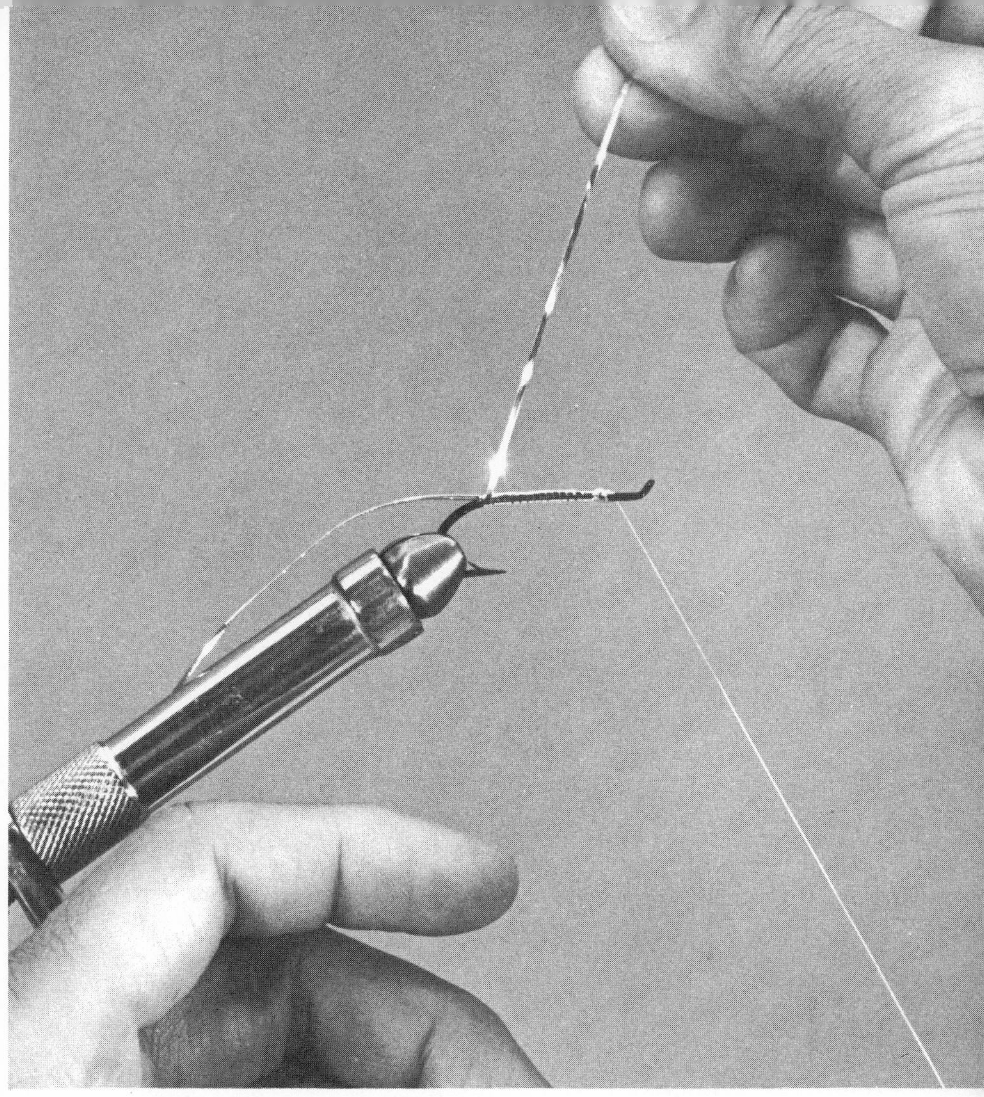

5d. When the flat tinsel covers the thread core, it will encounter the cut end of the tinsel on the oval tinsel strand. Make sure the flat tinsel covers it with at least two complete turns. The direction of winding for the flat tinsel changes here, directly above the hook barb. Wind it back over itself toward the hook eye, edge to edge with no overlapping. Tie off the tinsel as you did for the plain body, taper the end, turn back the point, catch it with a turn or two of thread, and secure the thread to the button.

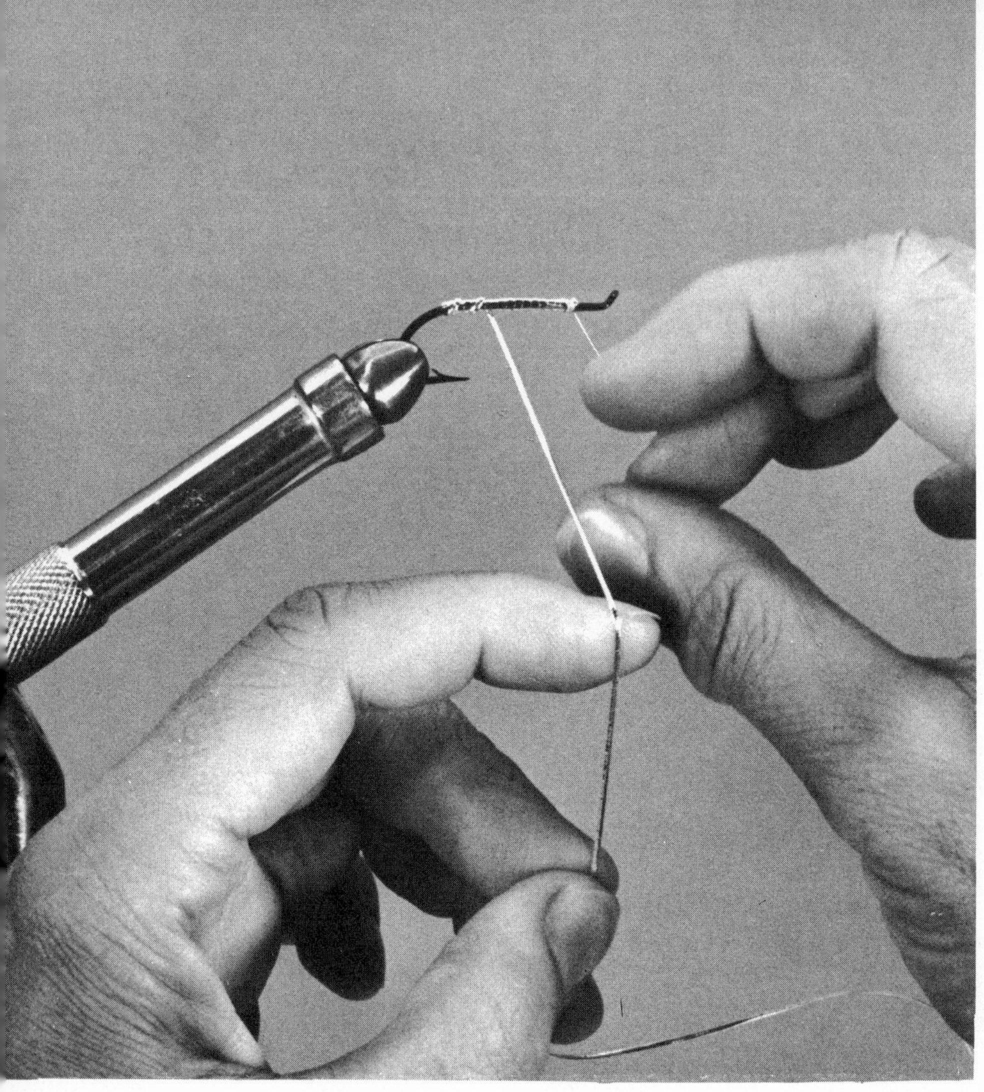

5e. To begin the oval tinsel rib, carry the strand down behind the hook and bring it up in front of the barb. Wind it around the hook in an even, open spiral toward the hook eye. Maintain a steady tension on the oval tinsel, so that the entire rib will be snug against the body and will not slip later.

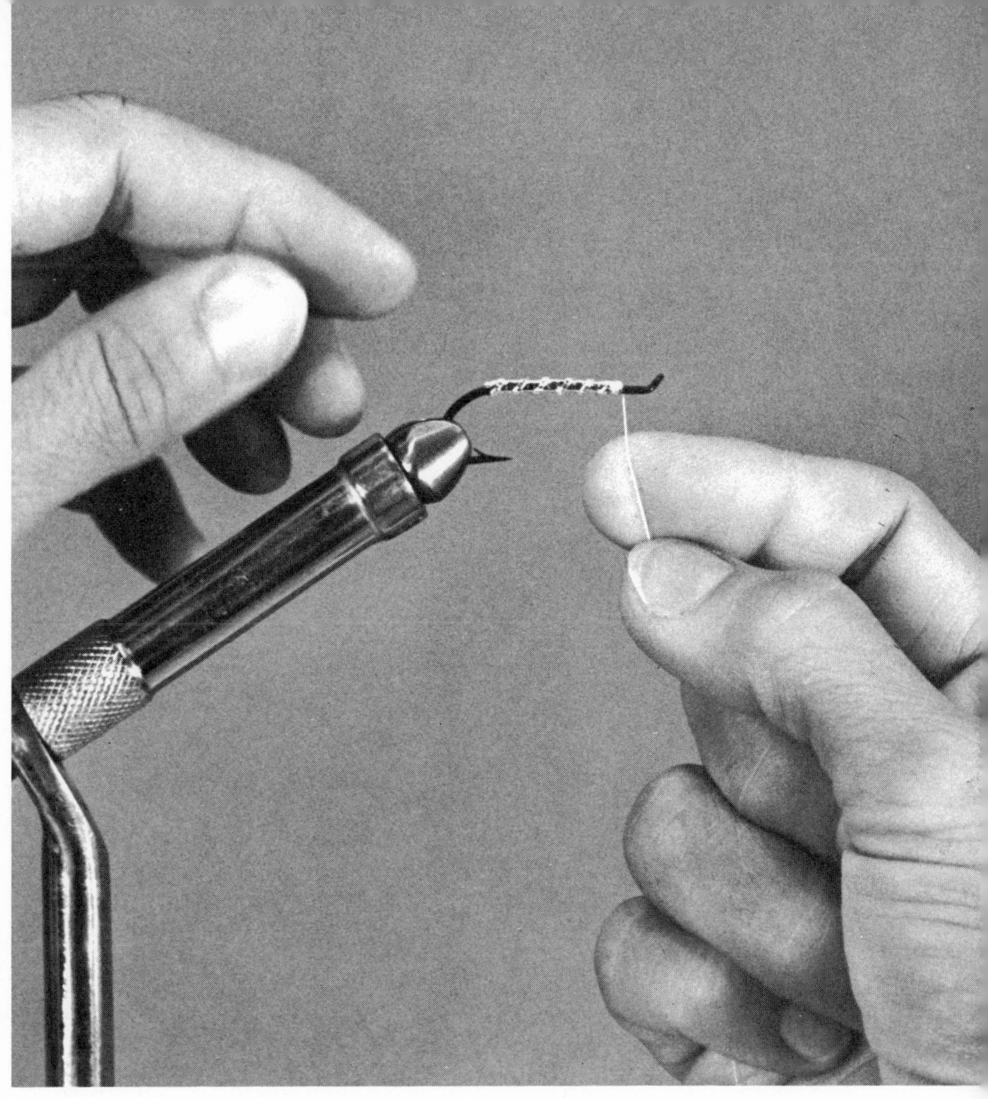

5f. Cross the oval tinsel with the tying thread to hold it, clip off the extra tinsel, and bind down the cut end, catching both the thread core and the fine tinsel covering. This ribbed body is now complete. Practice until the underbody is smooth and the ribs are evenly spaced and firmly placed around it.

Floss

Floss, whether of silk or of rayon or other synthetic fibers, is a material from which fly bodies can be fashioned. Silk floss, with its natural fibers clinging to each other more readily than do synthetic fibers, is easier to use for tying a smooth, tapered body. Rayon floss, sometimes called artificial silk, can be handled well with a little practice.

Floss is available in skeins, on spools or cards, in many colors. From skeins, the floss should be wound onto uniform cards and kept in a box, similar to a card index file, with every color visible and always ready for instant selection. This is a safeguard against undue tangling. The exposed surface of floss on spools may be protected by wrapping each spool with a band of paper held in place with a bit of Scotch tape.

Chenille is another material useful to the fly-tyer. Although technically not a floss, it is made of short silk or rayon fibers. These fibers are bound together by a twisted core of threads into a cord of silky pile. Wrapped on a hook, chenille resembles somewhat the fuzzy body of a caterpillar. It is available in several sizes and in a dozen or more colors, of which red, yellow, white, grey, wine, and black are the most often used.

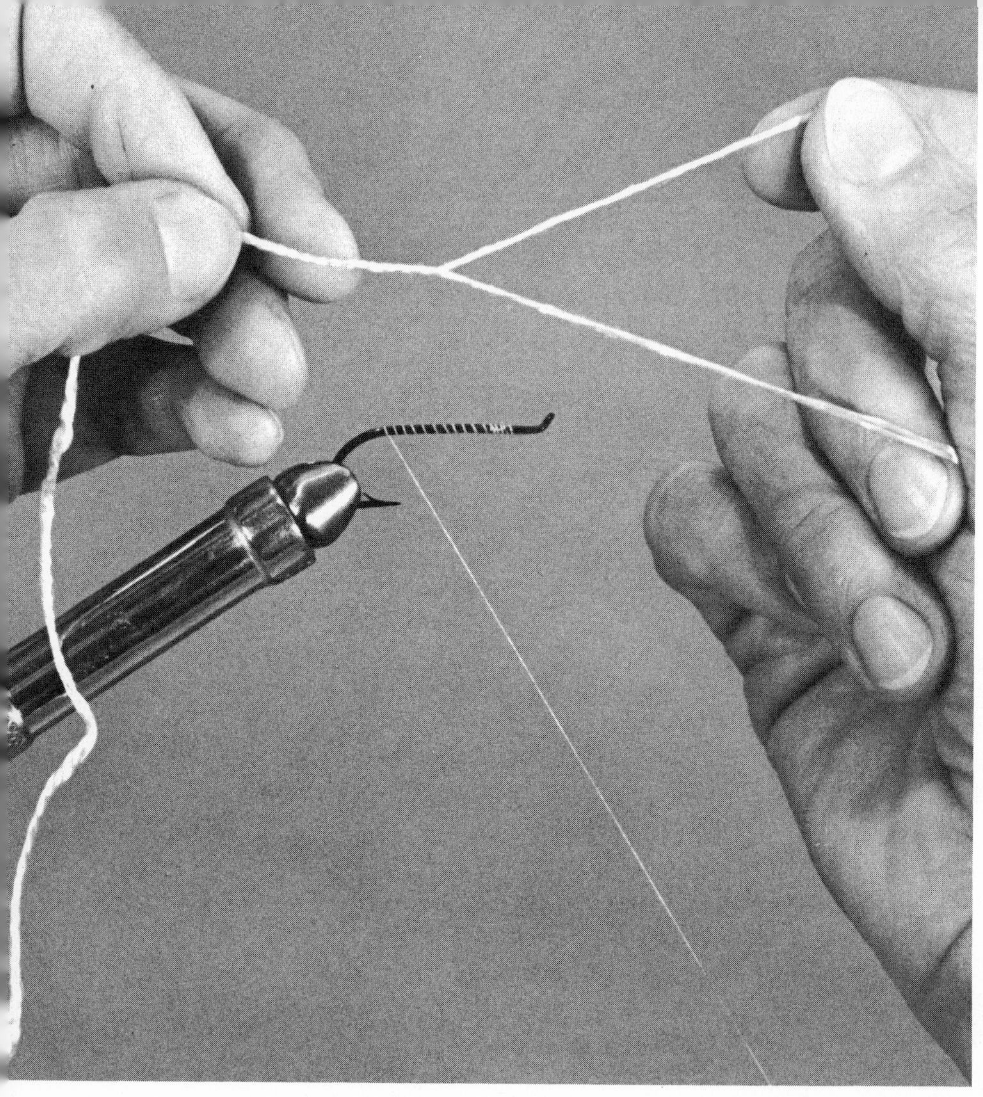

6a. This is rayon floss. As the strands are pulled apart carefully, the twist vanishes, leaving the floss slightly wavy. It must be separated before it is tied on the hook. The tying thread is attached at "wing position" and wound back in an open spiral toward the bend of the hook where the floss will be tied on above and just ahead of the hook barb. Rayon and other synthetic fibers tend to slip; keep them taut. The waxed thread will furnish a grip for the floss on the hook shank.

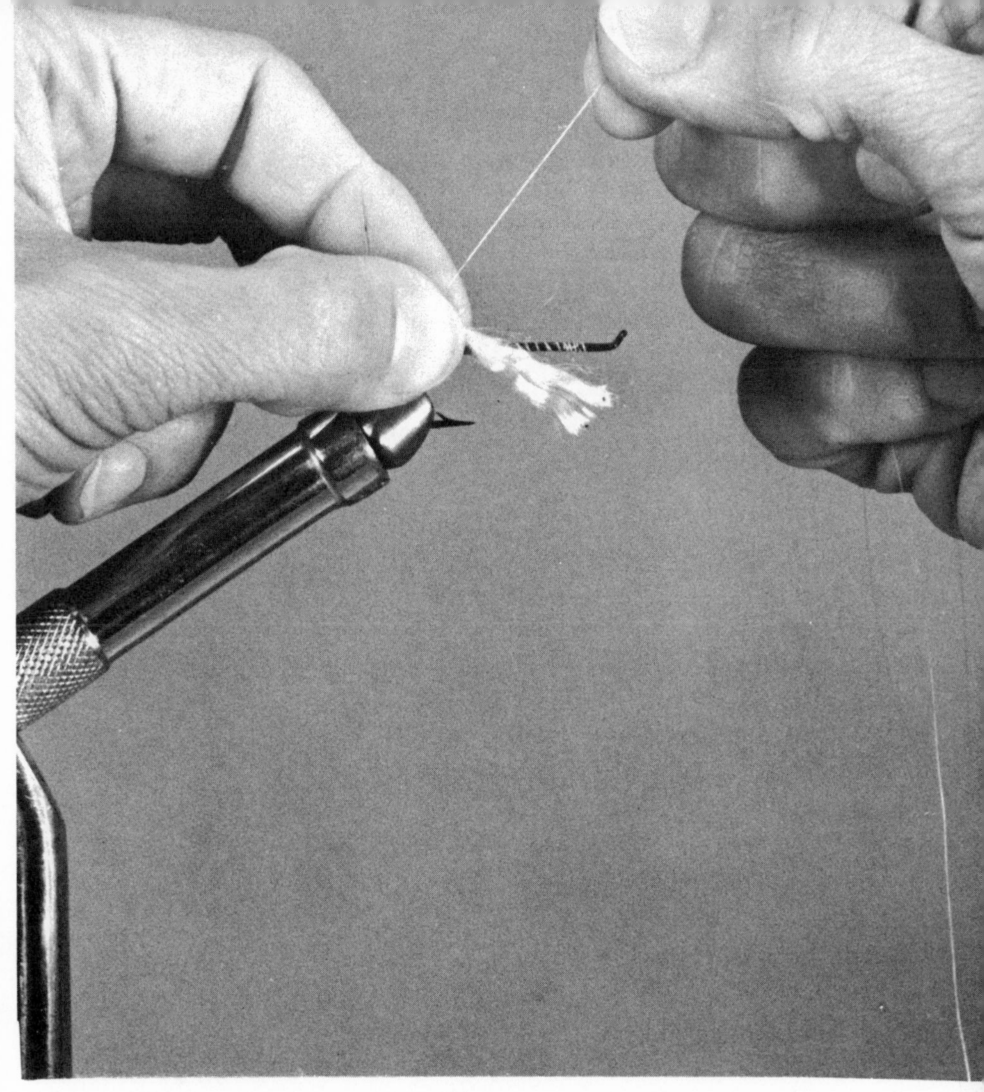

6b. Hold the strands of floss against the top of the hook above the barb with the left hand, and with the right hand release the thread from the button. Bring the thread *up* in *front* of the hook, slipping it between the left thumb and the floss. Bring the thread *down* between the floss and finger and continue *down* on the *far side* of the hook. Keep a firm grip on the floss and thread with the left fingers, and with the right hand pull gently downward on the thread. You will feel the thread sliding between the fingers of the left hand as it tightens over the floss and against the hook.

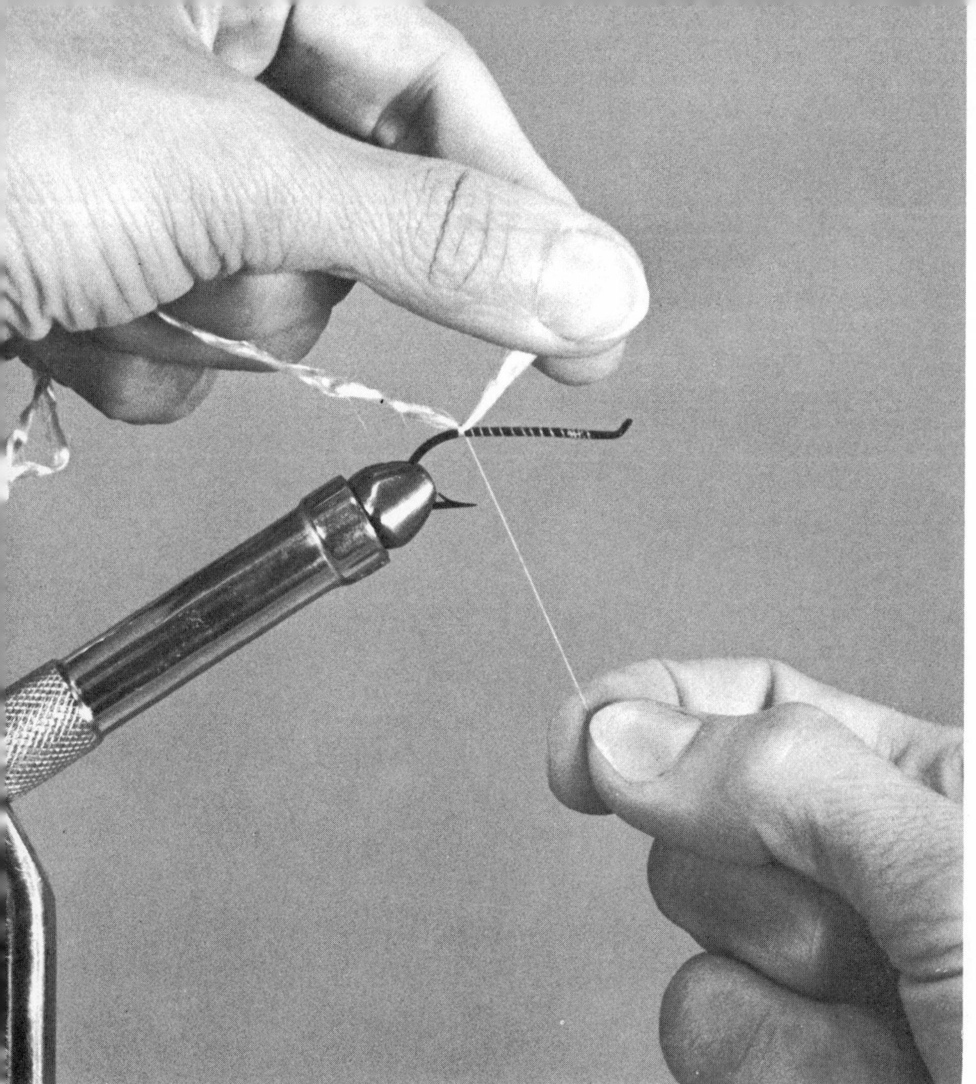

6c. The floss is now caught in place on top of the hook by the thread, but before opening the fingers of the left hand, repeat the process once more so that the floss will be anchored by two turns of tying thread. When the floss is tied on at "tail position," the short end of the floss may be used to pad the body, especially on a long hook.

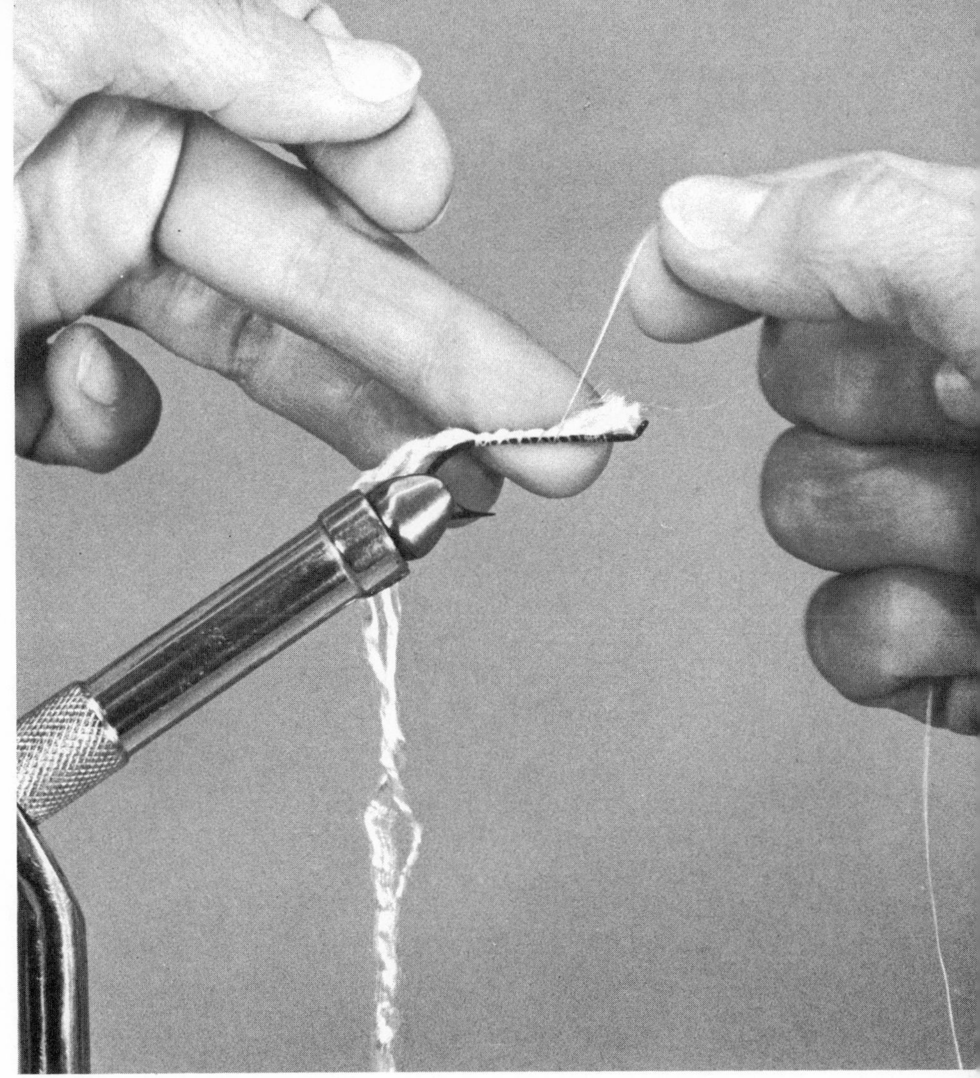

6d. Hold the short end of the floss forward along the top of the hook shank and bind it there with an open spiral of tying thread. Make sure the floss remains on *top* of the hook as the thread pulls against it.

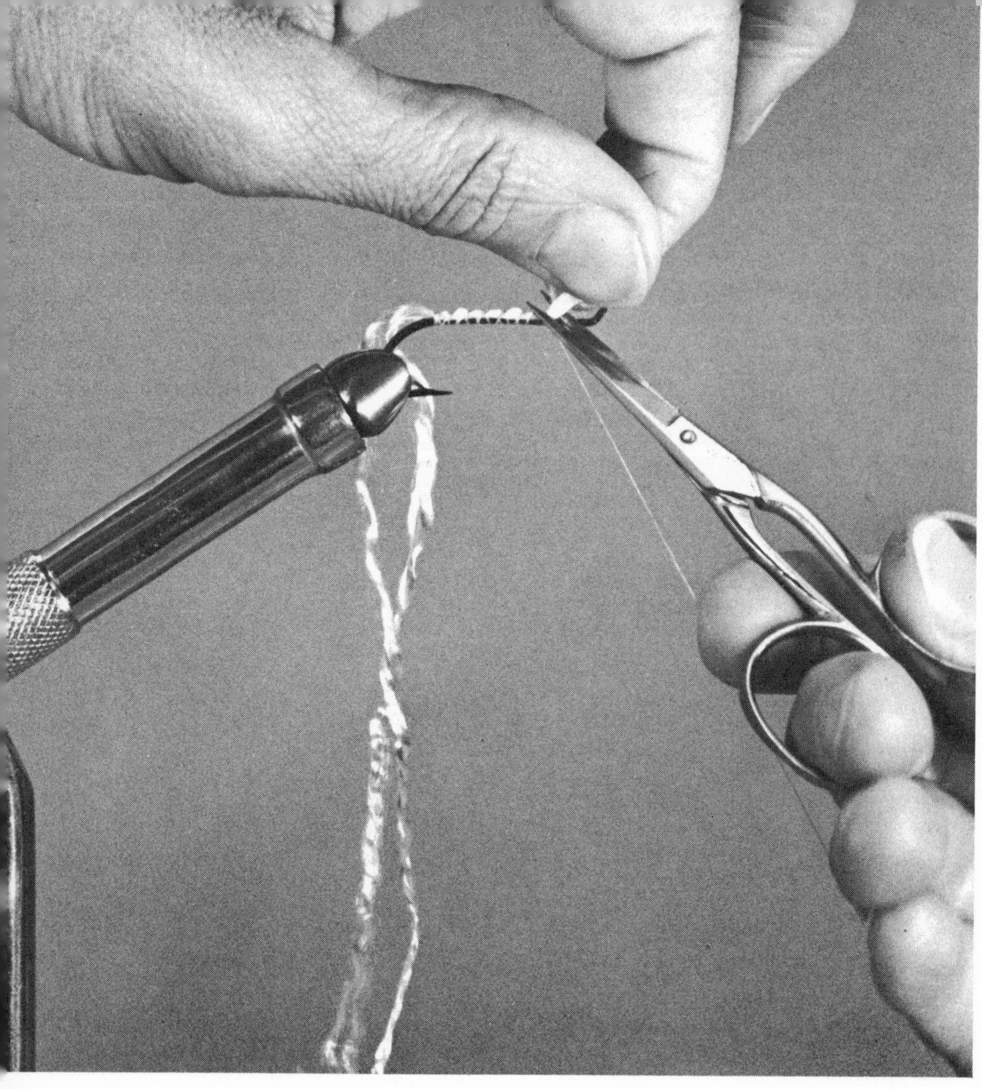

6e. When the thread reaches "wing position," secure it at the button. Lift the remaining end of the floss and cut it off close to the thread, at an angle to leave less bulk.

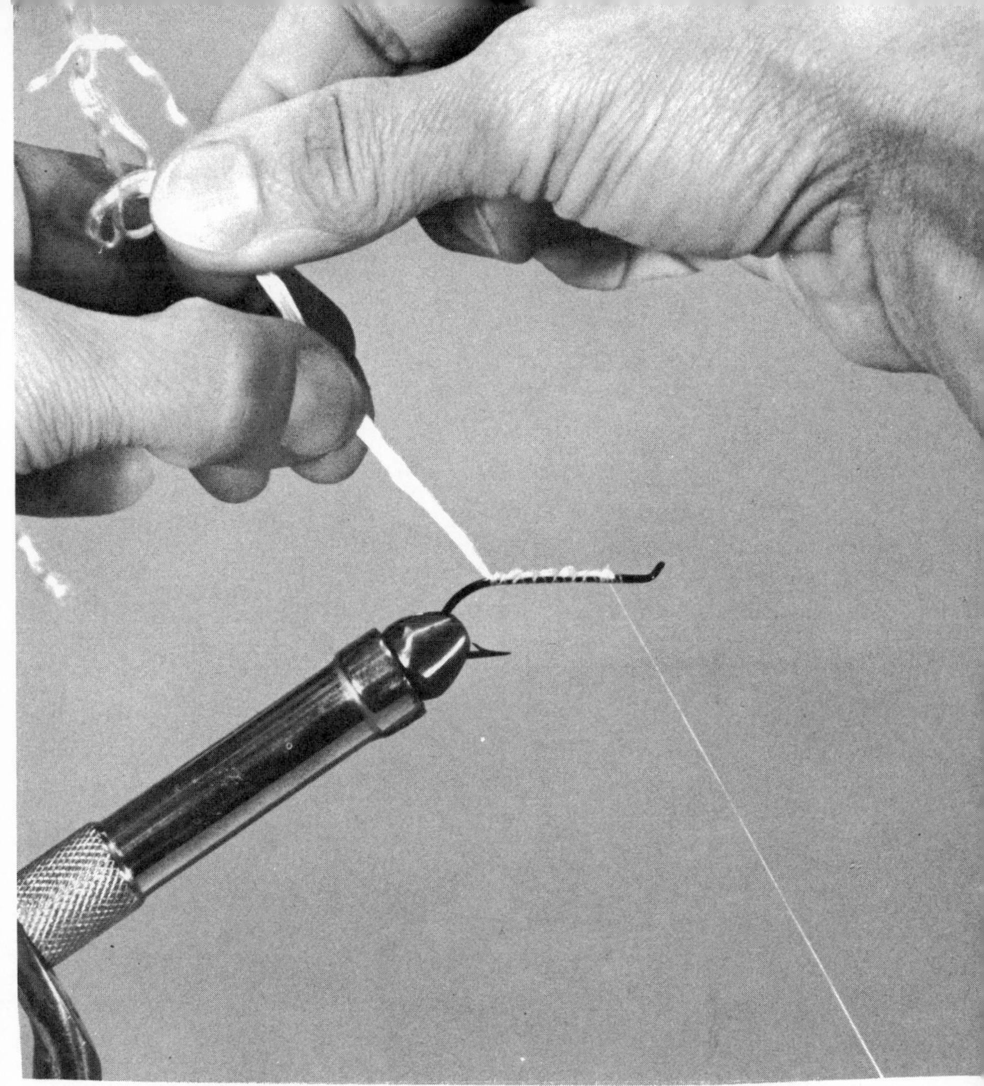

6f. Lift the long strands of wavy floss and straighten them into one strand by carefully smoothing them between thumbnail and finger. When the floss is a flat strand between fingers and hook, begin to wind it onto the hook. Keep the floss taut between hook and fingers.

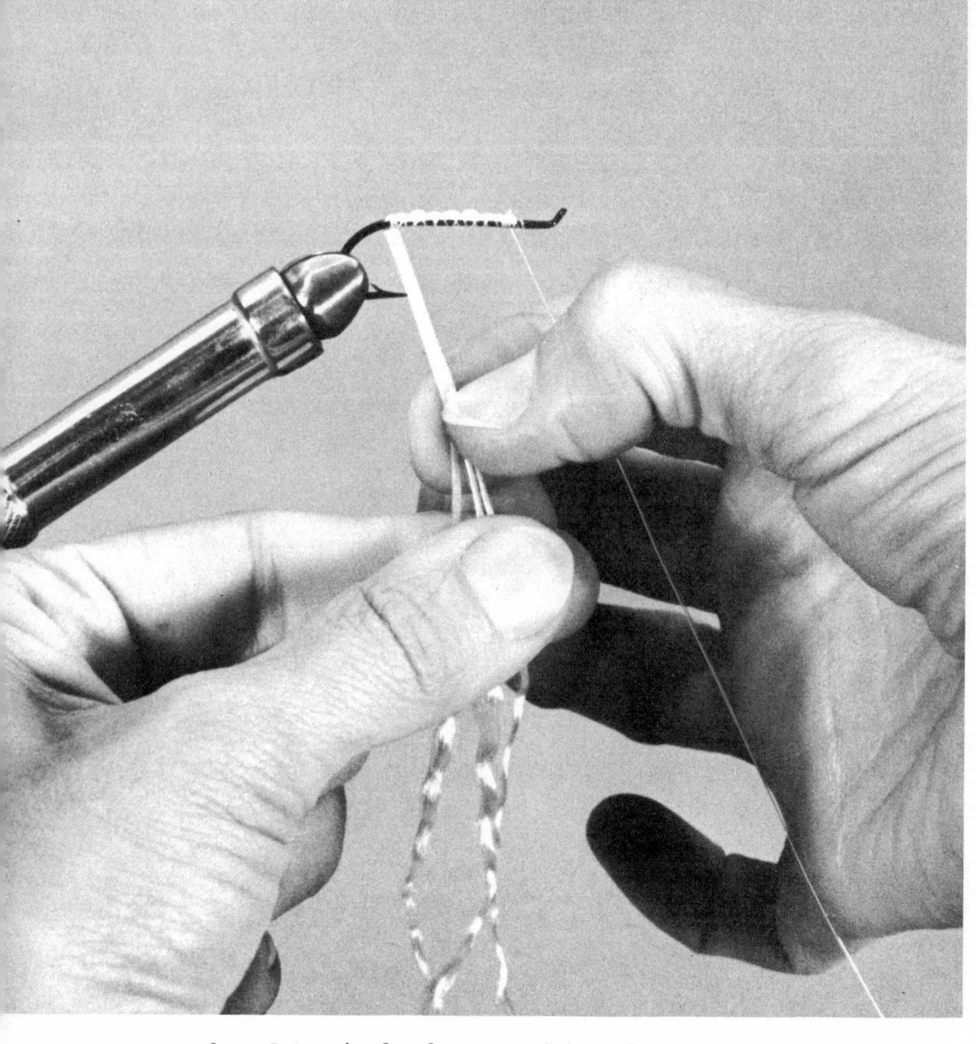

6g. Bring the flat floss strand down behind the hook and up in front. Take care to prevent any of the fine floss filaments from slipping back over the bend of the hook or catching on the hook point.

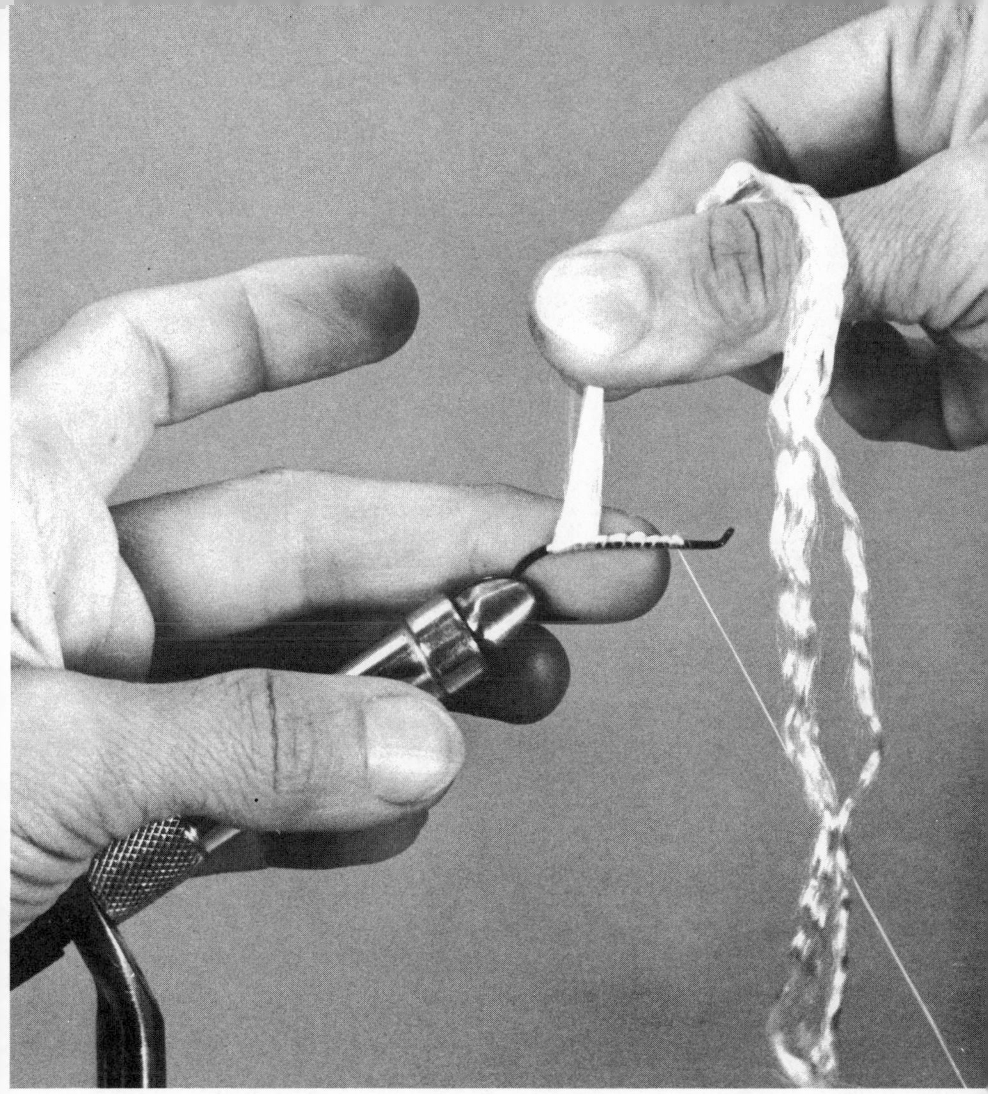

6h. Hold the floss slanting slightly in the direction of tying—in this case, toward the hook eye. Make sure the first turn of floss over the hook is immediately above the barb—not behind it—and covers the tying thread completely. Wrap the floss tightly, keeping it smooth. As each successive turn is wound around the hook, permit it to overlap the preceding one a little.

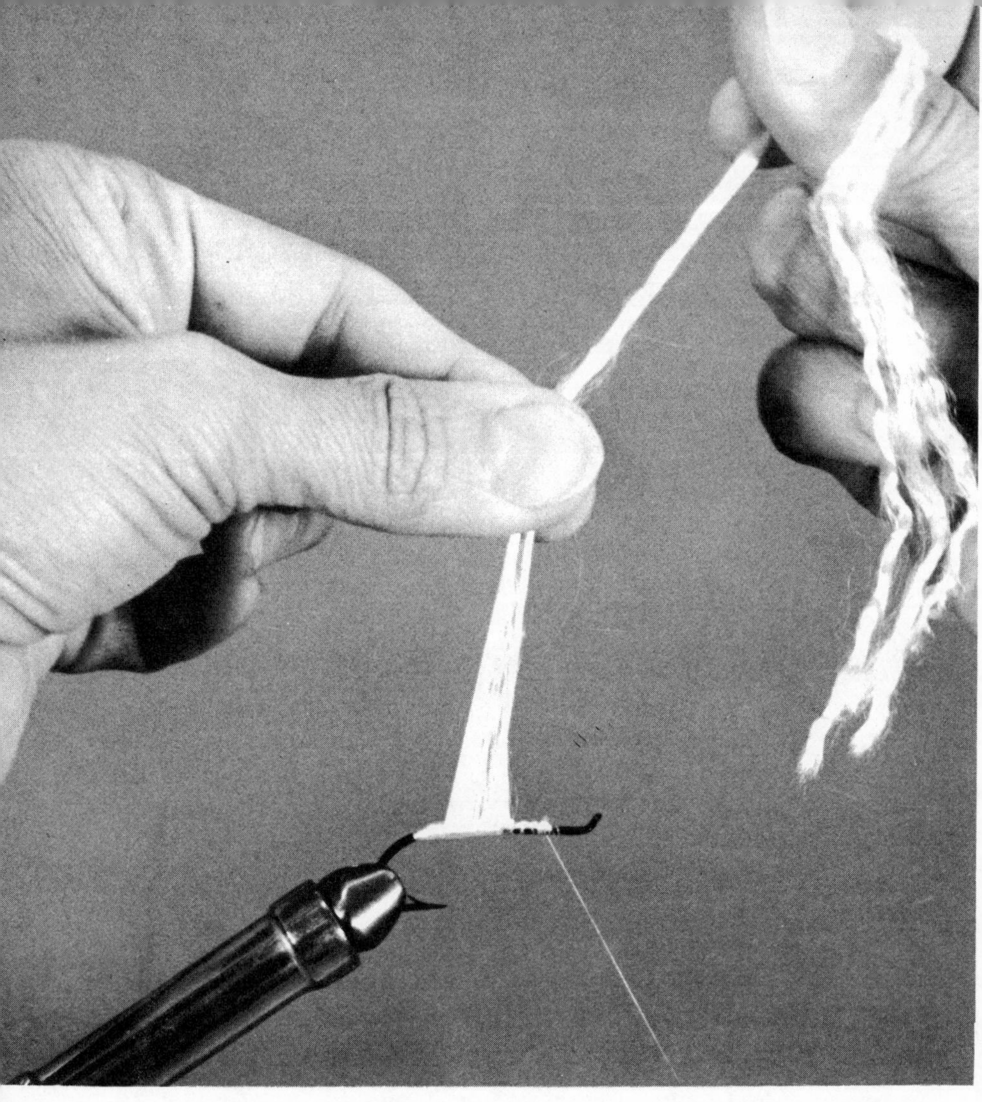

6i. By permitting the floss to spread somewhat at the hook as the winds around it are made, the body will become a little thicker in the middle of the hook as each turn of floss overlaps the preceding one a trifle. Keep the floss taut as it is carried down behind the hook and up in front and while passing it from one hand to the other.

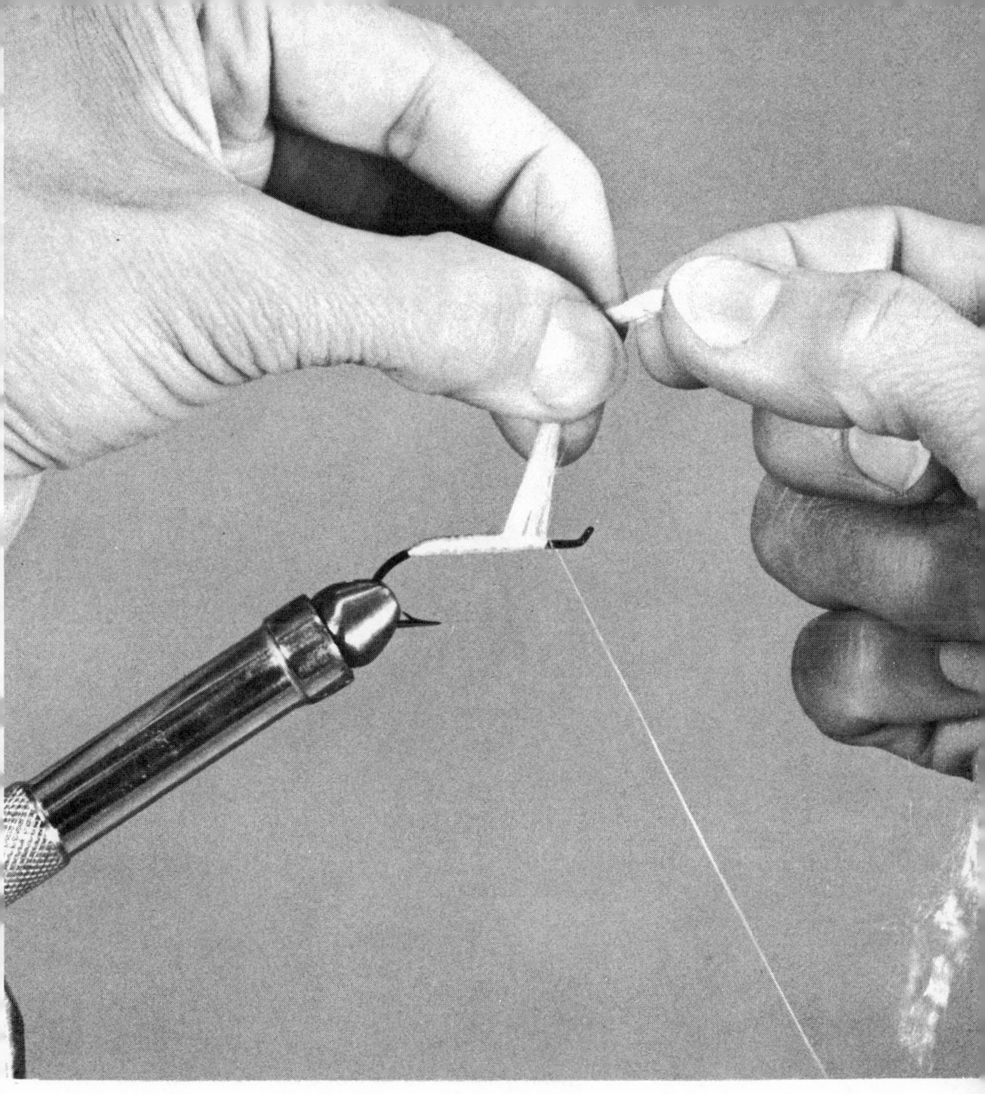

6j. As you approach "wing position," work the floss into a narrow strand by shortening the distance between hook and fingers. At "wing position" place the center finger of the left hand against the tying thread on the hook and with the right hand release the thread from the button.

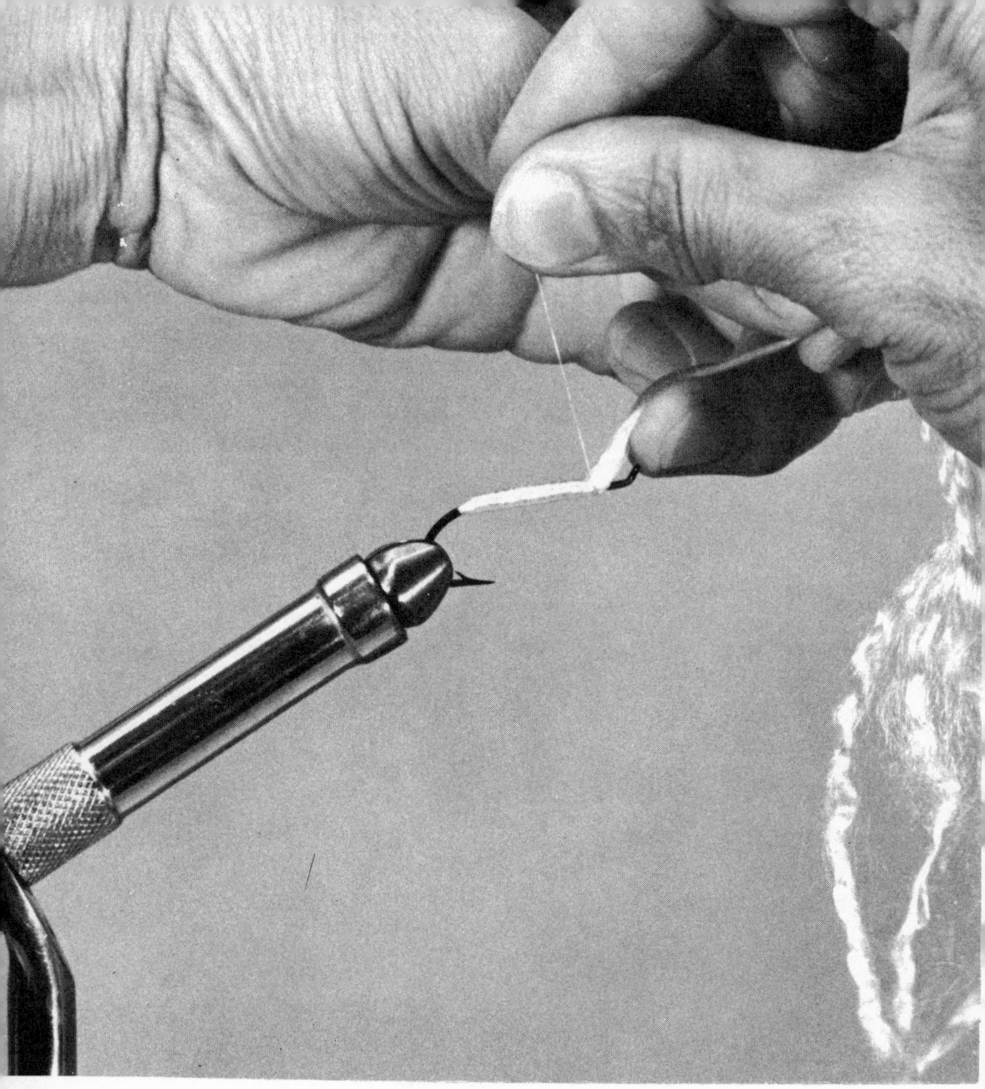

6k. Holding the floss taut in the direction of tying with the left hand, bring the thread up and across the floss to catch it against the hook and wind another turn of thread around the floss and hook to hold it. Secure the thread at the button.

6l. Clip off the excess floss at an angle close to the hook and bind down the tapered stub with two more turns of thread. The simplest floss body is complete.

Examine it critically. The surface should be "smooth as silk," tapered above the hook barb, the body itself firm and oval in shape. Now, remove the floss from the hook by carefully unwinding the thread until you can pick up the end of floss at "wing position." Unwind the floss from the hook and measure it, allowing just enough more for a comfortable fingerhold. This length of floss is all you will need to handle in the future for a hook of this size. Precutting the floss to the proper length before tying will prevent soiling a long strand through excessive handling. Practice with the used strand.

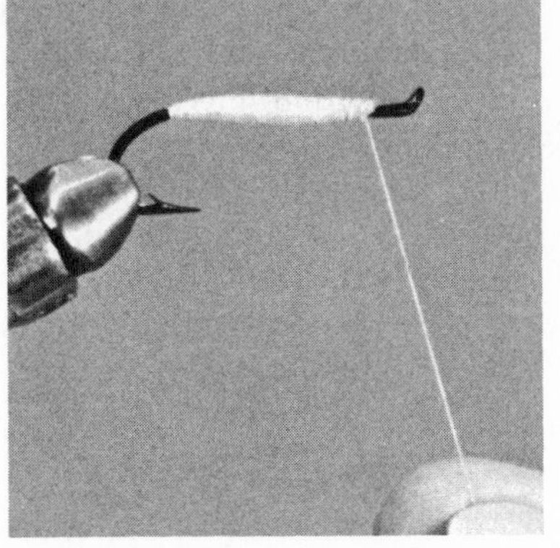

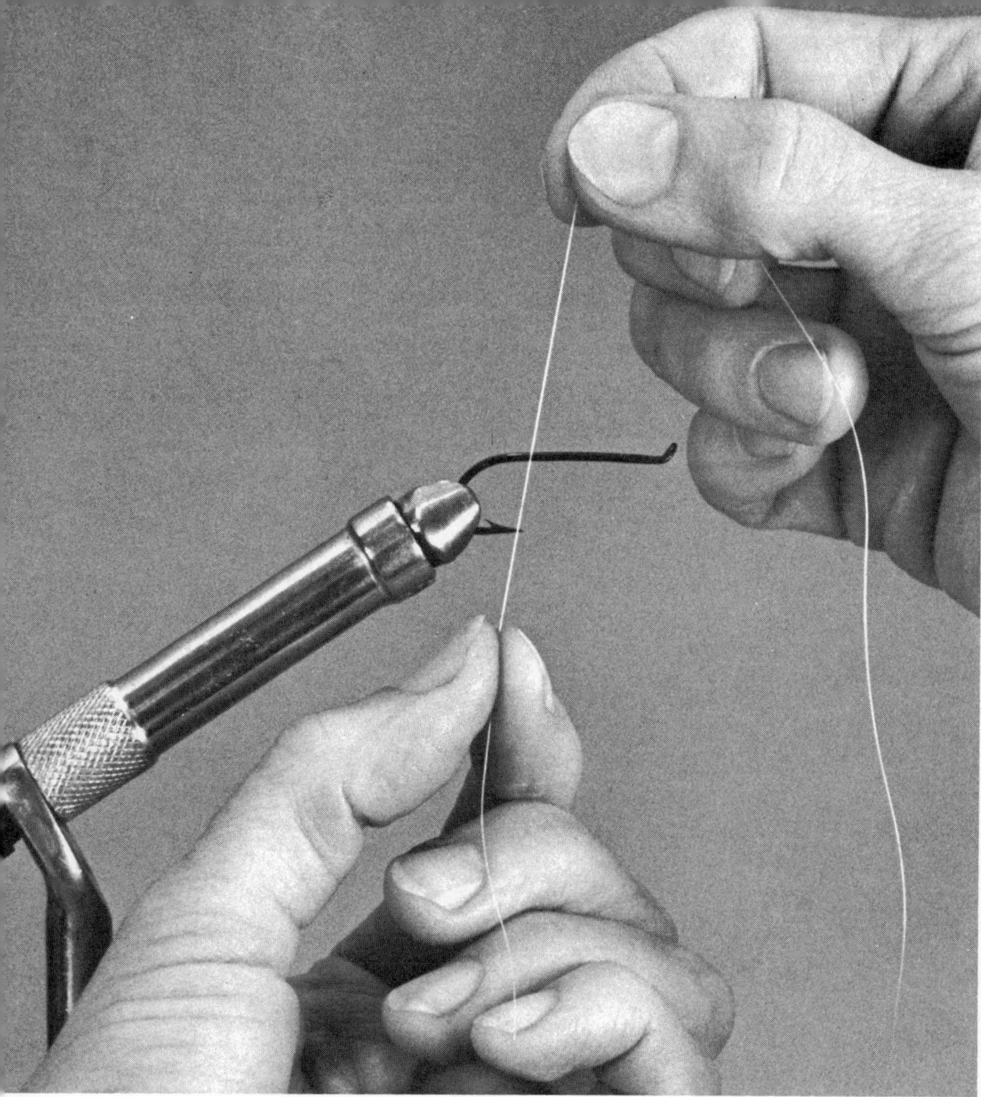

7a. To attach the thread at tail position, hold the short end of the waxed thread between the left thumb and forefinger. With the right hand, lay the thread against the hook directly above the point of the hook.

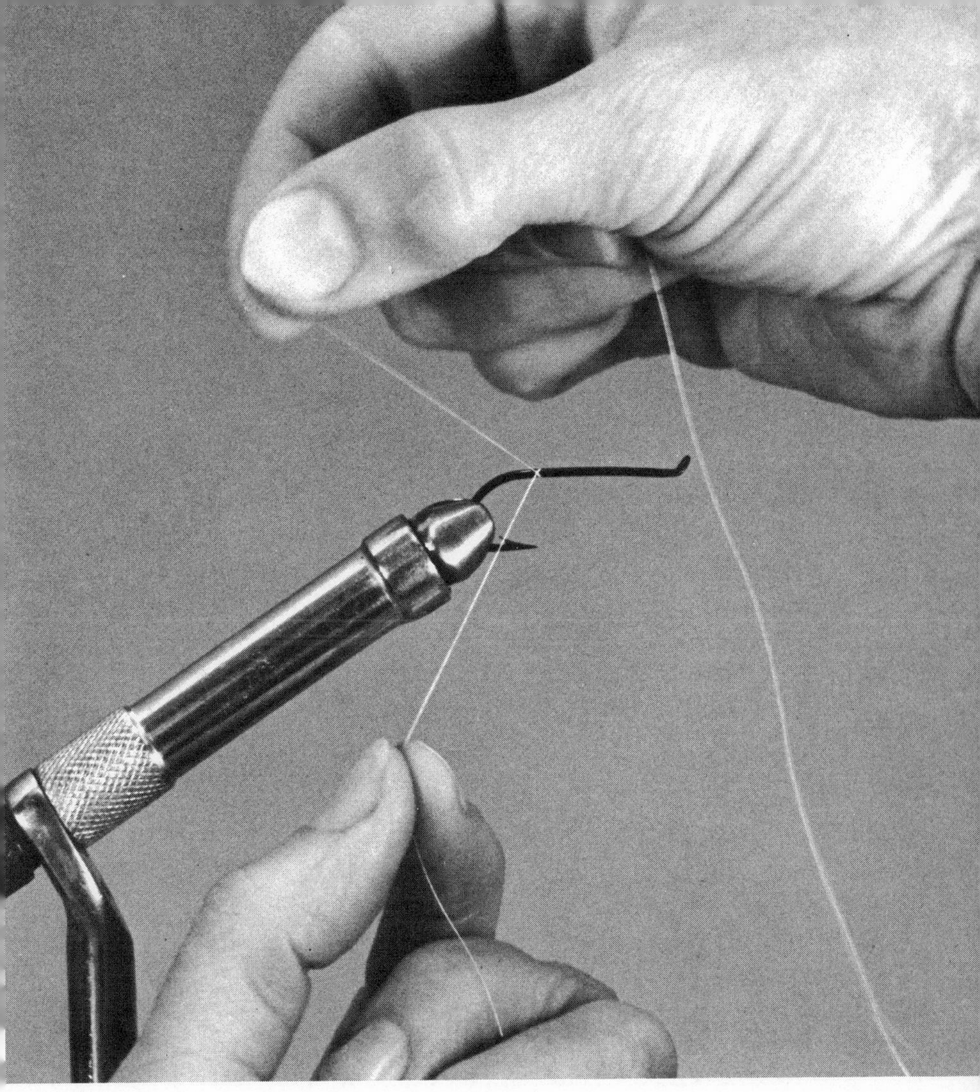

7b. With the right hand, carry the thread down behind the hook and up in front, crossing the thread held by the left hand.

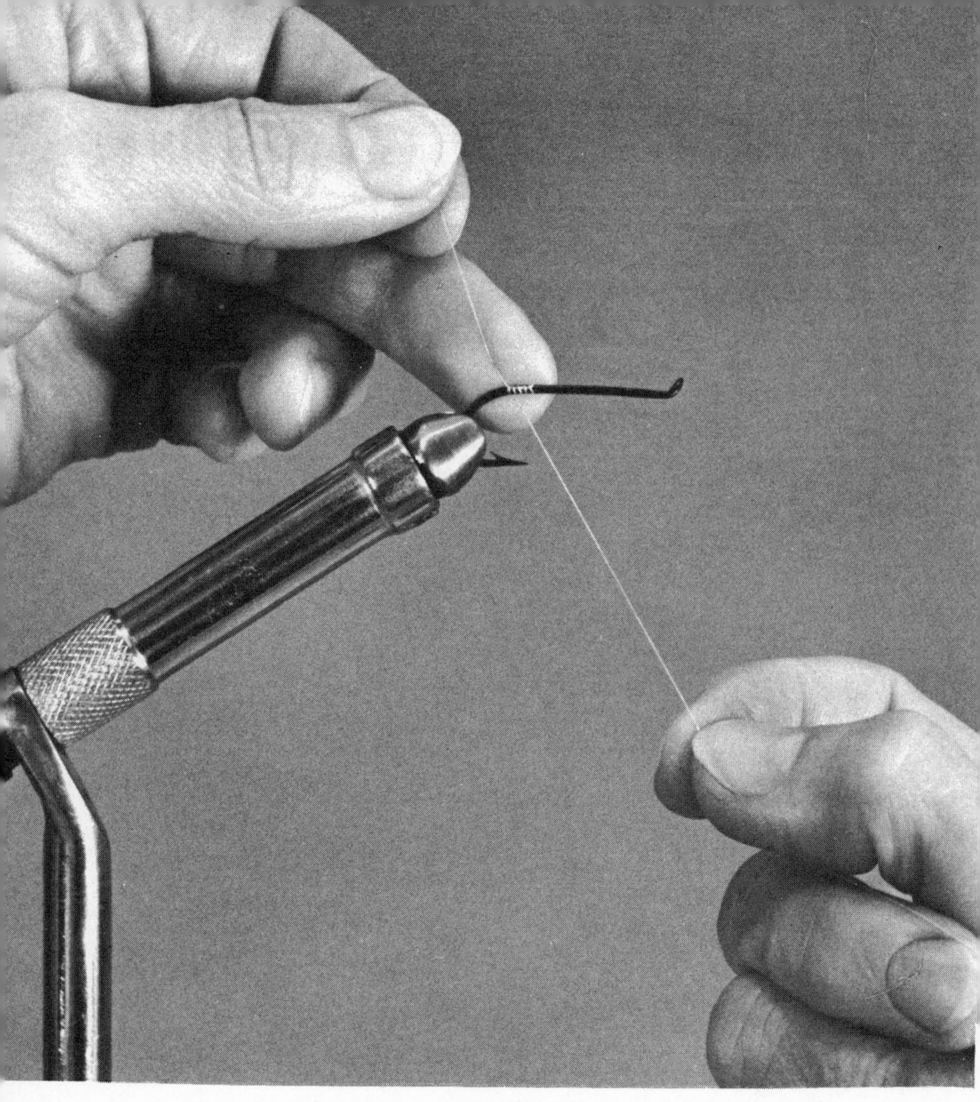

7c. Do this three or four times, making a close spiral towara the bend of the hook with the turns of thread ending just ahead of the barb. Secure the thread behind the rubber button.

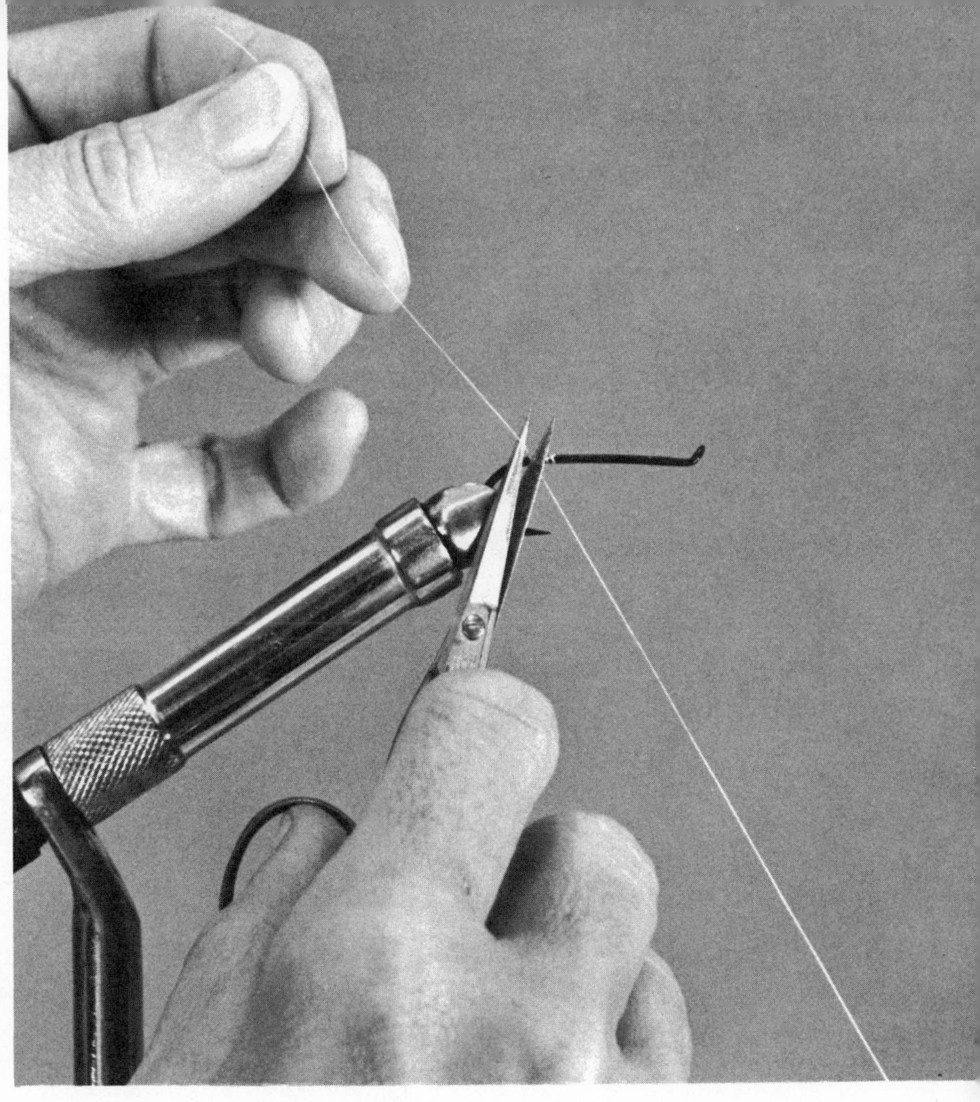

7d. Clip off the short end of the thread. The thread is now attached at "tail position."

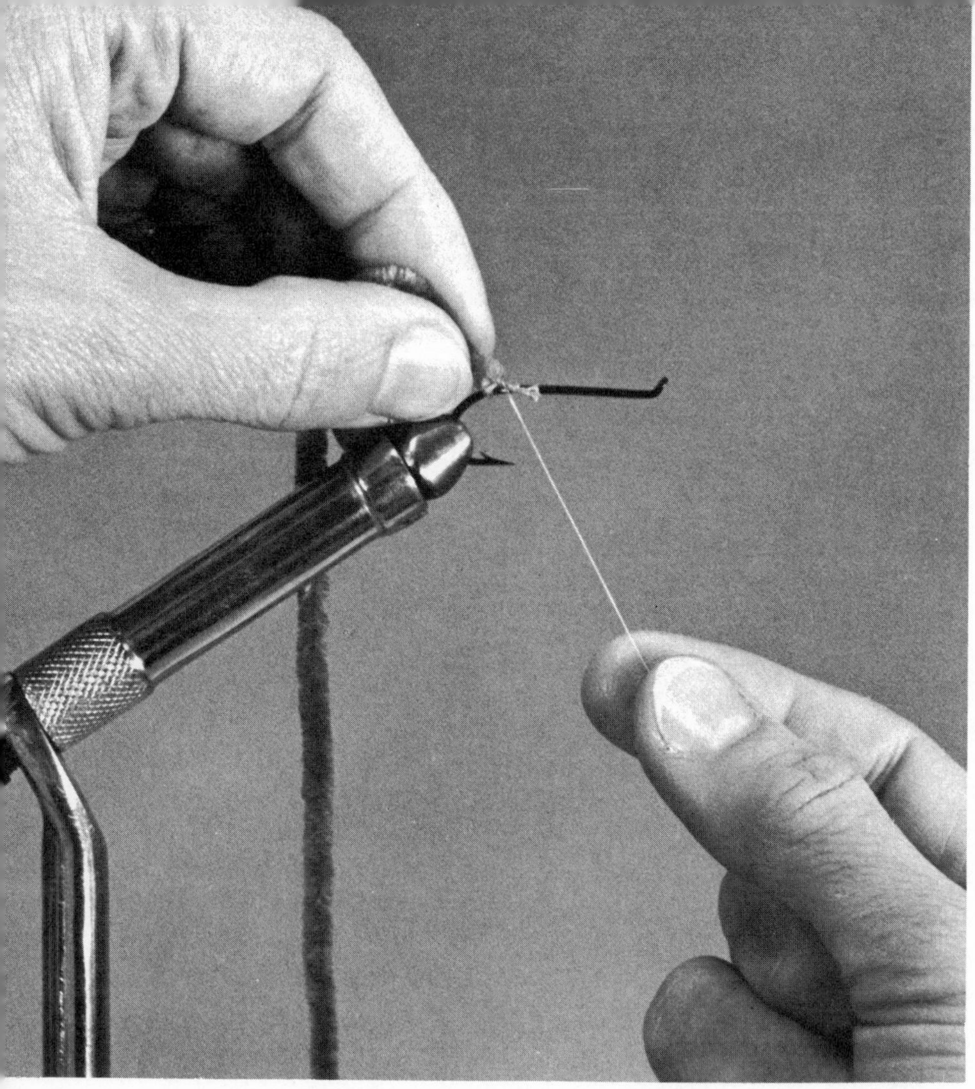

7e. Pull the fuzz from the end of a strand of chenille until ¼ inch of the thread core is exposed. Release the thread from the button with the right hand and bind the thread core to the hook shank directly *above* the barb, the thread now spiralling in the direction of the hook eye.

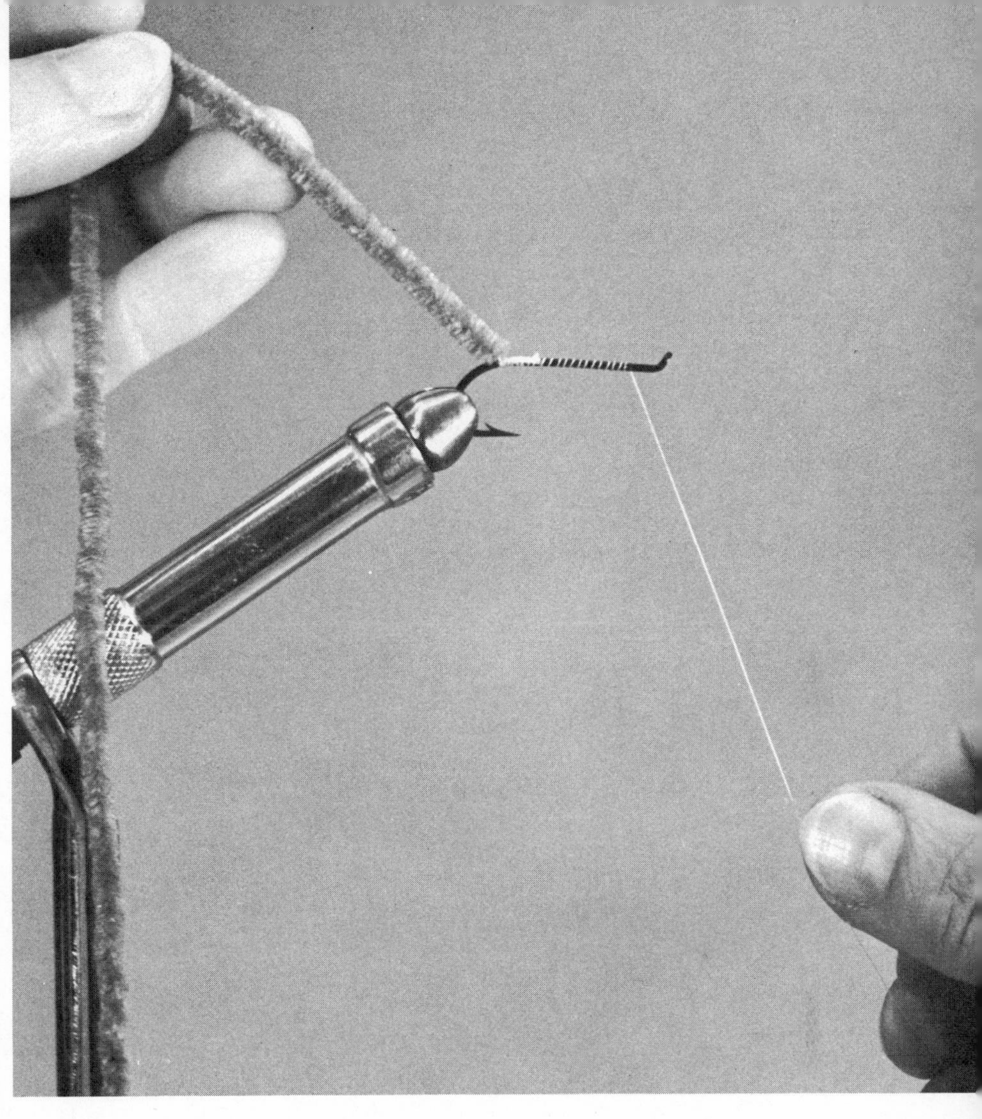

7f. Continue to wind the thread in an open spiral toward the hook eye until "wing position" is reached. Secure the thread at the button.

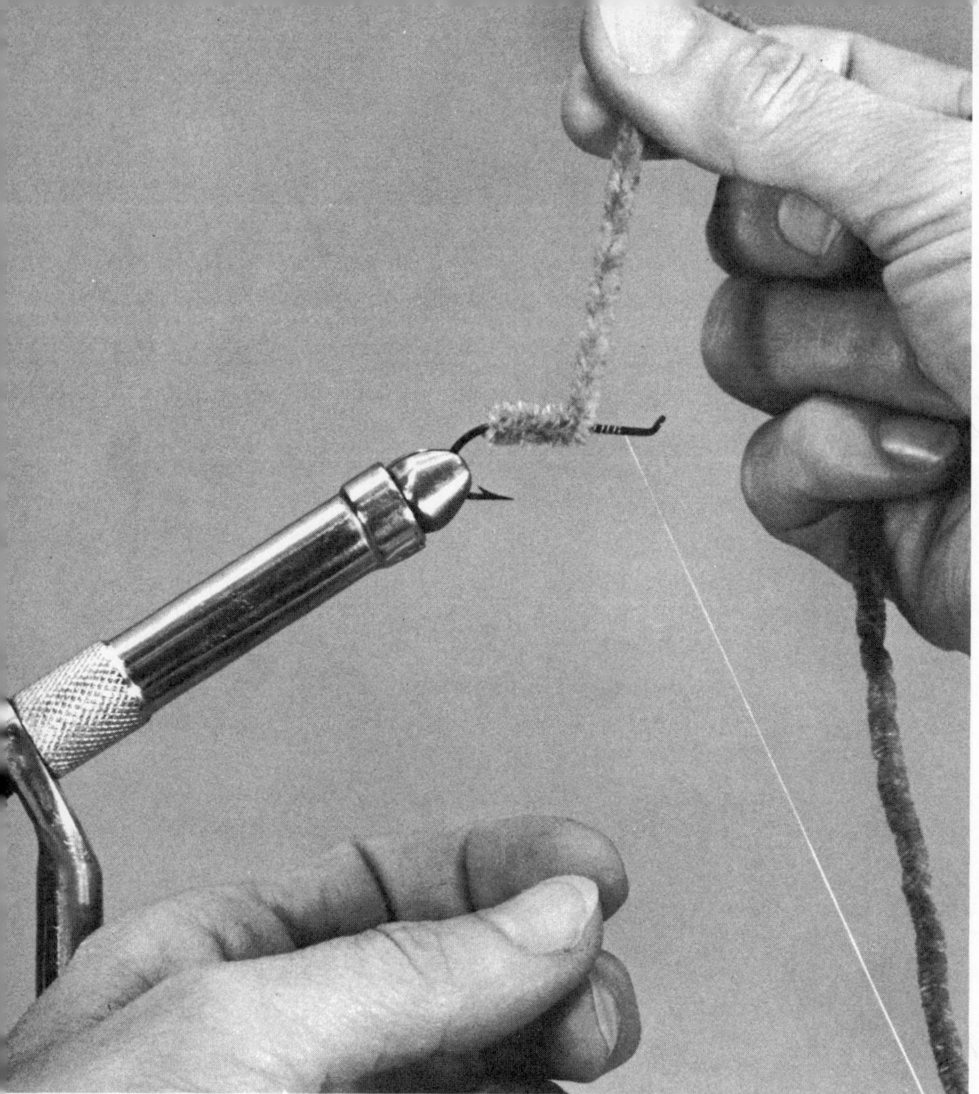

7g. Wrap the chenille around the hook in a close spiral, covering the hook and tying thread completely.

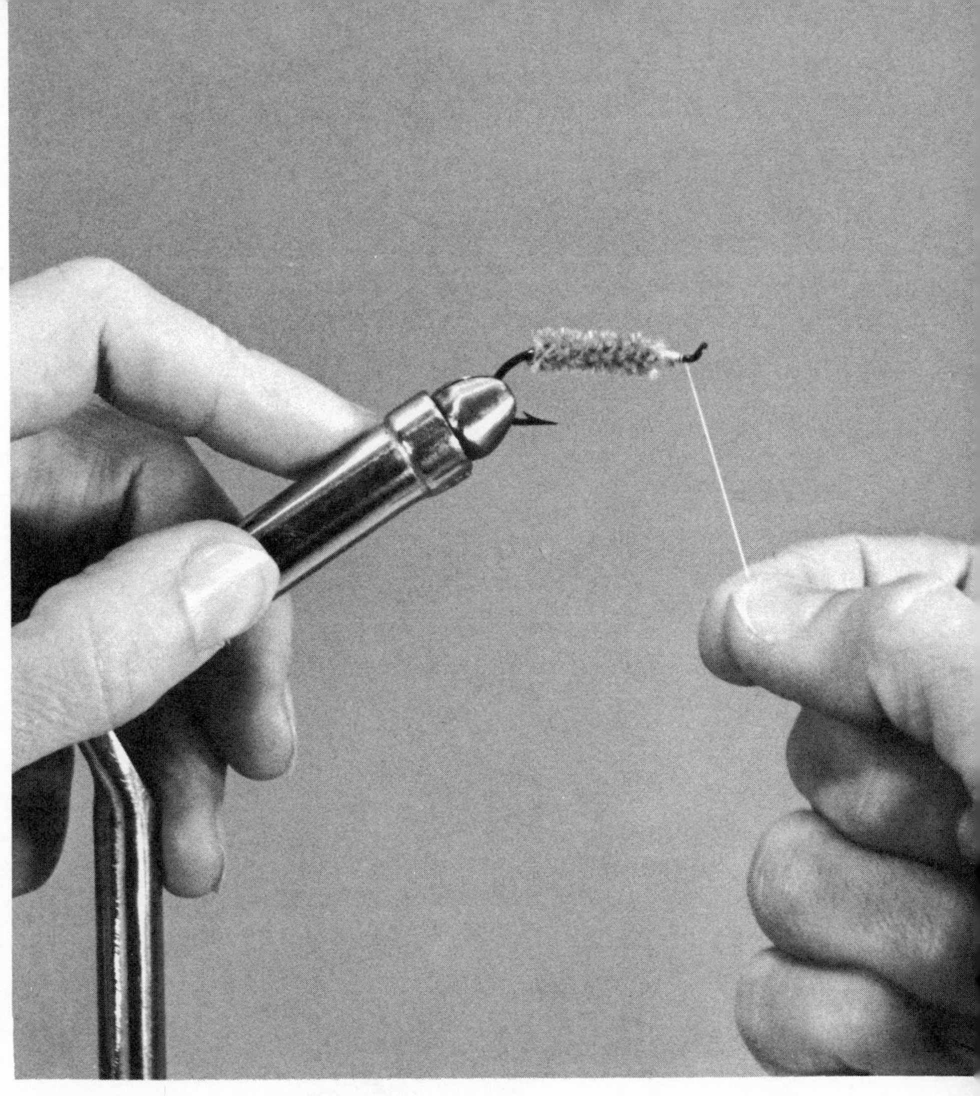

7h. At "wing position," release the thread and bring it up and over the chenille twice, binding it to the hook. Attach the thread to the button. Cut off excess chenille and bind down whatever chenille fibers or core may be visible ahead of the thread windings. The simple chenille body is now complete. This body can be made well with very little practice.

Wool

Wool is probably the most plentiful, colorful, and inexpensive material in the fly-tyer's stock. It has the distinction of being the oldest on record to be used for a fly body. Wool yarns may be obtained in small skeins or on cards containing a few yards each, in a great variety of colors and several weights and textures.

Yarn is made of strands of wool fibers twisted together. These strands may be separated before they are used for fly-tying or, if the yarn is not too heavy, it may be used just as it comes from skein or card.

Practice or emergency supplies of this material are not difficult to obtain, for there are usually small lengths of wool at home, such as the leftovers of knitting or mending projects. Anything knitted of wool and ready to be discarded—an old wool sock, mitten, or scarf—is a potential source of practice material. And for practice, any color of yarn is all right.

In an emergency, wool from an old tweed jacket could be another source of supply; its illusive color might conceivably match a particular hatch of insects on a favorite stream. A strand or two, sufficient for a few small flies, raveled from an inside seam would never be missed from the jacket.

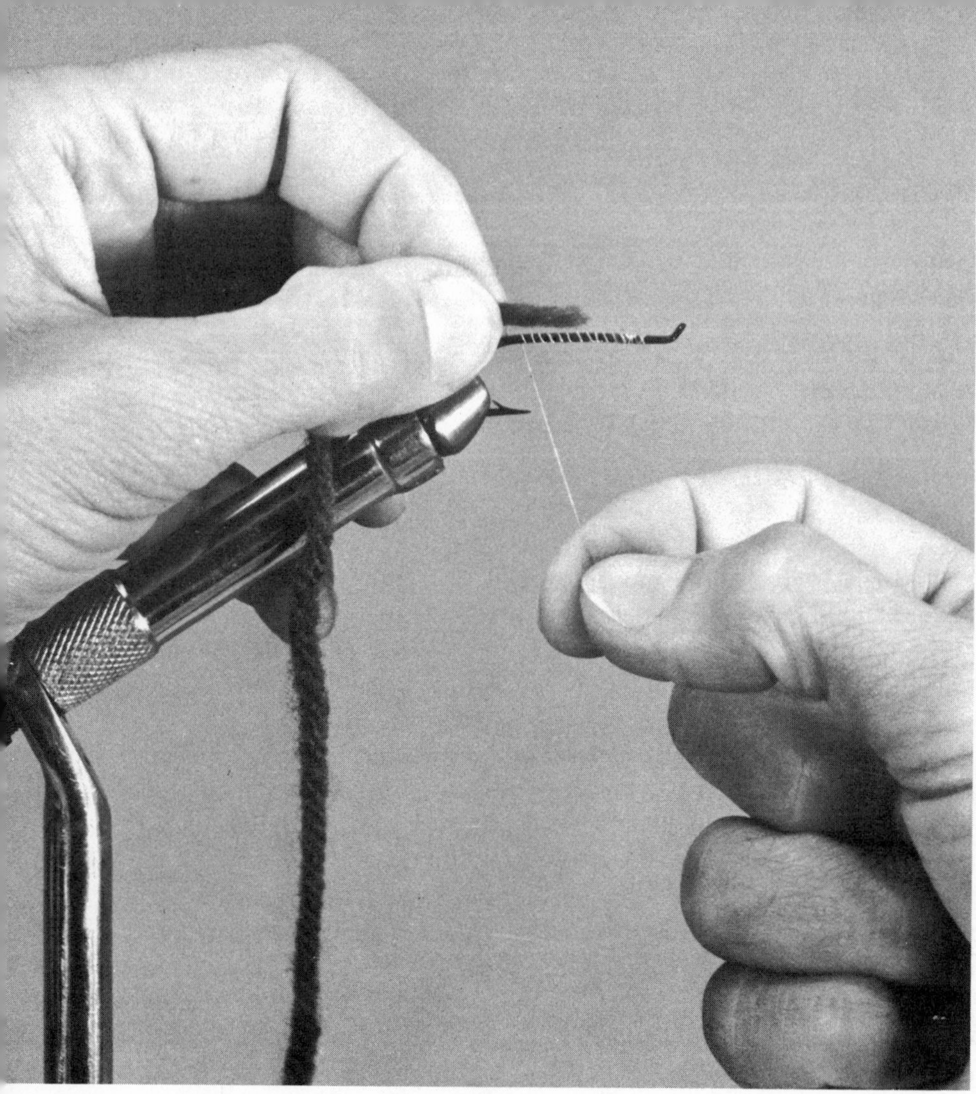

8a. On a hook this large, yarn of the size shown may be used without separating the strands. The thread is attached at "wing position" and wound down the hook in an open spiral to "tail position." Hold the yarn on top of the hook at "tail position" with the short end toward the hook eye.

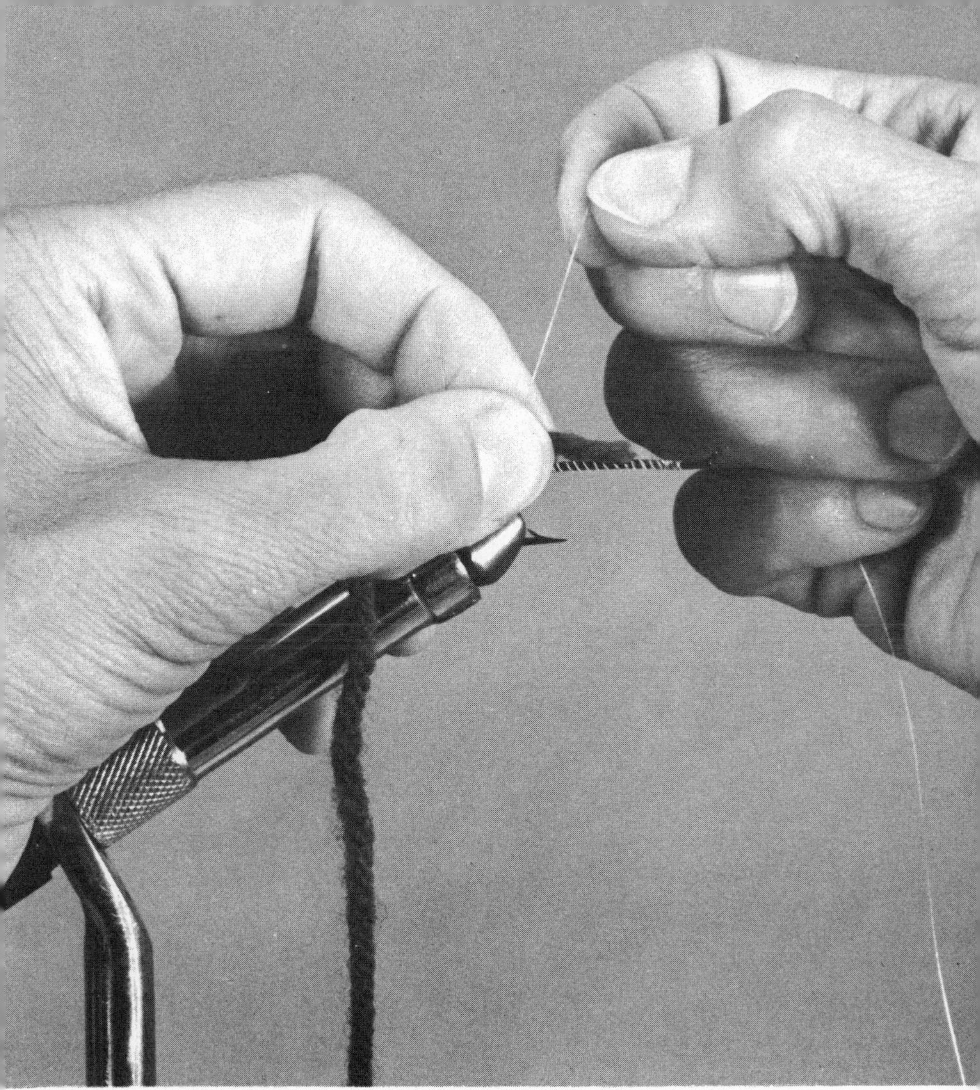

8b. Lift the thread in front of the hook, sliding it upward between yarn and thumb. Bring it down between yarn and forefinger on the far side of the hook and pull it snug, keeping the yarn on top of the hook.

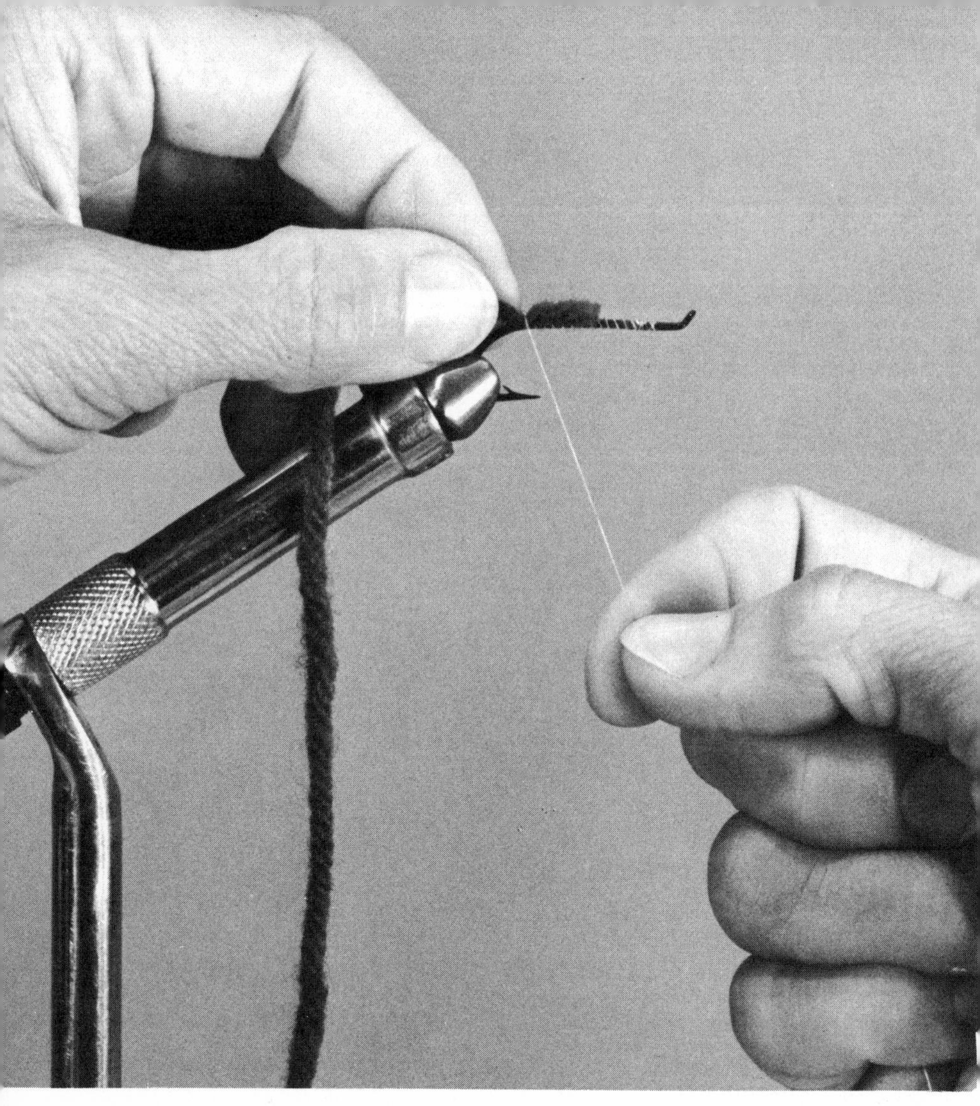

8c. Repeat twice, keeping the thread winding taut and in approximately the same place around the wool and hook. The yarn is now attached to the hook. Do not relax thread tension.

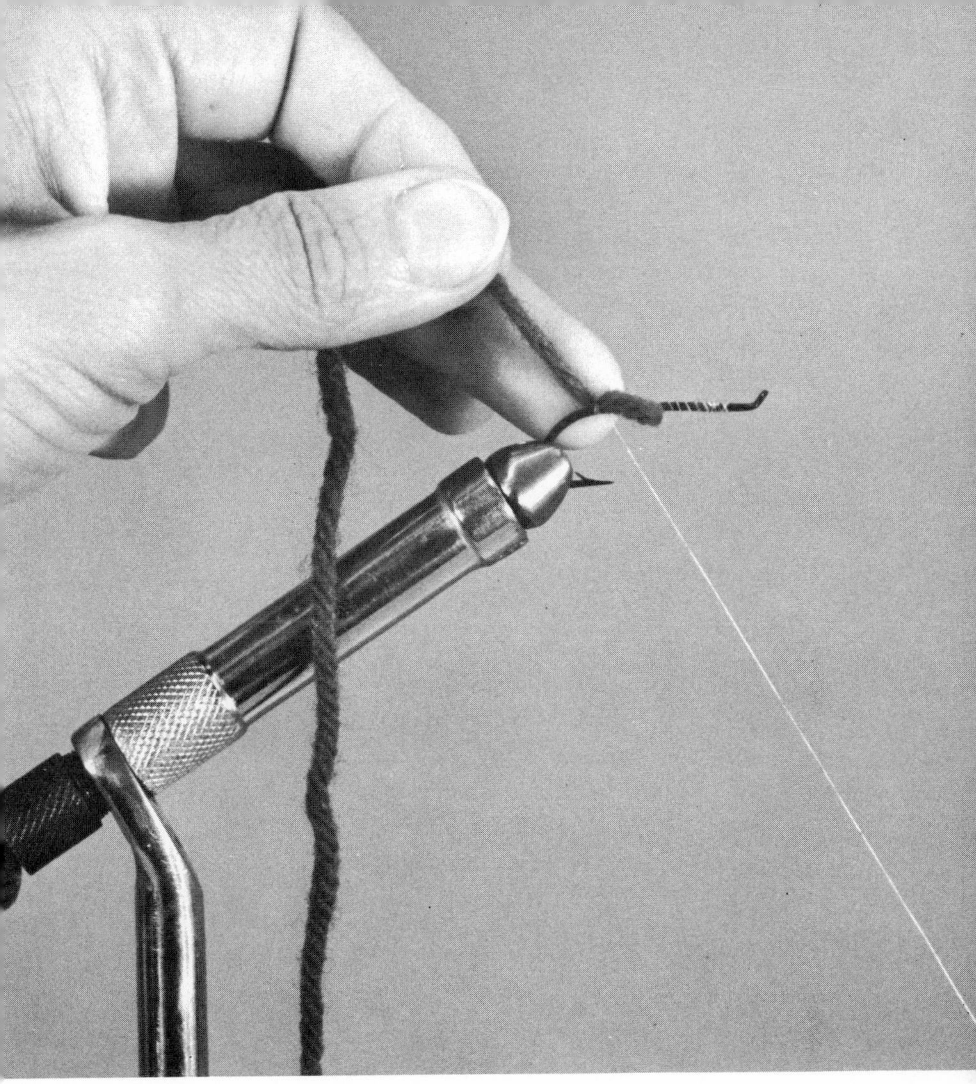

8d. Press the middle finger of the left hand against the windings while you catch the thread behind the button.

8e. Make a small loop of yarn against the middle finger of the left hand, letting the loop extend beyond the thread windings until it is even with the bend of the hook.

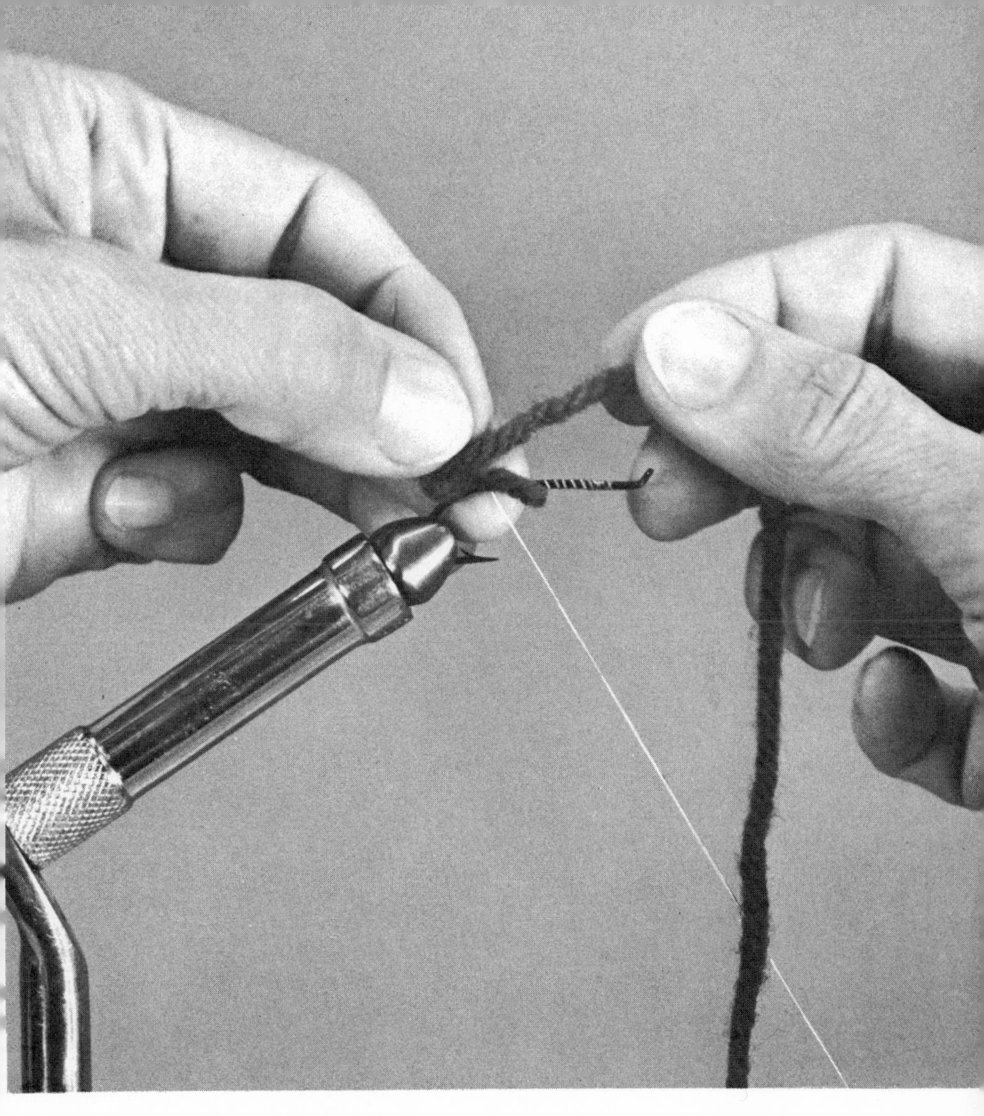

8f. Grasp the yarn loop with the left thumb and forefinger, pinching it on top of the hook while releasing the thread from the button.

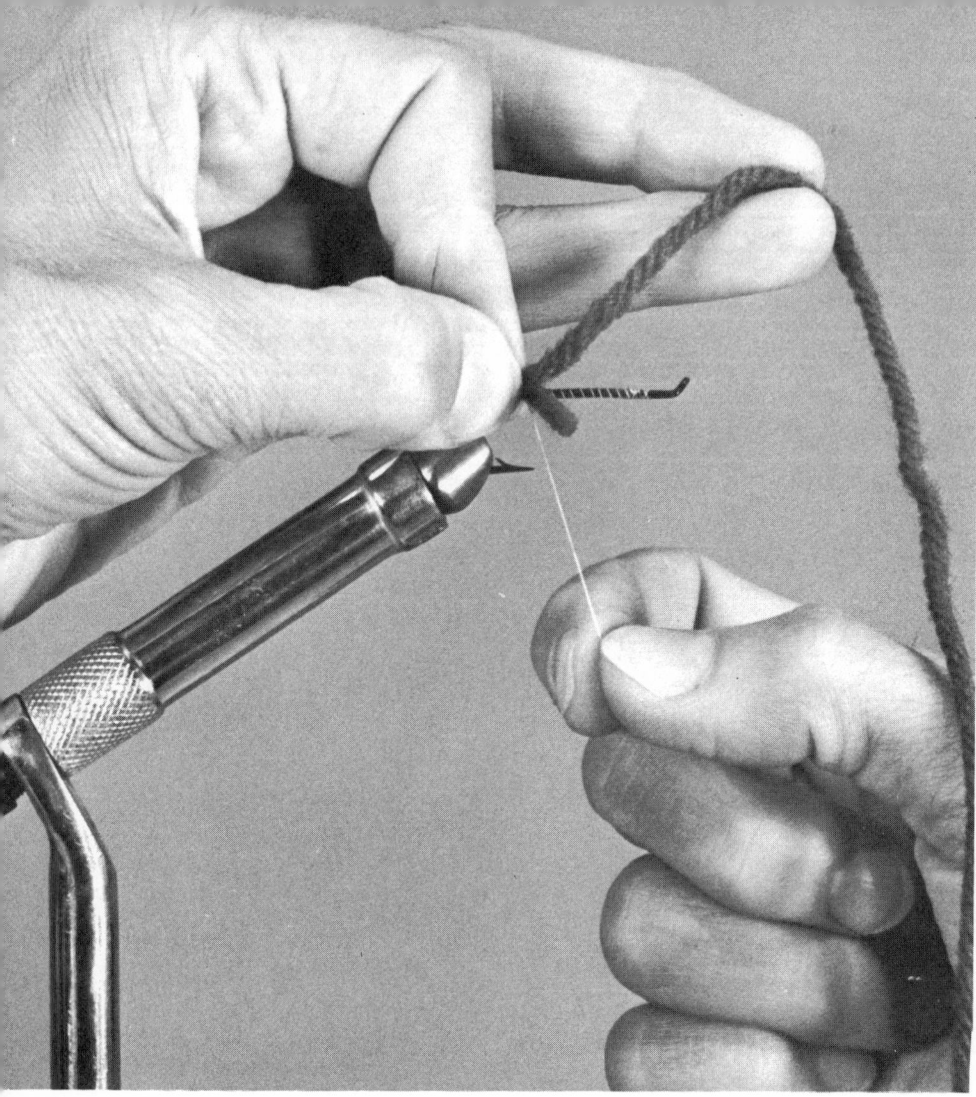

8g. Bring the thread up in front of the hook, between fingers and wool, and down between fingers and wool on the far side of the hook. Repeat. The extended fingers of the left hand hold the wool strand out of the way.

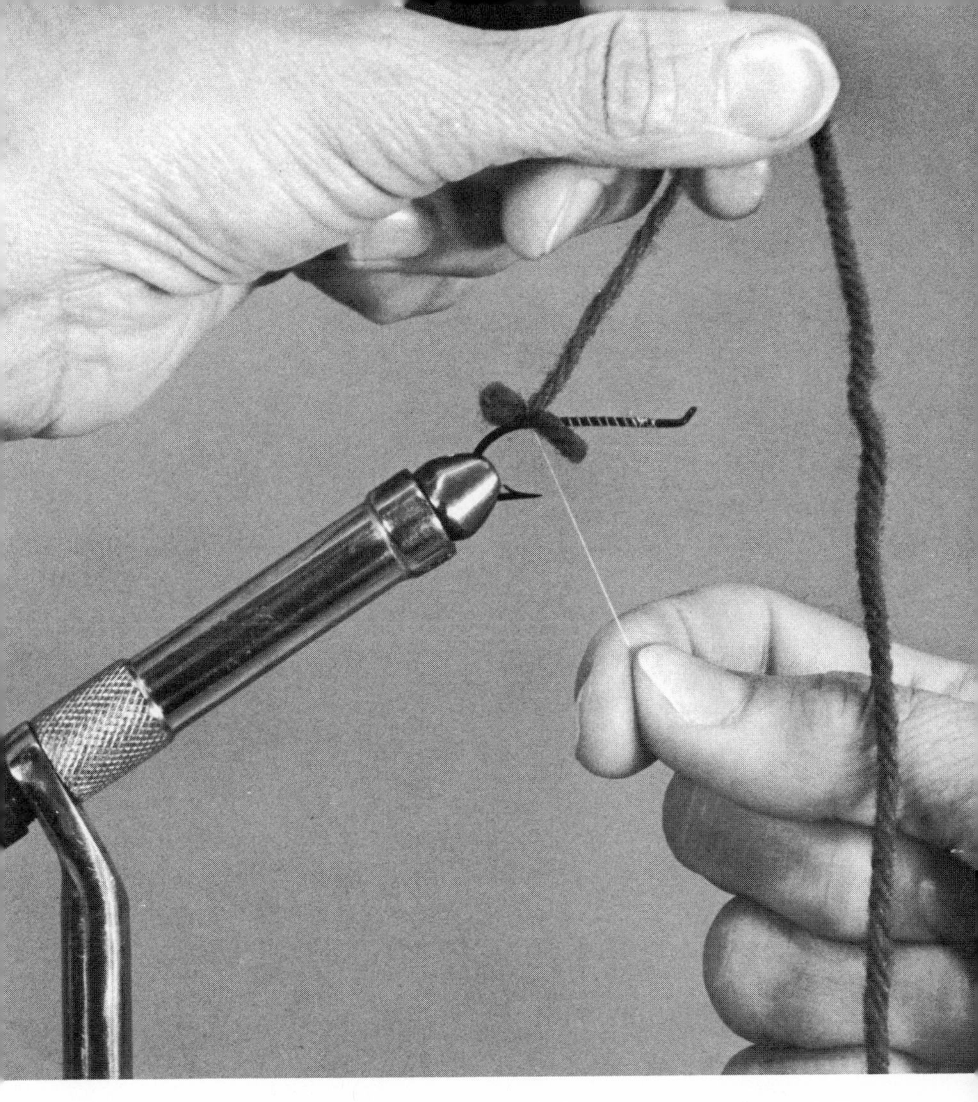

8h. The wool loop is held in place. Catch the thread behind the button and clip off the short end of yarn, tapering it.

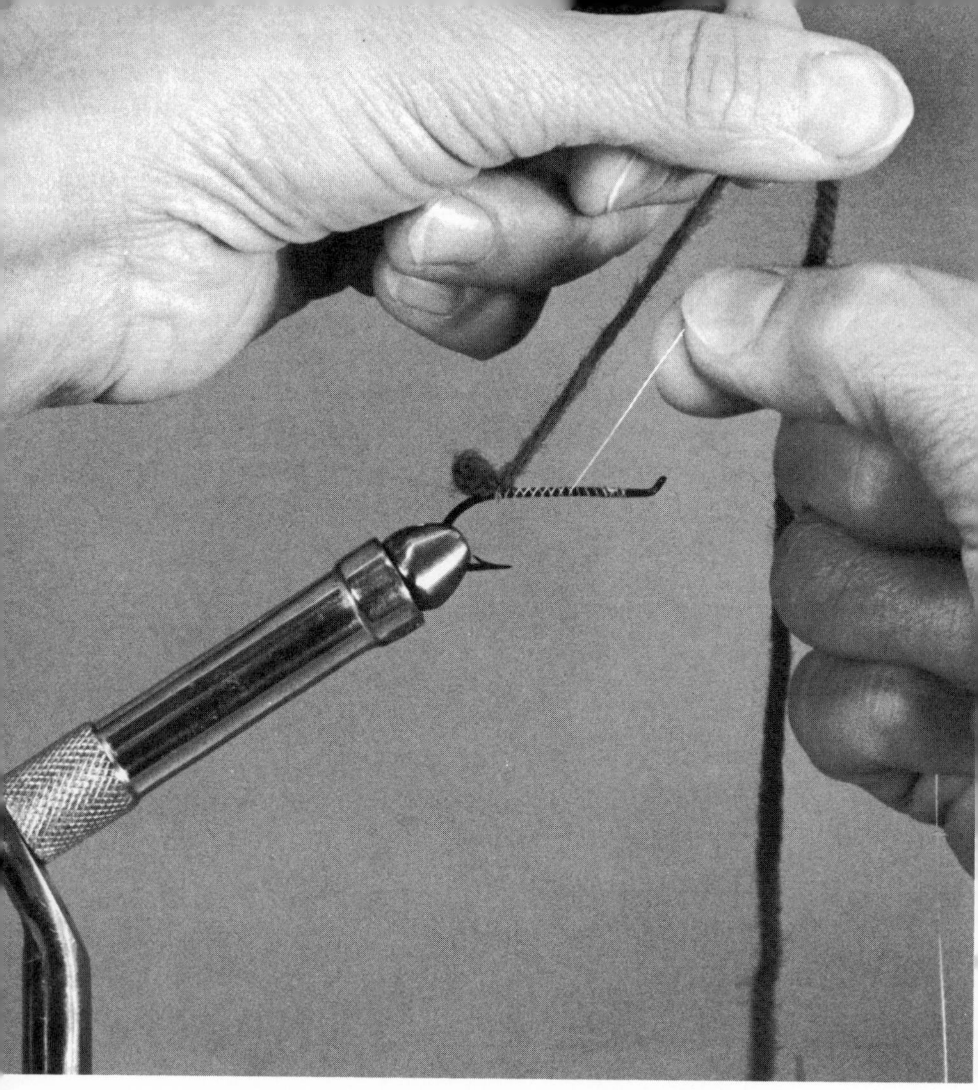

8i. Release the thread and bind the tapered end to the hook. Continue winding it forward along the hook in an even, open spiral to "wing position" and secure it at the button.

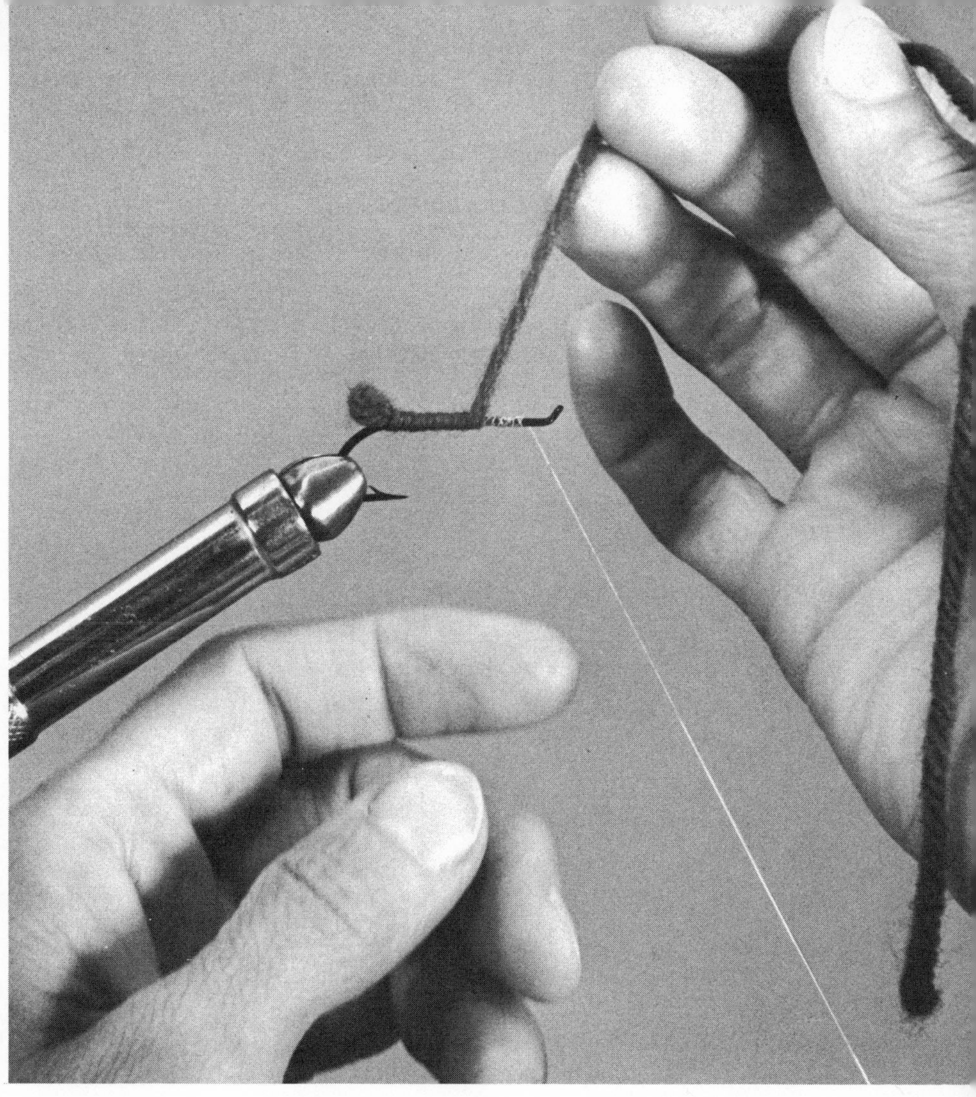

8j. With the right hand, carry the wool down behind the hook. Transfer it to the left hand when the right encounters the tying thread and bring it up in front, avoiding the hook point. As you wrap the wool around the hook, be sure the tying thread is completely covered. Hold the yarn at an angle in the direction of tying and continue to wind it, without overlapping, along the hook shank toward the hook eye.

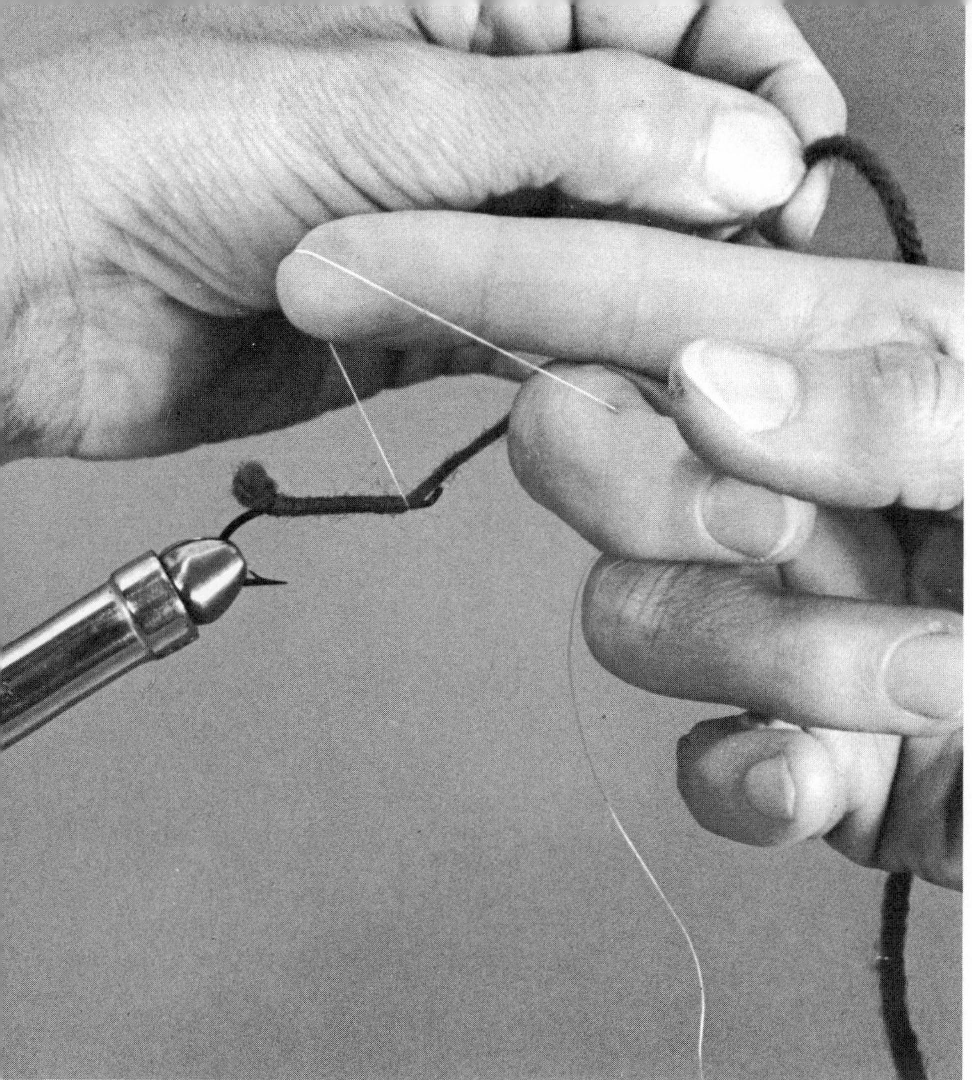

8k. When "wing position" is reached, release the thread and bring it up and across the yarn. Bind it there with another turn of thread. Secure the thread to the button. Cut off the yarn at an angle, tapering the end.

8l. Release the thread and bind this end neatly to the hook with two more turns of thread. The loop-end body is complete. By unwinding it and measuring the yarn, allowing a small amount for a finger grip, you will know how much wool is required for a body of this type on a hook this large. The wool unwound from the hook can be used again for practice.

Another simple body with a tag end can be made by holding

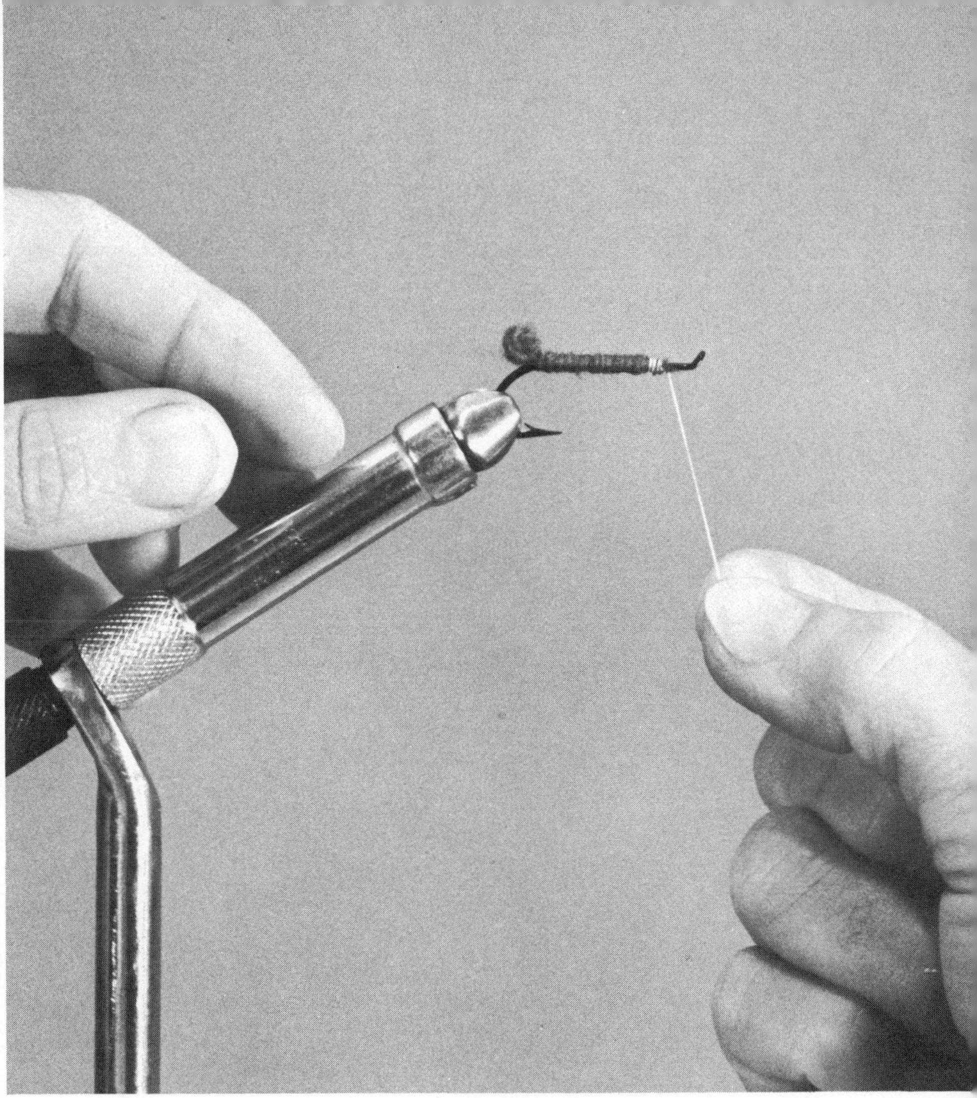

the wool yarn with the short end extending beyond the hook. Bind it in place and finish the body according to the previous instructions. Trim the short end of yarn even with the bend of the hook, holding the scissors vertically.

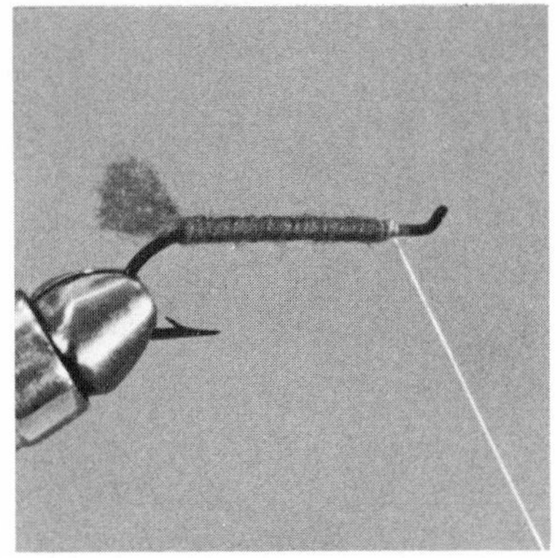

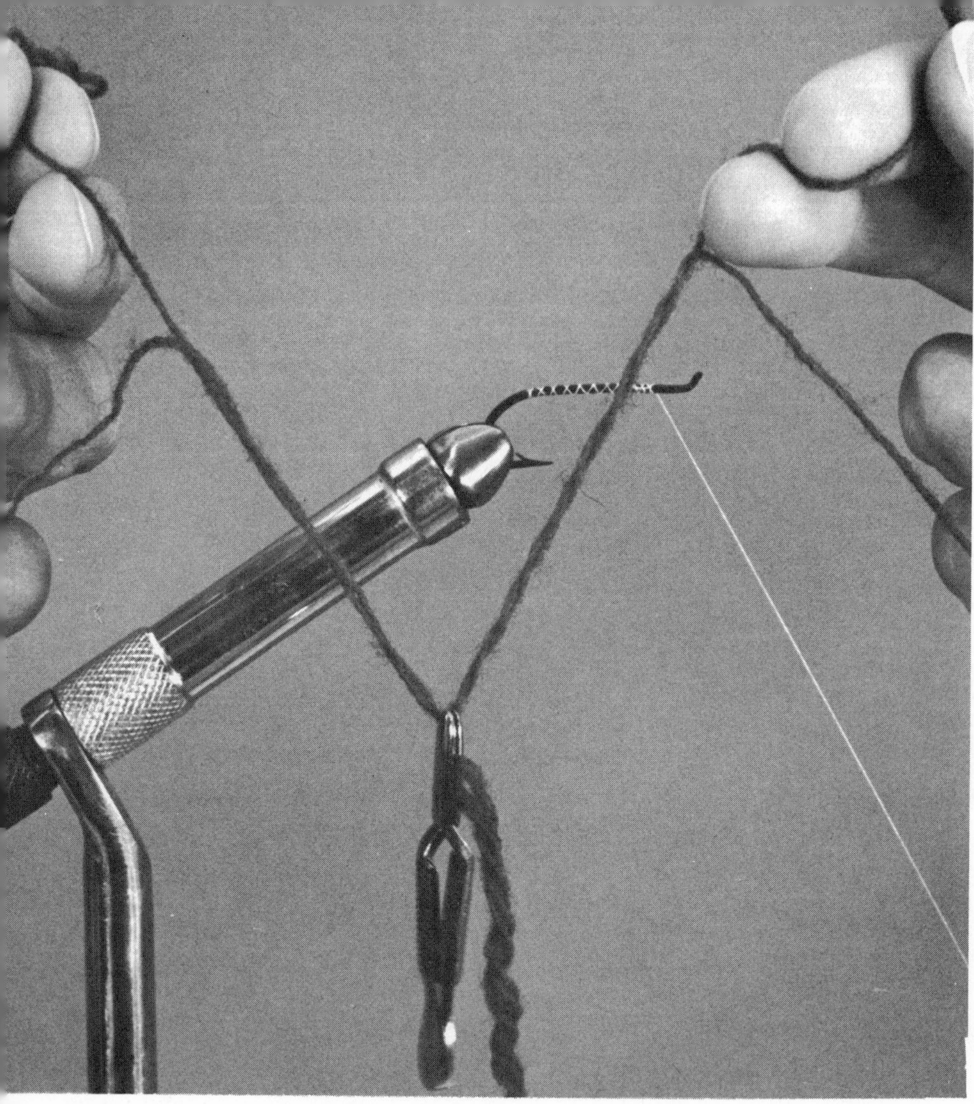

9a. The thread is attached to the hook at "wing position," wound back to "tail position," and forward again in an open spiral to create a base grip for the wool body. Separate the strands of yarn.

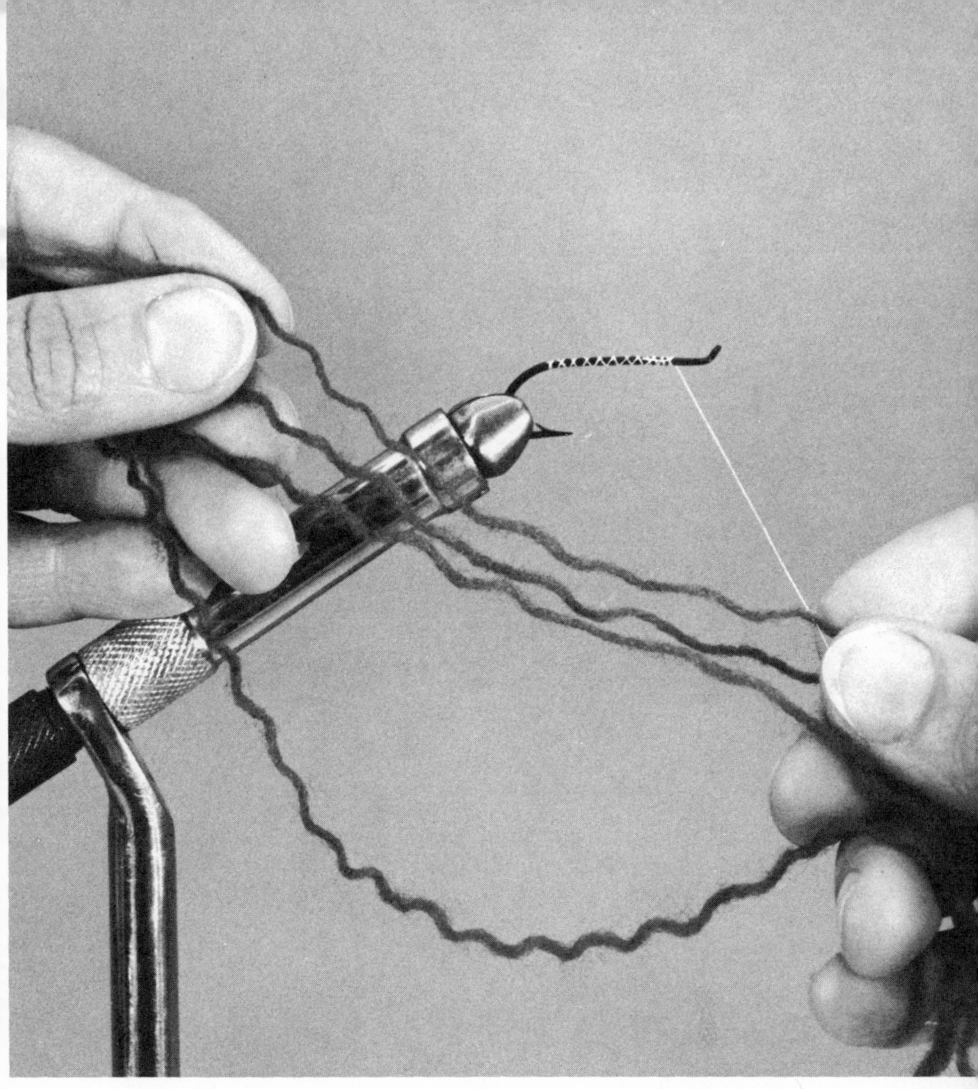

9b. The separated wool strands will be wavy. All of them may be used together on a hook this size. On smaller hooks, the strands used would be proportionately fewer.

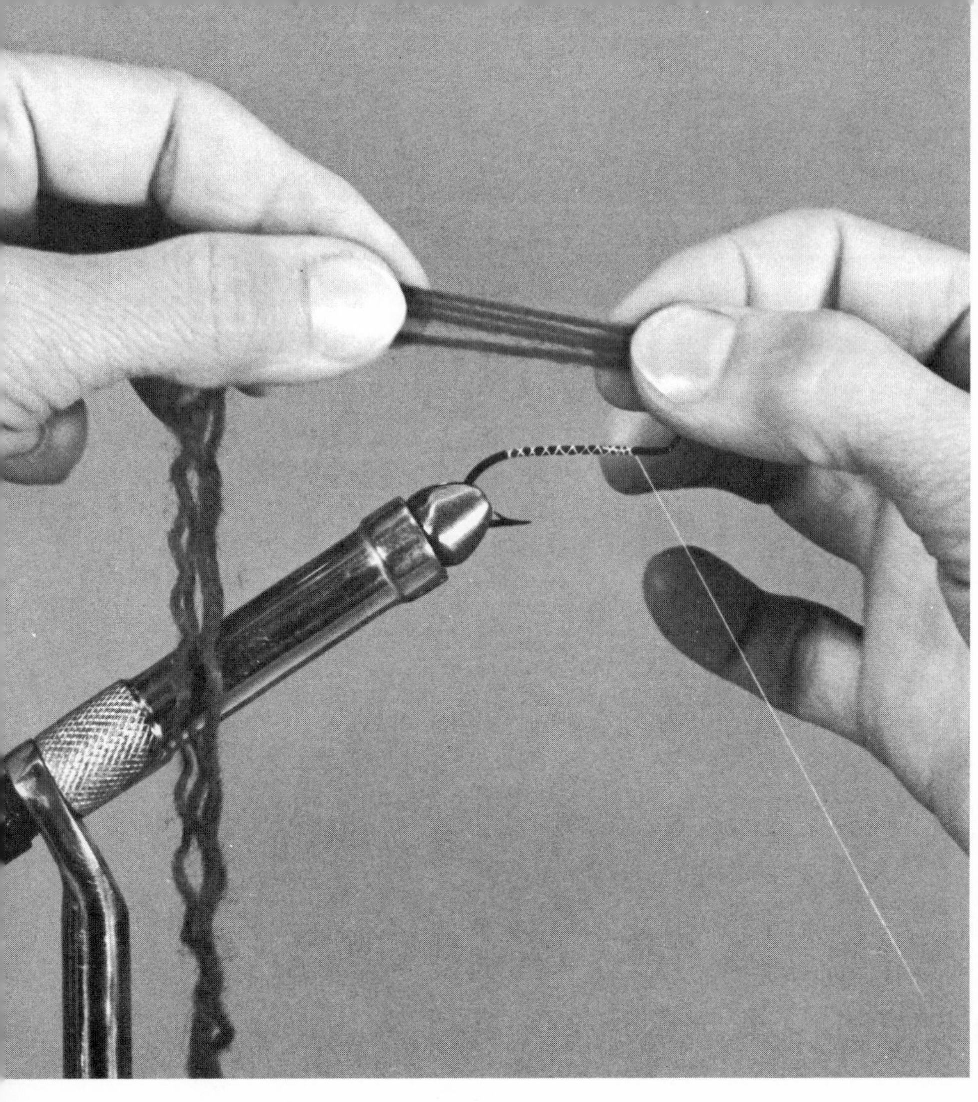

9c. When held together, a little tension will straighten the strands. They will be used as a single flat strand.

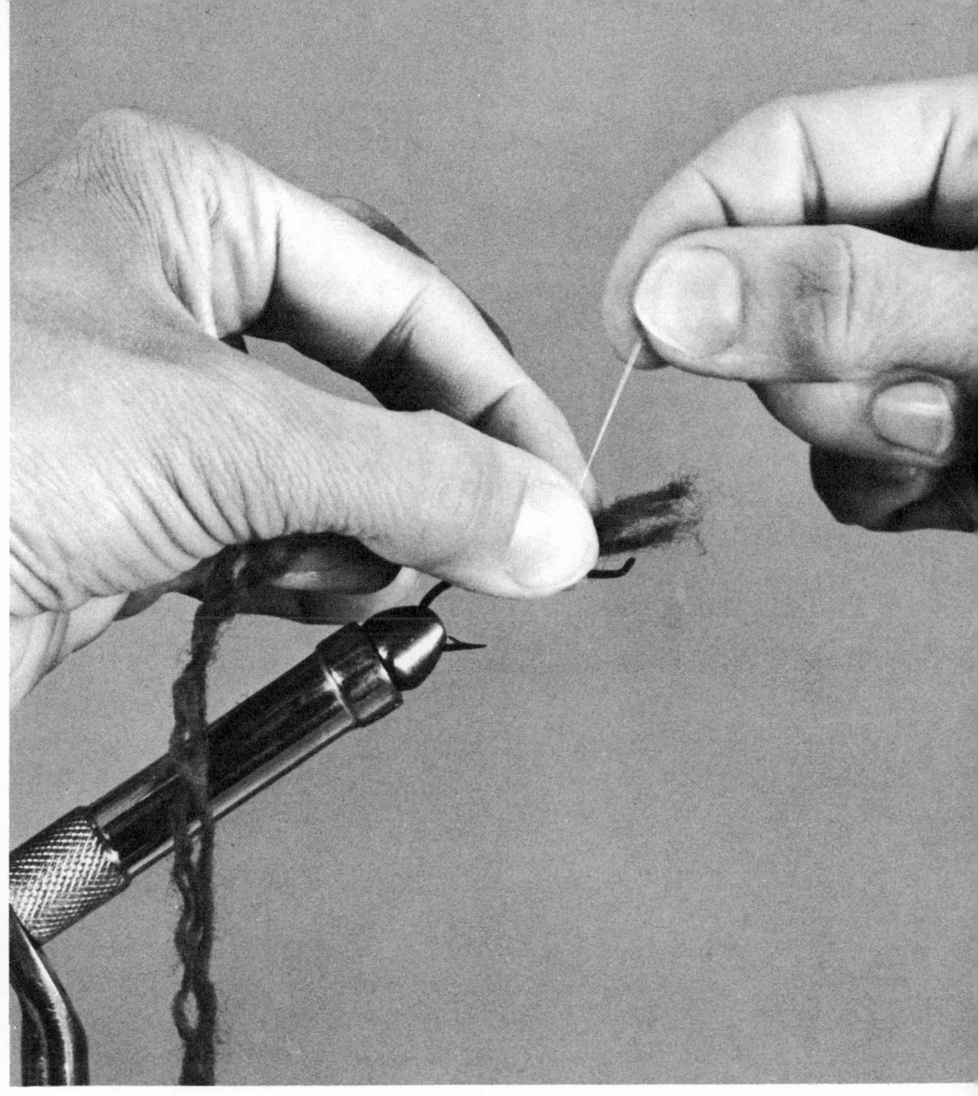

9d. Holding the strands with the left hand, ends slightly projecting toward the hook eye, attach the yarn to the hook at "wing position" by bringing the tying thread up and down between fingers and wool, as before. Repeat twice to anchor the wool to the hook.

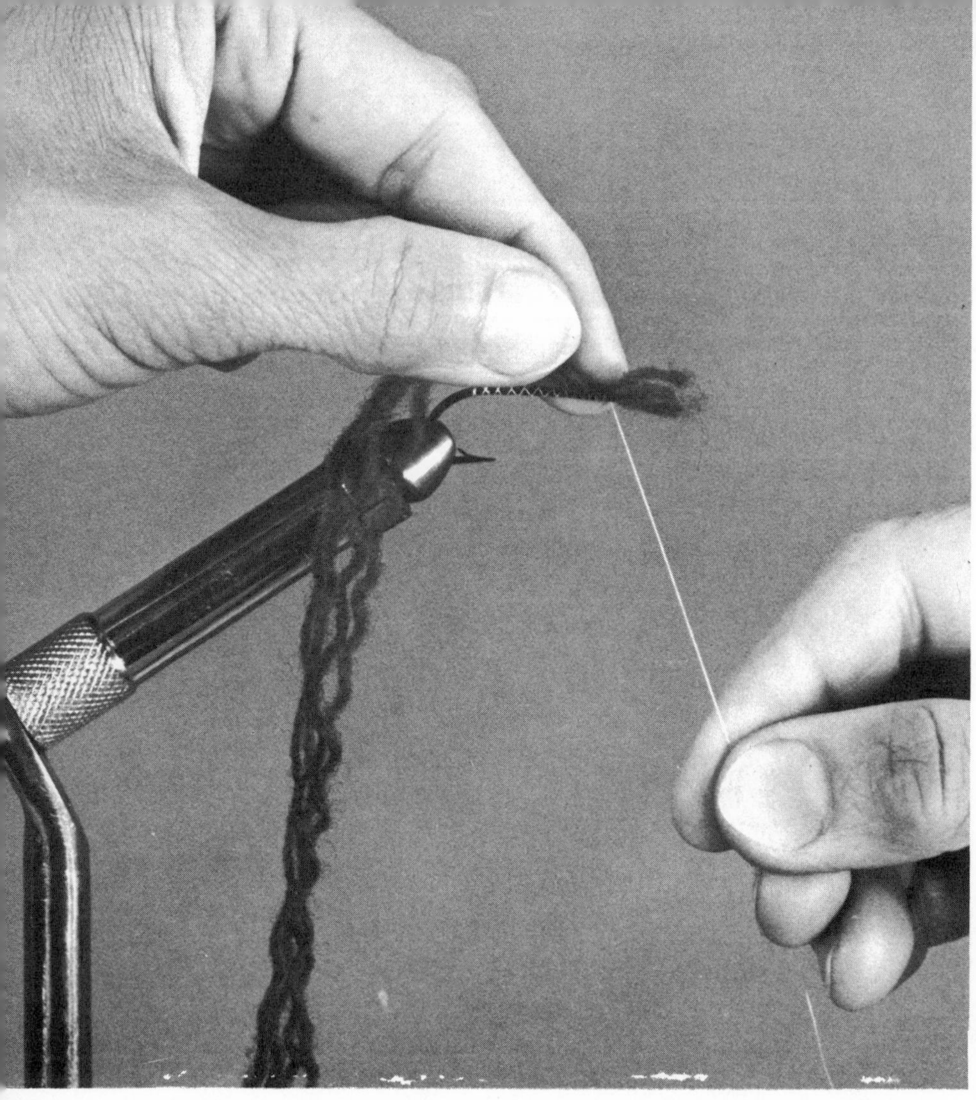

9e. Catch the thread behind the button. Press the tying thread against the hook with a finger until it is held securely by the button.

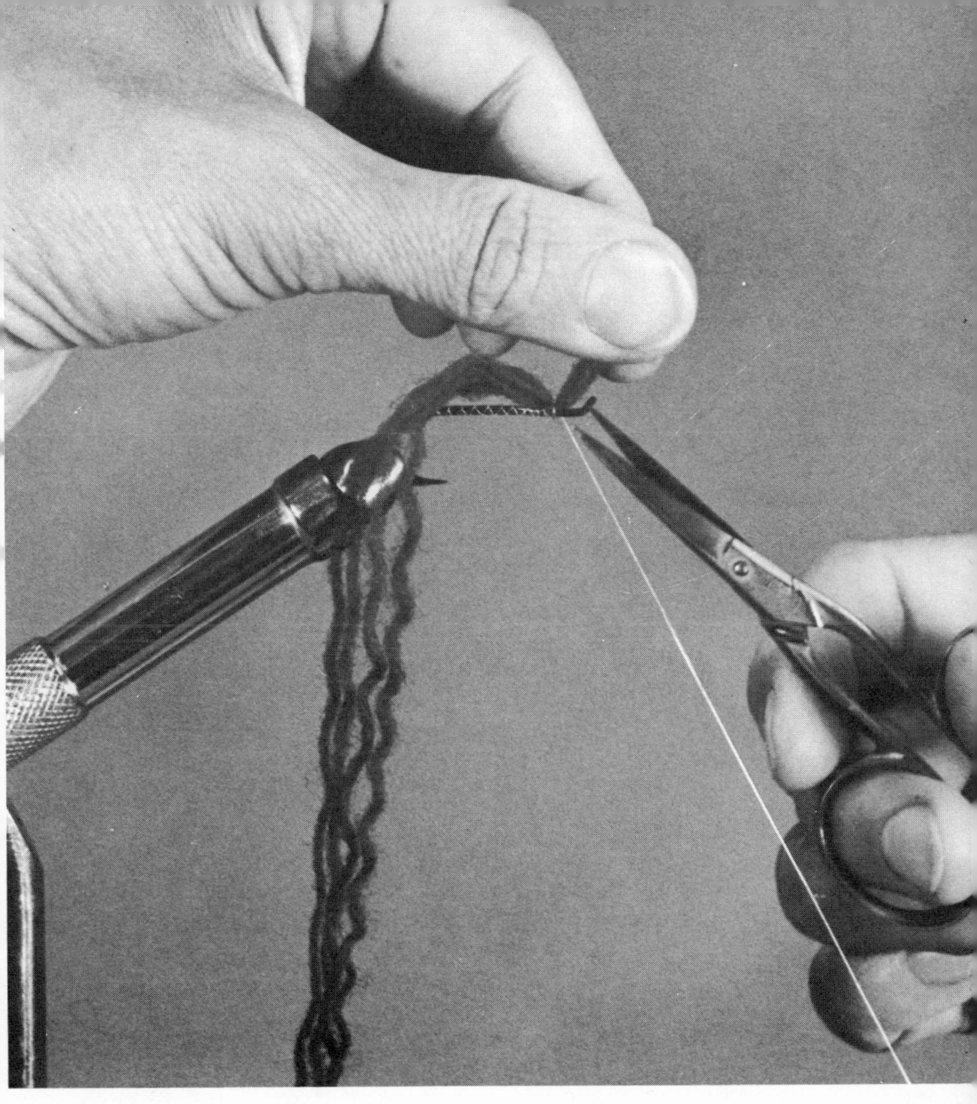

9f. Remove the excess end of wool, tapering it by clipping at an angle.

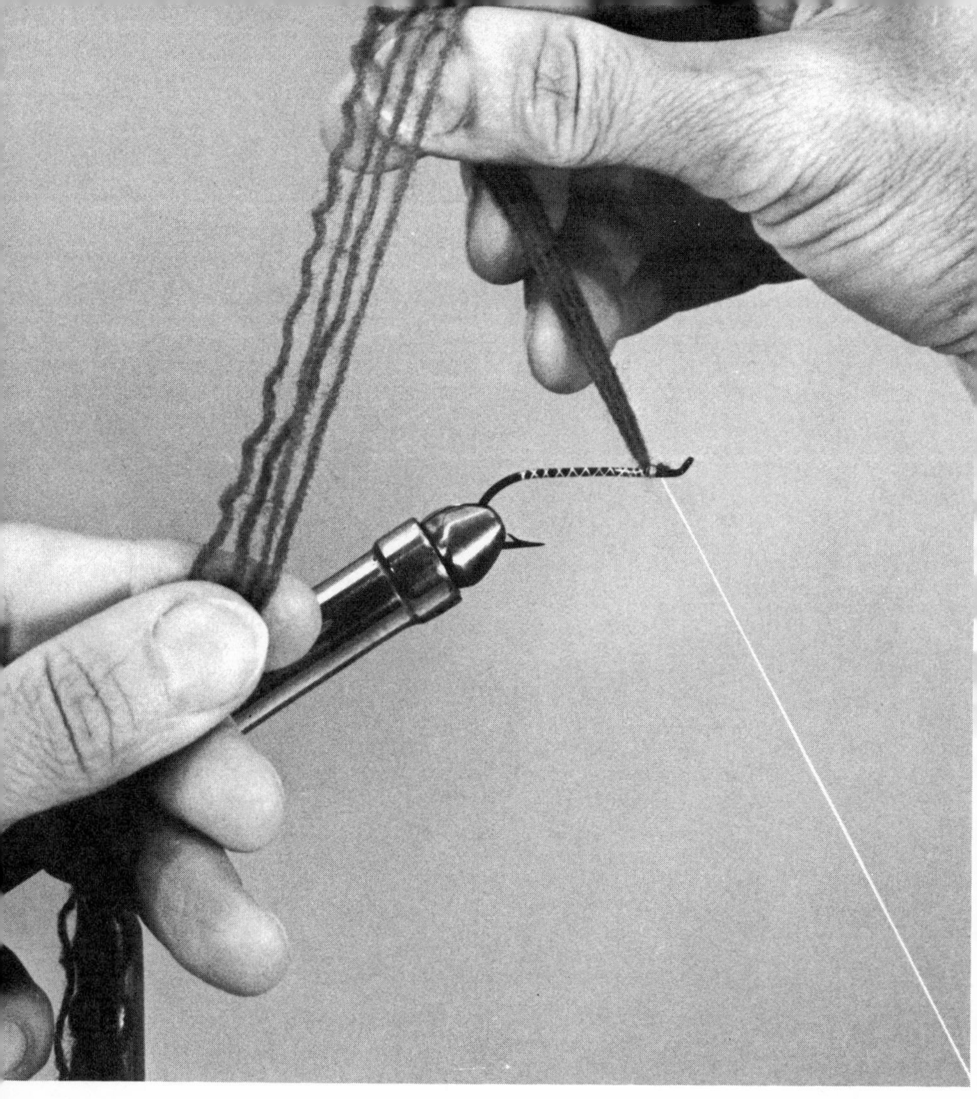

9g. Lift the wool strands, keeping them side by side. Keep the strands straight between hook and fingers.

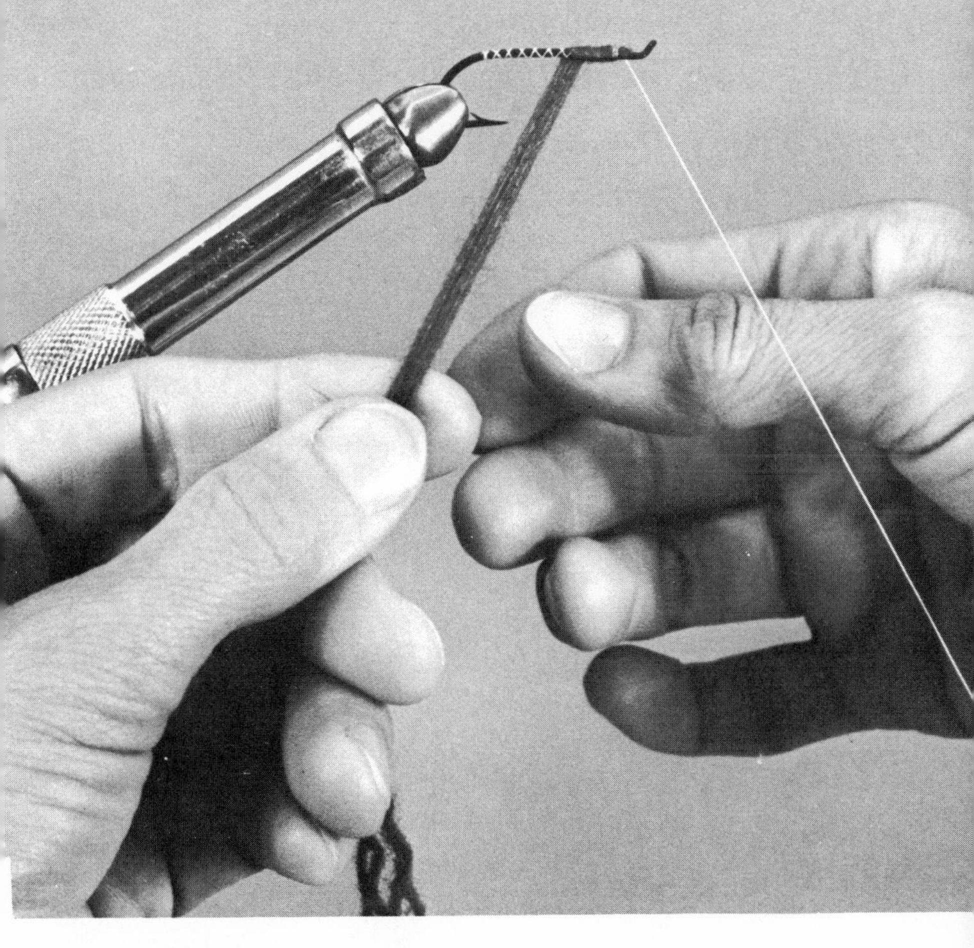

9h. Wind the wool around the hook, changing hands as necessary when the right hand encounters the tying thread. Keep the wool strands flat and slanting in the direction of tying. Do not overlap the windings. Avoid catching the wool strands on the hook point.

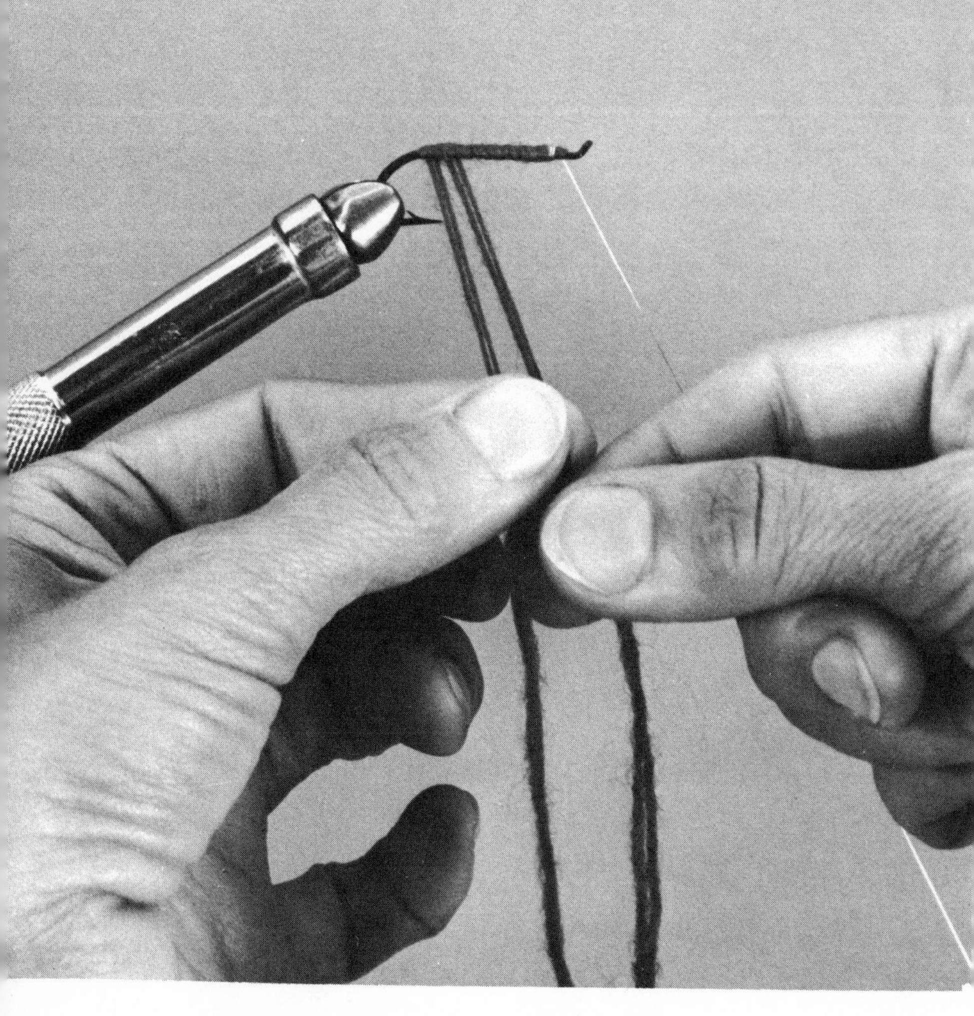

9i. Reverse the direction of tying above the barb and separate the strands slightly.

9j. The strands will now overlap as they are wound forward, increasing the diameter of the body in the middle, leaving the end of the body tapered.

9k. As the center of the body is reached, the strands are brought together and wrapping is continued with little or no overlapping of the strands.

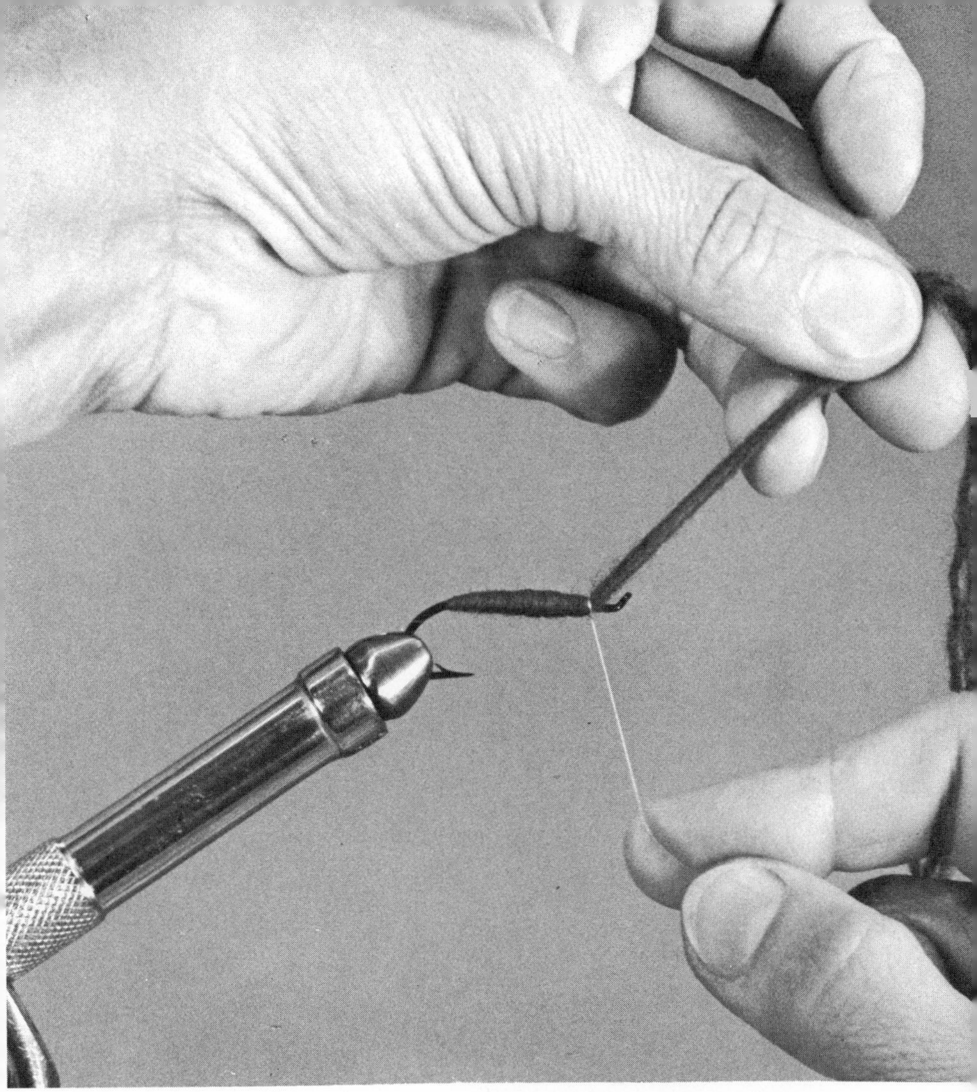

91. At "wing position," catch the wool with two turns of tying thread. Secure the thread and clip off excess wool.

Bind down the tapered end, thus completing the simple wool body. Unwind the wool, measure the strand, allowing the additional amount required for a finger grip. Use the unwound length for practice until the body can be made quickly, with a fairly even surface.

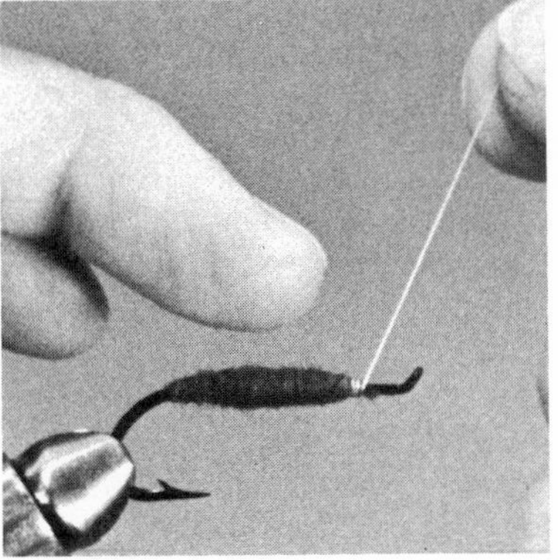

Dubbing — Wool and Fur

Wool yarn may also be used in another interesting way. Frayed, s shown here, the wool fibers are twirled or spun onto a waxed hread, which in turn is wound on the hook to make an exception-lly durable fly body. This process is called dubbing, and the body s called a dubbing body.

Two or more colors of wool can be combined in making dubbing, r wool and fur may be blended together in order to obtain trans-ucent or iridescent effects and a variety of textures.

Dubbing made from fur is soft, but once it is wound on a hook t is frequently impossible to unwind it. Many animal furs enrich he material stock of the fly-tyer and provide natural colors ranging rom white through cream, ginger, brown and grey, to black. When xposed to the bleaching properties of sun and water on the bodies f wet and dry flies, these natural colors are almost sure to be ermanent.

One of the animals whose fur is frequently used is the red fox; reamy, grey, or reddish-ginger bodies can be made from its thick elly fur. Furs, such as otter, mink, badger, muskrat, etc., having uard hair which can be used for wings and tails, also have a fine ndercoat that may be kept for use as dubbing.

Seal fur, which accepts dye readily, is used for the bodies of laborate and colorful salmon flies. A beginner in this branch of ly-tying should have very little difficulty after he has mastered the asic technique of tying dry and wet flies for trout and other fresh-water game fish.

Convenient to store in small quantities, a piece 2 inches square f any of these furs will furnish enough material for many bodies.

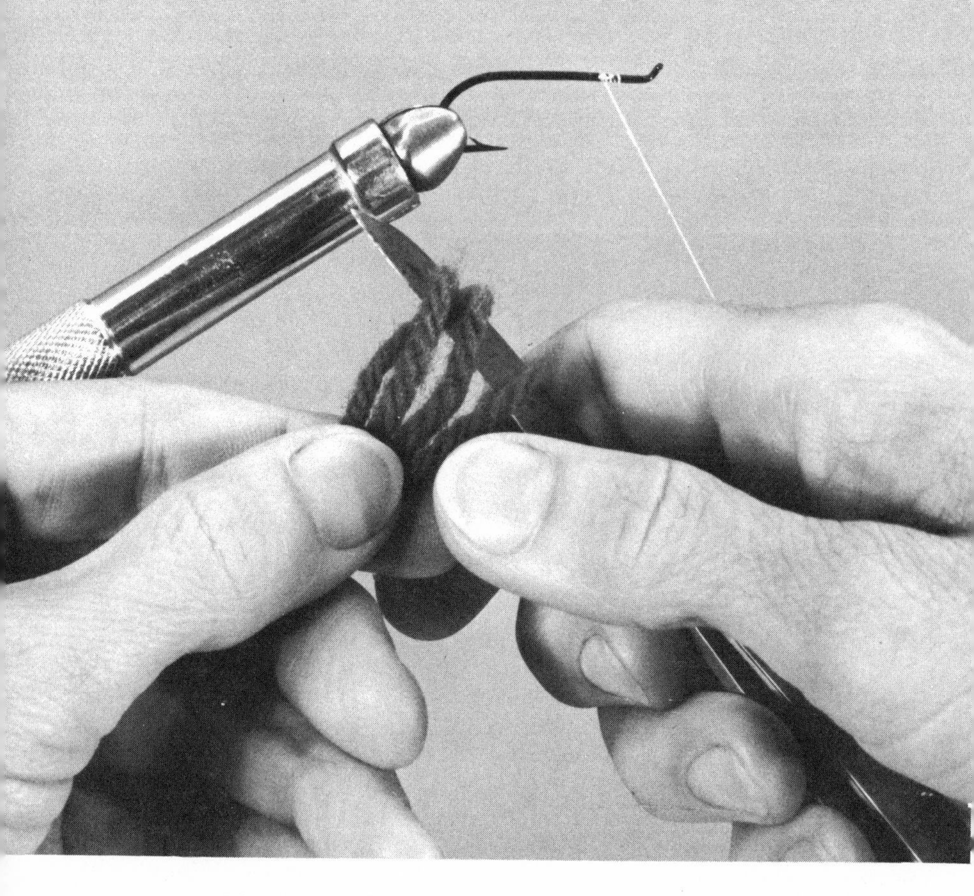

10a. Strands of wool yarn too short to be used any other way can be frayed and made into dubbing. Hold a few strands firmly in the left hand. A pocket knife with a fairly dull blade is held in the right hand, the blade edge toward you. Cut any loops.

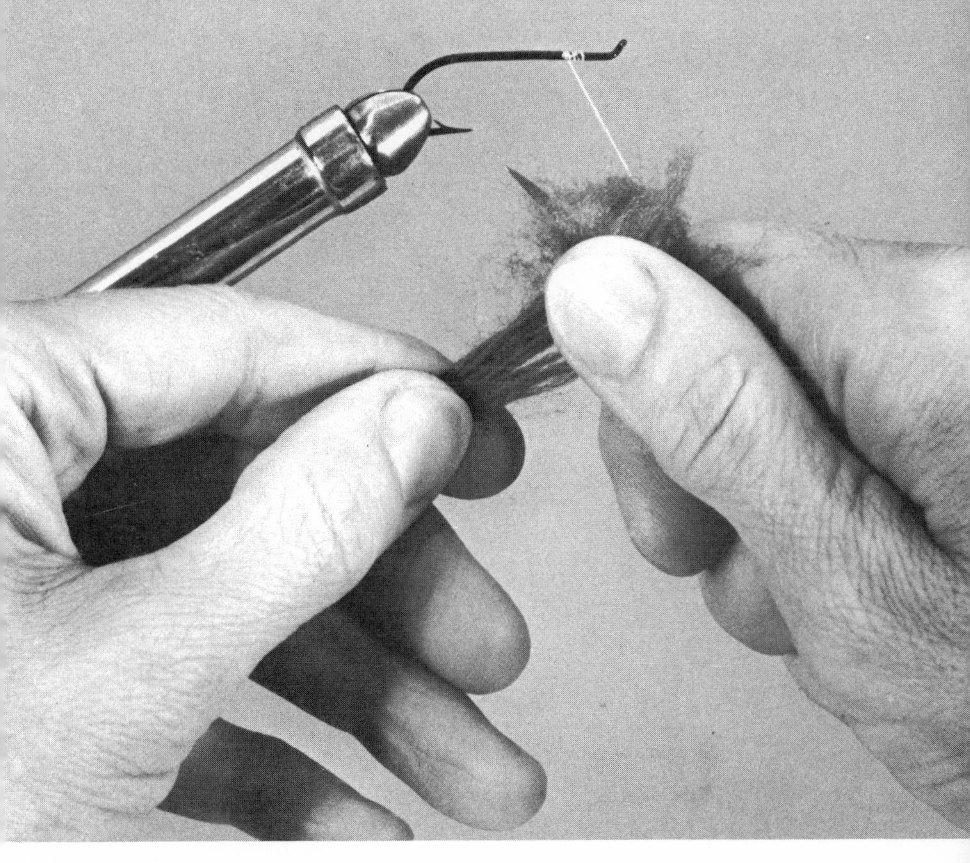

10b. With the thumb holding the yarn strands against the knife edge, scrape them with the blade. Fibers of the wool will pull away from the strands.

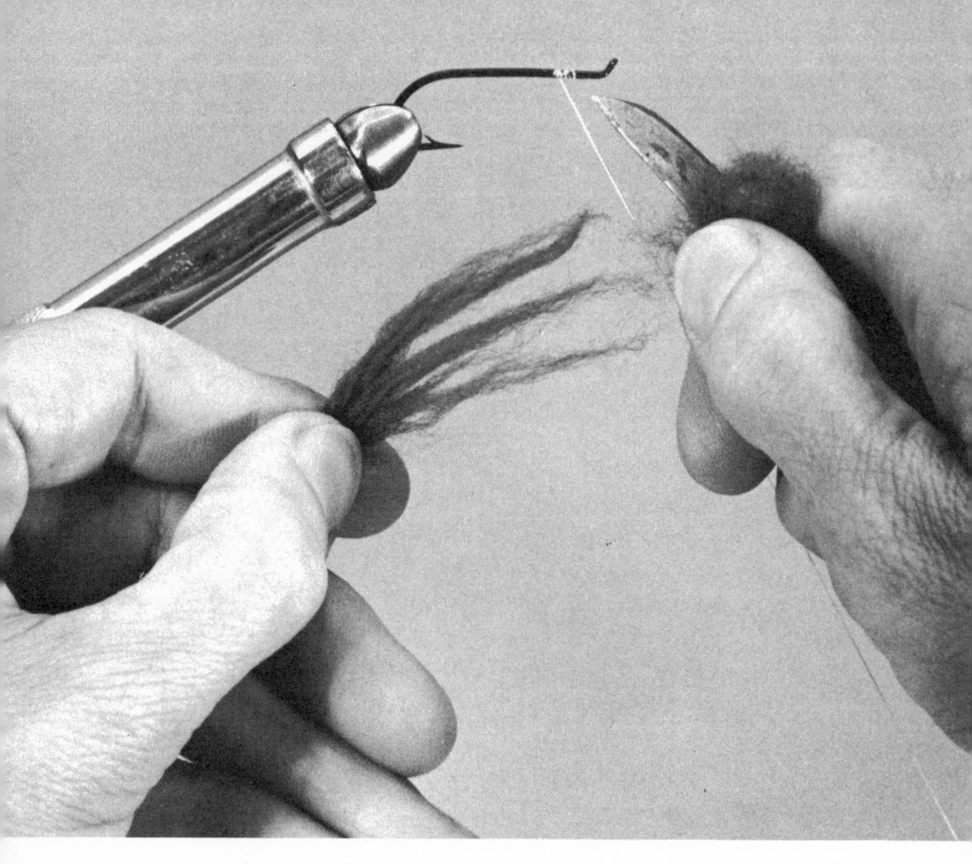

10c. Continue scraping until the yarn becomes a mass of fibers. This mass is dubbing.

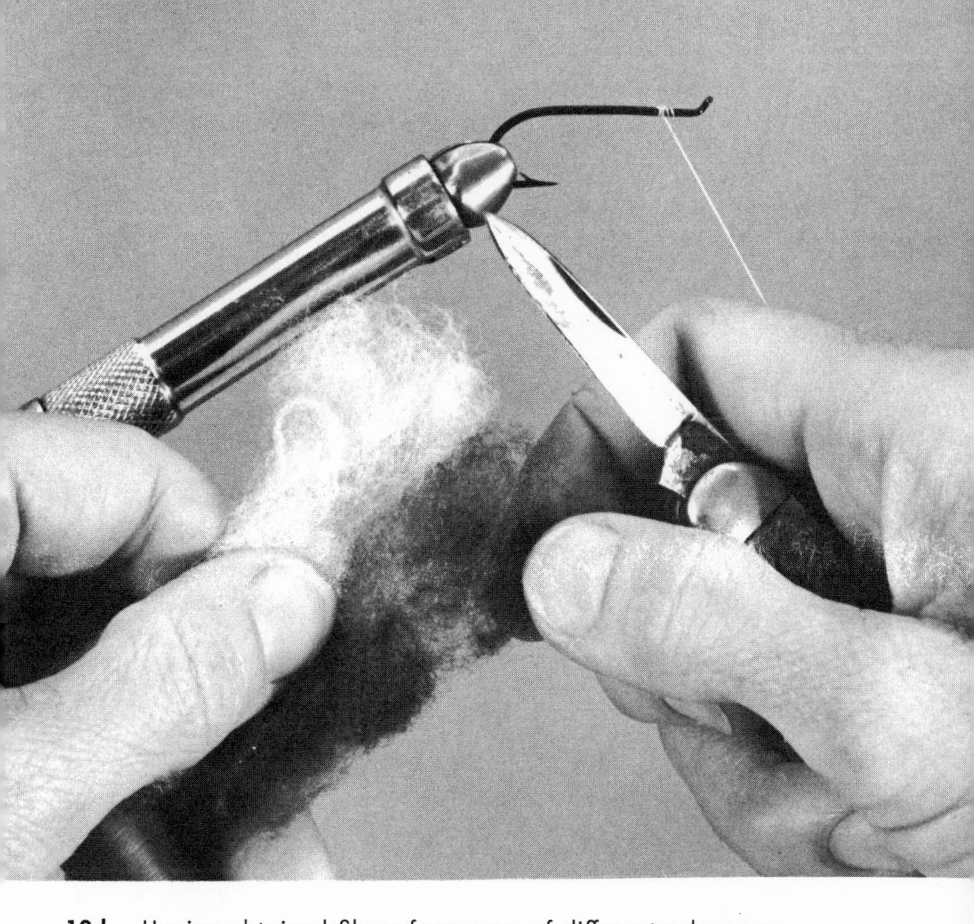

10d. Having obtained fibers from yarn of different colors, you can combine them. Hold the two masses together as you held the strands of yarn.

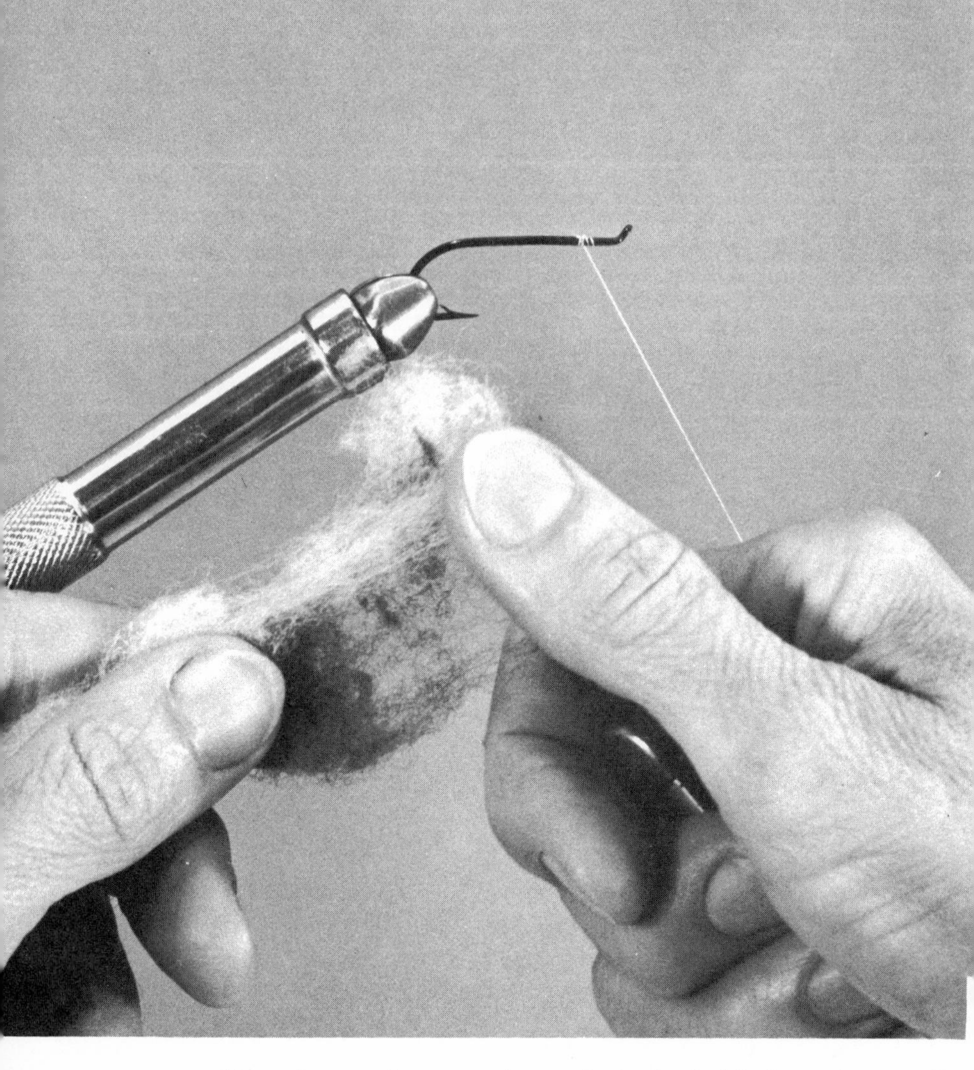

10e. Scrape them together with the knife blade and you will see the colors begin to blend. Continue until the colored fibers are evenly distributed throughout the mass of dubbing.

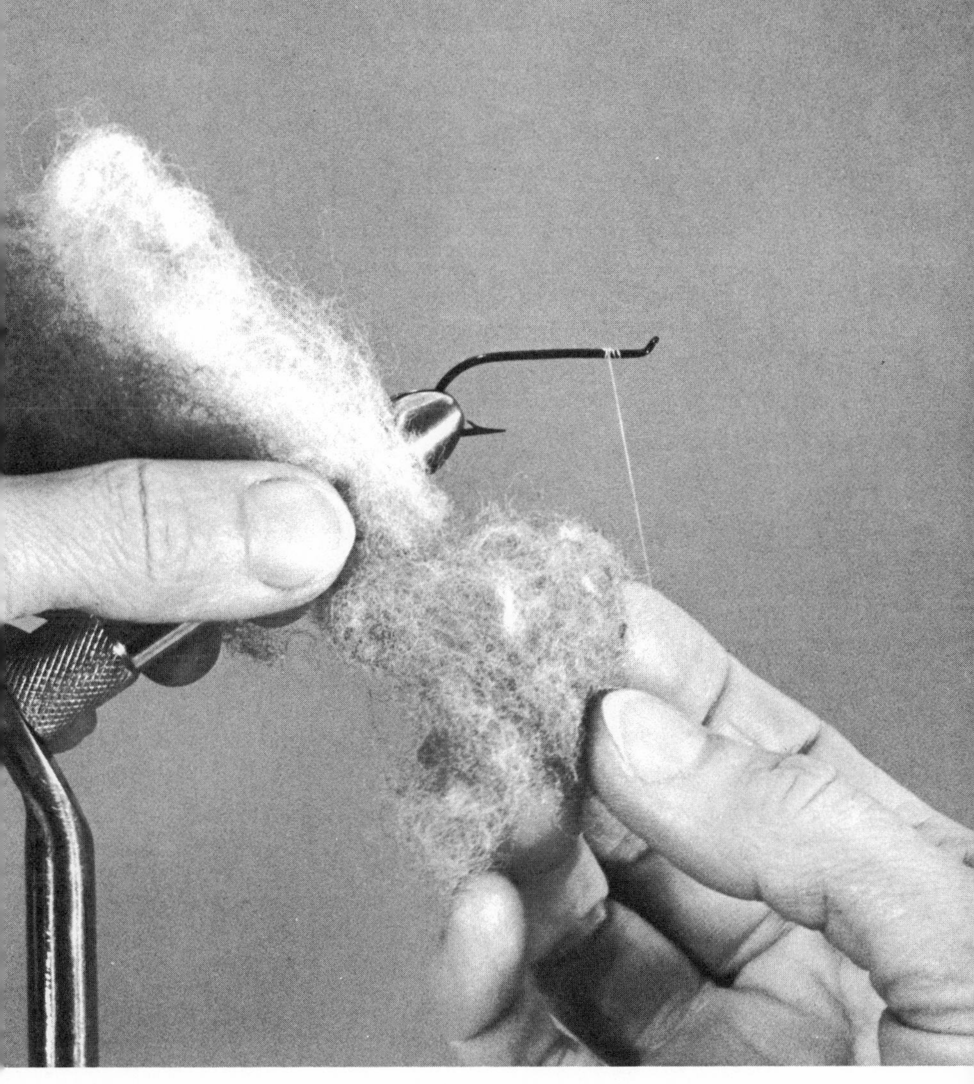

10f. Any combination of colors you want for dubbing can be made by blending the fibers together in this way, simply by adding as much or as little of any color you choose.

10g. Tying thread, well waxed, is attached to the hook at "wing position." Apply the dubbing to it by taking a few fibers between right thumb and finger. Hold them against the thread close to the hook and twirl them around the thread by drawing the thumb along the finger from the tip. Dubbing fibers will spin around the thread and be held by the wax.

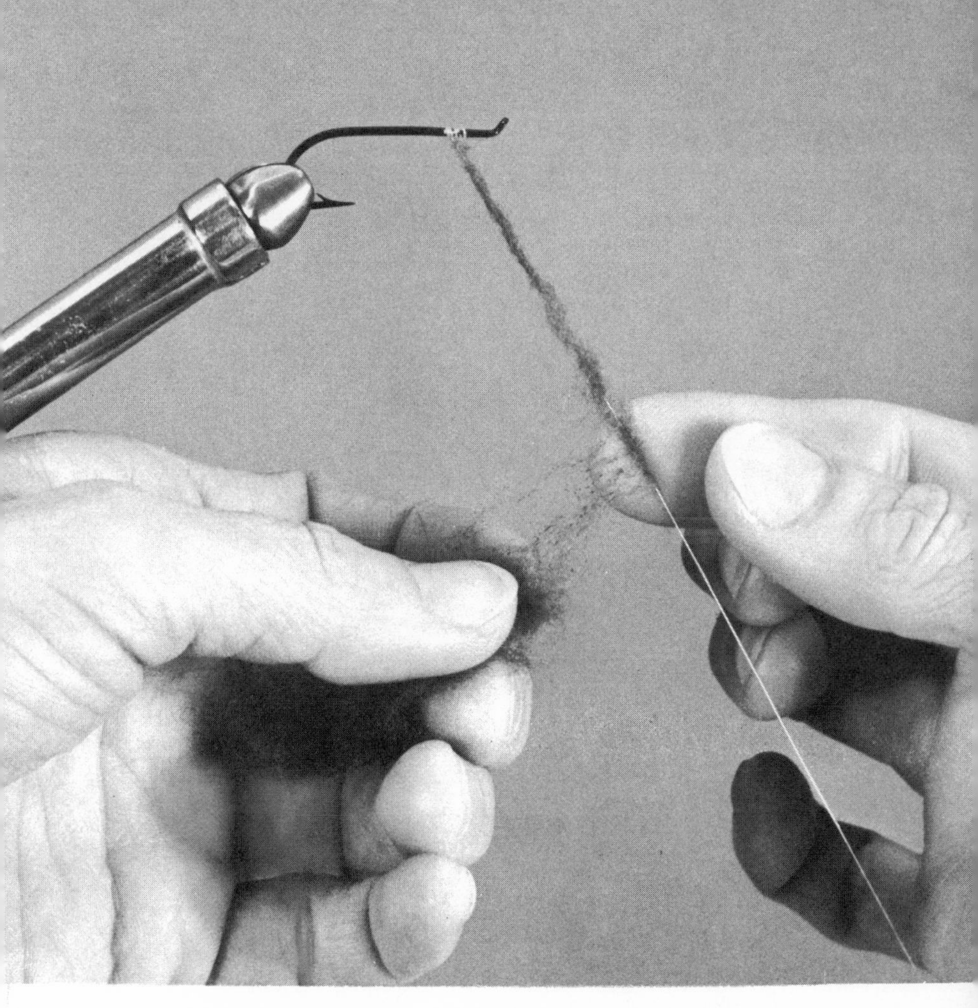

10h. When you have covered 2 or 3 inches of thread with dubbing, begin winding it on the hook. The tying thread is now the core of the material.

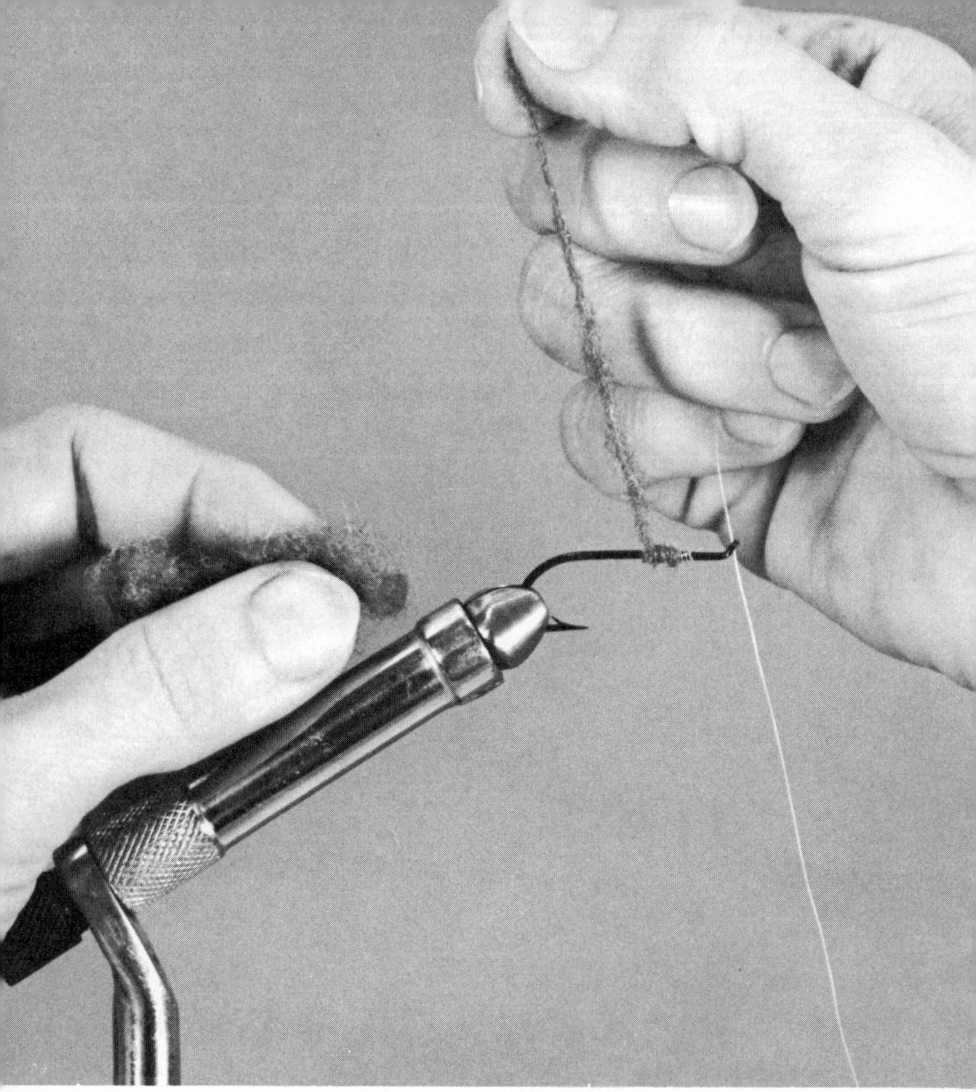

10i. As you wind the dubbing on, make sure the thread is entirely covered. Push the dubbing together if necessary to cover the thread.

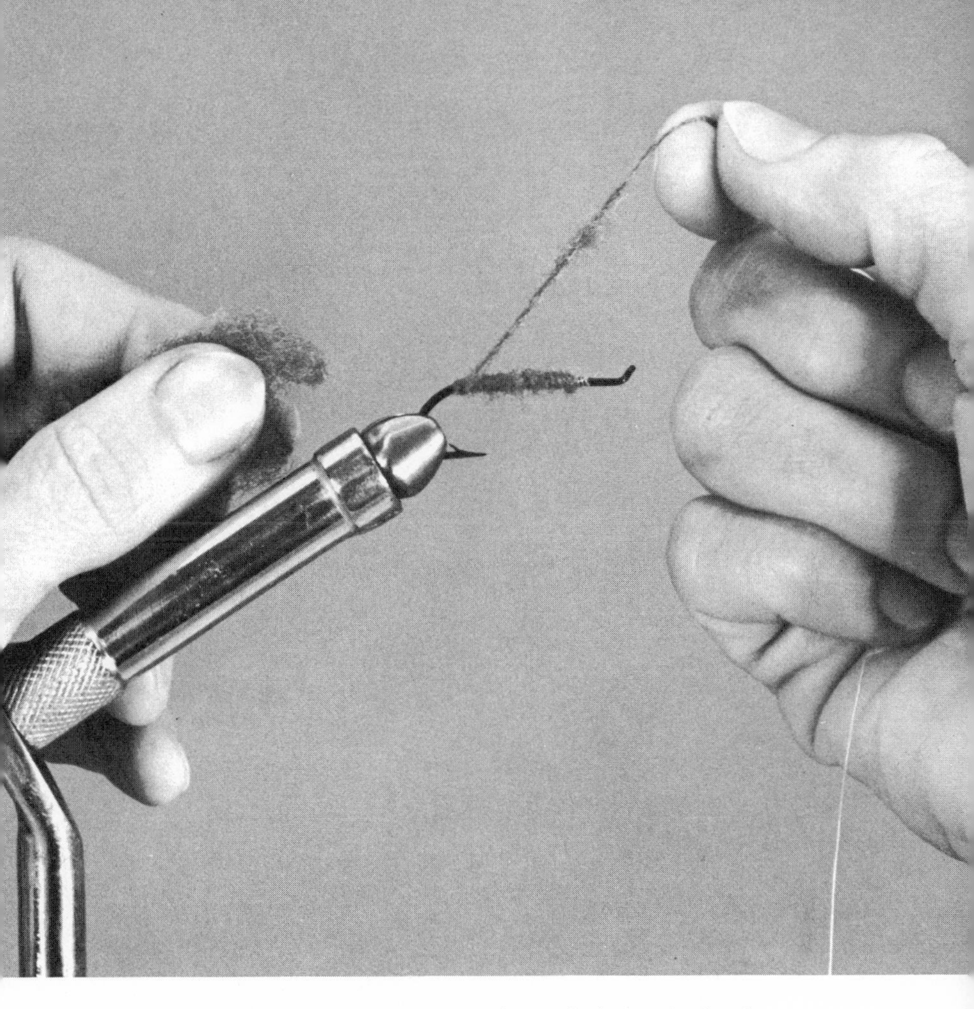

10j. Keep the body slim, tapering it at the end above the barb.

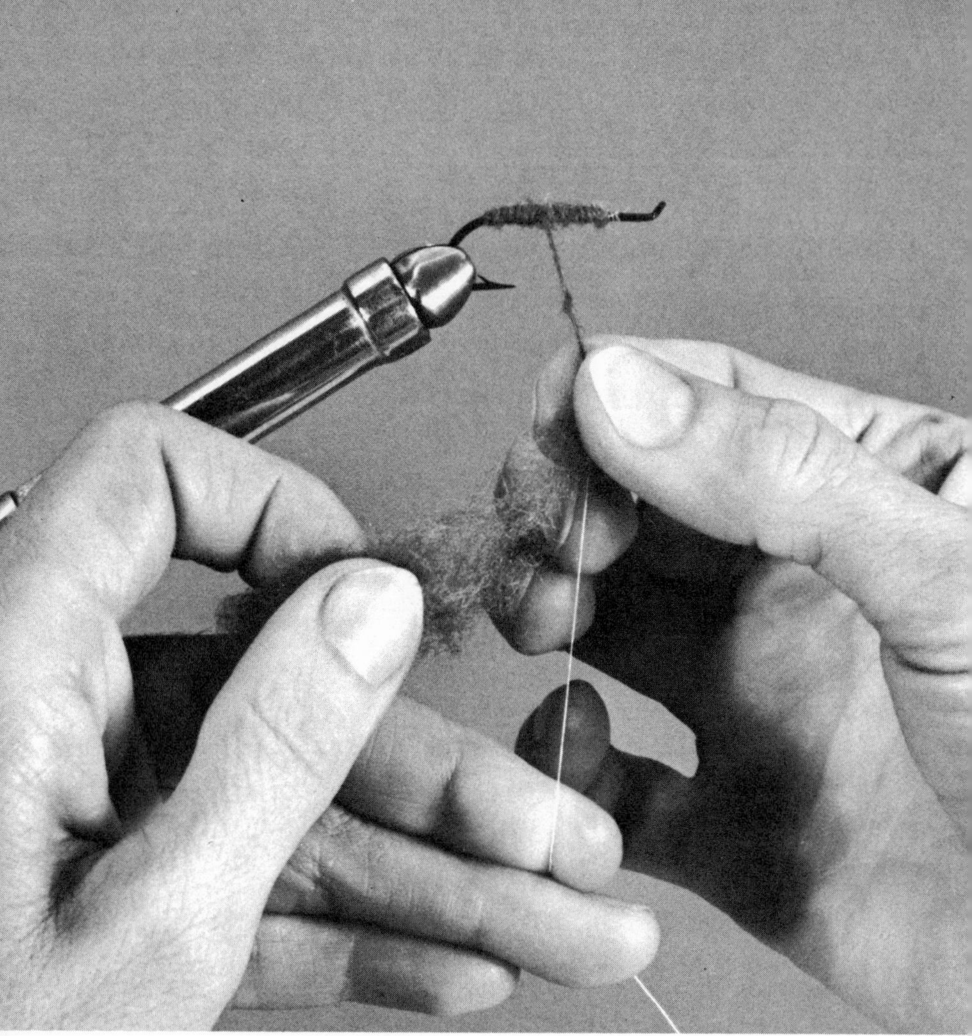

10k. Overlapping turns of dubbing a little in the center of the hook will help to build a slightly heavier body. Add more wax to the thread and apply more dubbing as required. When "wing position" is reached, any excess dubbing remaining on the thread may be scraped down away from the body with the thumb and first finger of the right hand as the thread is secured to button.

10l. The dubbing body is now complete, oval in shape, and tapered nicely above the barb and point, leaving maximum clearance between hook point and body. Practice until bodies uniform in shape can be made each time.

For a rougher appearance, strands of dubbing may be "picked

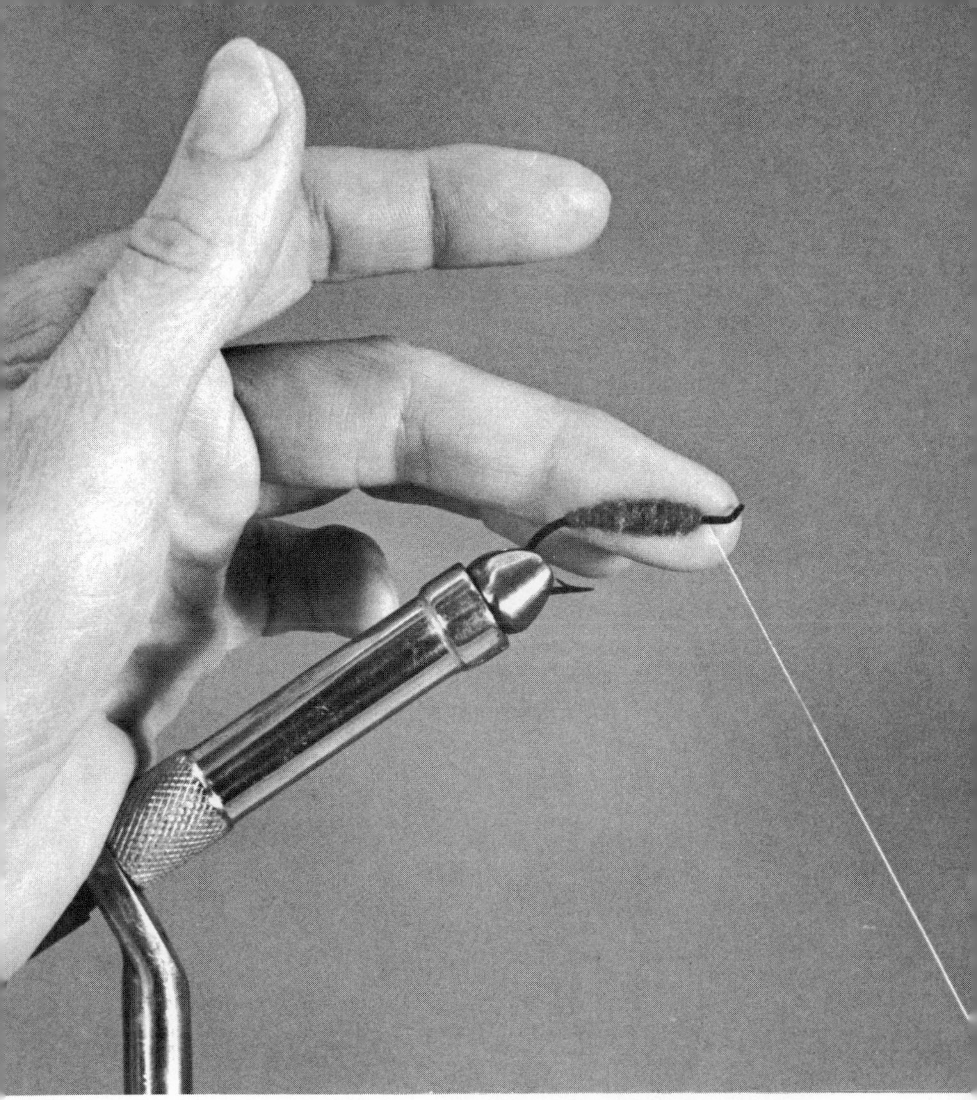

out" with the point of the stylet. Be careful to catch only wool fibers with its point and not the thread on which it was spun.

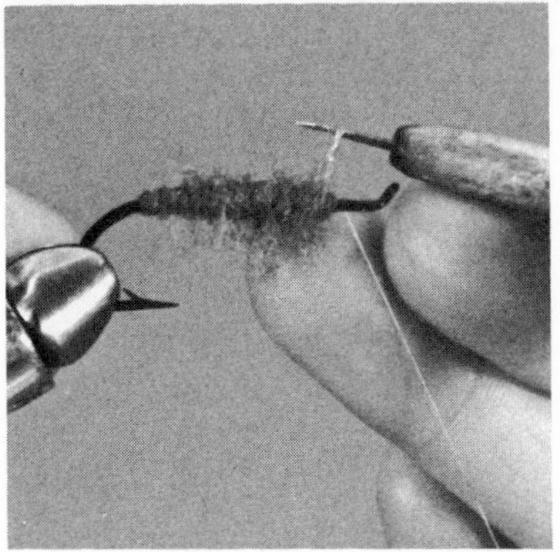

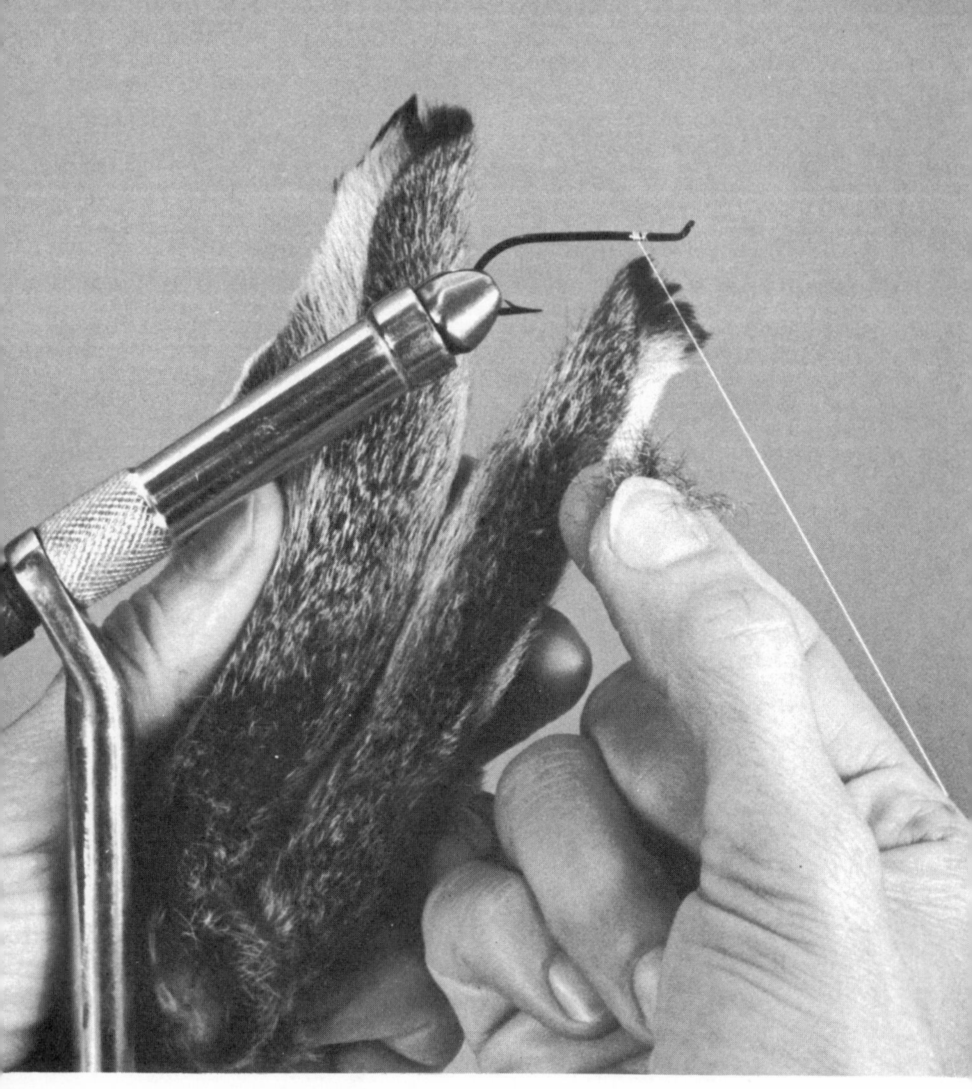

11a. When fur, or a short hair such as this from Hare's Ear, is used for dubbing, pluck the material directly from the hide and spin it onto the well-waxed thread which is attached at "wing position."

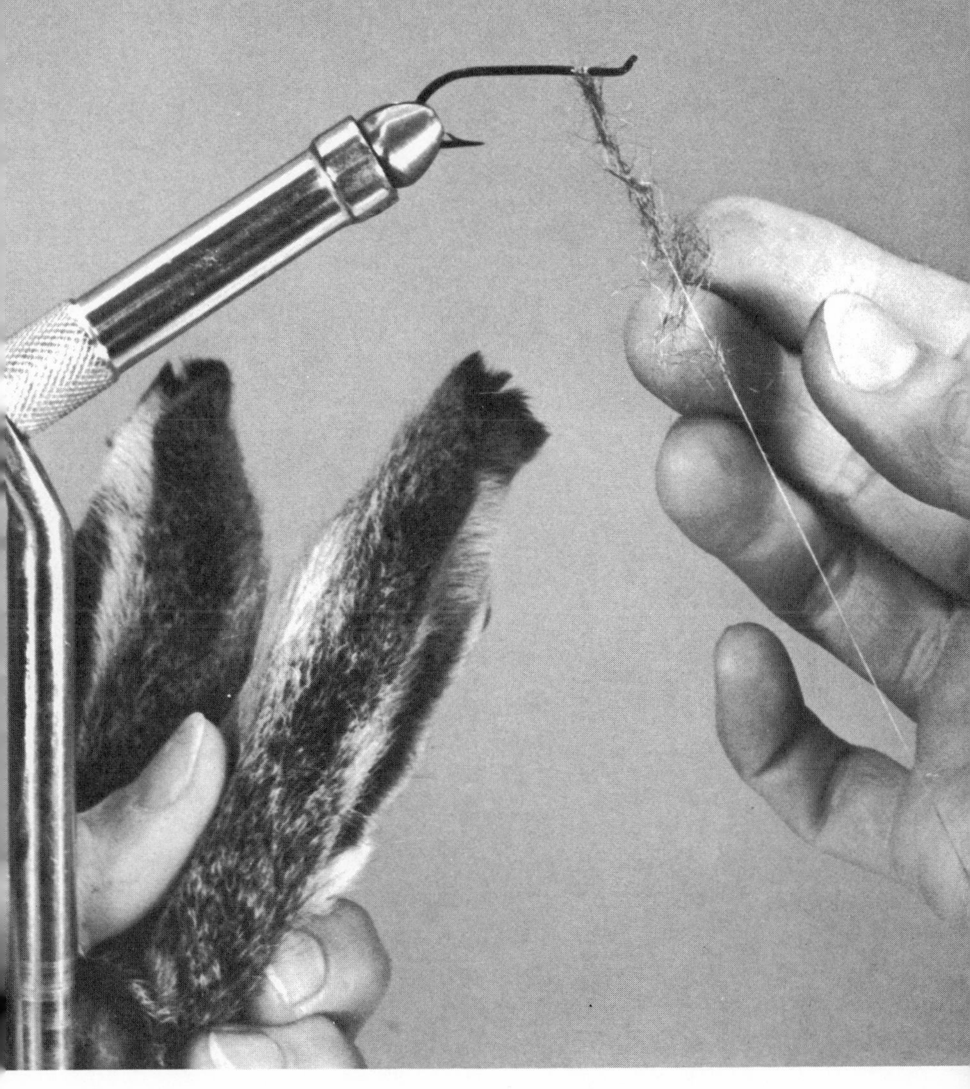

11b. It will require a little care to spin the short, stiff fibers of hair onto the thread. When an inch or two of thread is covered, wind it onto the hook. Replenish the wax on the thread when necessary and continue to pluck the hair or fur and spin it onto the thread.

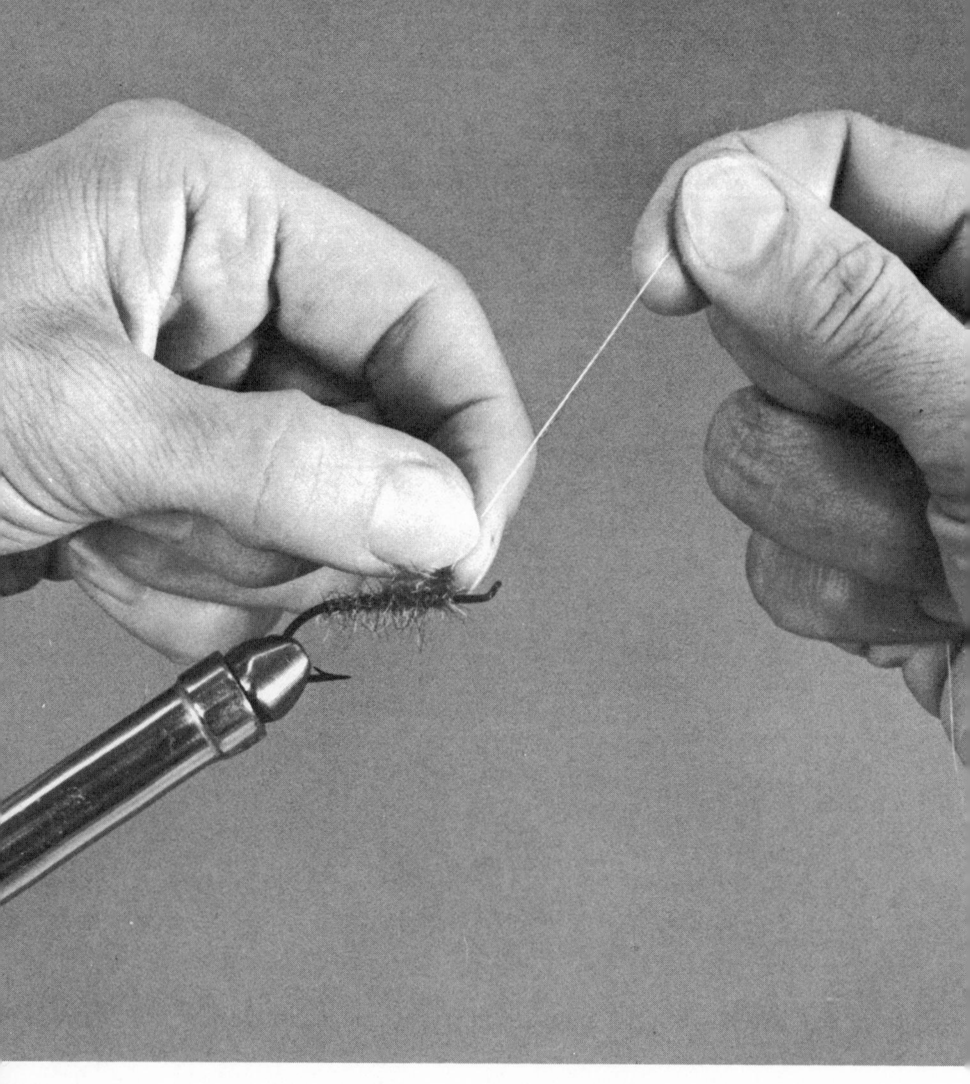

11c. Taper the body carefully above the barb and point and make sure all the thread is covered by the dubbing. As "wing position" is reached, scrape whatever dubbing remains on the thread downward toward the body and wind it around the hook, making the body slightly heavier at the front end.

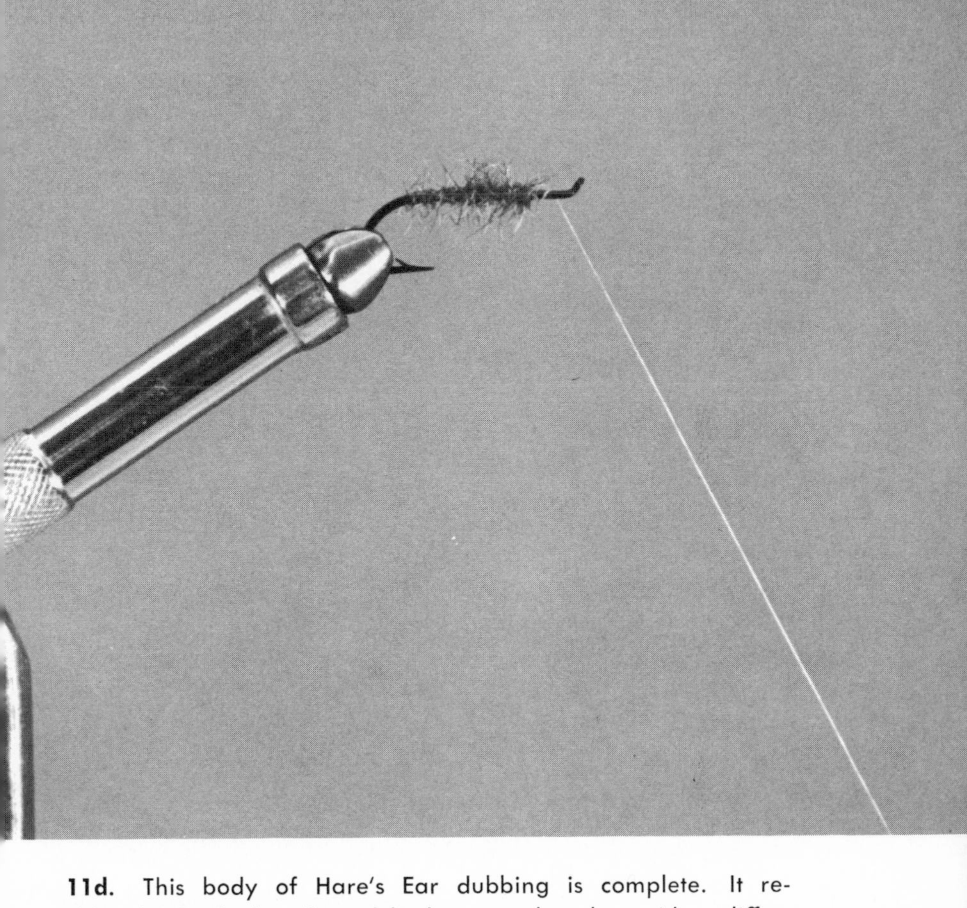

11d. This body of Hare's Ear dubbing is complete. It resembles the "picked-out" wool body somewhat, but with a difference. Practice plucking and applying this material to the waxed thread and winding it on the hook until you can do it quickly and uniformly each time. Soft furs that do not have guard hairs are easily spun into dubbing and applied to the hook in the same way.

Hairs

The North American white-tailed deer furnishes a different type of material from which innumerable bass and trout flies are made each year. For the fly-tyer's purpose, the body hair of the deer is considered hollow. The spongy, or pithy, center of the hair, enclosed by a smooth outer surface, compresses when the tyer's thread is drawn across it as though the hair were hollow, in effect similar to a bunch of soda straws tied tightly together. The ends remain expanded while the centers are forced to collapse into a much smaller space.

Because of its natural buoyancy, deer body hair is valuable for the bodies of dry flies, and with the addition of a water-repellent dressing the bodies will remain afloat almost indefinitely. Without the application of a protective floatant, a fly body of trimmed deer hair will eventually become saturated and can therefore be used for wet flies as well.

Flies made with deer hair often are less quickly rejected by the fish than hard-surfaced lures, many of which can be duplicated in appearance with deer hair.

Deer body hair is easily obtained, and since a little of it goes a very long way, it is one of the staples of the tyer's supply of material. A complete deer hide would probably furnish the average fisherman with more than enough flies for a lifetime of bass and trout fishing, but deer body hair can also be purchased in pieces a few inches square, an amount ample for several large flies or many small ones.

Handling deer body hair in tying will not be difficult if you remember to remove the fuzzy undercoat from the hair before tying, to use a small tuft at a time, and to maintain firm tension on the thread without breaking it.

Using a small tuft at a time is important and will prevent a larg amount of vexation. A large tuft will not fold around thread an hook properly but will shear the thread because of leverage exerte on it by the excess wedge of hair.

Caribou hair is similar to deer hair, and when used in the sam manner, it will produce a softer body. For handling moose mane see pages 180–87.

Unlike deer body hair, the tail hair of the deer does not have "hollow" quality. It ties in well, however, and is an excellent ma terial for wings and tails and for flies made entirely of long hair The length of hair for a fly should be carefully gauged so that th naturally tapered tips will not have to be trimmed away.

The back of the deer tail is greyish tan or brown, with the under side snowy white. It can be dyed easily. The best tails are thos with fine, slightly wavy or crinkly hair that averages approximatel 3½ or 4 inches in length. Tails with straight, coarse hair shoul be avoided. The crinkly or wavy hair will move with water current in an undulating way that seems to be attractive to fish.

Deer tails may be purchased boned and cleaned. If obtained raw the bone should be removed and the tail carefully washed in warm water with soap or detergent, rinsed thoroughly, and dryed. Sprin kling it with moth-repellent crystals before storing will keep the tai safe from moth damage.

A fresh deer tail is quite easily boned simply by making an in cision lengthwise down the back (dark side) of it, gripping the tip of the bone with pliers and pulling downward from the tip towar the base of the tail. The skin can then be laid flat and left to dr out, which it will do in a few days when exposed to the air. An deer fat clinging to the skin should be completely removed. When the tail is thoroughly dried, the skin becomes tight around the hai roots, and in this condition the deer tails may safely be stored fo an indefinite length of time.

Known by many romantic names (Kip, Ocali, Impala, Impali, Asi atic goat, etc.), the calf tail furnishes a hair that is widely used, an ex cellent, durable material for hair-wing flies. The tail, approximately 12 inches in length, is mostly white but may have a patch of reddish brown or black hair at the base. The hair is easily dyed and shorter than deer hair. It is soft, wavy, and of uniform length except at the extreme tip where it may lengthen abruptly into a tight corkscrew curl with a hard, almost glass-like, quality. All the hair can be used xcept this tip, which does not tie in well. These tails are available re-dyed, also.

The Grey squirrel, called Frosty because of its white-tipped dark air, and the Fox (Rusty) squirrel are the two most common sources f hair with horizontal color-barring. They are used for fly wings, ils, and shell-back nymphs.

While hair from many exotic animals is imported for use in fly-ying, these mentioned here are the ones found in every fly-tyer's asic stock of materials. Whenever any of the various hairs can be ubstituted for a feather in the construction of a fly, the result will e a longer wearing, more durable product.

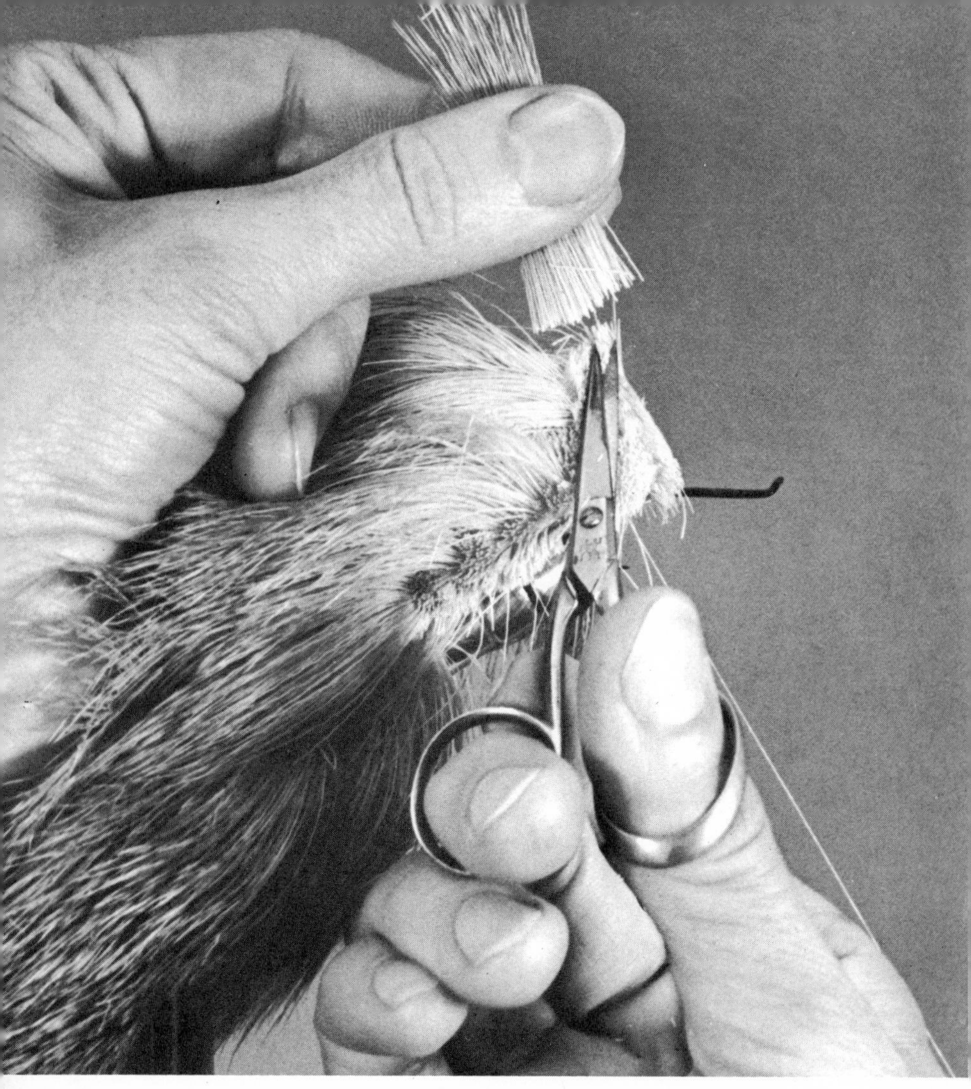

12a. Be patient with this body; it is not difficult to tie. Attach waxed thread to the hook at "tail position." Clip a small tuft of deer body hair close to the hide. Drop the piece of hide into your lap so there will be no need to reach out on the table for it each time you want another tuft. Run the points of the scissors through the cut ends to remove all fuzz.

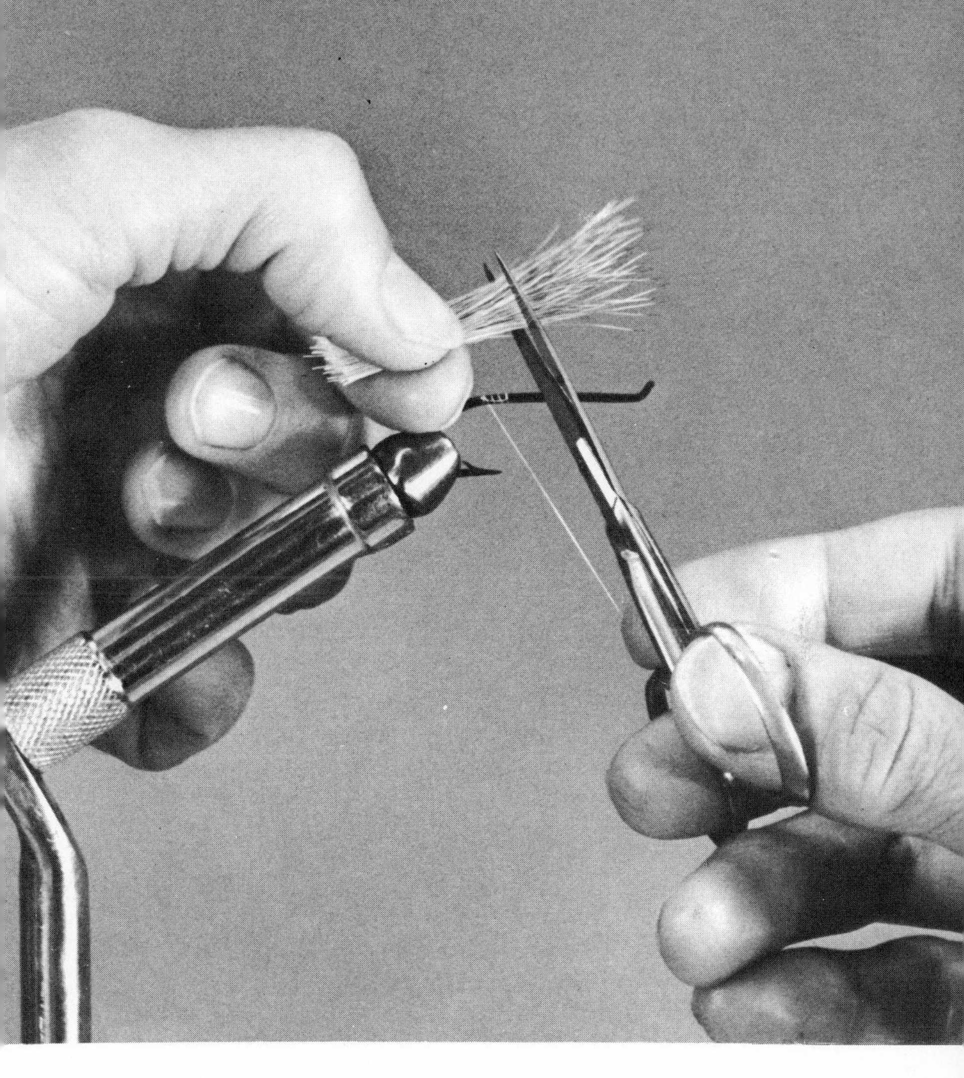

12b. Clip off the tips of the hair, leaving a short tuft between the fingers.

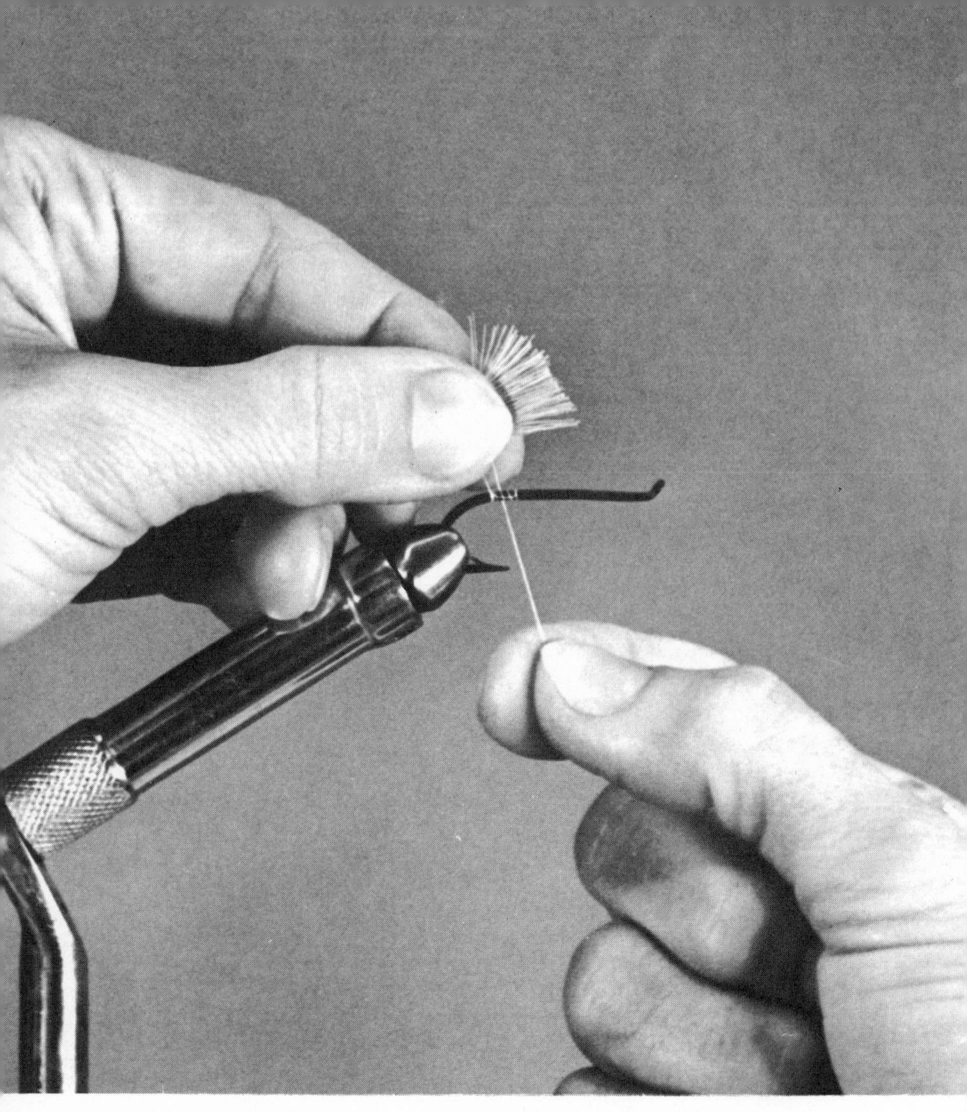

12c. Holding the hair tuft above the hook, over the barb, bring the tying thread up in front of the hook, slipping it upward between thumb and hair and downward between hair and finger on the far side of the hook. Examine this photo closely and you will see the thread going up in front of the hook and down on the far side of it. Between the fingers the thread goes over the tuft of hair. As you pull the thread downward, you will feel the thread sliding between the fingers of the left hand.

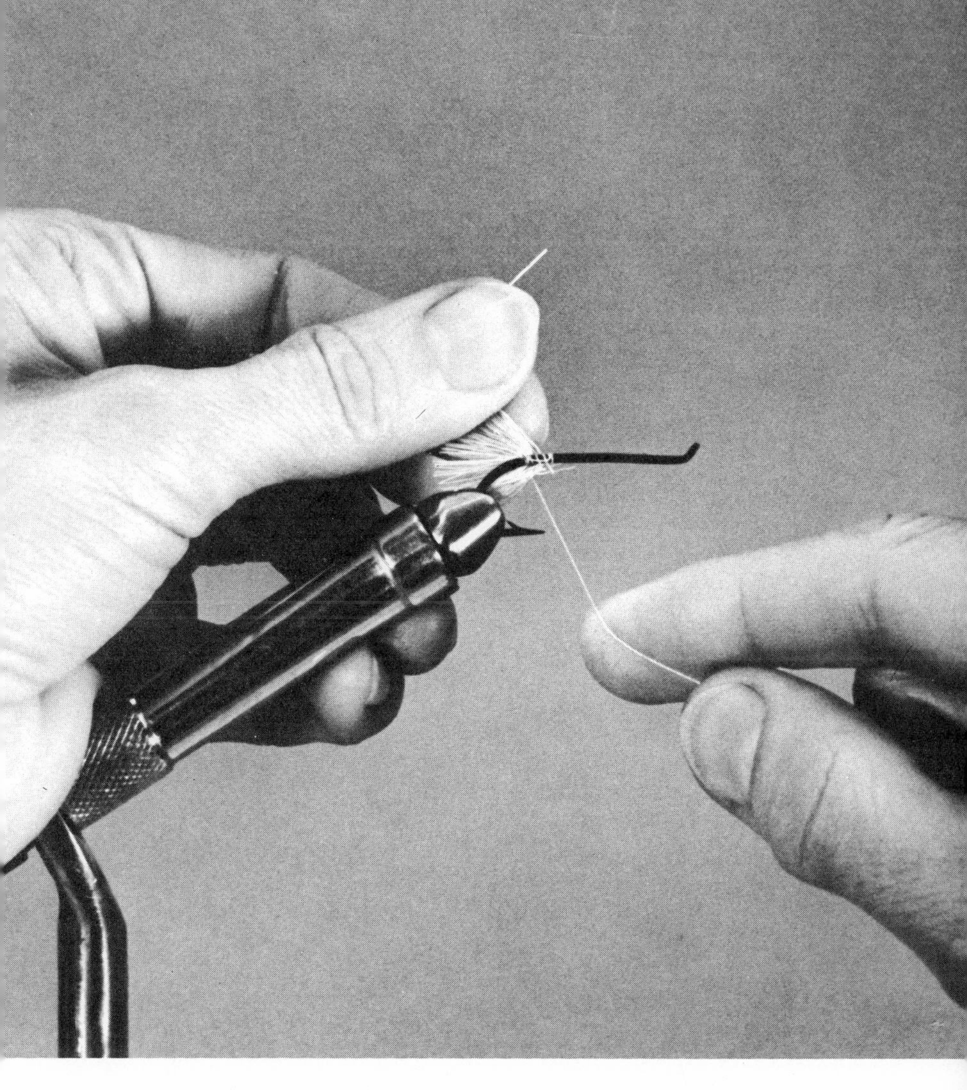

12d. Maintain a firm grip on the hair and keep it on top of the hook until the thread has pulled the tuft down to the hook. Keep the tying thread taut. As you draw the thread toward you beneath the hook, allow the hair to be pulled from between the fingers. It will appear beneath the hook, folded around the thread. The thread is wrapping the center of the hair tuft around the hook.

12e. Lean forward and look along the hook shank at the tuft of hair as it is being drawn around the hook. This is what you will see. Grip the hair, holding it folded around the thread as you draw it upward and over the hook, as close as possible to the first turn.

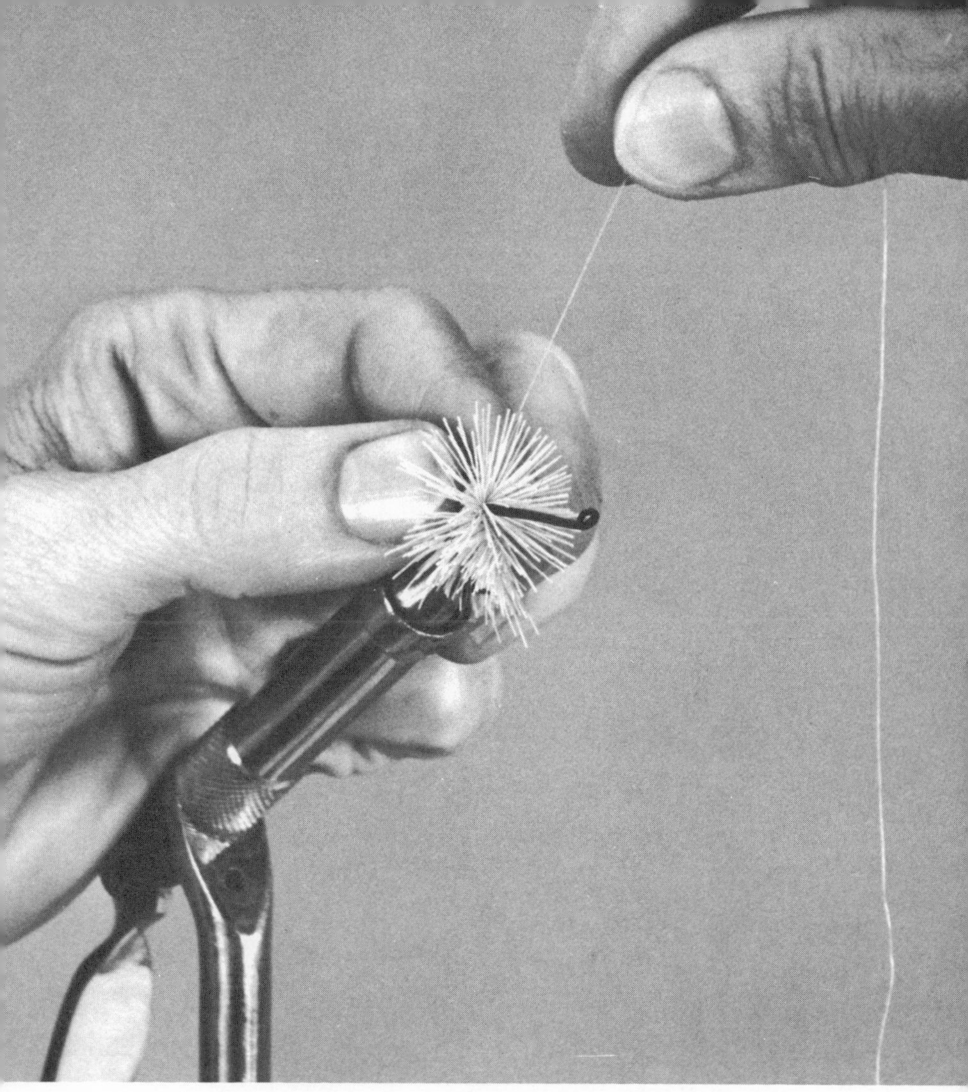

12f. Wind the thread once more around the hook through the hair. The first tuft is now wrapped around the hook and all turning motion of the hair should have ceased. It is firmly held to the hook as long as tension on the thread is maintained.

12g. Bring the thread down, preparatory to attaching it to the button. Before securing it, reach forward of the spun tuft and encompass it with all the fingers of the left hand.

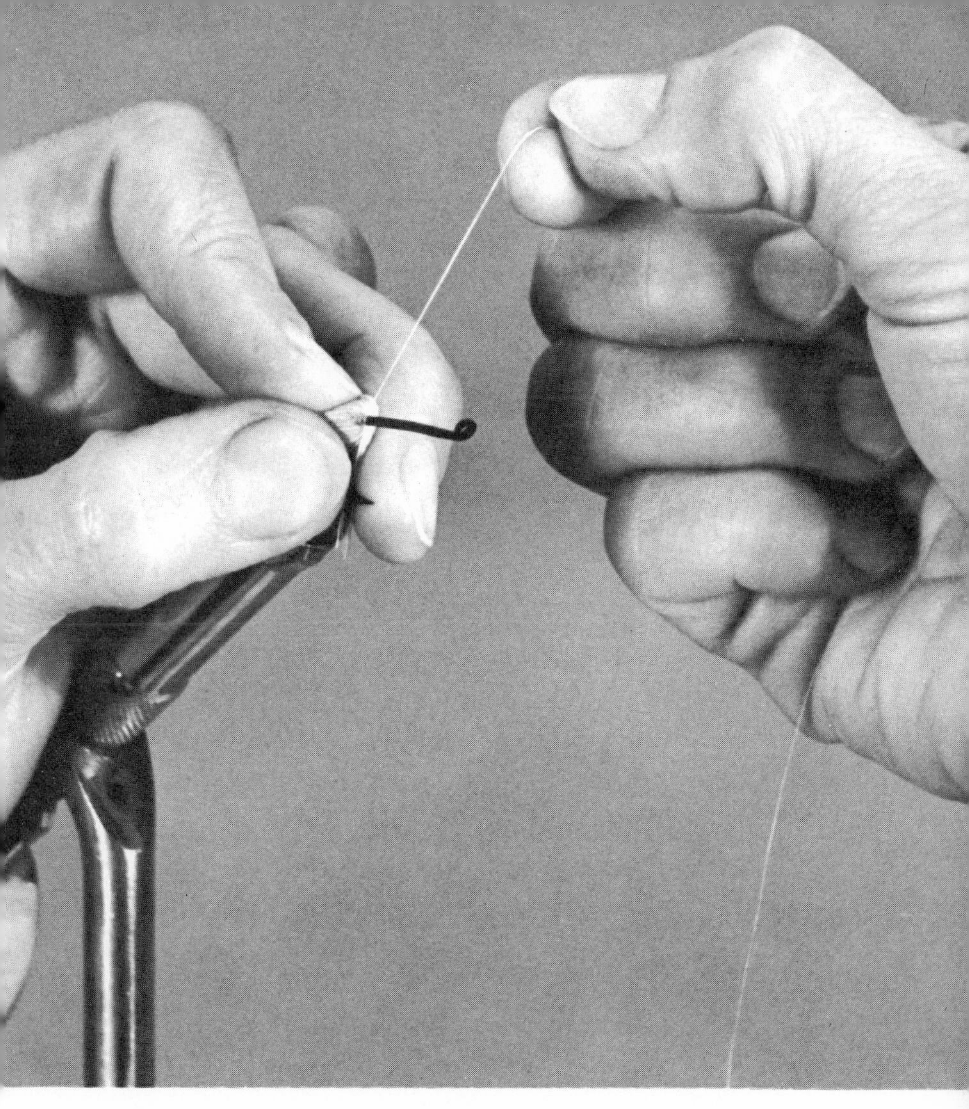

12h. Draw the entire ruff of hair backward and wind one more turn of thread tightly around the hook immediately in front of the hair. Secure the thread to the button.

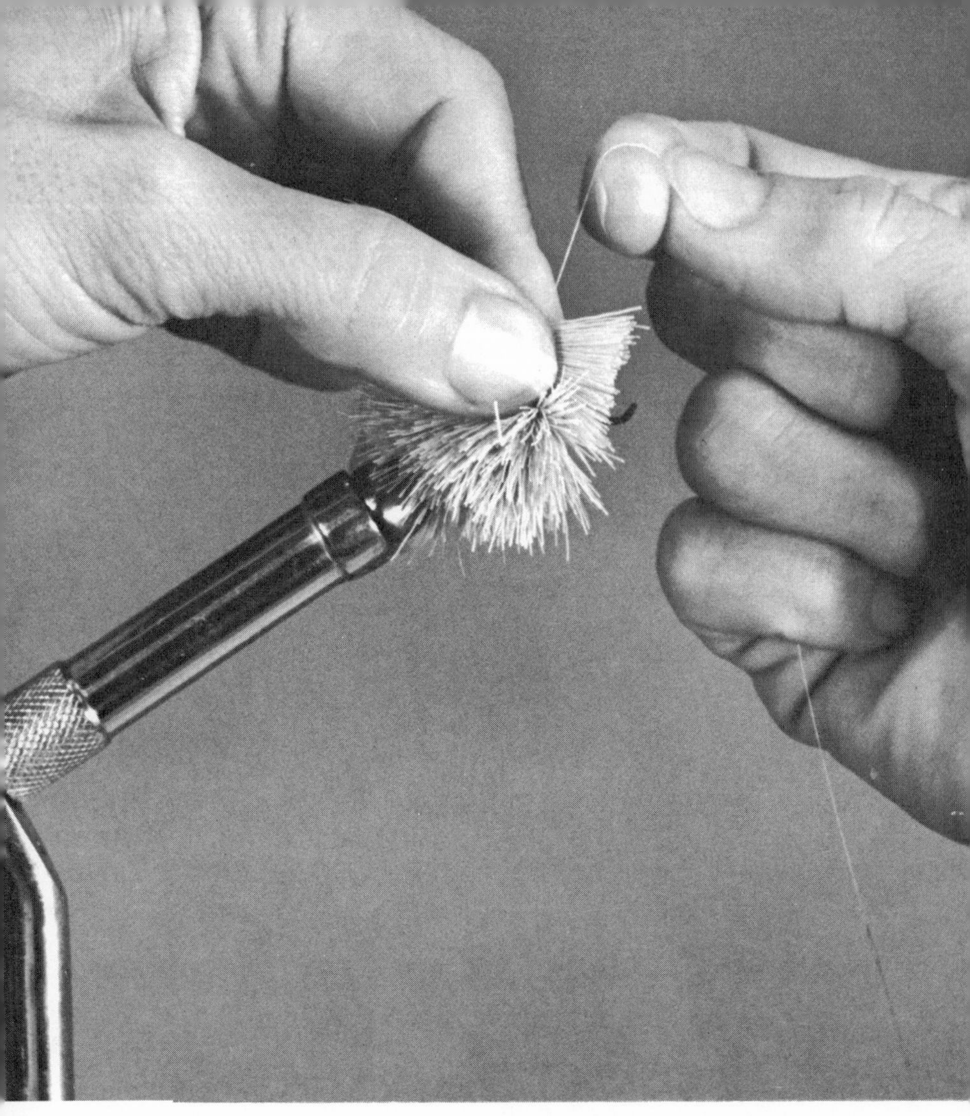

12i. Select another slim tuft of deer hair, trim it, and tie it on exactly as you did the first, as close to the first tuft as possible.

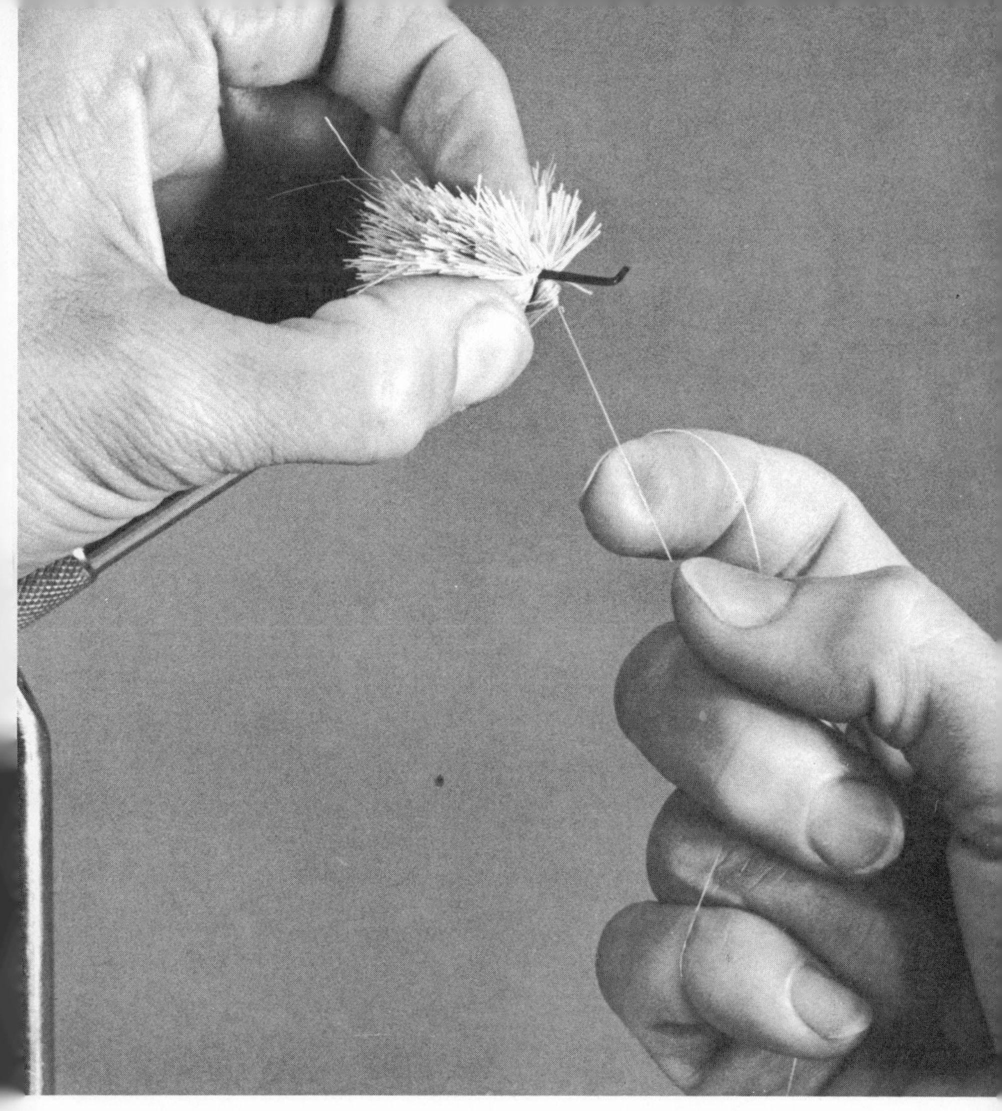

12j. Hold the hair backward out of your way as you draw the tuft around the hook, enabling yourself to see exactly where the hair is being wound on. All turning motion of the hair should cease after the thread has made two complete circuits of the hook. If the turning motion is still noticeable, you may have used too heavy a tuft. Unwind it, keeping the thread taut. Secure the thread, cut a fresh tuft taking less hair, and continue as before. Add further tufts until the hook shank is filled with hair.

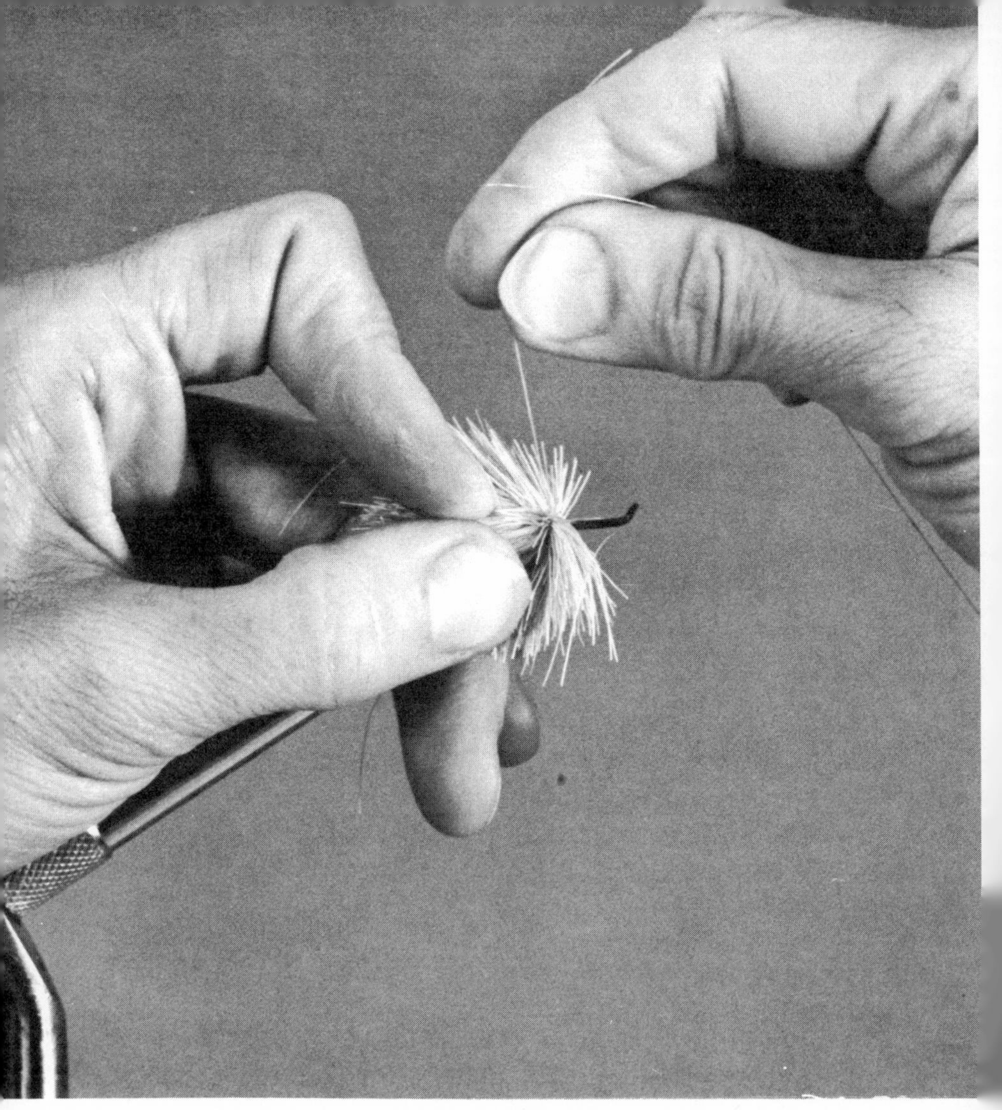

12k. As you approach "wing position" and are securing the last tuft of hair, you may make two more turns of thread through the hair, using a scalloping motion of the right hand to guide the thread between the standing hairs. Keep the thread taut, of course. Now, hold all the hair back and bring the thread up in front of the hair as close to it as possible. Tie a wrap knot there using three turns of thread. Having practiced the wrap knot earlier, you should have no difficulty with it now.

13a. The hair body is now complete and ready for **trimming**. Remove it from the vise for greater maneuverability. The simplest shape to trim will be the straight taper.

13b. Hold the hook by the eye. The tying thread wound snugly around the fingers will aid in maintaining a firm grip on the hook. The first trimming will clear the underside of the body. Hold the barb and point upward. Slide the scissors into the hair directly beneath them and clip away a small amount of hair at a time, clearing the space between point and hook shank.

13c. Using the hook point as a guide, trim the bottom of the fly level. Cut the hair as close to the hook shank as can be done without digging the points into the closely packed hair. Leave the hair a trifle longer near the fingers than at the extreme end.

13d. With the underside of the body flat, the first cut to be made along the side can now be gauged. For a body of this size and shape, the finished width nearest the eye should be about ½ inch. Hold the body with the flat side toward you, eye down. Slide the blades of the scissors into a little of the hair at the side. The base of the blades will be approximately ¼ inch from the hook shank, the tips touching the shank at the bend of the hook. This first straight cut will be a guide for following ones.

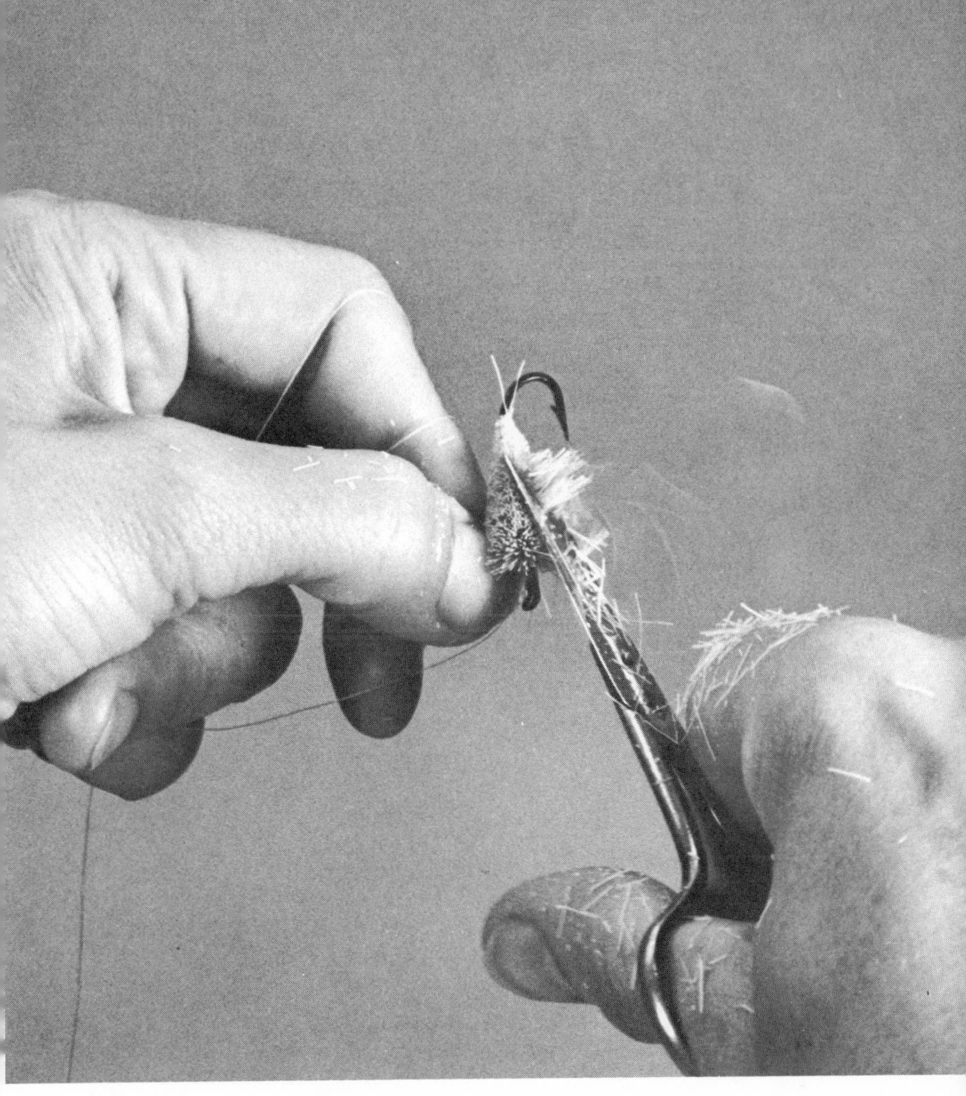

13e. Keep the base of the scissors at the same distance from the hook and continue to make straight cuts around the body, the tips of the scissors just clearing the hook shank each time.

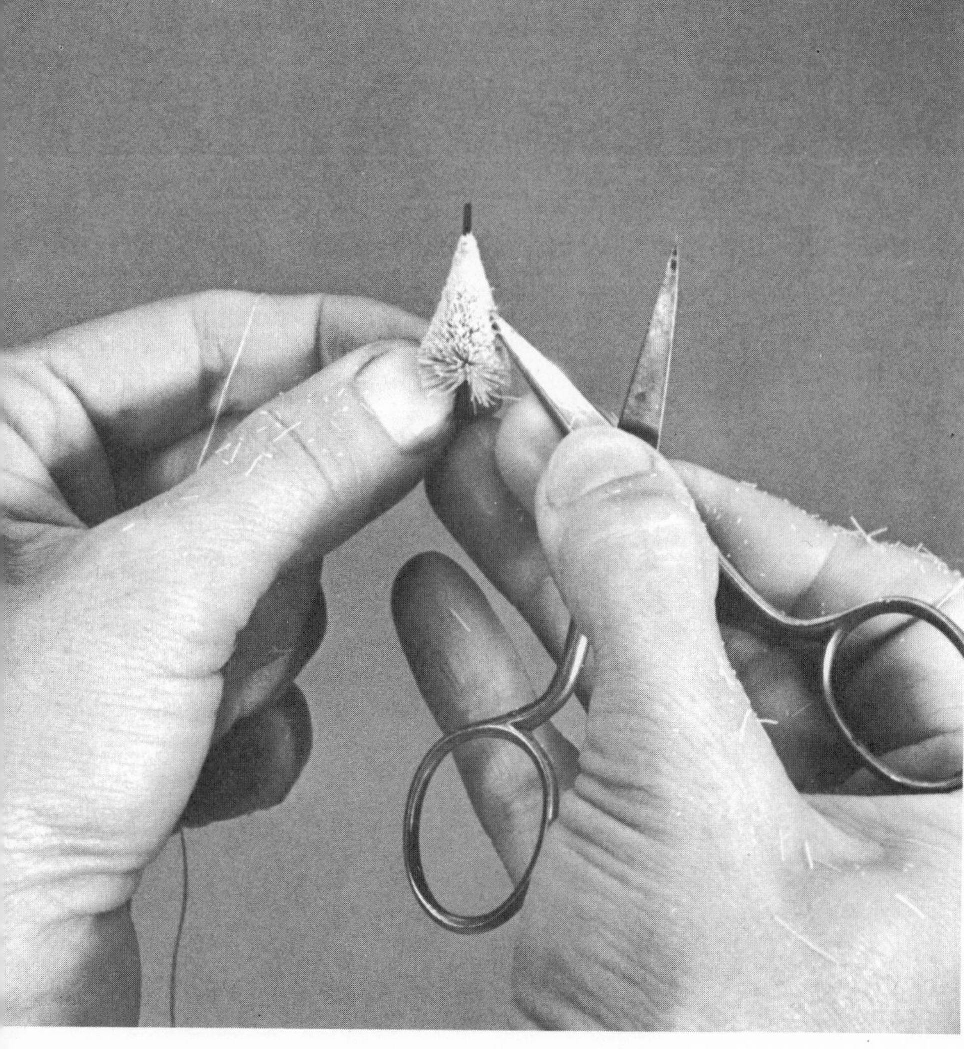

13f. Gradually a neatly tapered body will emerge. When the long hair has been trimmed away, run the point of a blade gently through the surface of the body hair with a combing motion. This will raise any hairs that may have been bent down while tying.

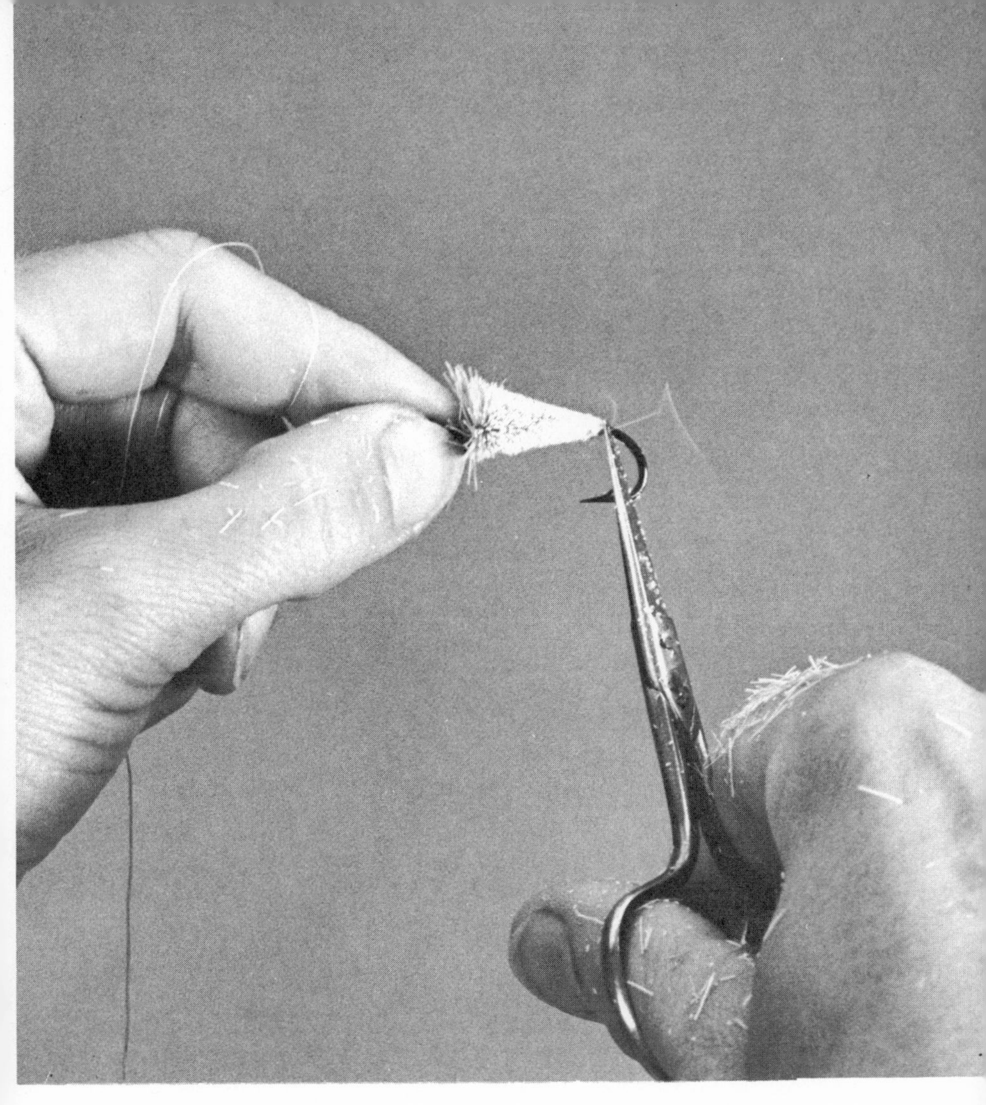

13g. Remove all protruding hairs by clipping them even with the surface.

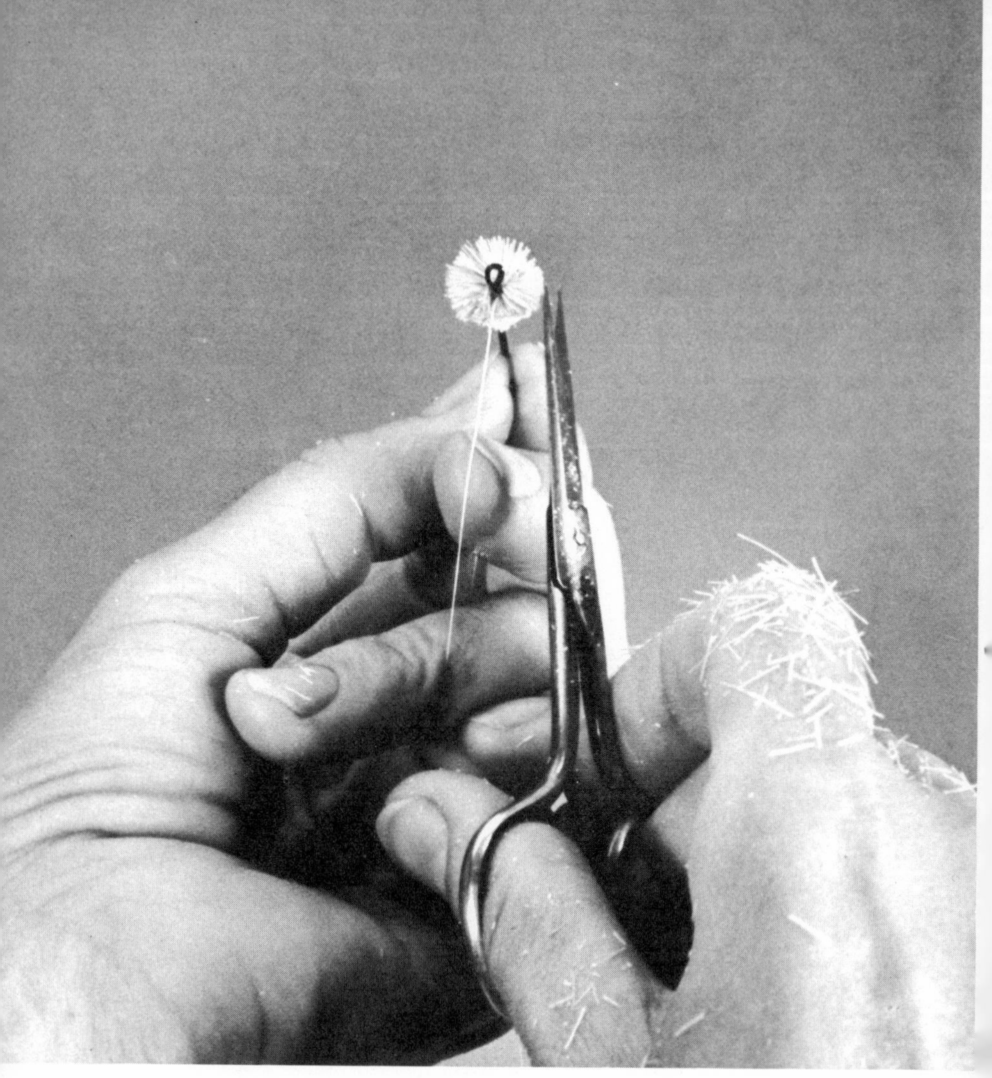

13h. From directly in front, the body should be symmetrically trimmed around the hook, with slightly more above the hook than directly below.

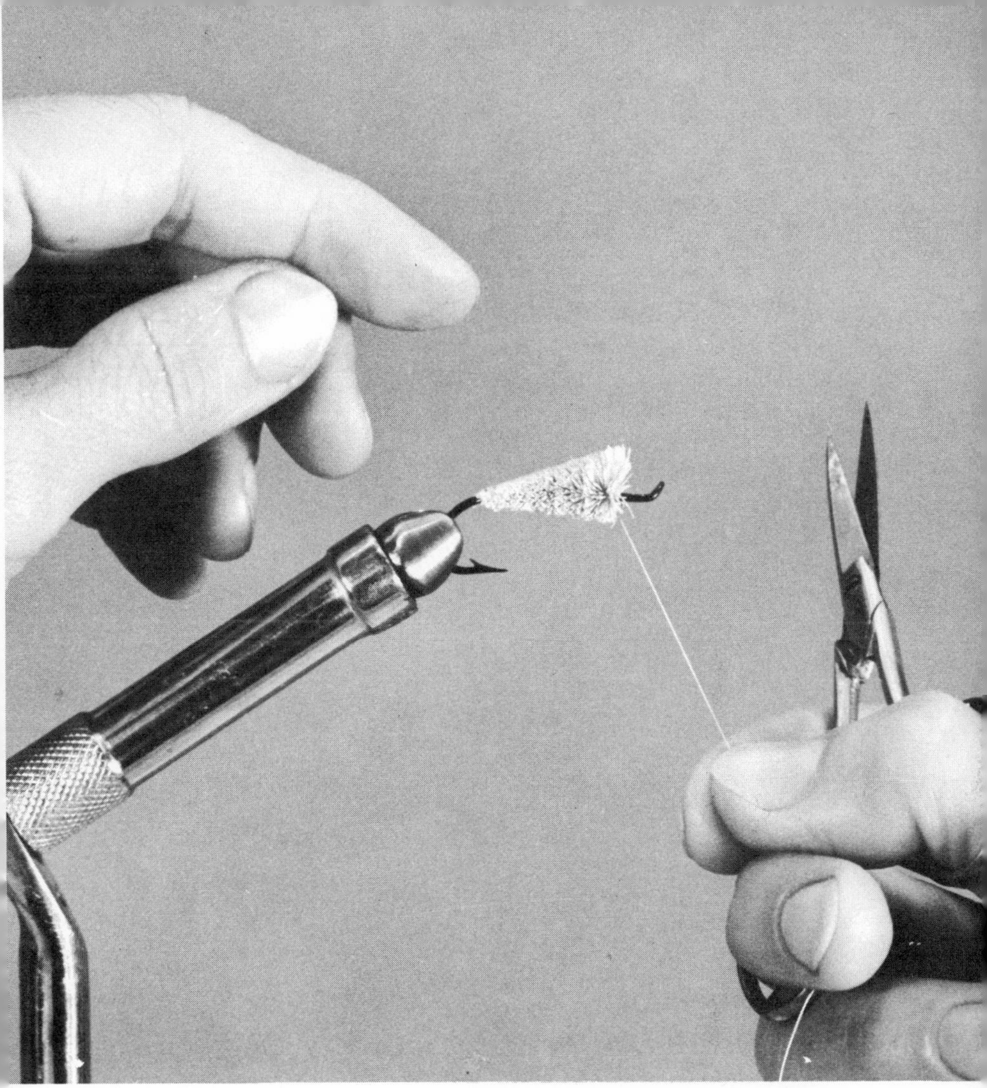

13i. The body, carefully rimmed, is now complete. Pracice tying and trimming until you an produce uniform bodies every ime.

By using very short tufts of hair, body that requires **little or no rimming** will result. This can be sed for fishing just as it is. On a maller hook, a body like this made f tiny tufts of hair is used as a ymph.

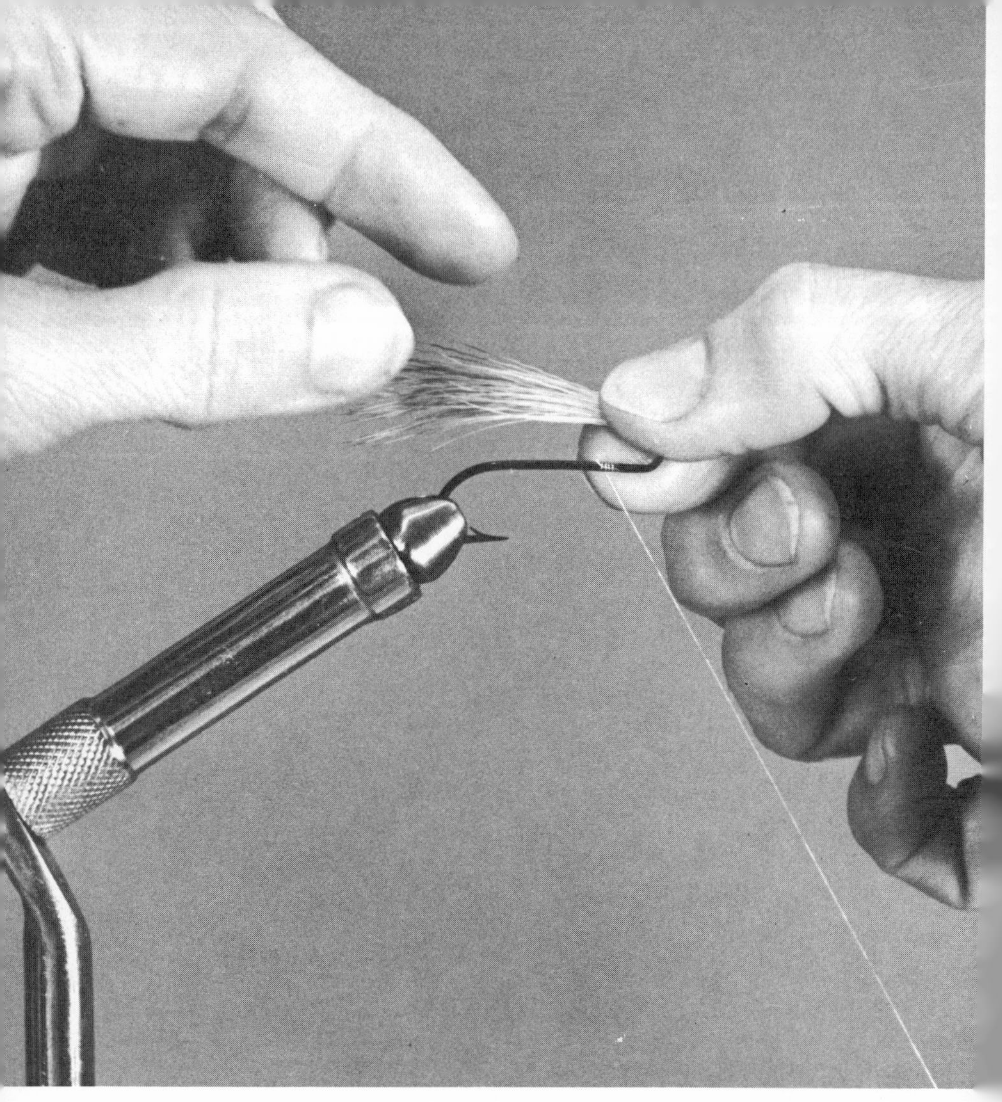

14a. Another body that requires **little or no trimming** is made by cutting a small tuft of hair and removing the fuzz from the cut ends, this time leaving the natural, tapered tips. Make sure they are fairly even. Hold the tuft against the hook, butt ends in the right hand, and adjust the length, permitting the tapered ends to extend a short way beyond the end of the hook.

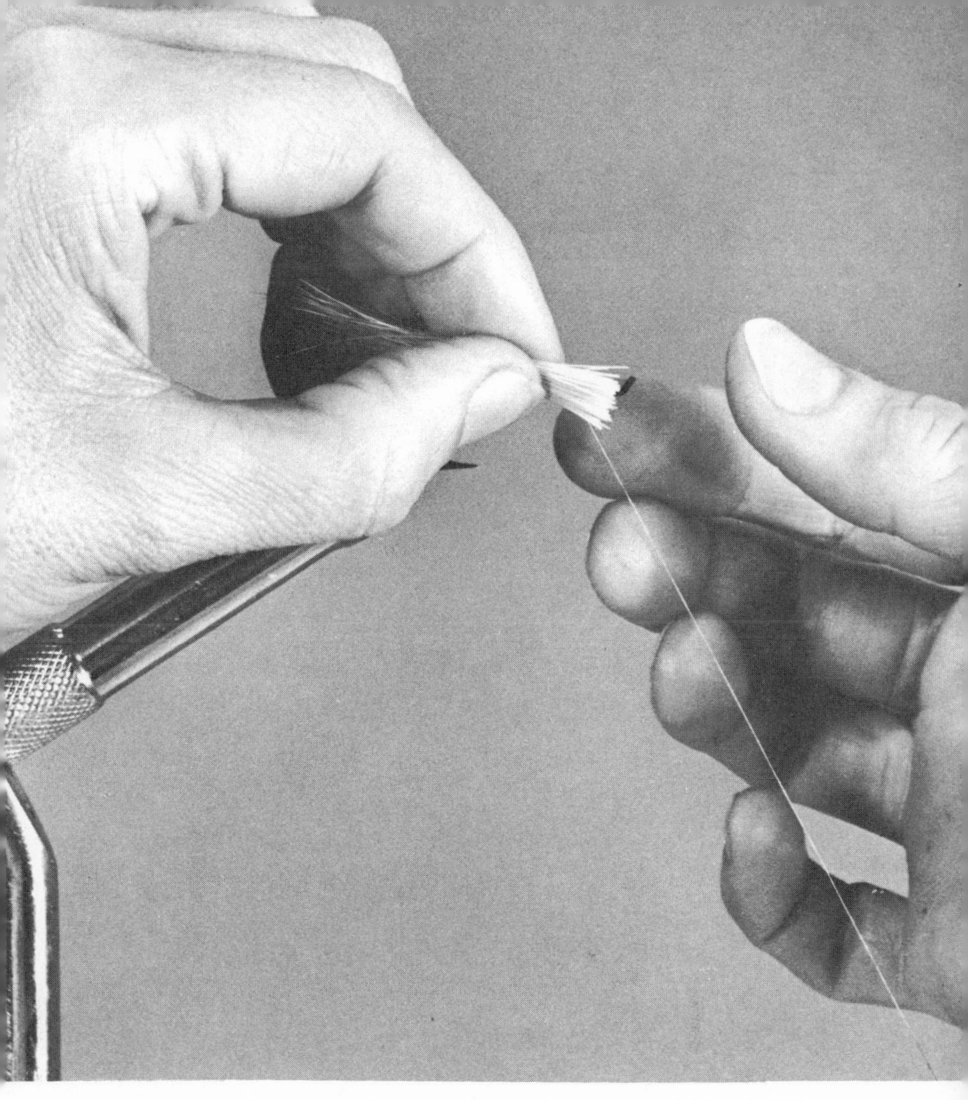

14b. Grip the tuft with the left hand, just above "wing position" as it is held there by the right hand. The right hand can now release the thread and bring it up in front of the hook, slide it between fingers and hair, and slowly ease the hair around the hook.

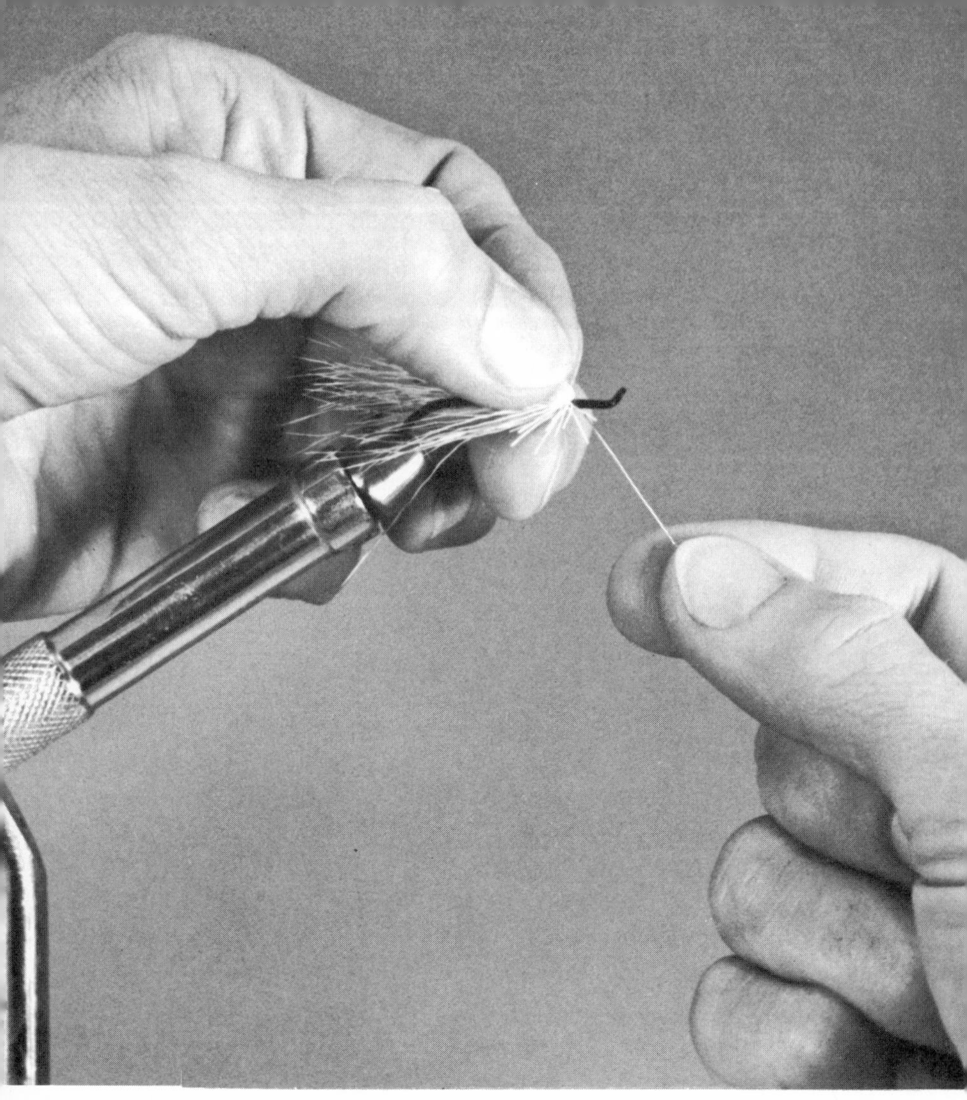

14c. When the hair completely circles the hook, wind another turn of thread through it, then hold it back and wind one more turn of thread in front of the hair and as close to it as possible.

14d. Another very short tuft with the natural ends removed may be added in front of the cut hair, and as close to it as possible. If still another small tuft is needed to fill in the space between "wing position" and the base of the hook eye, add it now, leaving just enough room for the head. Carefully draw all the cut hair back and tie a wrap knot, ending at the base of the hook eye. Clip the thread and rewax it. Make sure the long hair is evenly distributed around the hook and smooth it down as close to the hook as possible.

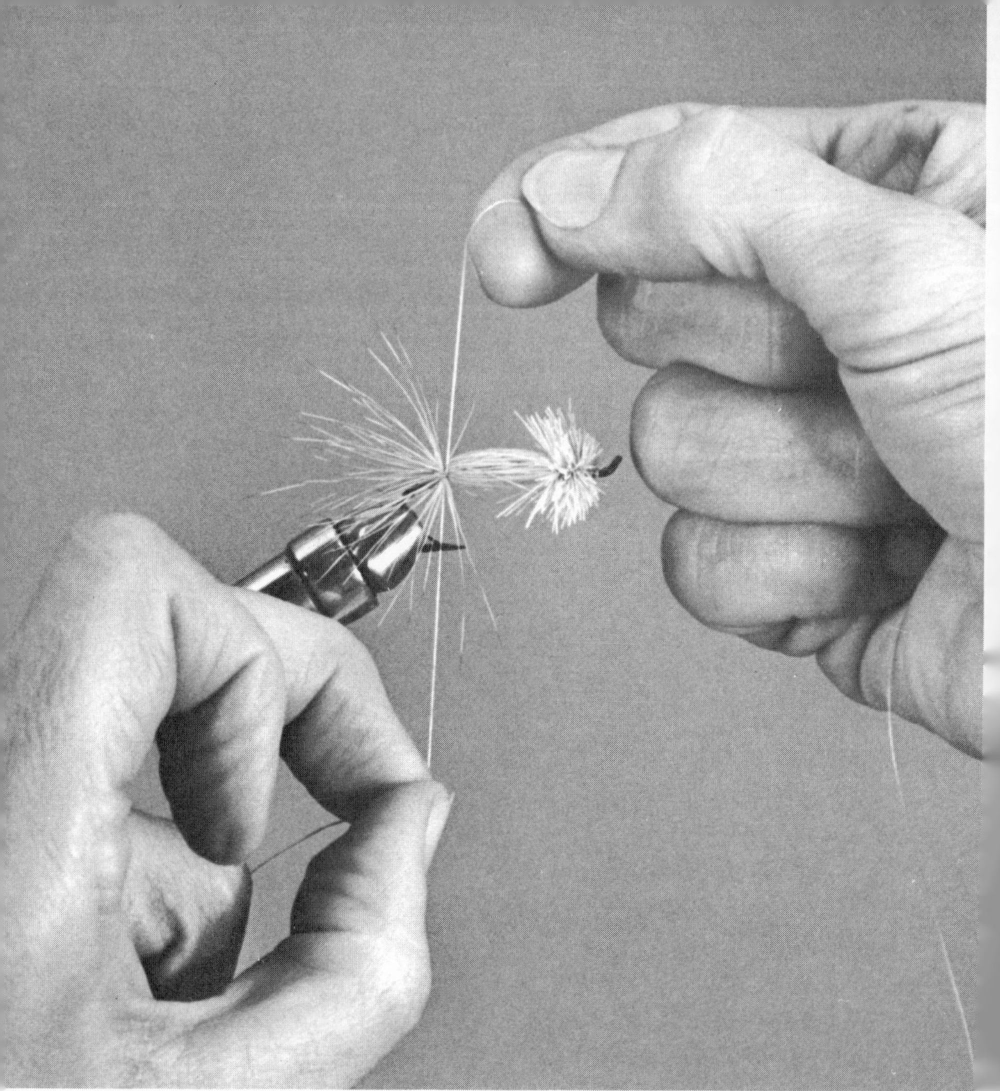

14e. Now, take the short end of thread in the left hand as though about to attach the thread to the hook at "tail position." Gently place a loose turn of thread completely around the hair and hook, above and slightly in front of the hook barb. Slowly tighten the thread. As the loop tightens, it will draw the hair against the hook. Keeping it taut, bring the thread down behind the hook and up in front, across the thread held by the left hand. Repeat this three times. Drop the short end with the left hand and proceed to make a wrap knot directly over the thread windings. A narrow band of thread will result, held securely in place by the wrap knot.

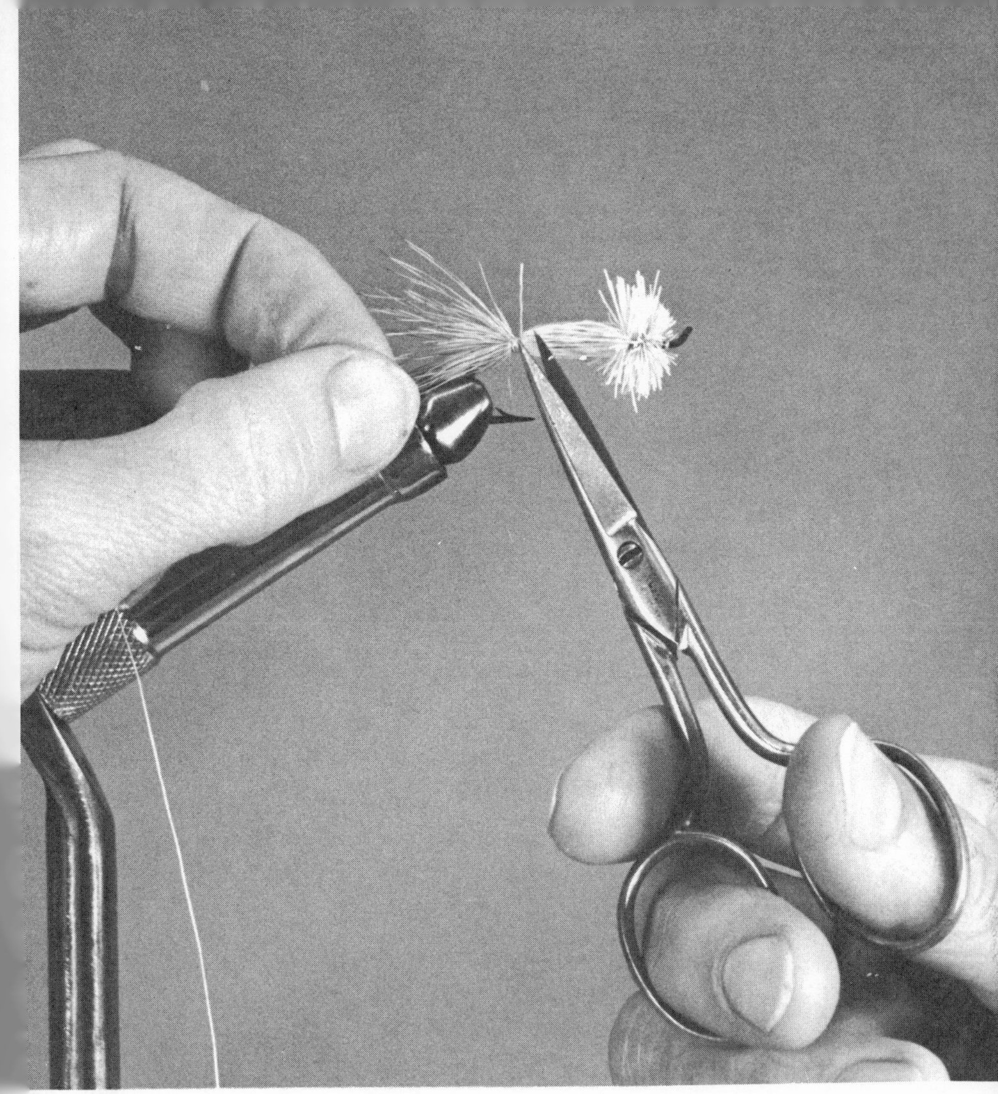

14f. Clip the tying thread and the short end of thread close to the winding. Carefully cover all exposed thread with head-varnish or lacquer, holding the hair out of the way while doing so. This fly may be left as it is, without further trimming, or the tuft at the front can be shaped a little more if desired.

15a. Hook in vise; thread attached at "tail position." Clip a small tuft of hair from a tail of Asiatic goat or Bucktail. Remove all the short, fine hairs and soft undercoat from the base of the tuft. The natural ends of hair are tapered and should be used without trimming.

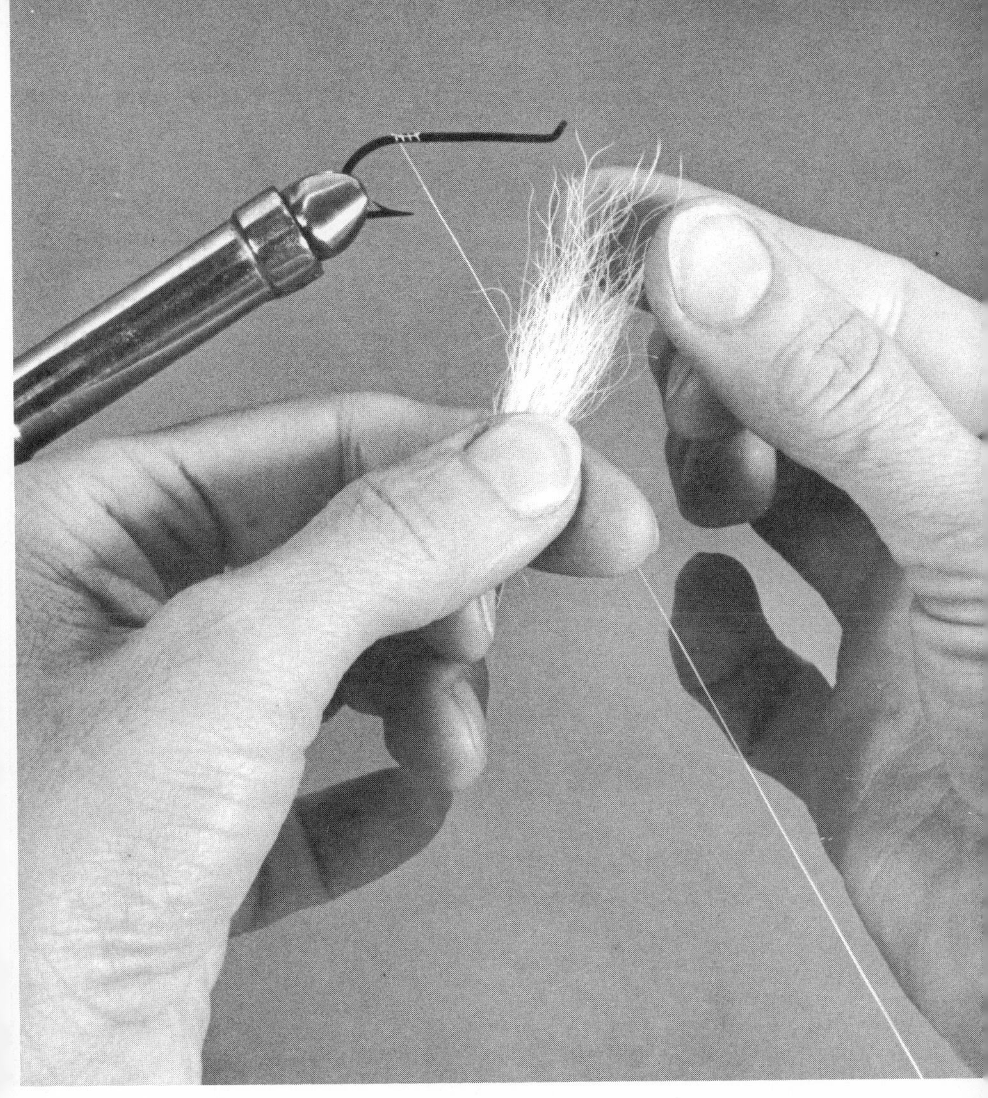

15b. Remove any hairs having broken or cut ends. Even up the tips of remaining hairs by pulling the longest ones gently from the tuft, leaving the major portion undisturbed.

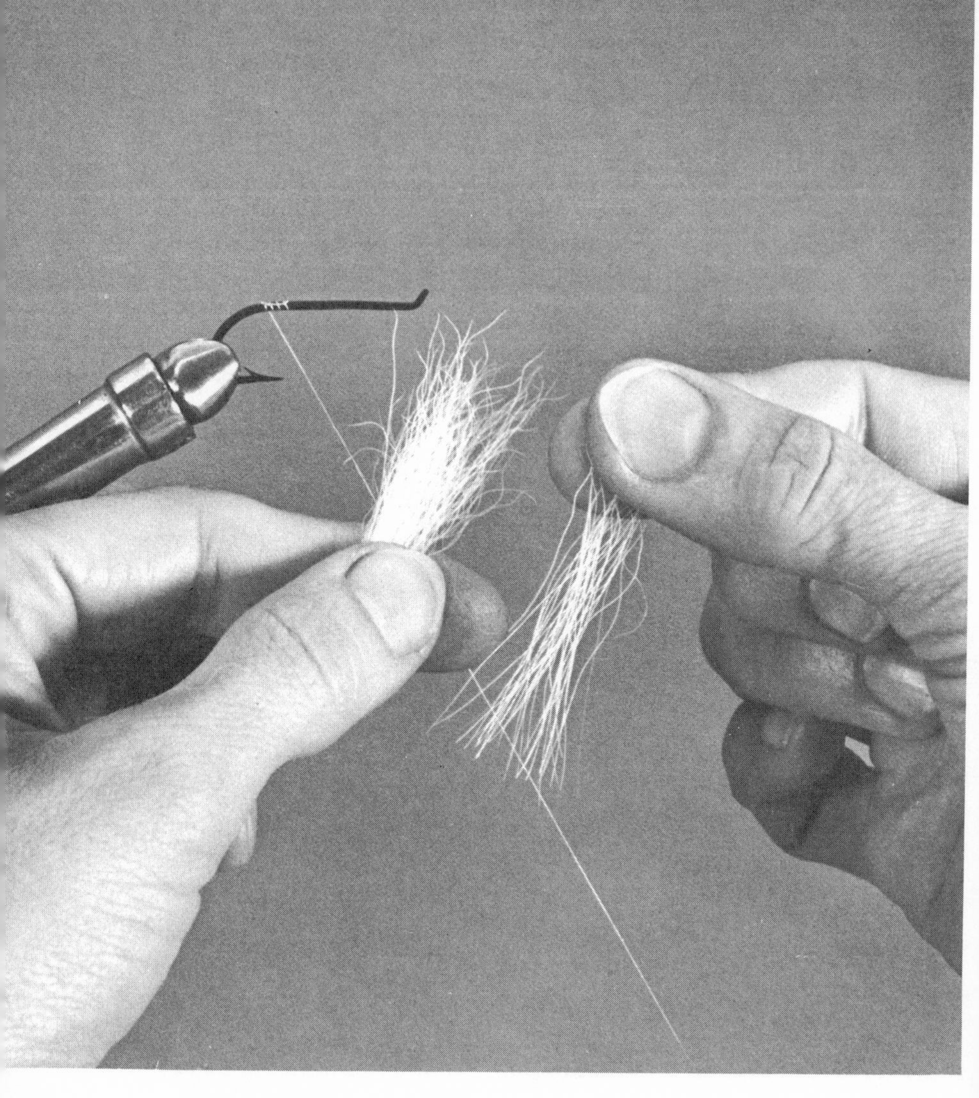

15c. Either discard them or replace them lower in the tuft so the tips are even. Do this a few times, until the tuft is neater and more uniform in appearance.

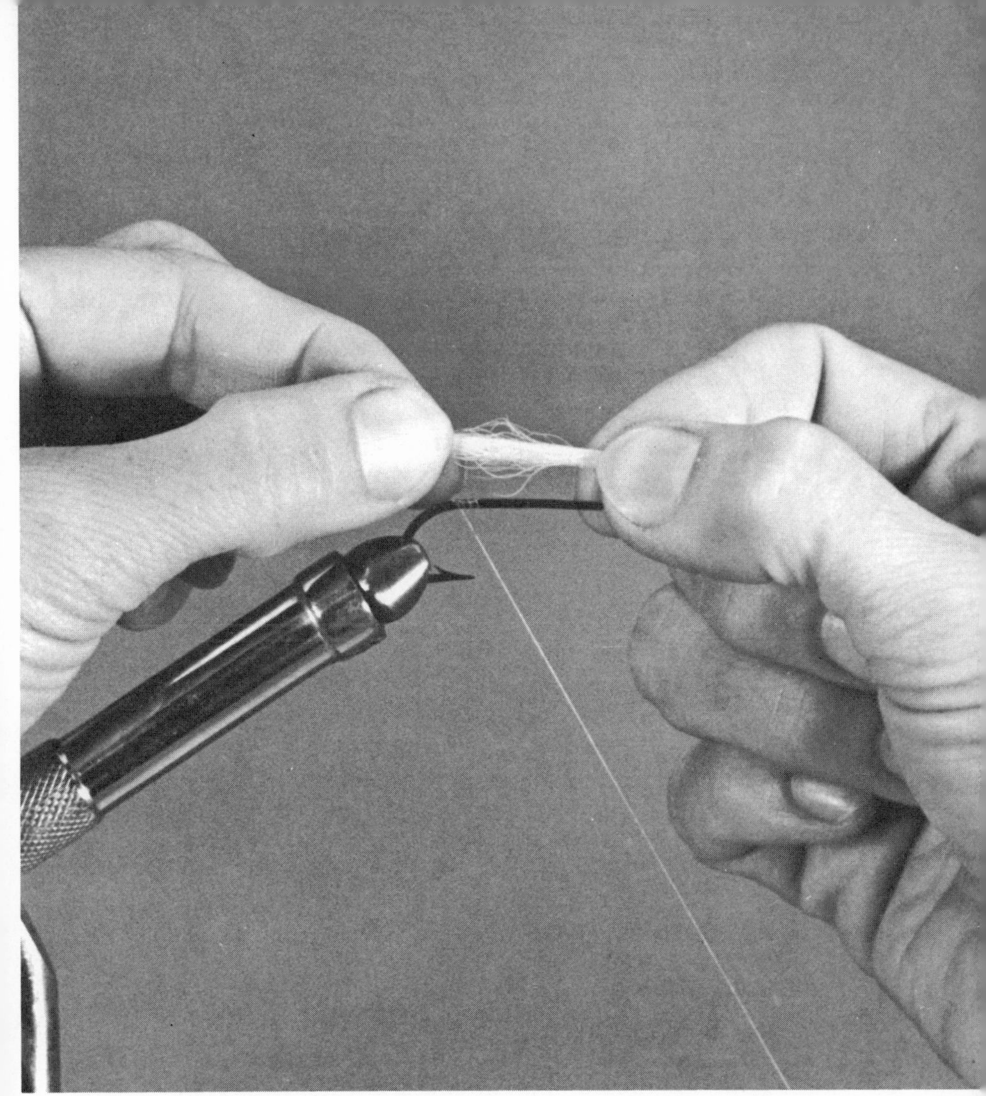

15d. Hold the cut ends of the tuft in the right hand and determine the length of the tail by measuring it against the hook. An average length for tails is approximately the length of the hook shank.

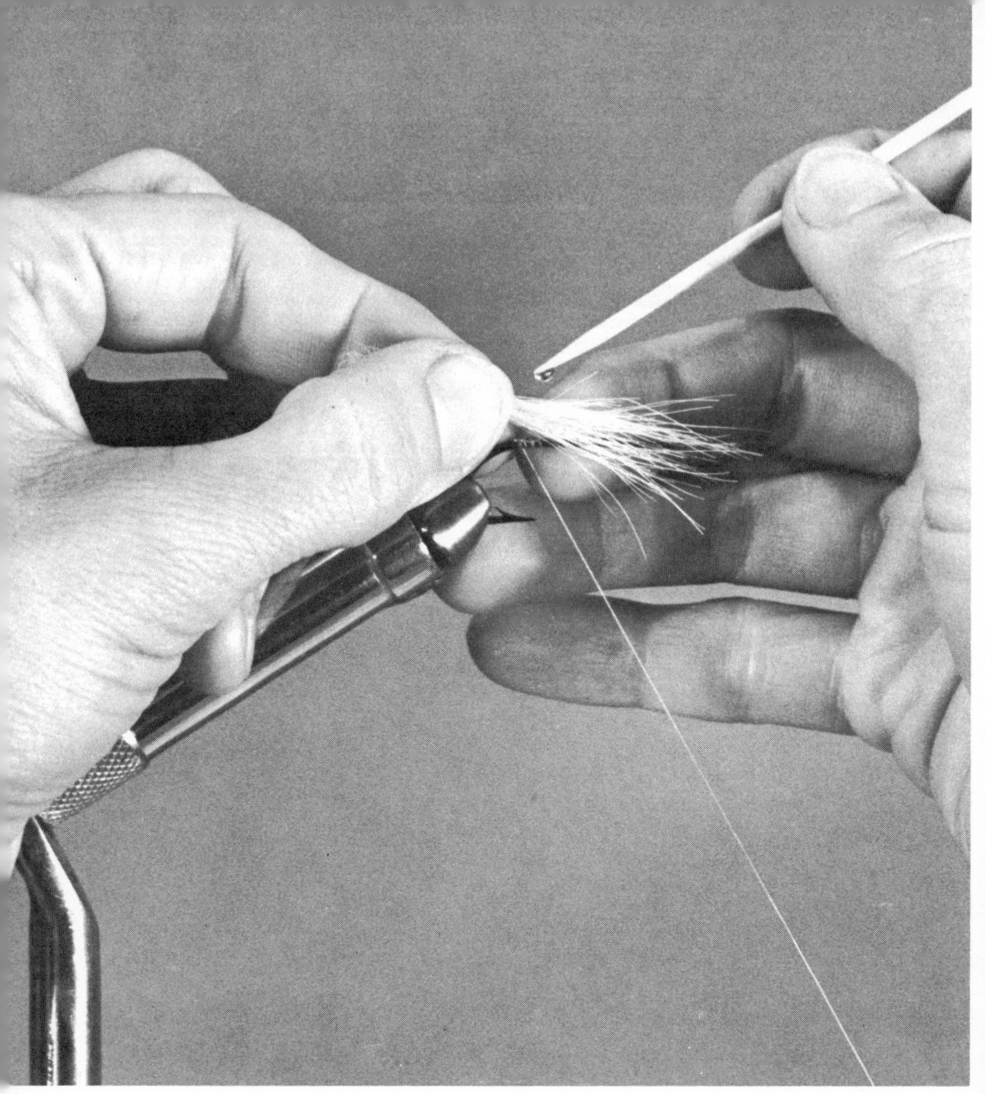

15e. Having gauged the length, grip the hair tuft with the left thumb and forefinger, the tips touching those of the right hand. Hold the tuft at "tail position" and put a drop of head-varnish or lacquer on the hair where the tying thread will cross it, immediately in front of the fingers.

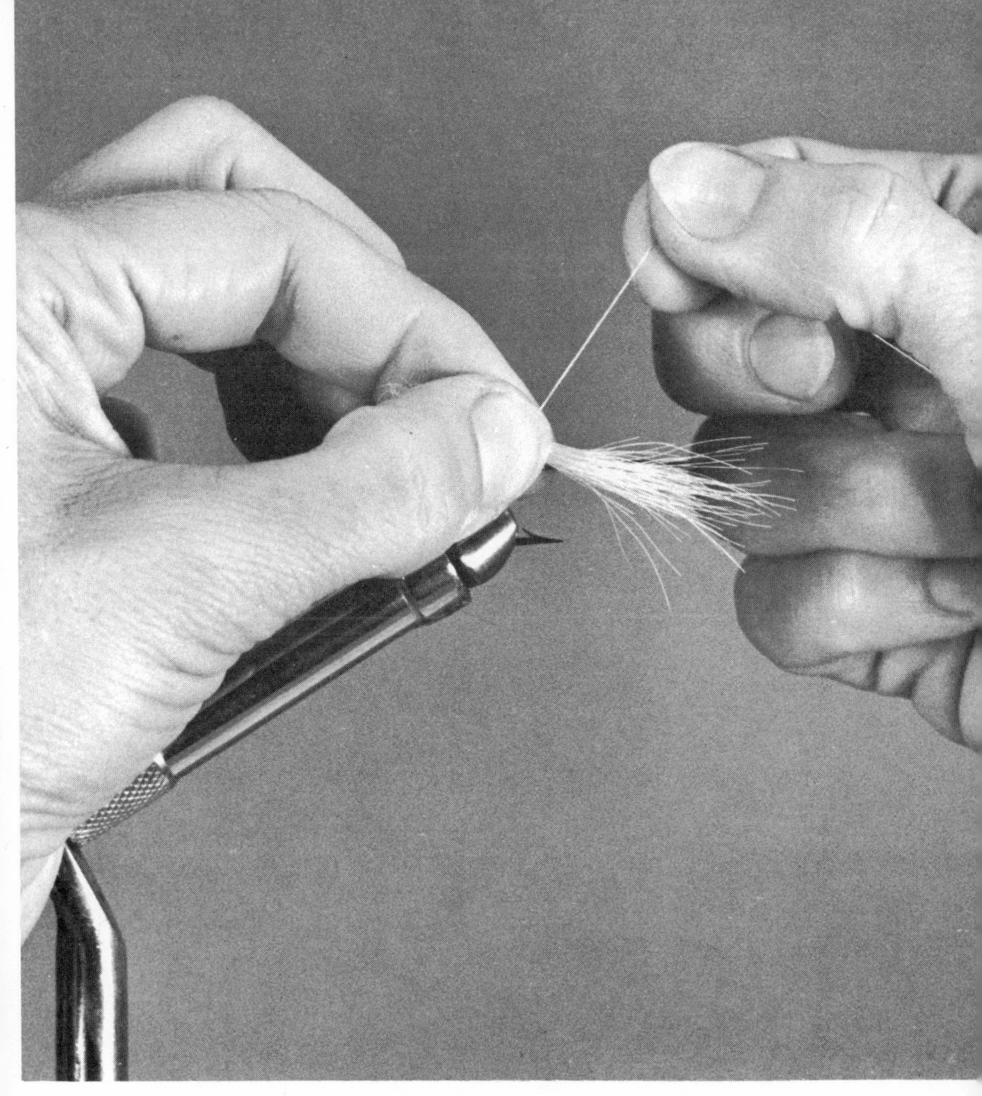

15f. Release the tying thread and bring it up in front of the hook, sliding it upward between thumb and hair tuft. Bring it down between tuft and forefinger on the far side of the hook.

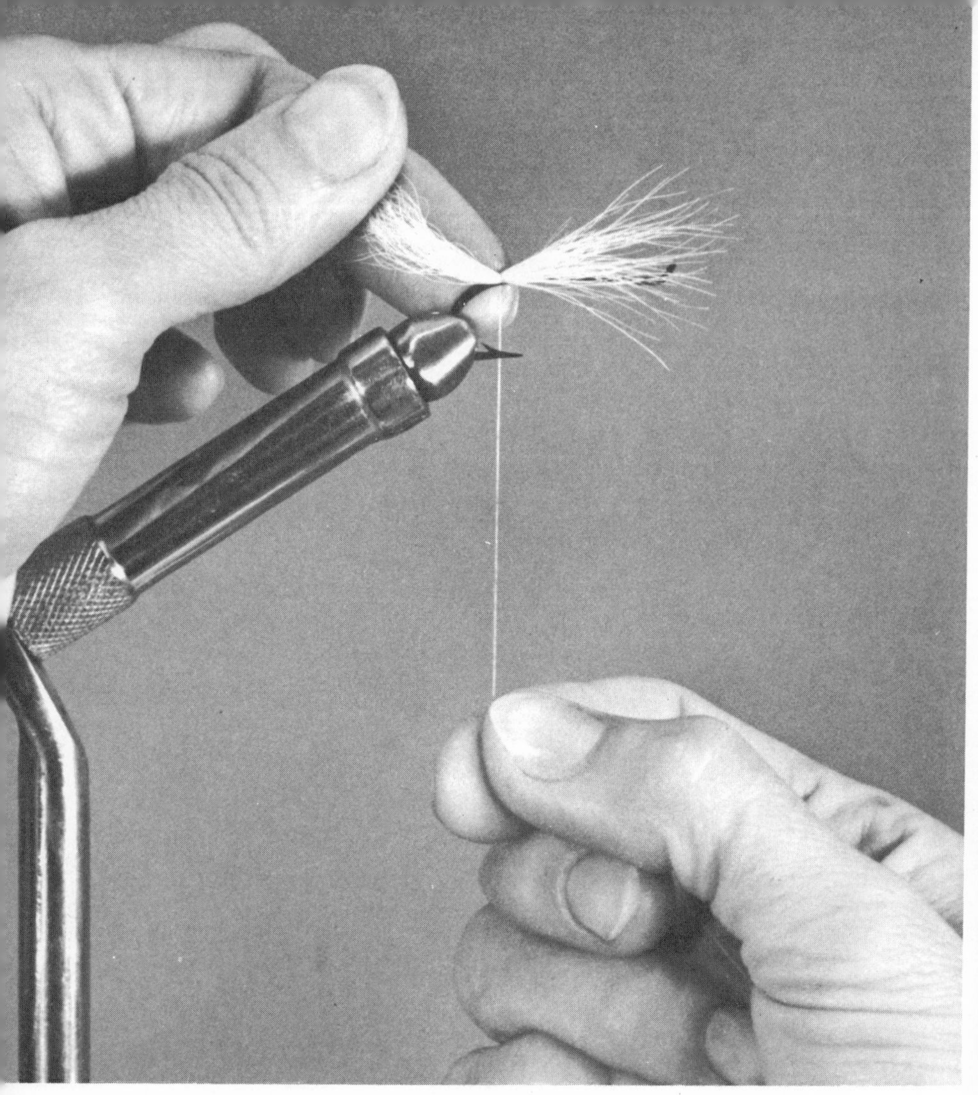

15g. The thread should cross the hair slightly ahead of the barb. Keep the hair on top of the hook. Do not let it be pulled around under the hook by the thread. Another turn of thread as close as possible to the first will anchor the hair. Keep the tying thread taut.

15h. Lift the hair tuft and carry the thread around behind it, keeping the thread tight at the hook. When the thread has crossed beind the tuft and is on the far side of the hook, release the hair with the left hand so the right may pass by and bring the thread forward and toward you *above* the hook shank. Again grip the hair tuft with the left hand and carry the tying thread behind it. This time bring the thread down on the far side of the hook and up again in front in the usual way. One complete turn of thread now circles the base of the tail.

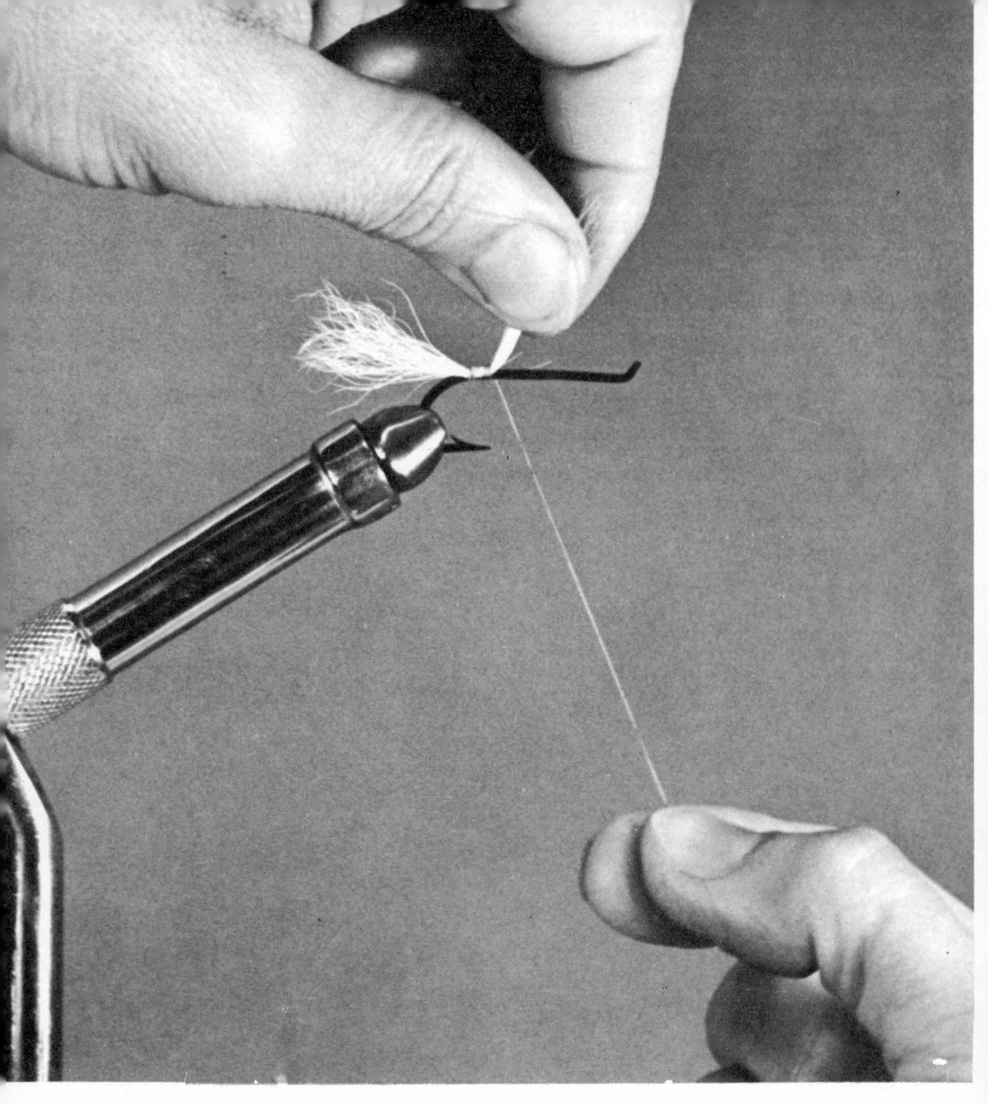

15i. Make two more turns of thread over hair and hook, keeping the hair on top of the hook, spiraiing the thread forward. The tail is now bound to the hook.

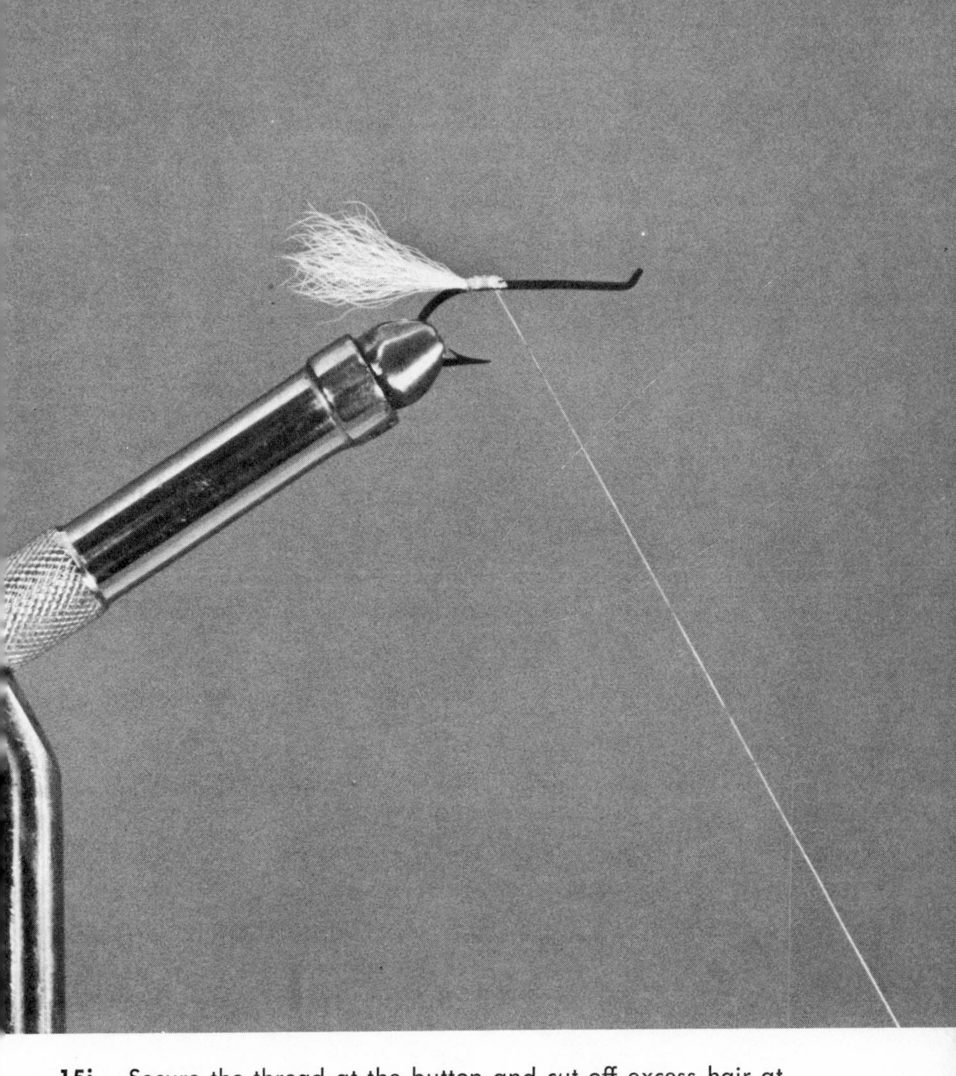

15j. Secure the thread at the button and cut off excess hair at an angle to taper the ends. Examine it. This amount of hair is fairly heavy, suitable for a body such as the trimmed deer hair body. Less hair should be used for a tail on a wool, dubbing, silk, or chenille body.

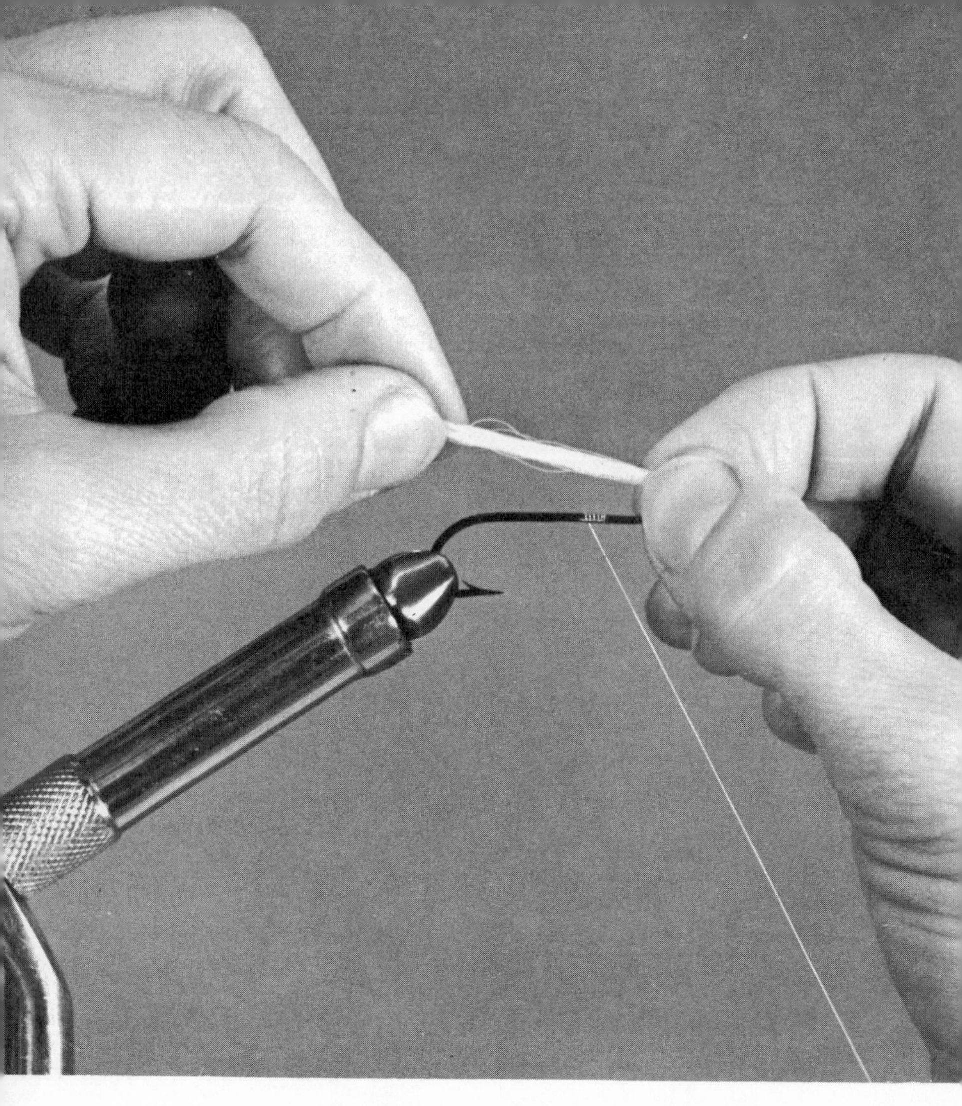

16a. The thread is attached at "wing position." For the single hair wing, streamer type, a slim tuft of hair is selected and cut from a Bucktail. Even the natural ends as for the tail. Remove fuzz from the cut ends of hair and measure it against the hook to determine the length. This wing will extend not more than the width of the gape (distance between point and hook shank) beyond the bend of the hook.

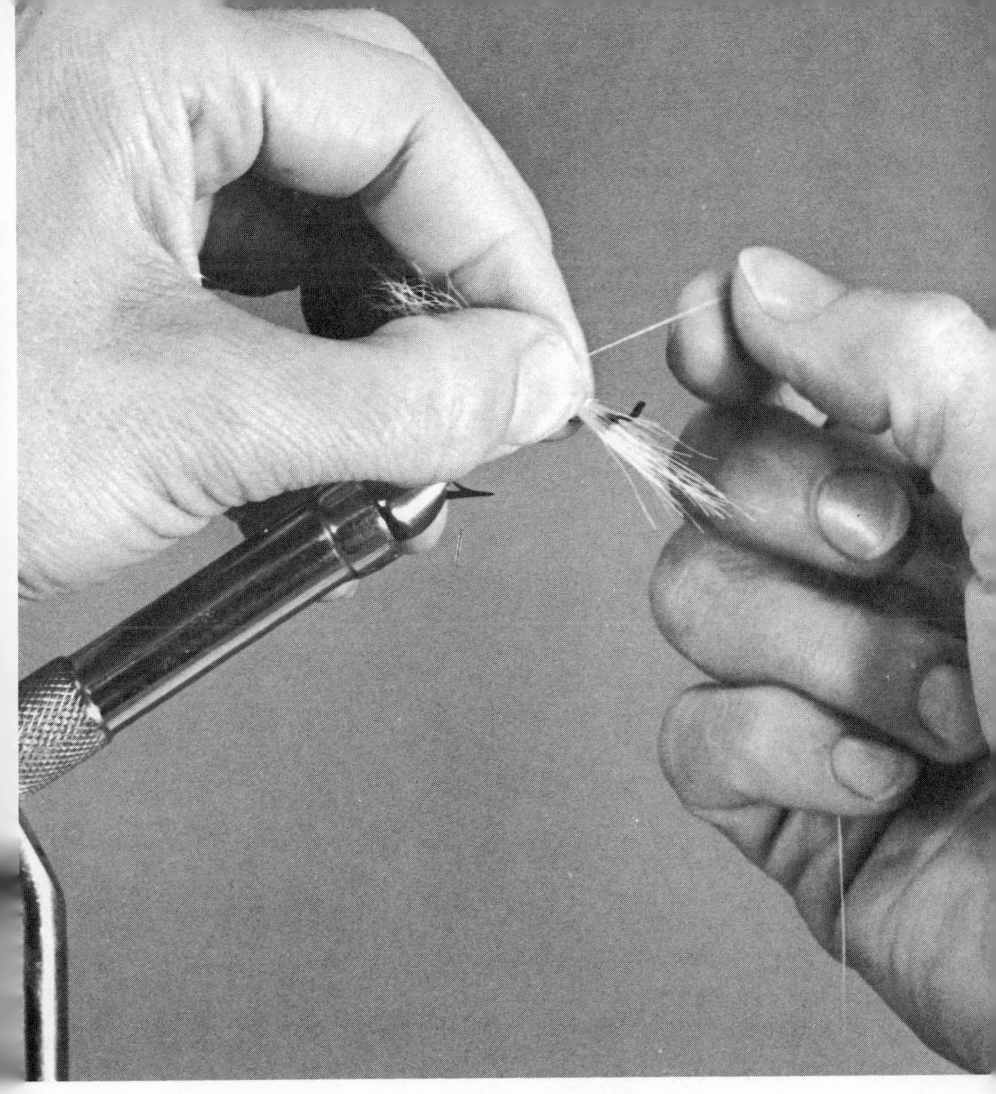

16b. Let go with the left hand and regrip the hair tuft with the left fingertips touching the right ones. Place a drop of head-varnish or lacquer on the hair where the tying thread will cross it. Bring the tying thread up between the fingers and across the hair at this spot. Two complete turns of thread around the hook and hair will anchor the tuft.

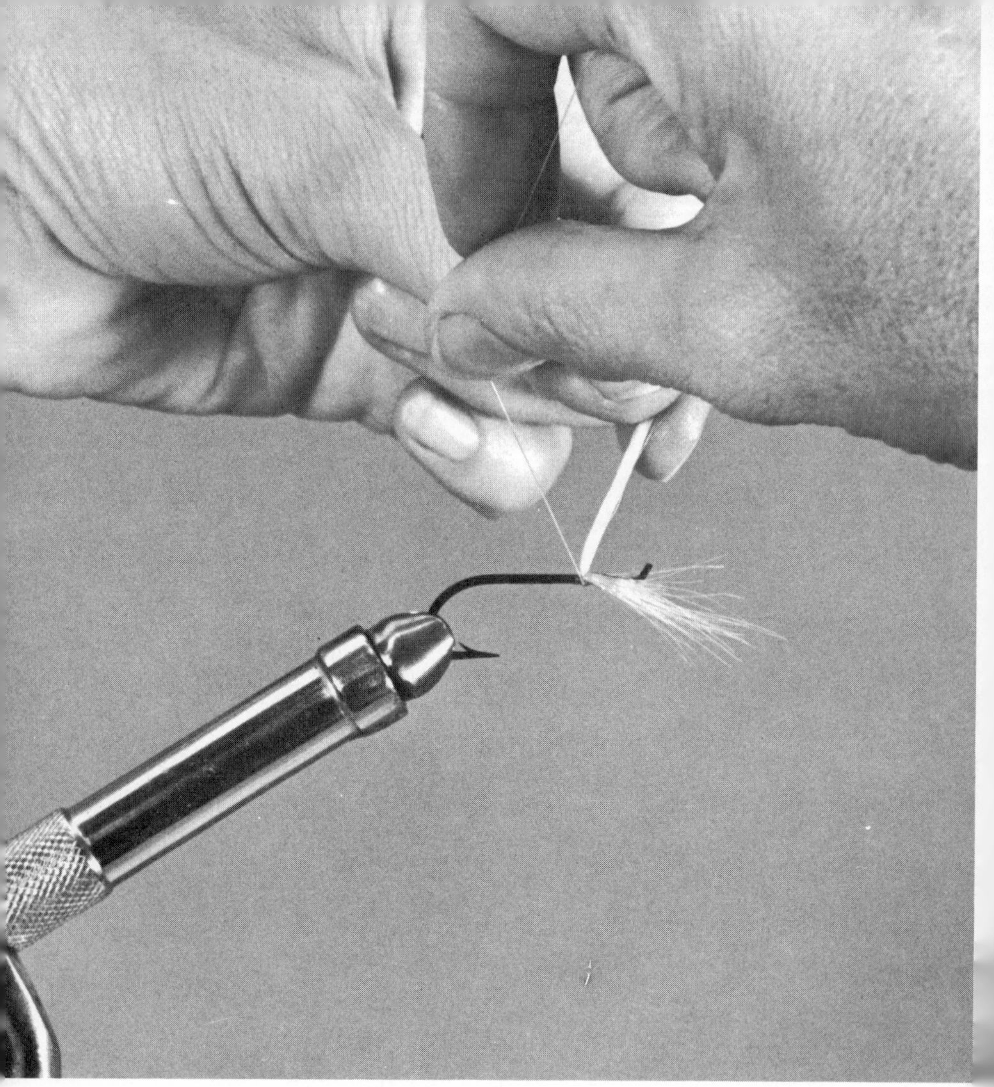

16c. Raise the tuft with the left hand, carrying the thread around behind it.

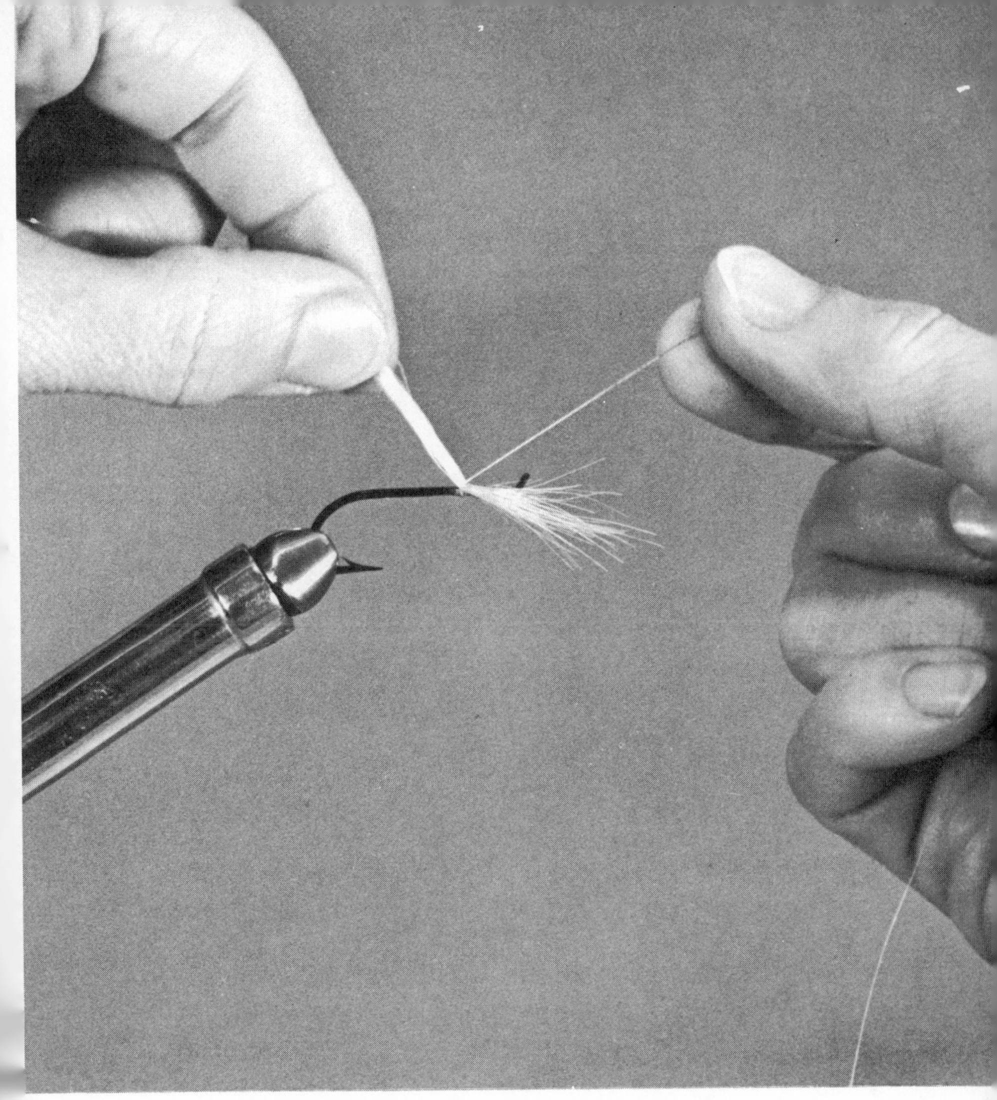

16d. Bring the thread forward on the far side of the hook and toward you, above the hook. Carry it around behind the tuft of hair again, this time bringing it down behind the hook and up in front in the usual way, changing hands as necessary.

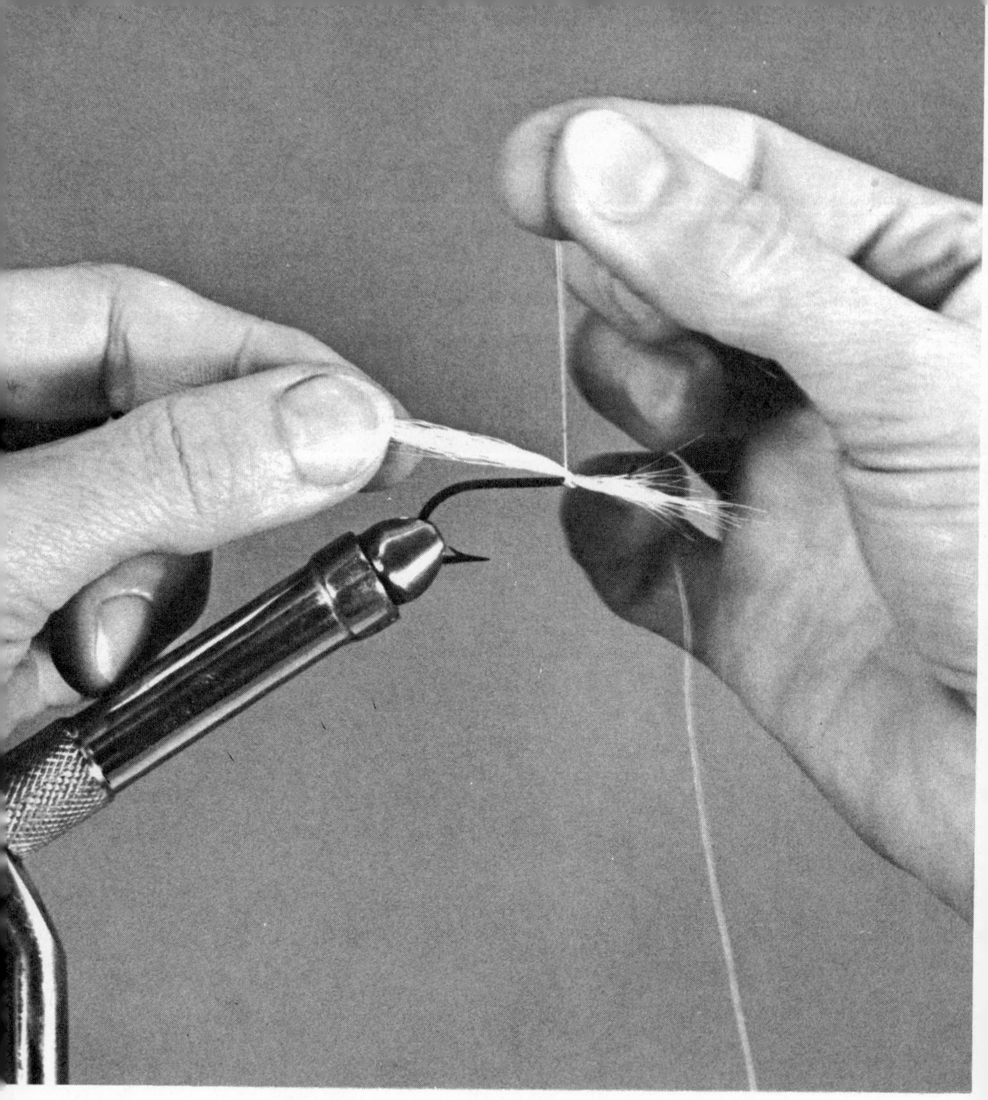

16e. The wing is now circled by one complete turn of tying thread. Hold the hair tuft down fairly close to the hook shank and put one turn of thread across the place where the circling thread meets on top of the hook. This will hold the wing down in its proper position. With the next two turns of thread around the hair and hook, make a gentle spiral forward.

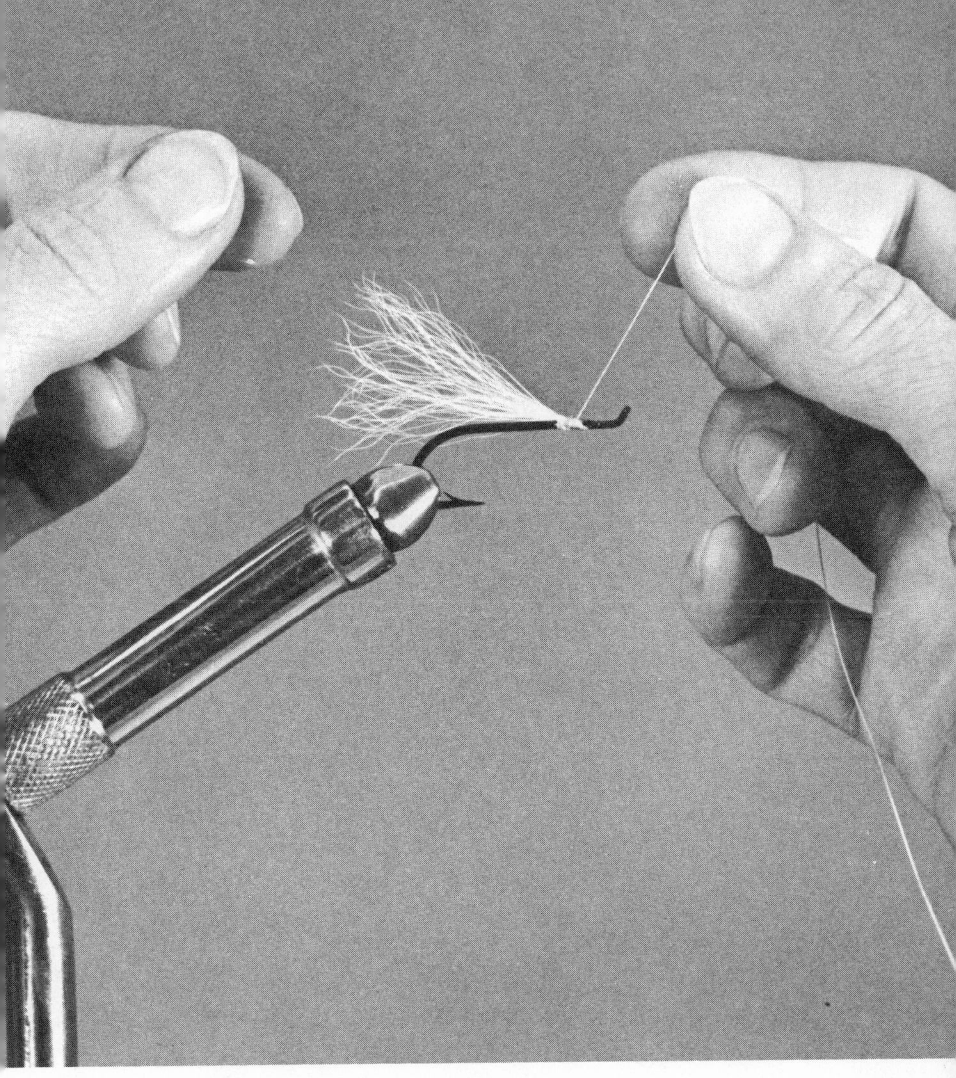

16f. Secure the thread to the button and cut off surplus hair at an angle to taper it. One more turn of thread over across the cut ends will be sufficient. The streamer-type hair wing is complete. Practice until you have mastered setting it at the proper angle. A streamer wing should lie back along the hook shank. (A wet-fly wing should not extend much beyond the bend of the hook.)

17a. By easing a small tuft of squirrel tail hair backward against the direction in which it grows, the ends of hair will become more even and the horizontal color bars more distinct. When the tips are as even as you can make them, cut the tuft free.

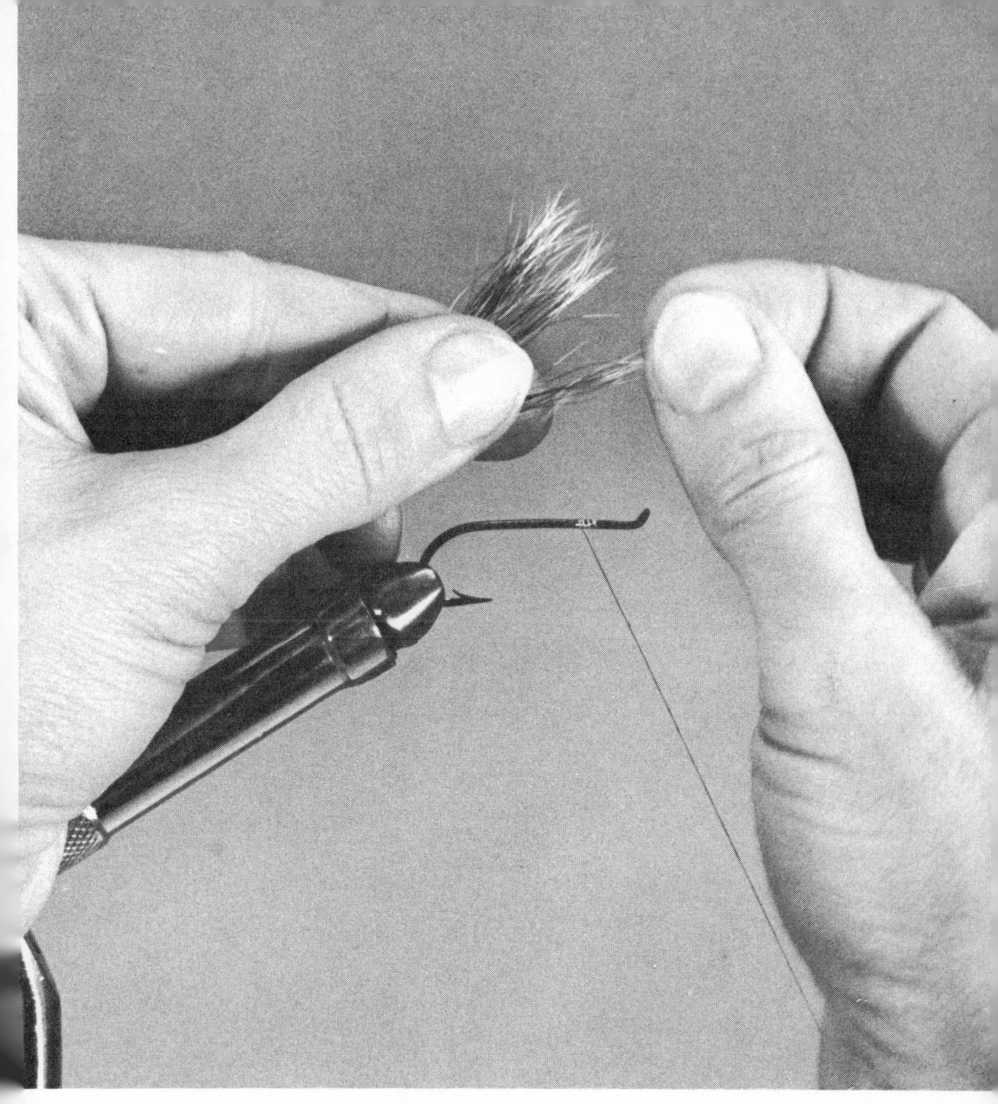

17b. Remove any hairs that may be exceptionally long. Remove any fuzz from cut ends. Measure the hair against the hook for length, approximately the length of the hook shank for this type of wing. Place a drop of lacquer or head-varnish on the hair where the thread will cross it and secure it to the hook as you did the streamer wing.

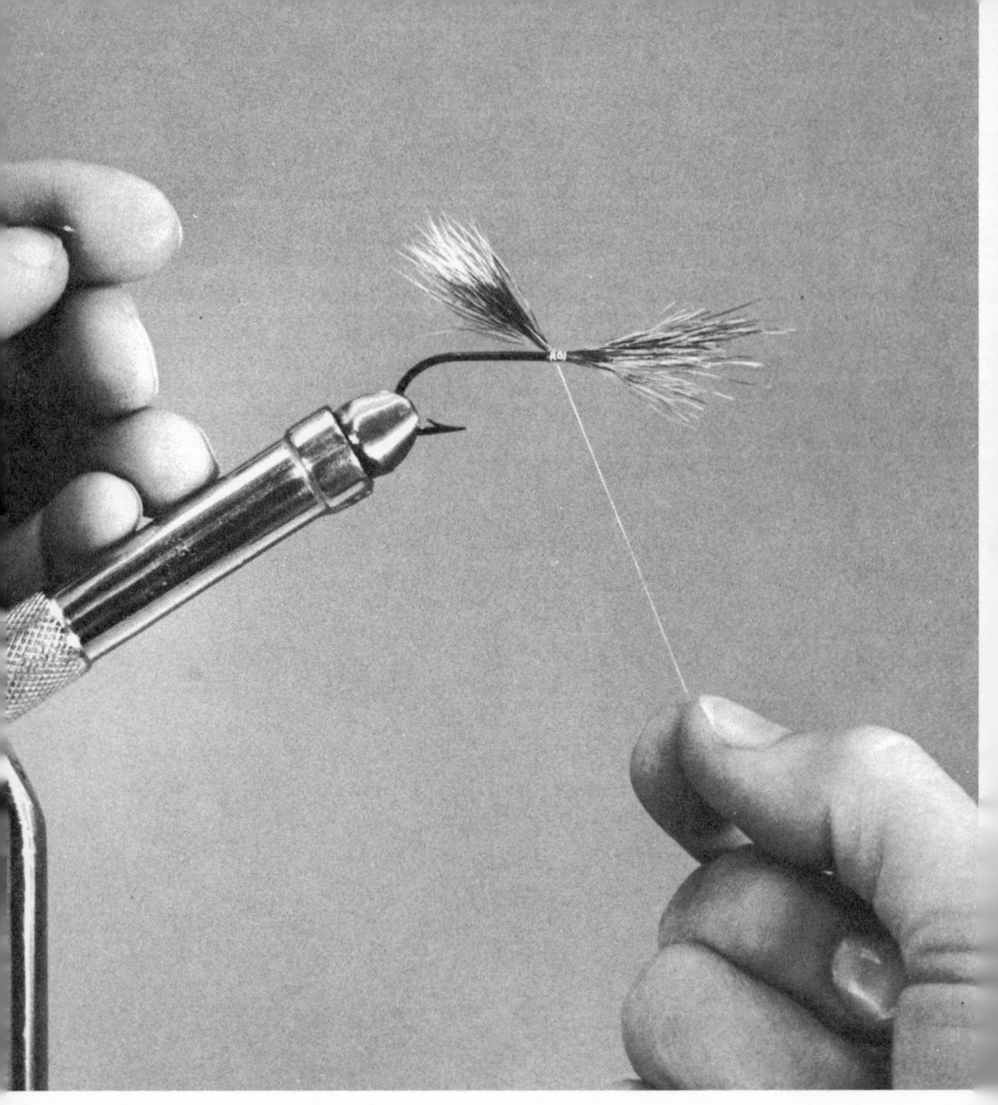

17c. After circling the tuft with tying thread, hold the wing at a higher angle from the hook than you held the streamer wing and put another turn of thread across the juncture of the circling thread and the hook.

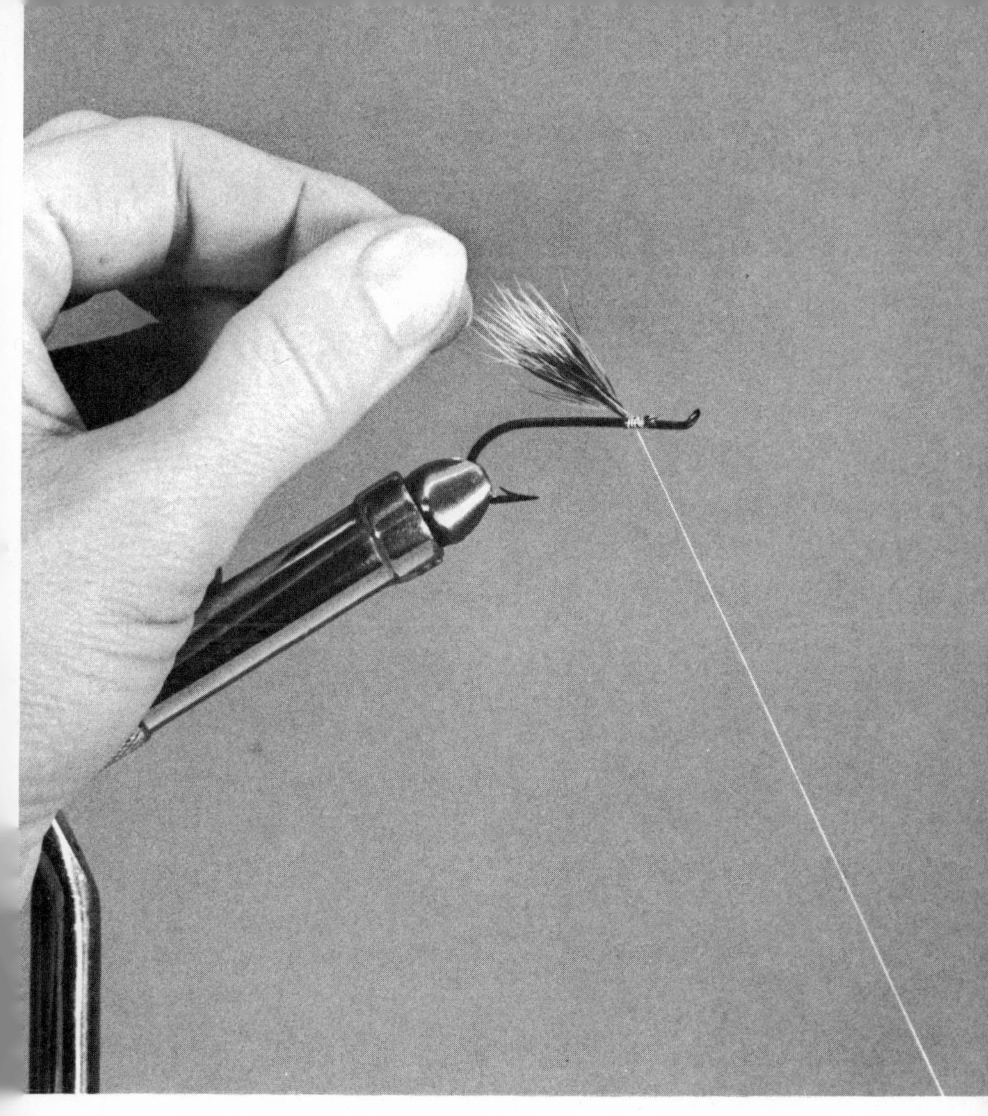

17d. Place another turn of thread forward of it, secure the thread to the button, and clip off excess hair at an angle to bevel it. Wind two more turns of thread over the clipped ends to bind them down and the single hair wing, of the type used for dry flies, is completed. Practice binding this hair wing securely to the top of the hook and setting it at the proper angle. For wet flies the wing angle is slightly lower.

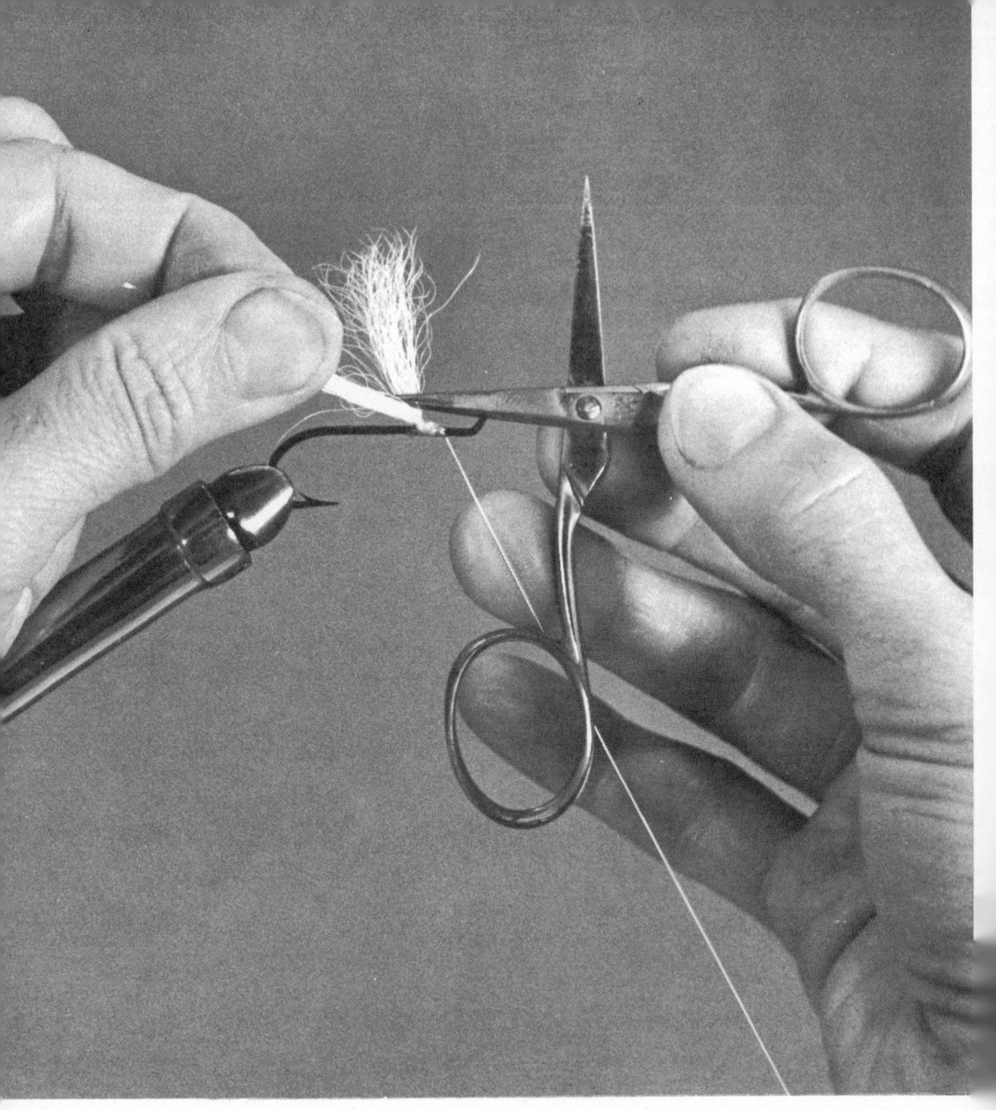

18a. Select a tuft of Asiatic goat for this wing, using a little more hair than was used for the preceding wing, since this one is to be divided. Remove all fuzz from the cut ends, make the natural tips even, and fasten it to the hook. Circle the hair tuft with thread and secure the thread to the button. Divide the wing by inserting the scissors, holding the blade parallel to the hook shank.

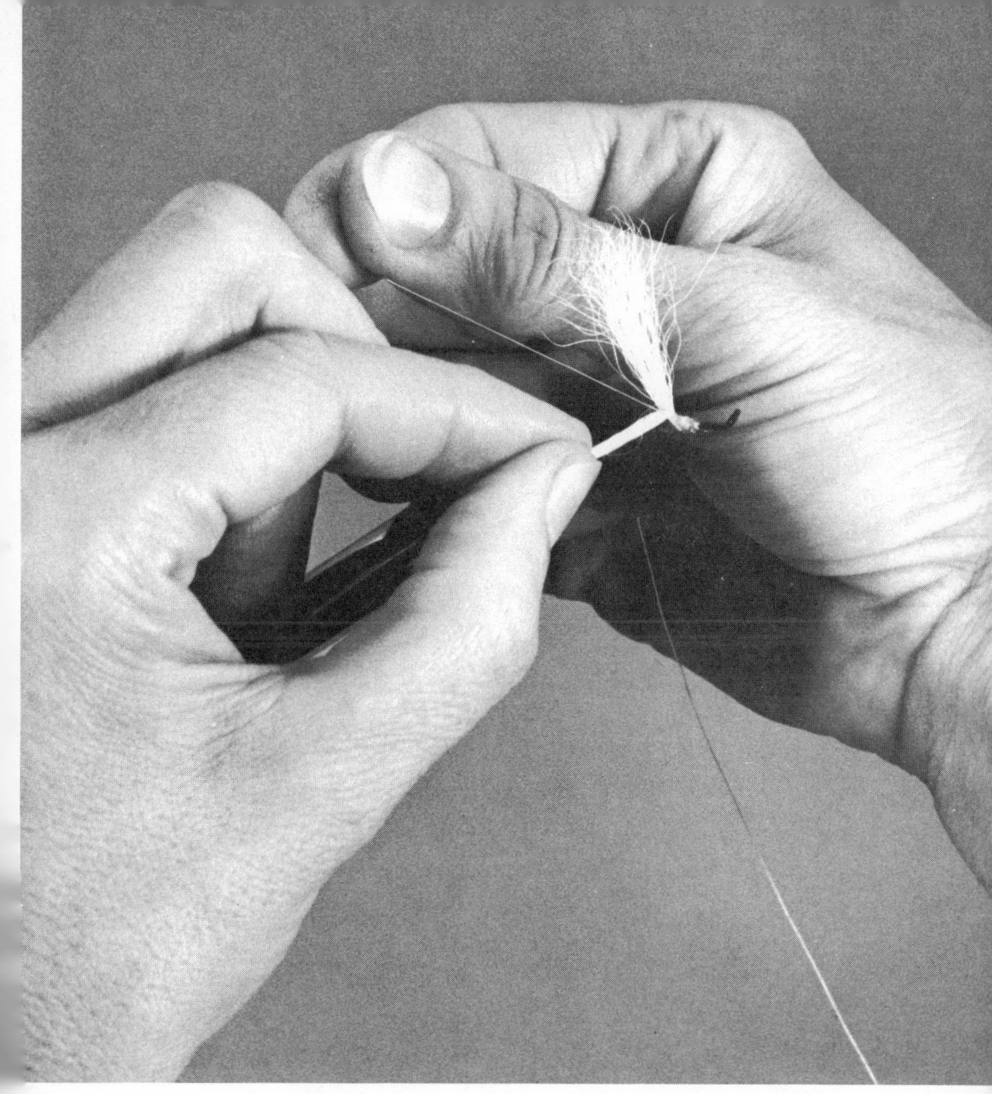

18b. Hold the near half of hair toward you and with the right hand release the thread and carry it back between the tufts of hair and down on the far side of the hook. Keep the thread taut.

18c. With the left hand release the hair and take the tying thread from the right hand. With the right hand hold the near tuft forward. With the left hand bring the thread toward you beneath the hook.

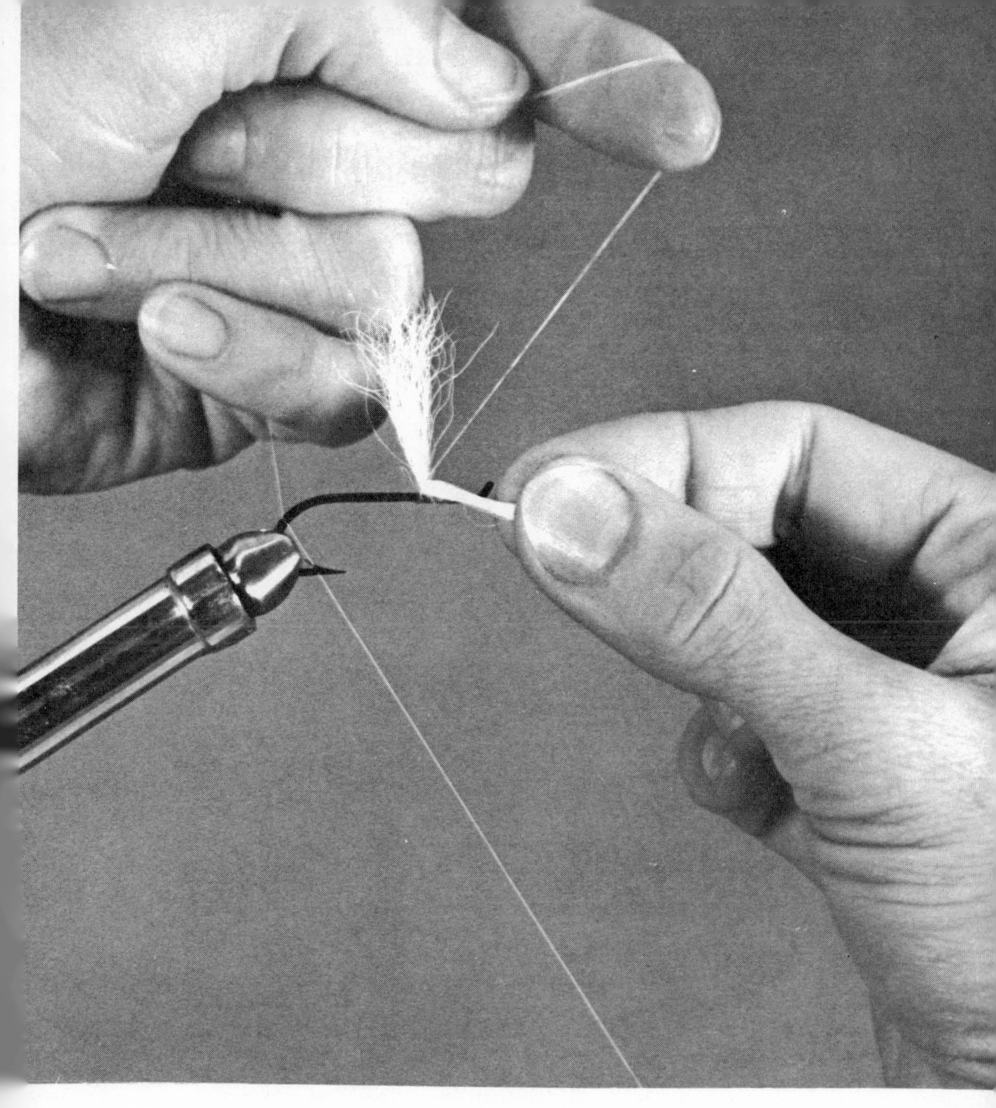

18d. Continue with the thread up and over between the tufts of hair. Keep the thread taut.

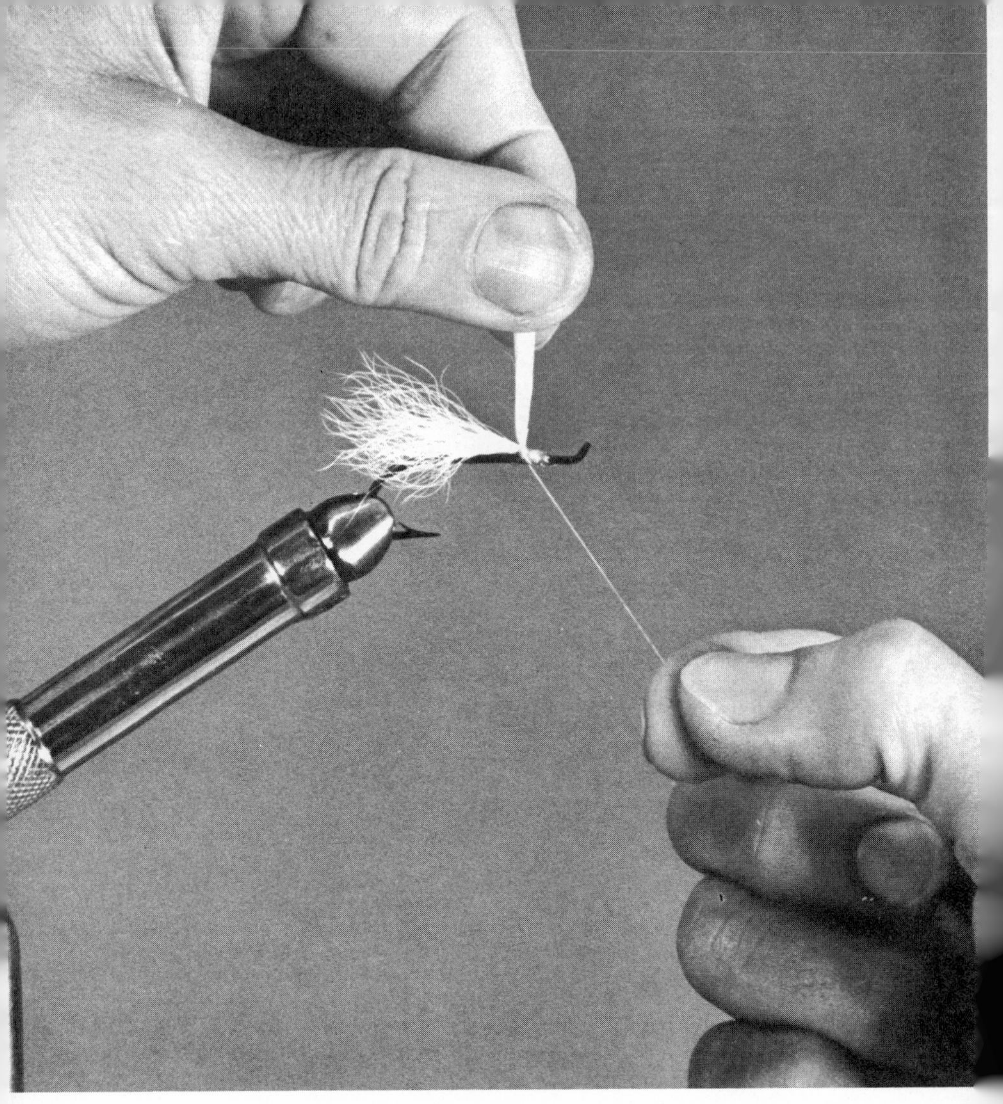

18e. Grip the thread now with the right hand, freeing the left. Bring it down on the far side of the hook and up in front in the usual way. The tufts of hair are now separated by the thread crossing between them.

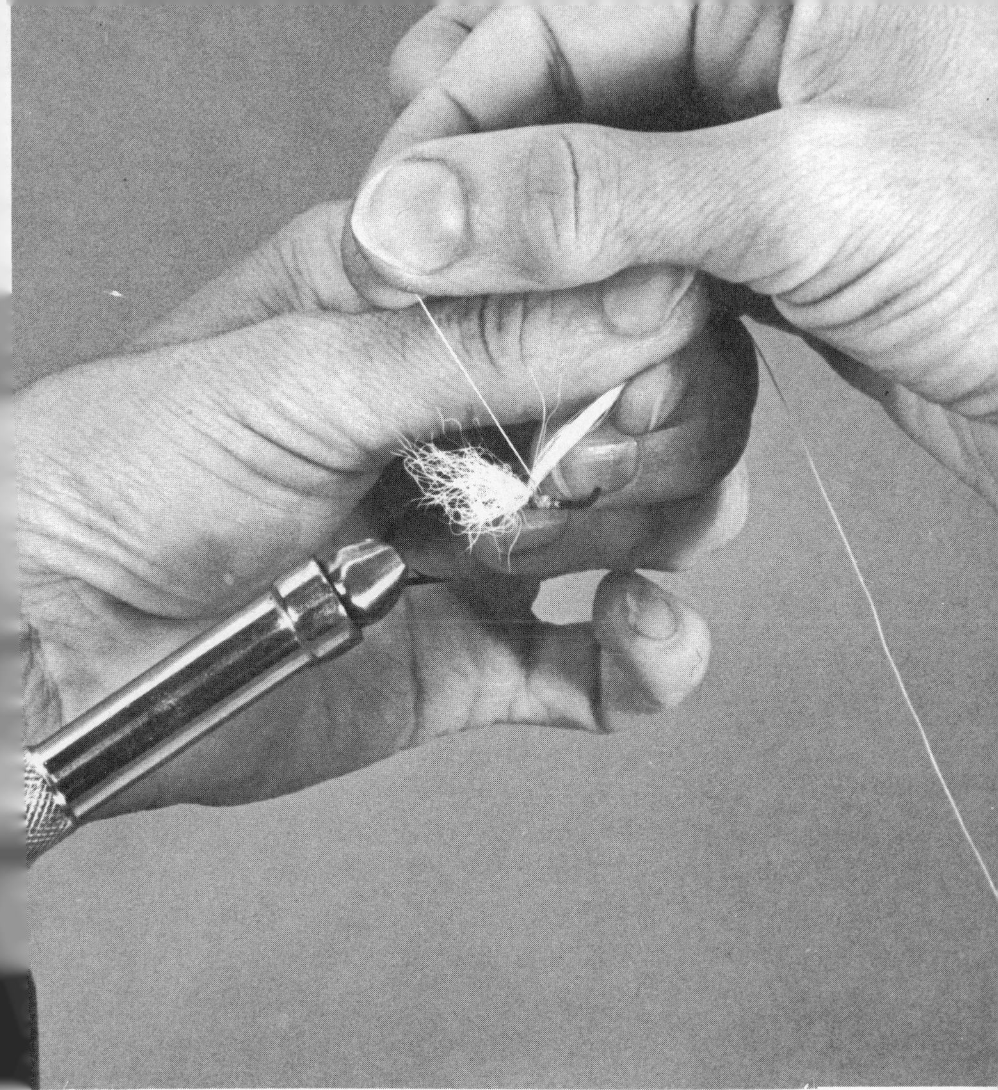

18f. With the left hand hold the far tuft. Carry the thread back between the tufts and circle the far tuft with thread, changing hands when necessary, bringing the thread toward you above the hook and through again between the wings from right to left, carrying it down this time on the far side of the hook and bringing it up in front, behind the near tuft of hair.

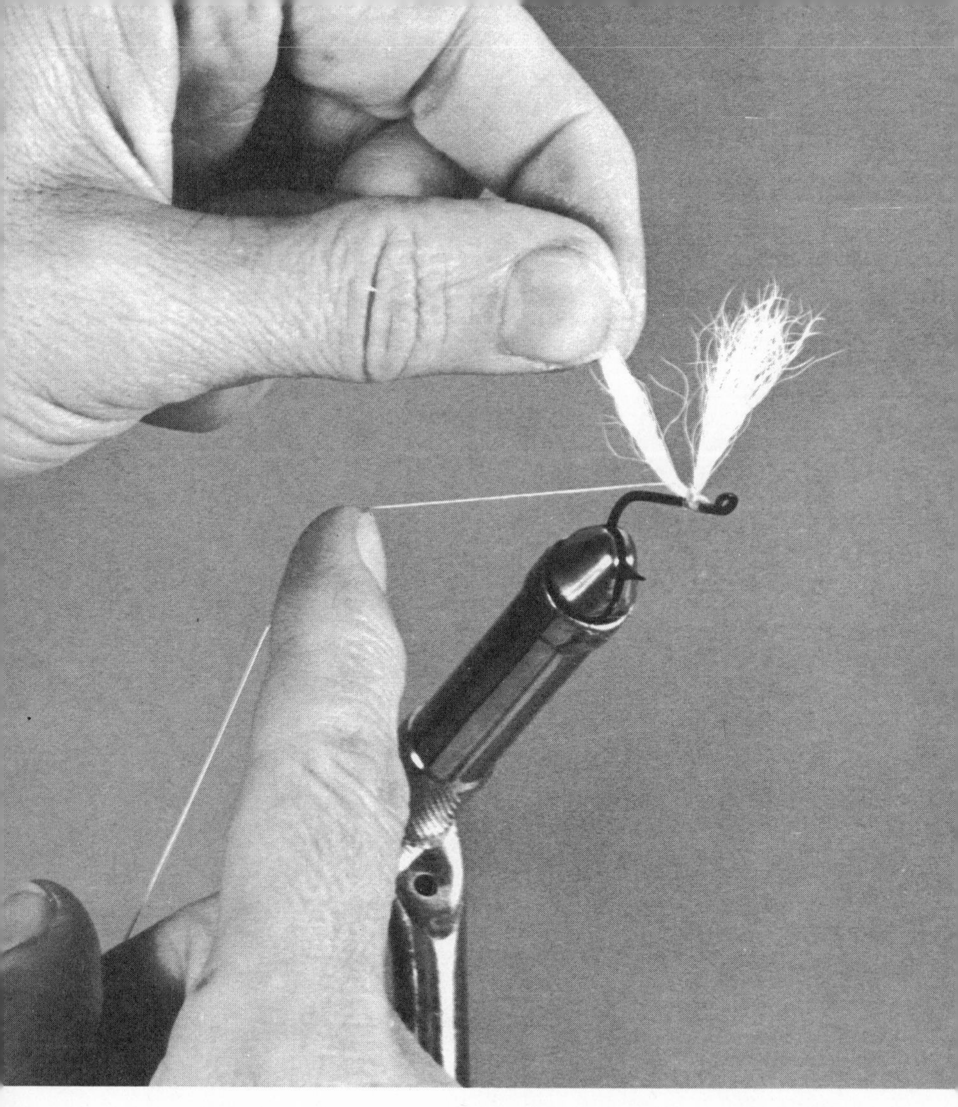

18g. Carry the thread up and forward between the tufts of hair and circle the near tuft completely by carrying the thread around it above the hook and forward between the tufts once more, this time taking the thread down on the far side of the hook, ahead of the wings, beneath the hook, and up in front in the usual way.

18h. Place one more turn of thread around the hair and hook mmediately in front of the divided tuft and the wing is complete. he angle of the **V** between the wings can be adjusted by the angle t which you hold them as you circle each one with the tying thread. ractice this wing until you can divide it evenly and are able to set he two halves at the same angle each time. Crossing the thread etween the tufts and circling each one with it will become a simple rocess once you have familiarized yourself with it through practice.

Quill

For slim, almost weightless bodies, quill is a favorite material. Two readily available sources are hackles and peacock herl, and for the herl there is an excellent substitute—moose mane. There are other sources but only the latter two, easiest to use and to obtain, will be considered here.

By gently scraping a single, long, bronze or greenish flue of a peacock plume between thumbnail and forefinger, the colored barbules are removed without much difficulty and the quill is freed.

To prepare several quills at a time, the whole tip end (or eye) of a peacock plume may be dipped into a liquid laundry bleach until the colored barbules have dissolved and the quills are bare. This must be done carefully, of course. Enough liquid bleach to cover the tip end clipped from the plume may be poured into a shallow glass or china bowl. The moment the colored barbules have disappeared, remove the quills from the bowl quickly and rinse immediately in a cup of water to which approximately ½ teaspoon of soda bicarbonate or ammonia has been added. Thoroughly rinse again in clear, warm water. After the quills have dried, they are ready to use or to be stored for future use.

The long hairs of moose mane require no preparation. The hairs, although similar to deer body hair, are longer and coarser. Grey (or greyish-brown) and white hairs are often found on the same piece of hide. By using one of each together, the resulting body will have a segmented appearance much like the herl-quill body, but with more contrast.

Both the peacock quill and moose-mane "quill" should be tied in the base, for the tips are the weakest area of both.

19a. Removal of the colored barbules from the whole tip end of an eyed peacock plume leaves the quills intact.

19b. A light and dark stripe on each quill is clearly defined. Each quill is a little wider at the base than at the tip.

19c. Remove quills by clipping them close to the main shaft.

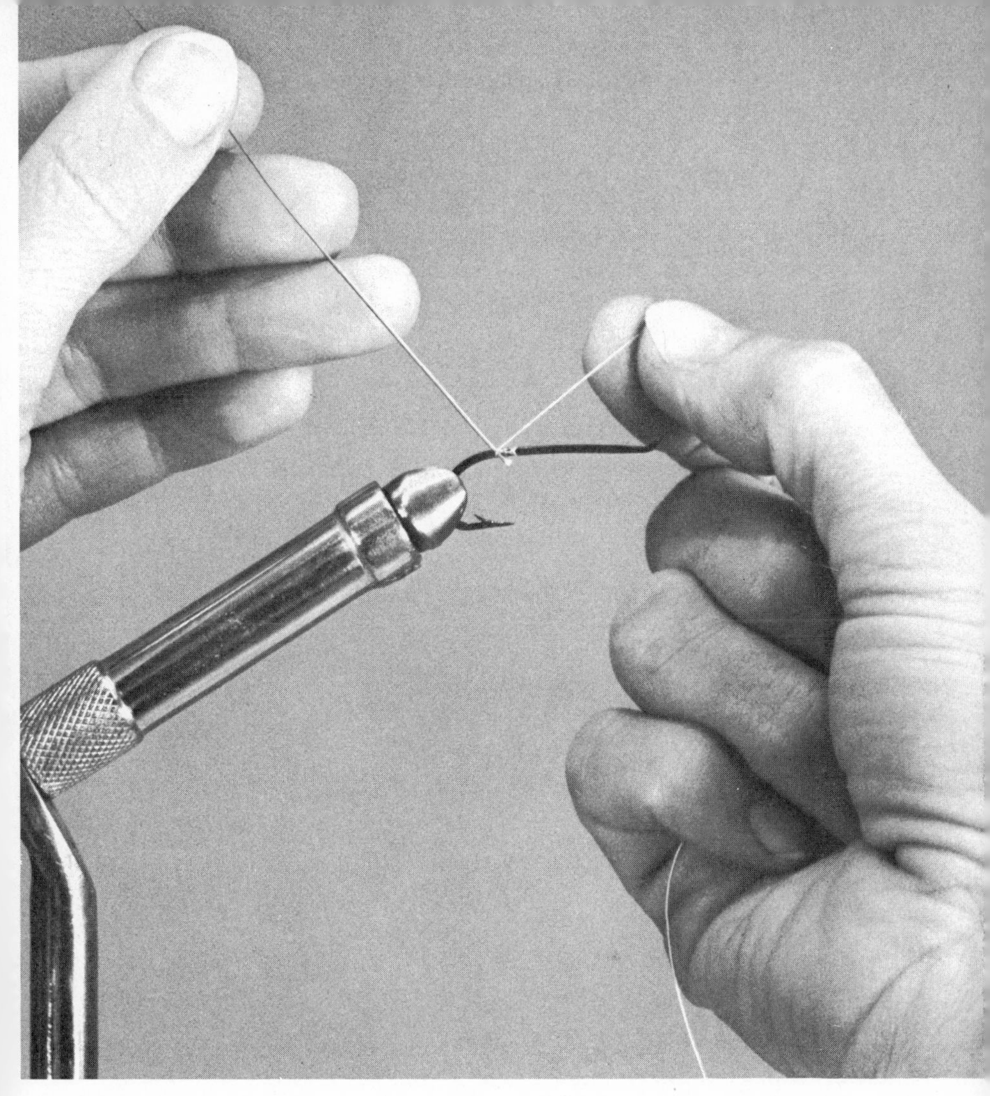

19d. With the thread attached at "tail position," bring it up and across the base of a single quill held flat against the hook, dark stripe to the left. Bring the tying thread up and across the quill once more.

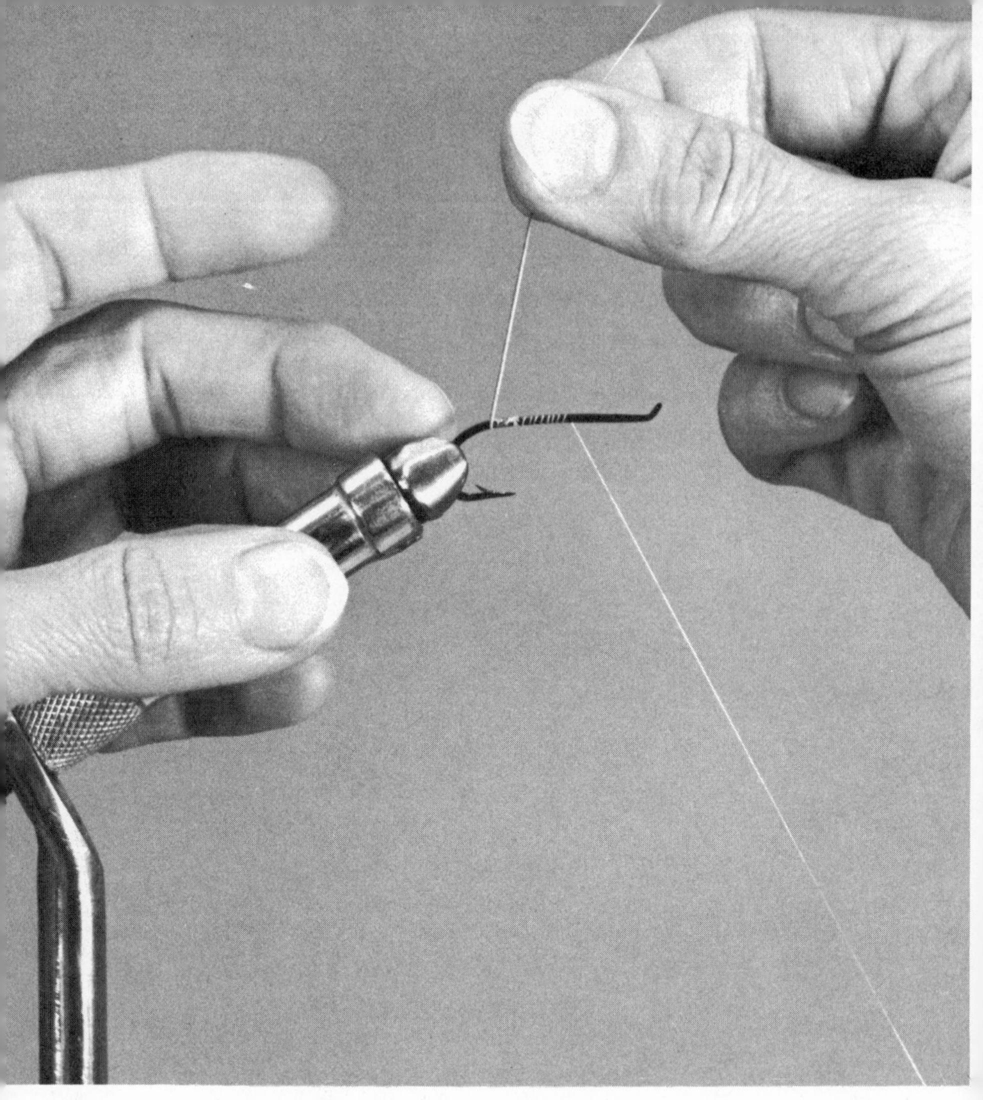

19e. Wind the thread in a close spiral toward the hook eye, far enough to be out of the way while you wrap the quill around the hook. Keep the quill flat, each turn edge to edge without overlapping.

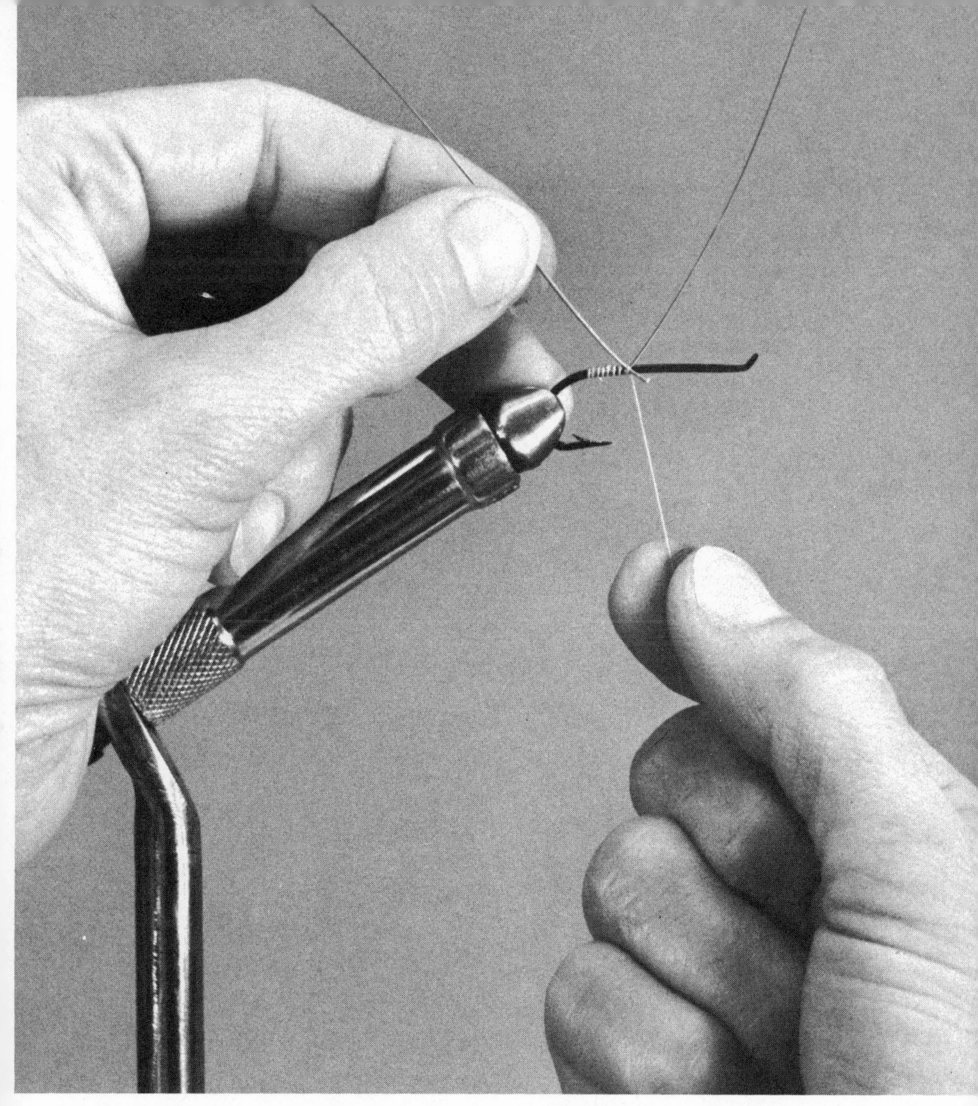

19f. As the quill narrows, the stripes become fainter and the quill becomes weaker; therefore, a second one will be tied in. Release the thread from the button and *unwind* it, back to where the first quill is becoming narrow. Cross the thread over the quill, to anchor it to the hook and tie in the second quill at that point, the turns of thread making a close spiral but not crossing each other. Again wind the thread forward in a spiral, to be out of the way.

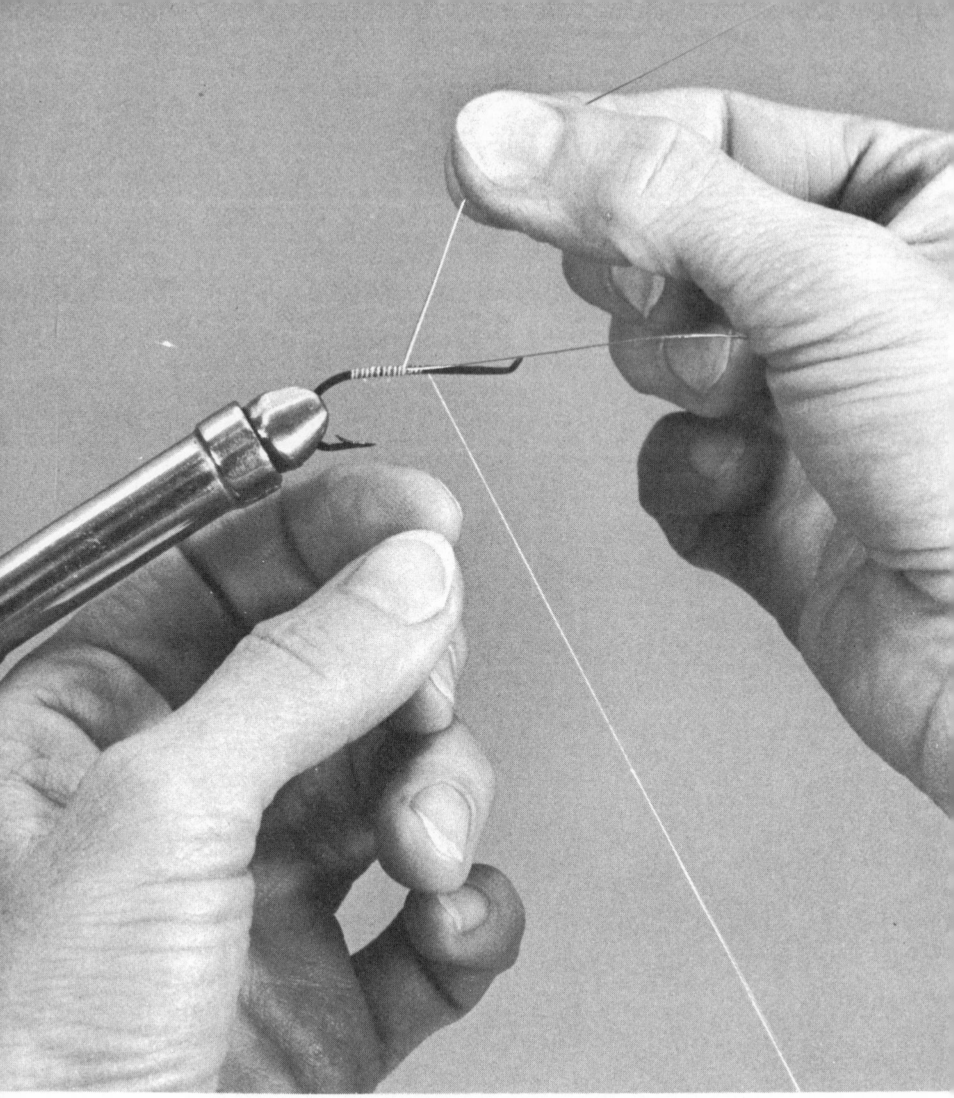

19g. Wind the second quill over the thread and the ends of quill lying along the top of the hook. These ends will serve as a base for the quill being wound on. By keeping the turns of quill edge to edge, the thread and quill ends will be smoothly covered.

19h. As the second quill narrows perceptibly, unwind the thread again to that place and cross the quill with the thread. Add another quill in the same way. These additions should be done so

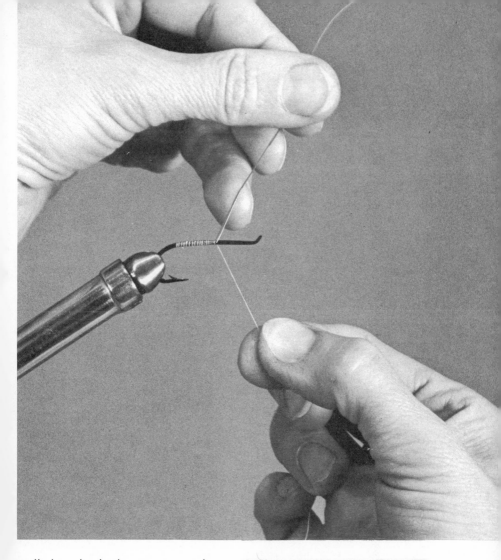

well that the body appears to be made from one continuous length of quill. When "wing position" is reached, clip off the remaining ends of the quill. Two more turns of tying thread close together over the quill is enough to hold it securely. This body is complete, but unwind these quills now and use them for practice. Steaming will straighten them again for you.

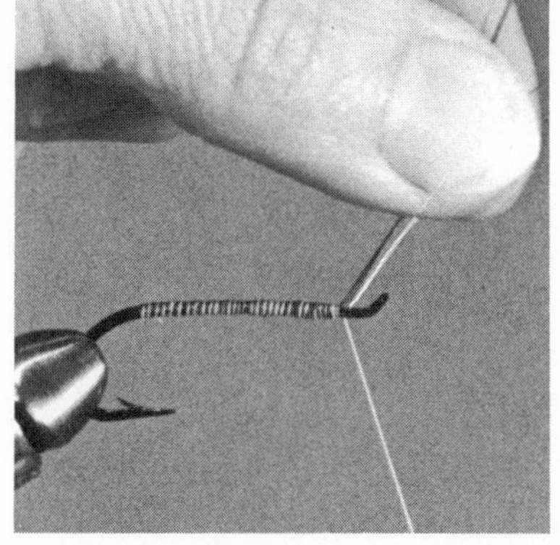

20a. The individual hairs of moose mane are usually longer than the quills of peacock feather.

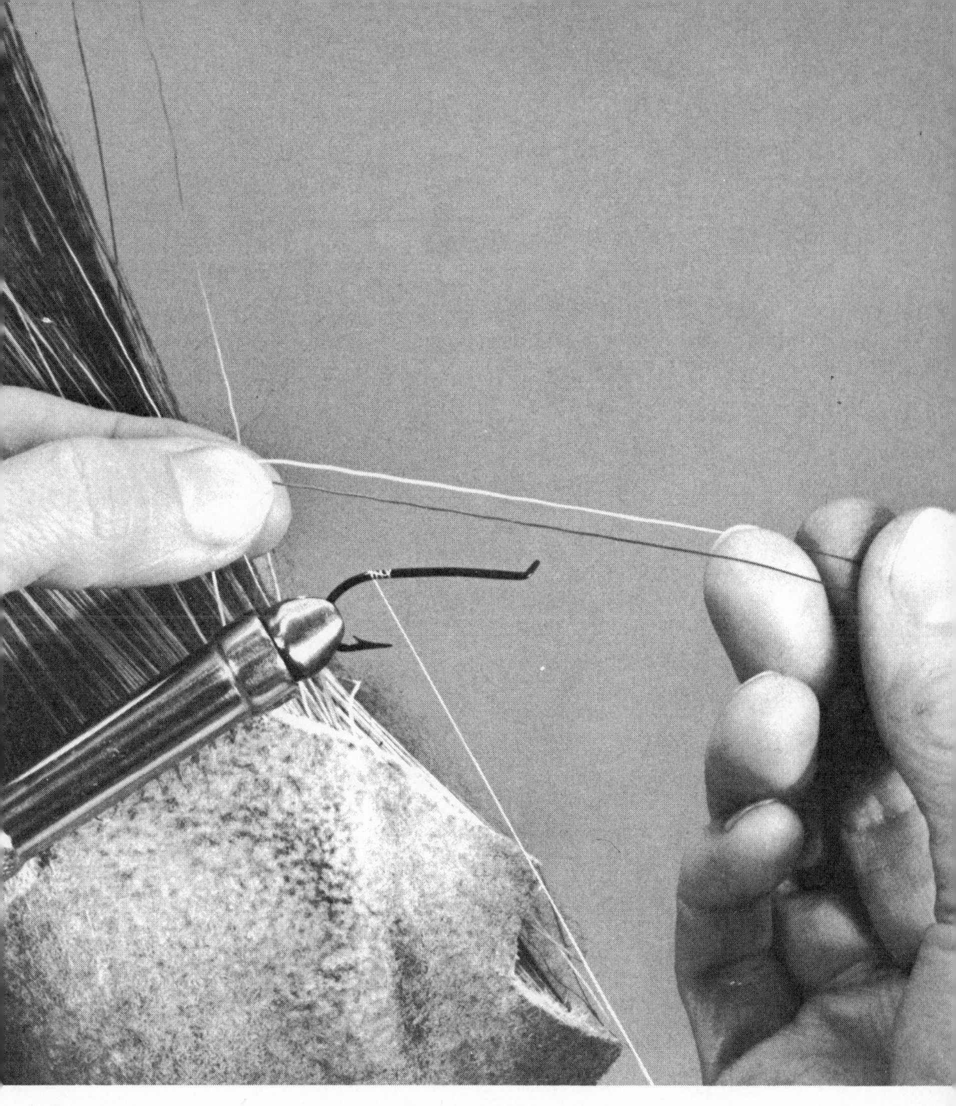

20b. Select a light hair and a dark one of nearly equal length.

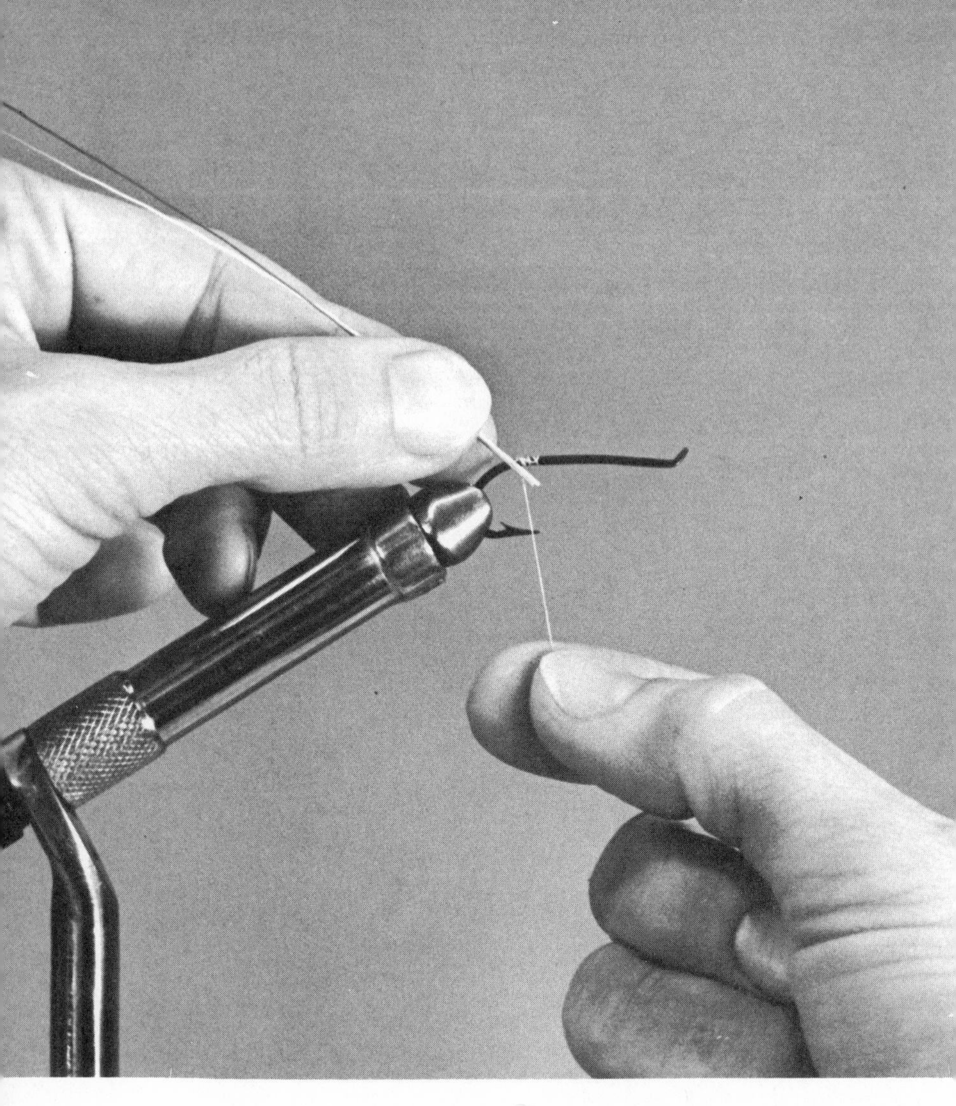

20c. Tie them in together at "tail position," the base of each held against the hook above the barb, the dark hair to the left of the light one.

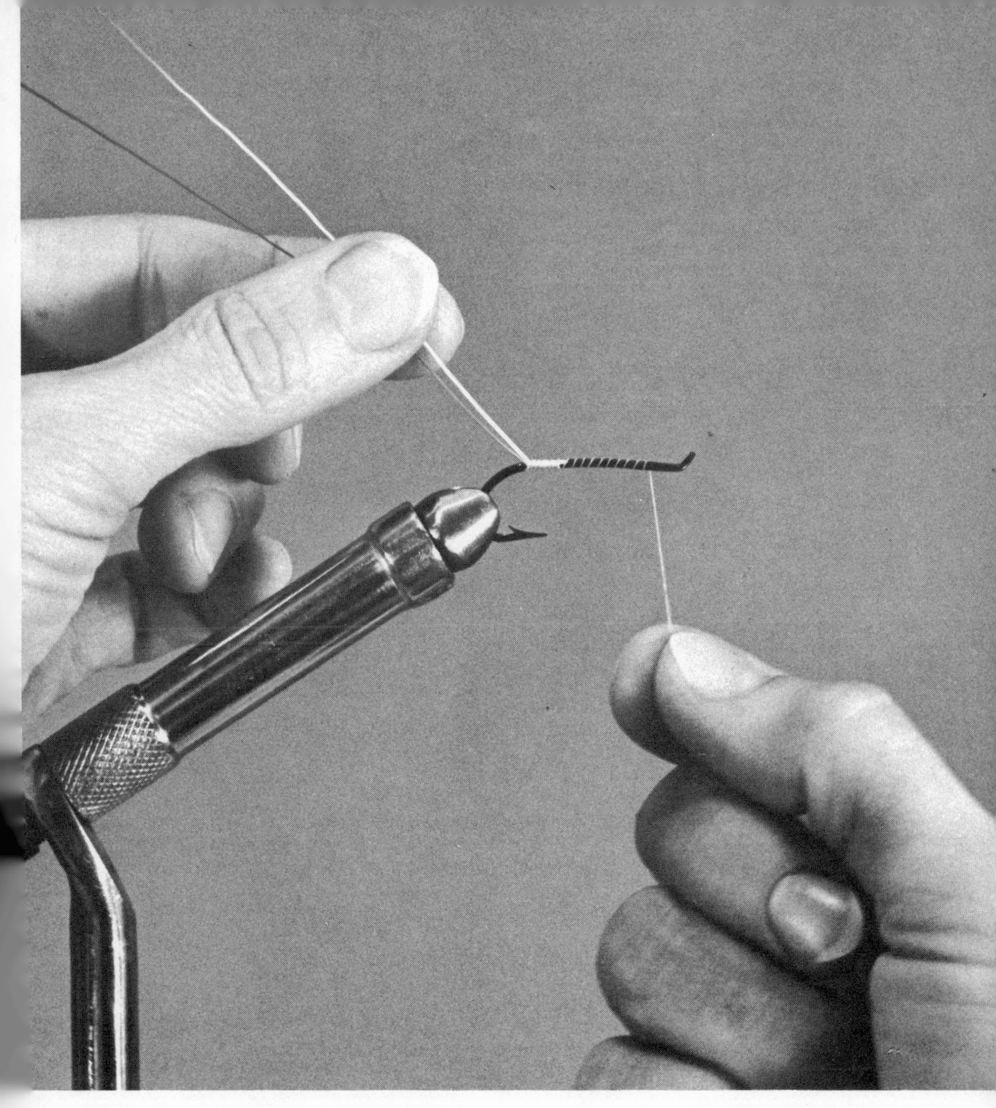

20d. Wind the tying thread forward in a close spiral to "wing position" and secure it at the bottom.

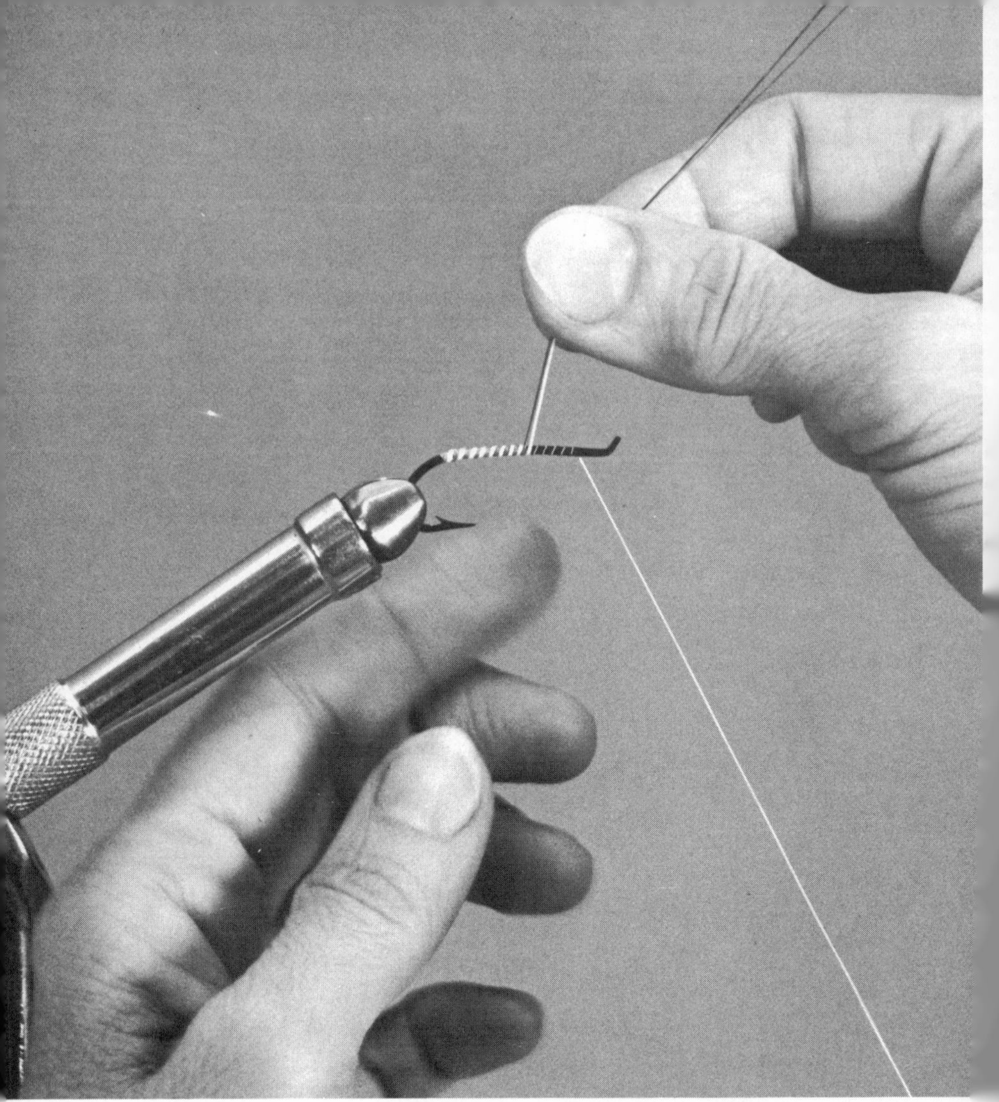

20e. Wind the two hairs together around the hook. Keep the dark hair to the left. The stripe simulates that of the peacock quill, although the barring has greater color contrast than the peacock quill. A monotone body can be made by using either the light or dark moose hair separately.

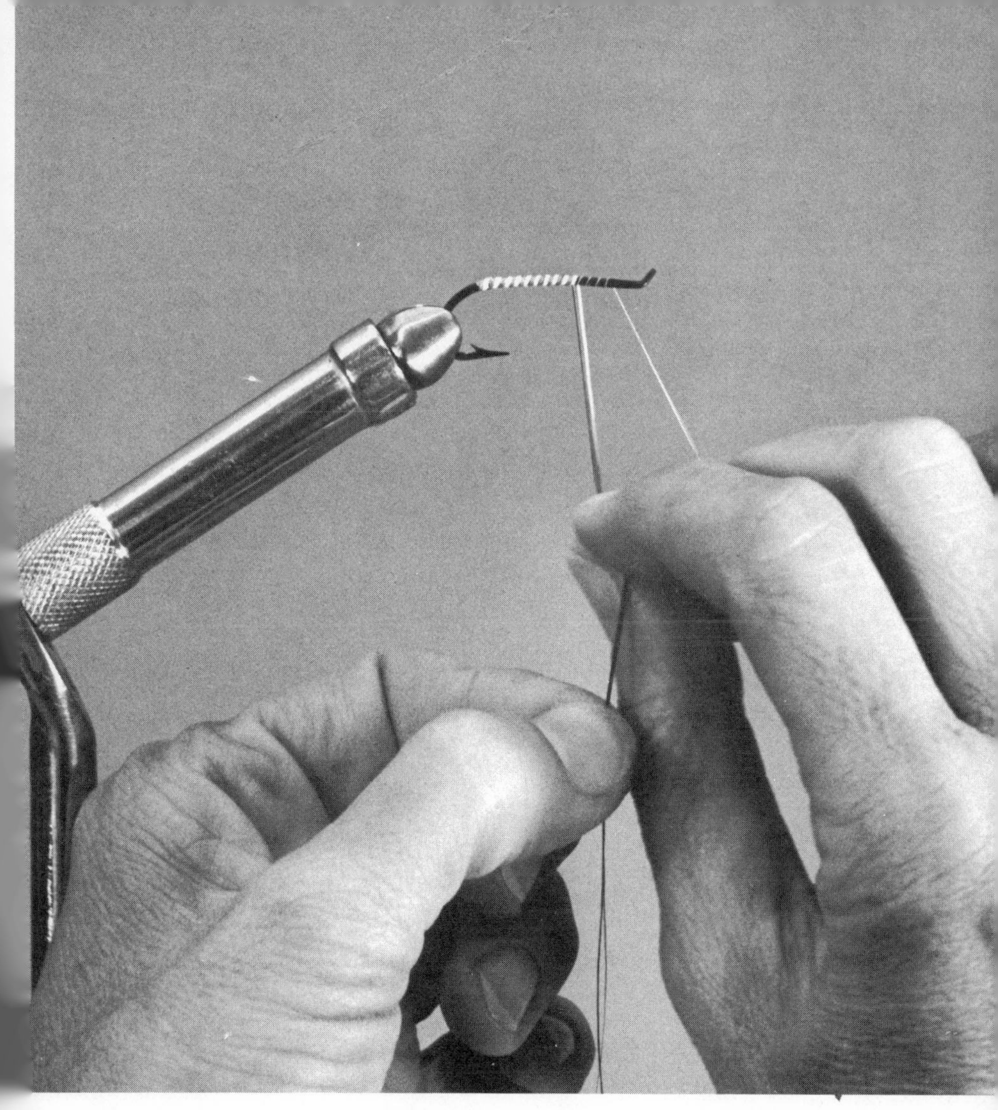

20f. Wind the quills side by side, edge to edge without overlapping. Cover the thread completely.

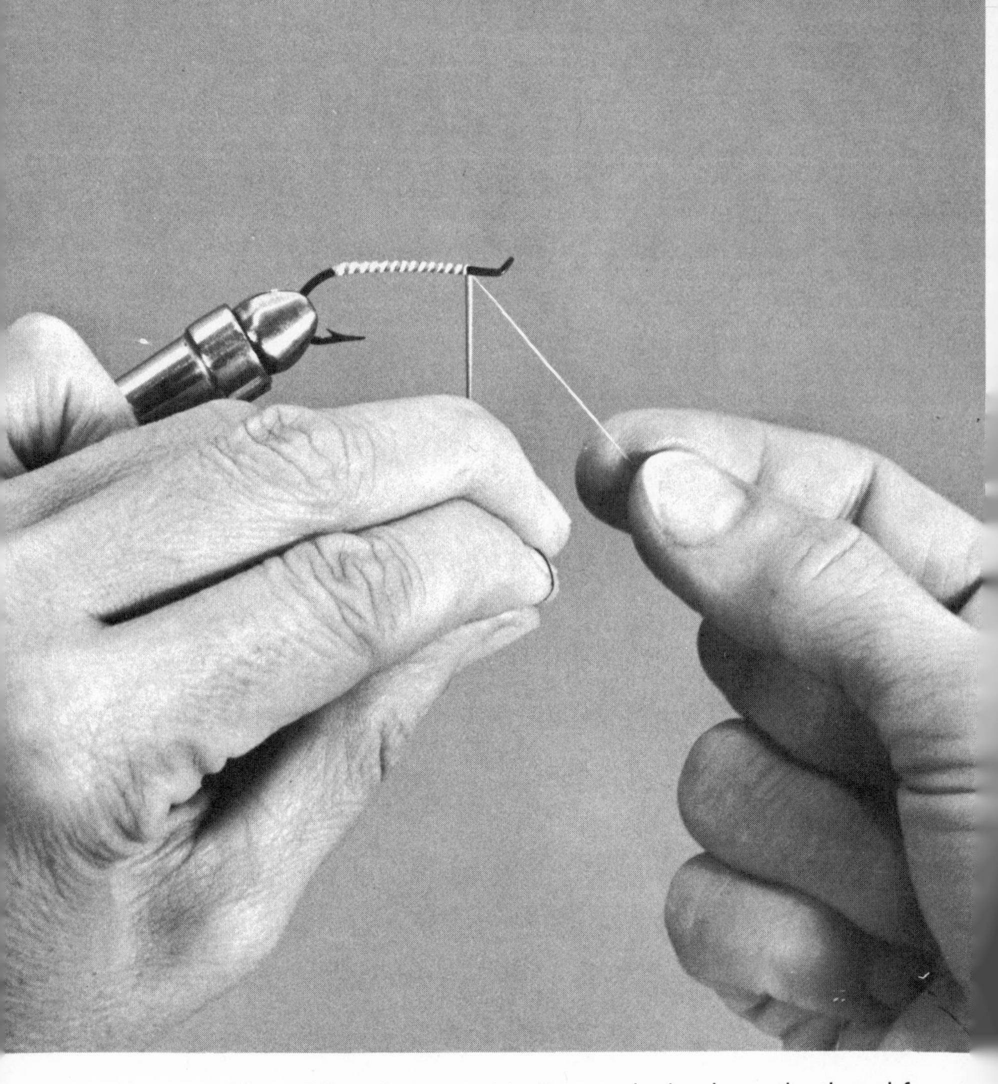

20g. When "wing position" is reached, release the thread from the button and bring it up and across the moose "quill," twice.

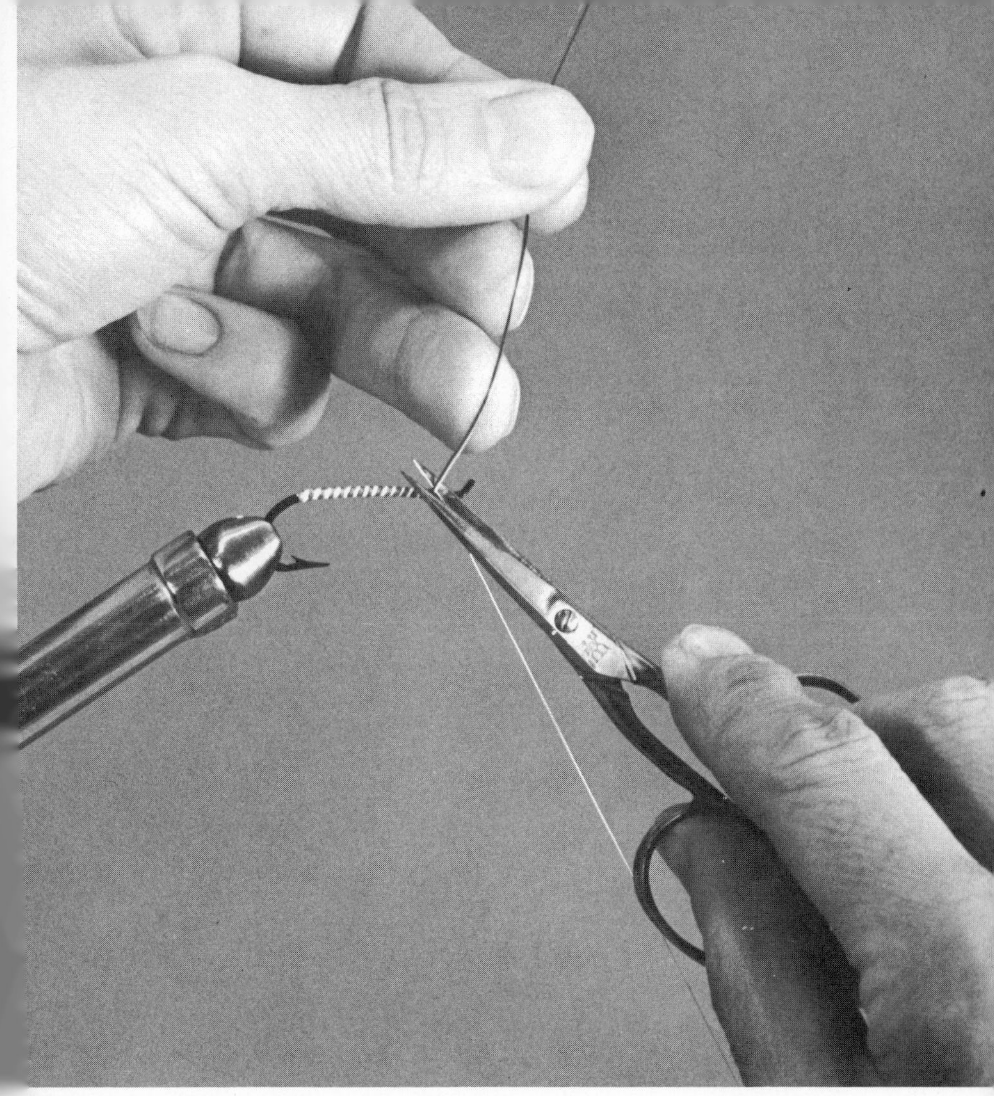

20h. Clip the hairs close to the tying thread and bind the cut ends to the hook with one more turn of thread. The "quill" body is complete; a little practice should master this body quickly.

Feathers

From an infinite variety of feathers, the fly-tyer may choose those that meet his specific requirements. Carefully selected for form, quality, texture, and color, they also must be sorted for size to correspond with the size of hook on which they will be used.

Plumage suitable for the fly-tyer's purpose is obtained almost entirely from male birds, the females having soft, usually drab feathers and, by comparison with the male, of poor quality.

Feathers found on the neck and back (saddle) of a prime cock are called hackles. It was once believed that only birds bred for fighting could produce hackles of a quality worthy for fly-tying, yet cockfighting has been abolished in many countries and domestic breeds continue to furnish many excellent hackles.

Neck hackles, available on the skin, are shorter than saddle hackles but have the advantage of being pre-sorted for size. Tiny in length and width at the top of the neck, they gradually increase in size, becoming bass-size hackles at the lowest edge of the cape.

Saddle hackles, available strung, must be sorted; but the advantage here is that the hackles are of greater length, with a thinner, more limber stem (or quill) than those found on the neck.

Hackles are also available loose (in bulk) but usually contain a large proportion of waste feathers and are tedious to sort.

Hackles for the dry fly should have glossy, fairly stiff flues (barbs) of even length and with very little web along a limber or flexible stem. The purpose of the hackle on a dry fly is threefold: to represent either the legs of a natural insect or the motion of its wings in flight, to add wind resistance, which will help the fly drop lightly onto the surface of lake or stream, and to aid in keeping the fly afloat.

While the wet-fly hackle should also have a fairly thin and limber stem, a generous amount of web is desirable along it at the base of the flues. The barb itself may be softer than those of a dry-fly hackle. The soft and webby fibers absorb water quickly, helping the fly to sink and then move limply with the water currents, imparting a lifelike quality to the fly.

Wing feathers of birds such as the various ducks, the goose, and turkey are used for winging both wet and dry flies. The feathers should be obtained in pairs well matched for size, color, and marking, and the barbs should cling strongly together out to the very edge. For practice-tying, "slate" goose or white goose wing feathers (called broad quills) are comparatively inexpensive and probably the easiest ones to handle well within a short time.

Tail feathers of several pheasants are used in strips for both wings and tails on flies. Only the center feather is equally balanced in length of flue and marking; the others should be obtained in pairs.

Feathers such as guinea, grouse, or partridge, which are used for wet-fly hackles, or teal, mallard, wood, or summer duck flank and breast feathers which are used for winging dry flies, may be obtained by the dozen or in quantities of an ounce or more at a time. Although these are in bulk, they are not difficult to sort for size and quality. Any feathers that might have extraneous material adhering to them should be discarded. Close packing may crush the feathers out of their natural shape and curve, but steaming will restore them quickly.

A word here about steaming. A teakettle spout will direct th steam into a stream which is ideal for steaming feathers of all kind If a gas flame is used for boiling the water, care must be taken t keep the feathers from its direct and scorching heat, which will de stroy delicate feather tips in an instant. Live steam will not injur the feather at all. Hold the feathers to be steamed with a pair o fly-tying pliers for safety and keep your fingers out of the steam.

Many other beautiful feathers are available to the fly-tyer. Th airy maribou feathers, a stork contribution to fly-tying, are used a whole tips or in strands combined with a hair like bucktail. Strand of ostrich plumes and peacock tail feathers are beautiful body ma terials for flies. The peacock sword feather is used in strands fo wings and tails or combined decoratively with wings of differen texture. Other decorative feathers are also available but will not b considered here, since practice with them would be an unnecessa waste of money and material. Once the more common feathers can be handled well, there will be no need to practice with the expensive ones, for you will be able to handle them well also.

To judge for good quality in feathers of any kind, look for a glossy appearance of the "right" surface, definite color, and a pliant response between the fingers. Feathers having a faded look; that are harshly dry to the touch, possibly leaving a powdery coating on the fingers; or whose barbs seem brittle and are easily dislodged from the stem or quill—these feathers, which may have been removed from a sick or diseased fowl, are unsatisfactory even for practice-tying. Feathers found to be still partially encased in a transparent sheath are not fully developed and usually cannot be used to good advantage. Try always to obtain the finest feathers available; never be satisfied with less than the best.

21a. Herl for fly bodies should be taken from the largest, glossiest-eyed peacock plumes available. Steam them and the colored barbules will stand out from the quill strands. Hold the highly colored side of the plume toward you. The strands immediately below the eye have the longest and thickest barbules and those on the left of the center shaft make the finest herl bodies. Compare them with the lowest strands where only the barbules above the quill show at all, diminishing in size the farther down they are on the plume. The quill of the strands is flat. The colored barbules are found only along the front edge of each quill, the other edge being bare. The barbules that rise upward from the quill are longest; those below tend to lie flat along the quill.

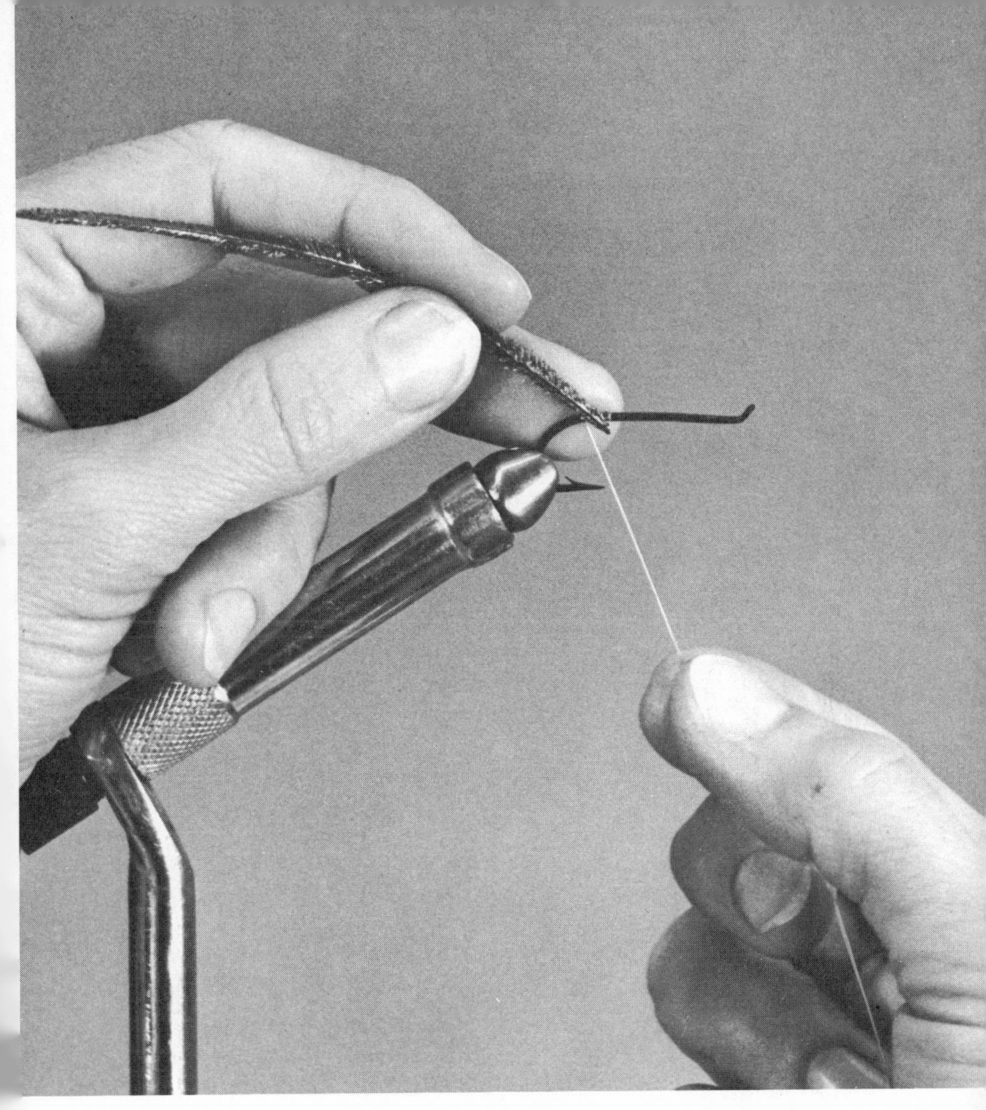

21b. Select a strand of herl near the eye on the left side of the peacock plume. Keeping it in the same relative position, with the glossy side toward you and the longest barbules up, hold the quill base flat against the hook at "tail position" and bring the tying thread up and across it.

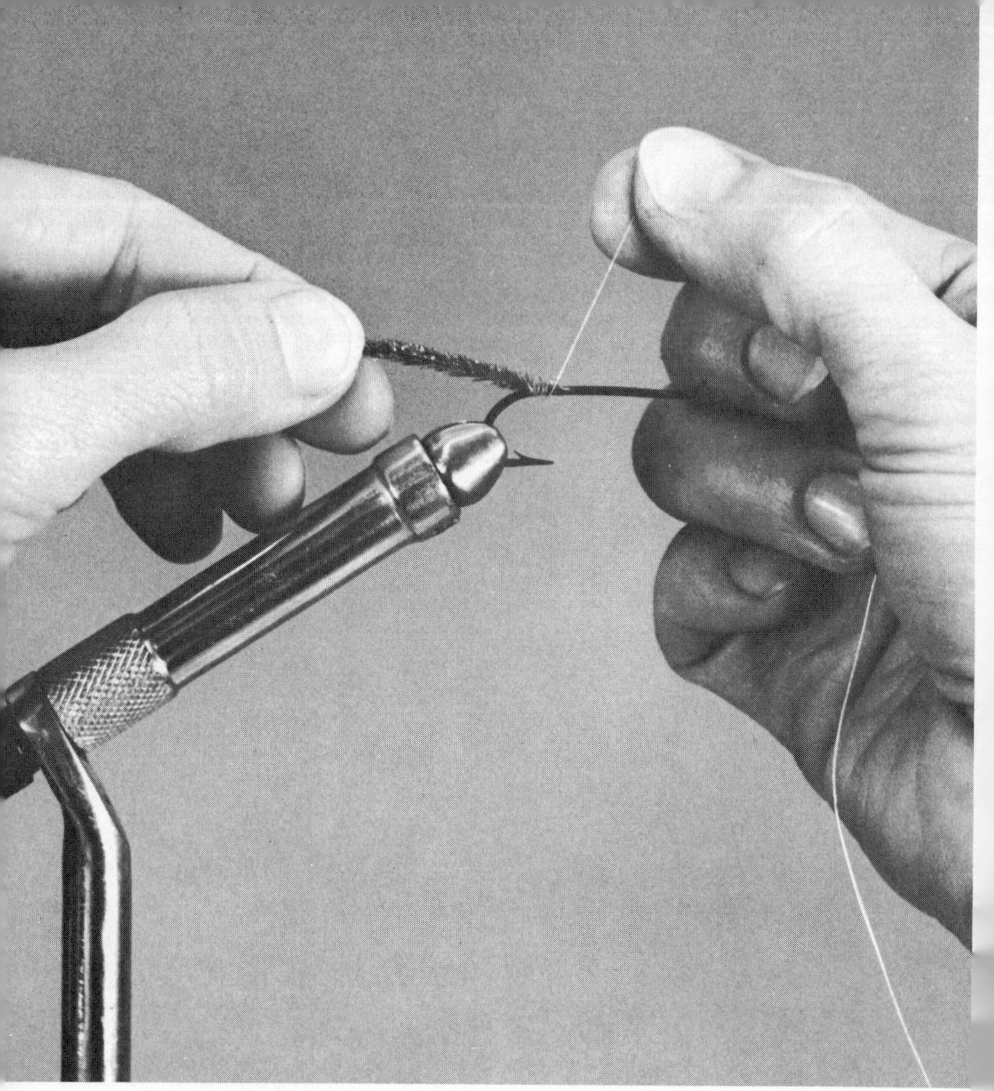

21c. Make sure the bare edge of the quill strand is toward the eye of the hook. Bind the quill end against the hook with a close spiral of tying thread and secure the thread to the button.

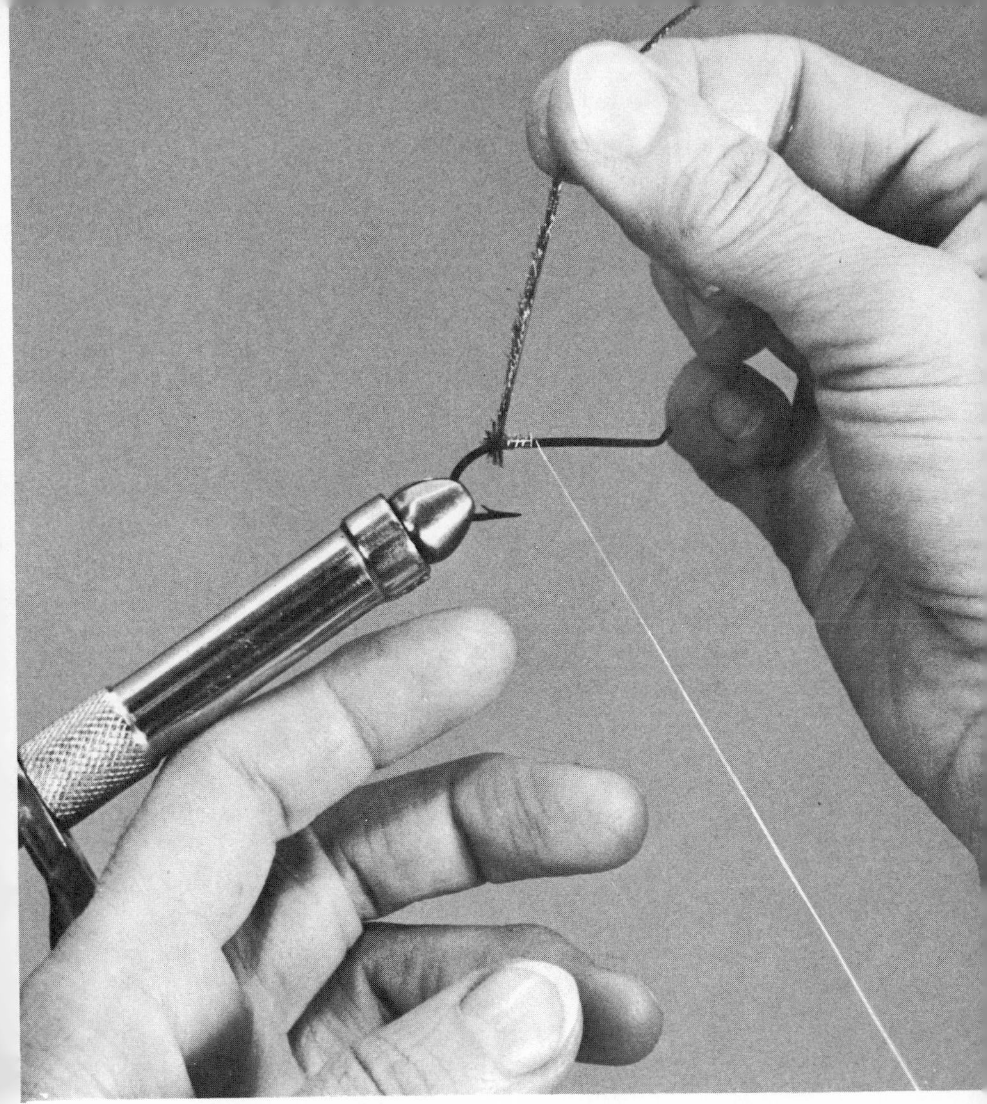

21d. As you begin to wind the herl around the hook, the bare edge of quill will be noticeable along the hook ahead of the barbules, which will radiate around the hook. As the turns of quill overlap, keep the colored barbules as close as possible to those of the preceding turn, hiding the quill entirely.

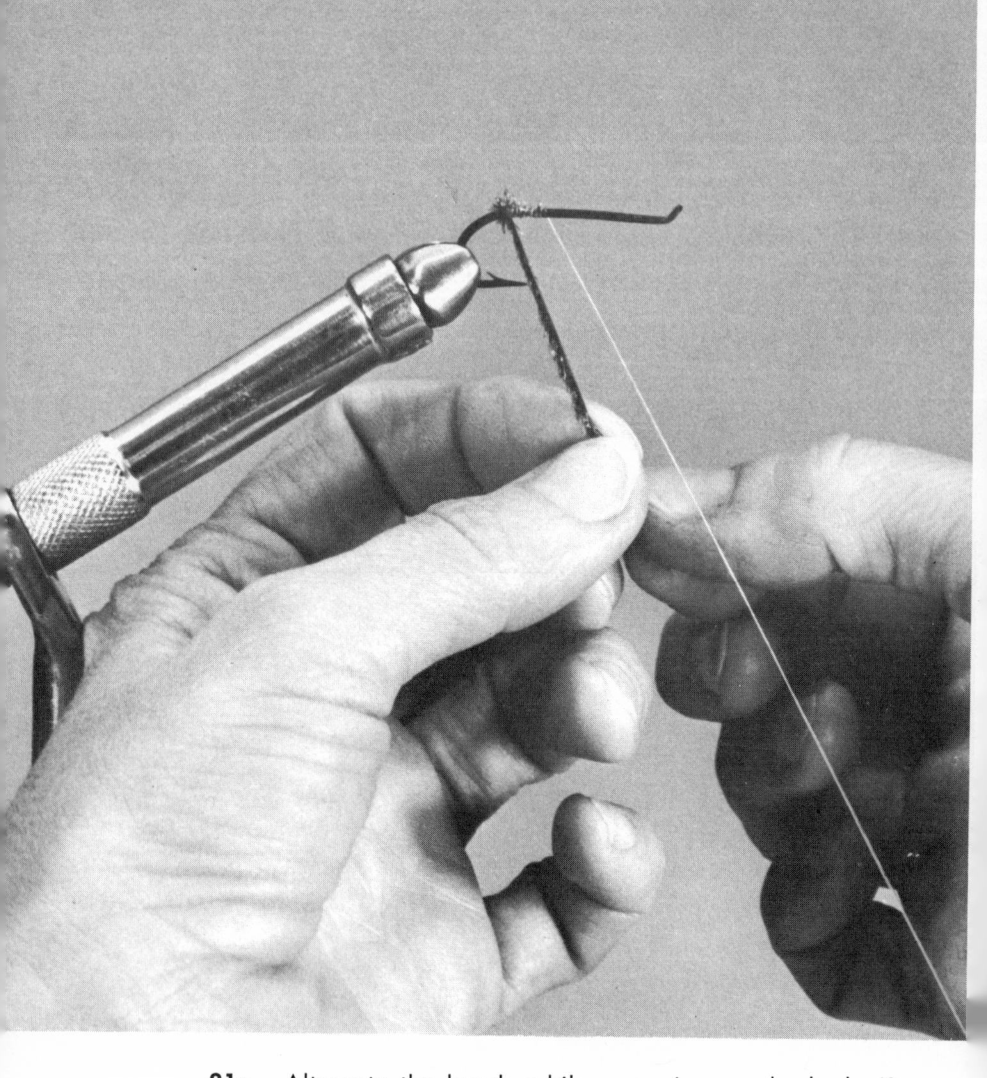

21e. Alternate the hands while wrapping on the herl. Keep the quill flat, with the bare edge forward.

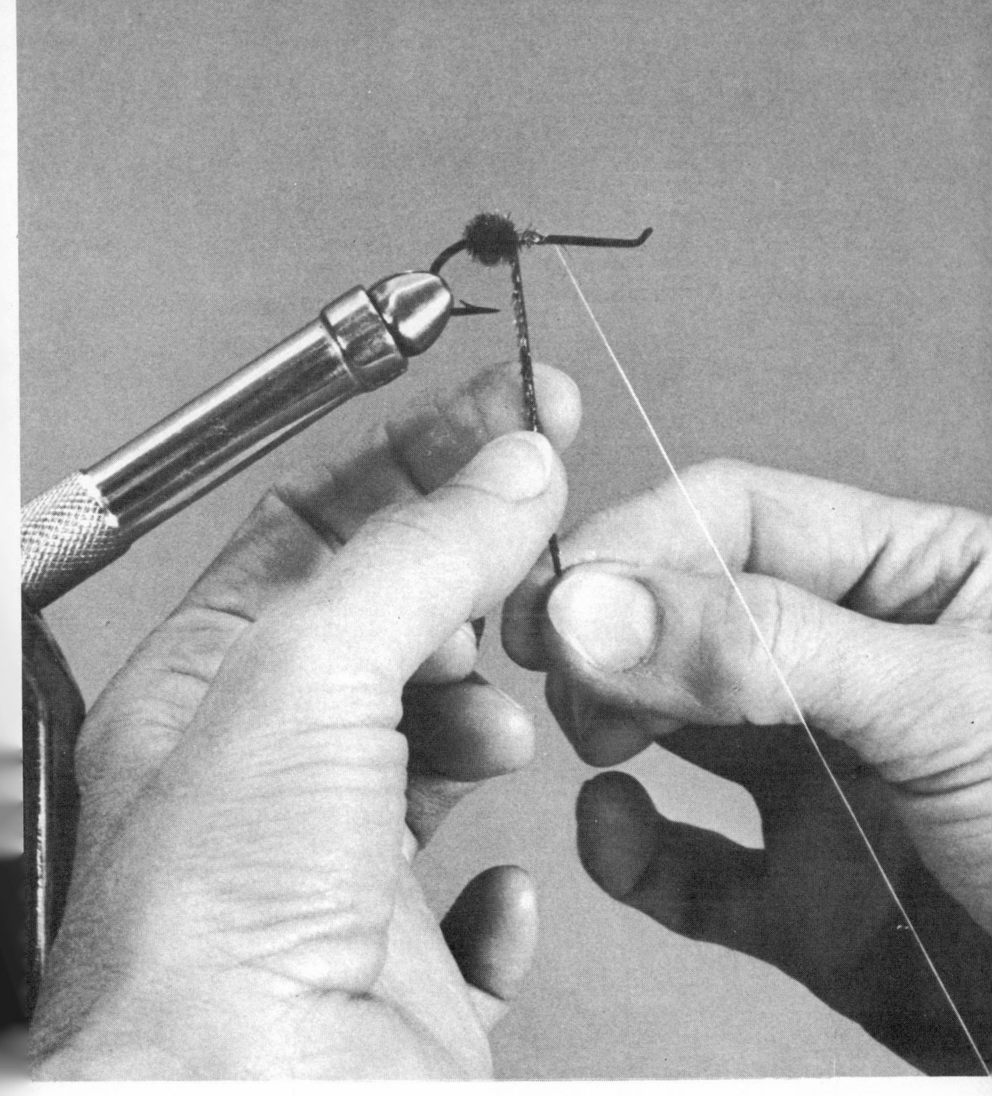

21f. The longest barbules are in the center of the strand. As you continue to wind the herl, the length of the barbules will begin to grow smaller as you near the tip of the strand. At this point, unwind a turn or two of tying thread if it extends beyond.

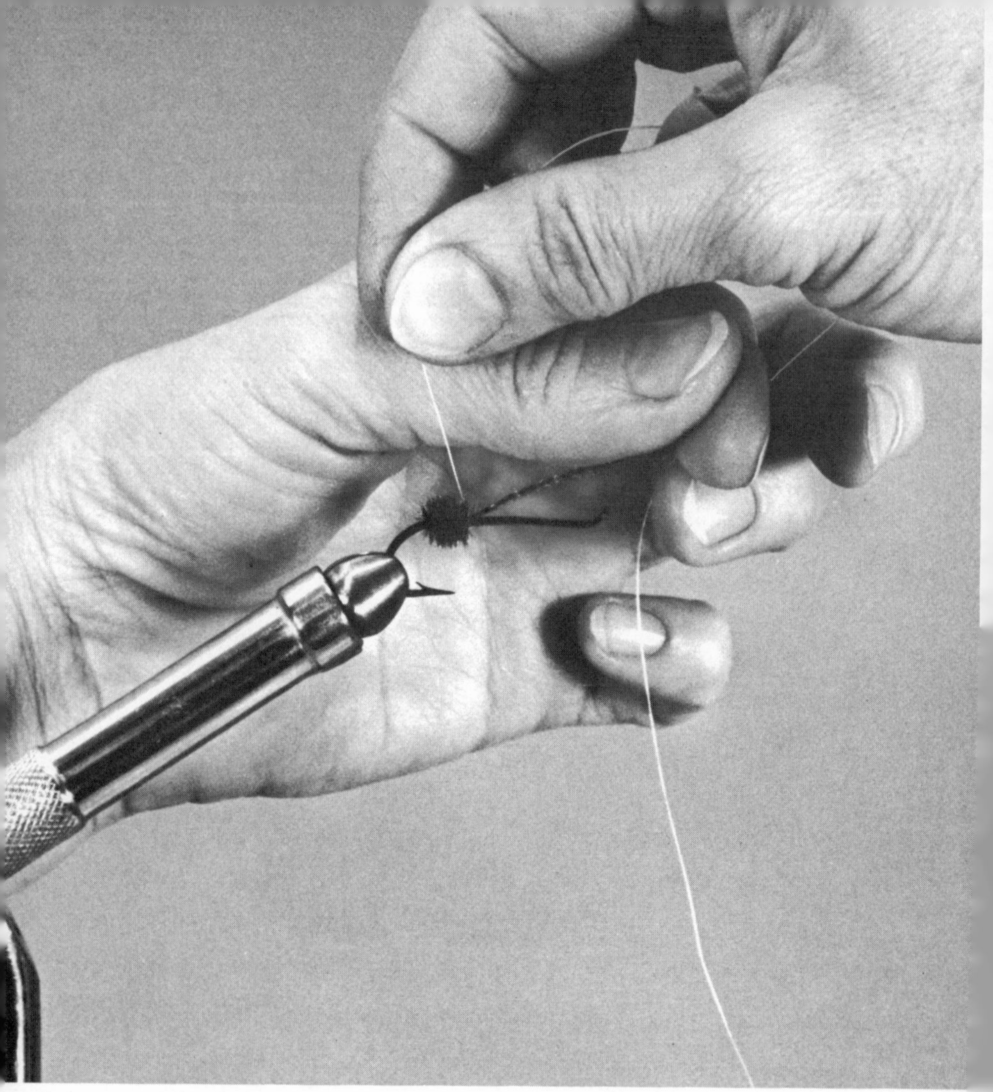

21g. Bring the thread up and across the herl twice to secure it. This first section is all you would need for a fly body on a small-sized hook.

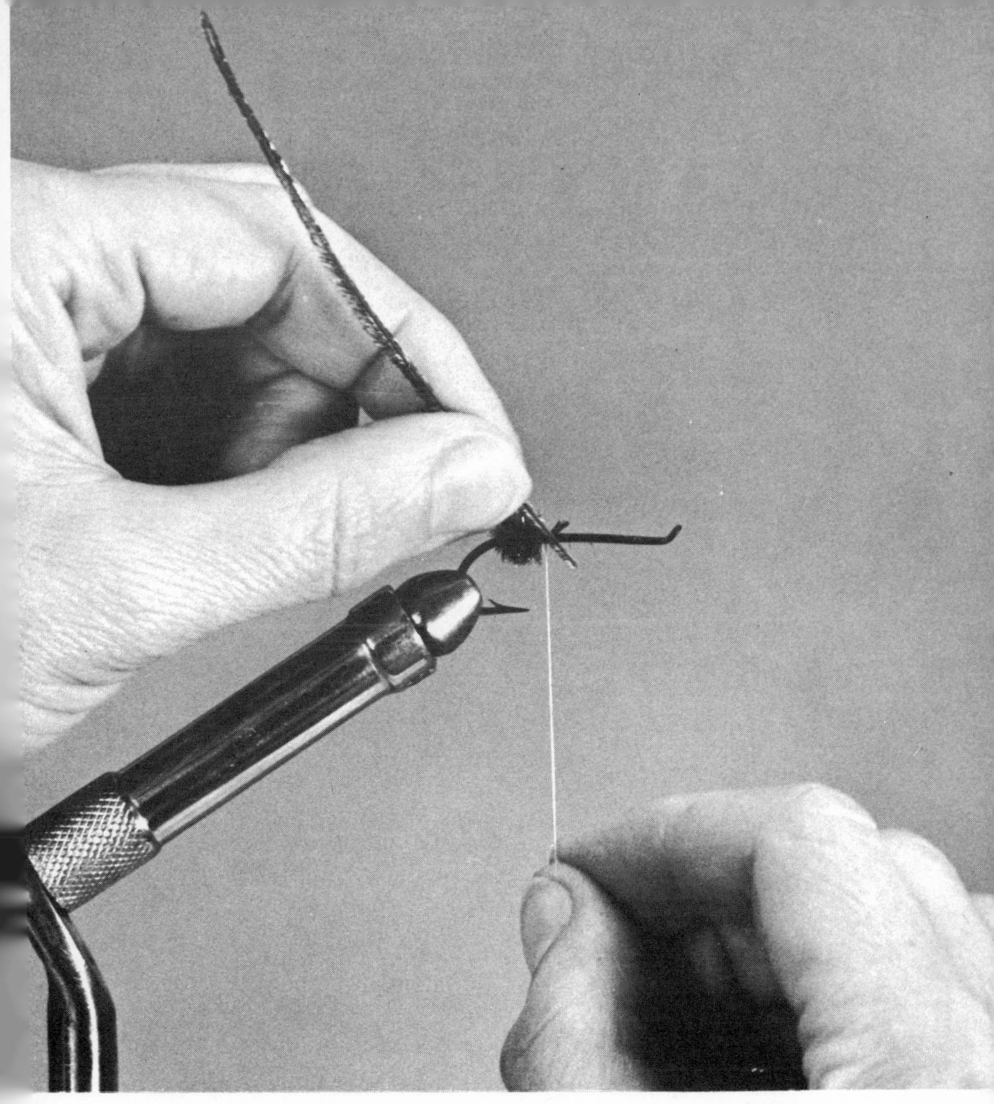

21h. As close to the first section as possible, tie on a second herl strand taken from the same side of the same peacock feather, and hold it in the same position as the first, flat against the hook, bare edge of the quill toward the hook eye. Secure it there with the tying thread.

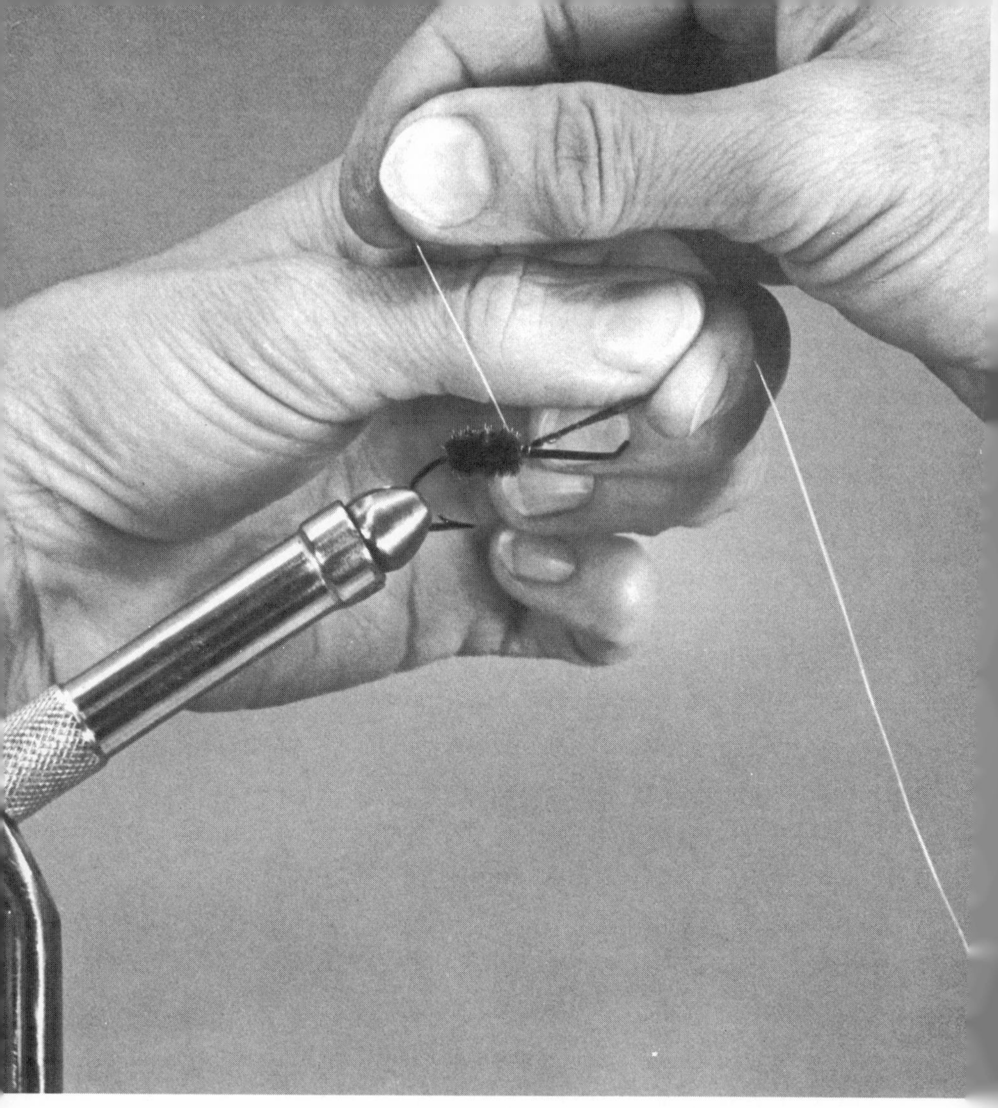

21i. Wind it carefully *through* the last two turns of herl of the first section, with a scalloping or zig-zag motion of the winding hand, so that the two will intermingle, then forward again, each turn of the colored barbules as close as possible to the preceding one. This will give the body an even appearance, showing no break between the sections. When the widest part of the herl has been reached, secure it with the thread and add another strand.

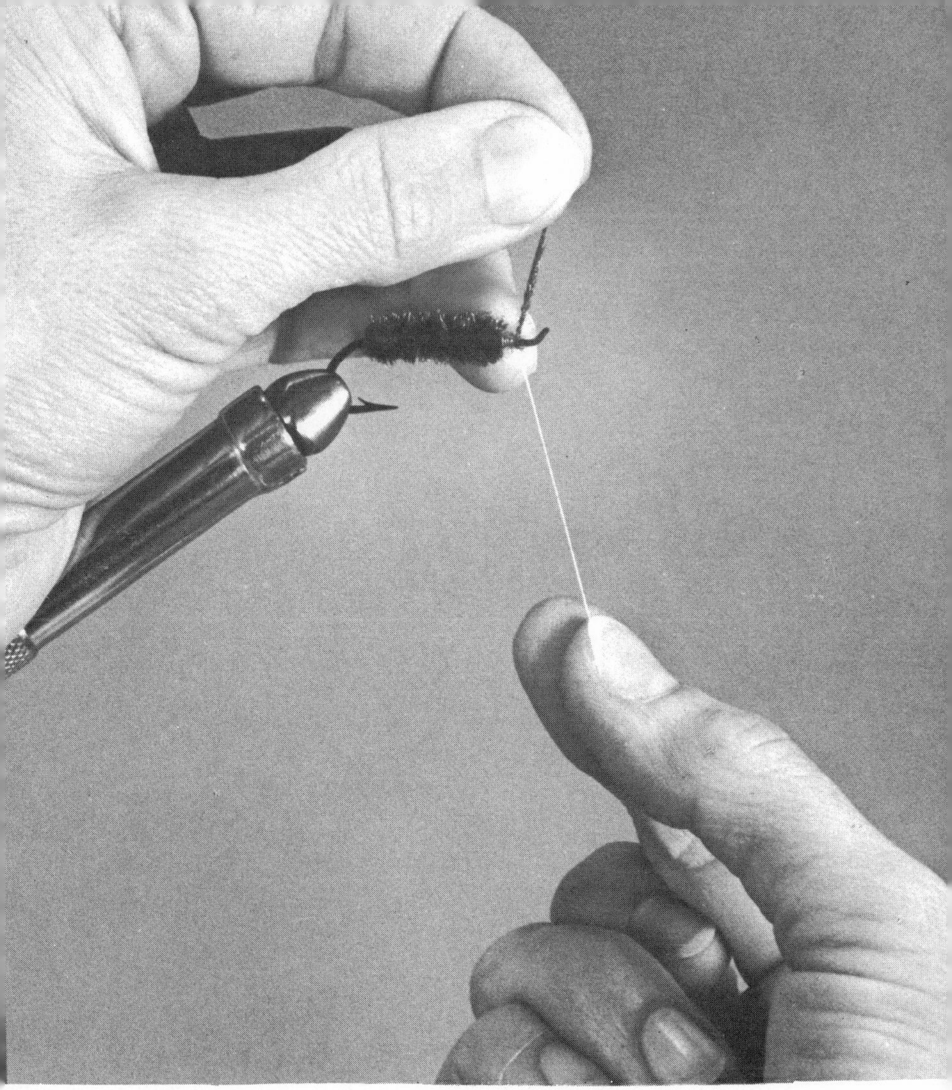

21j. Continue to add herl
ands in this manner until the
ok is covered to "wing position."
Clip off the remaining end of
rl. This is the only method for
ng this beautiful herl body.
actice until no breaks are notice-
le between the sections. Be
reful to select only the best
ands for this body, and always
ep the quills flat on the hook.

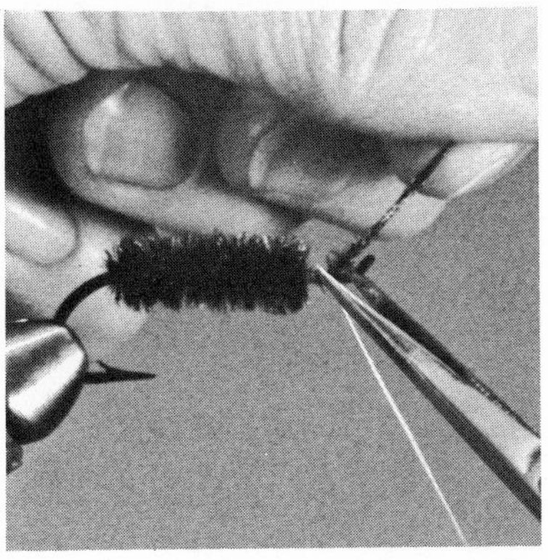

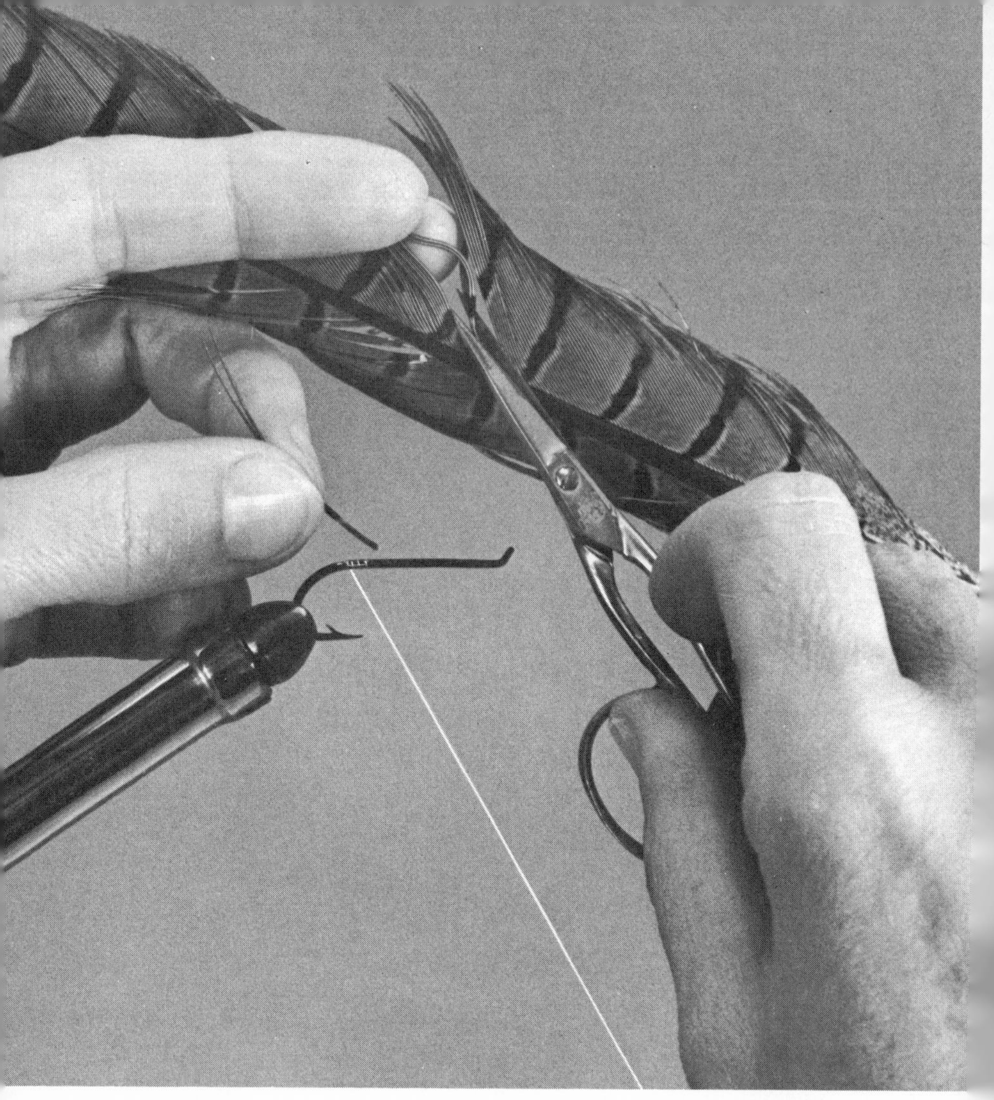

22a. The center tail feather from any adult male bird of the pheasant family is evenly matched on both sides of the center quill. The barbs (or flues) are of equal length and their natural curve is of equal strength.

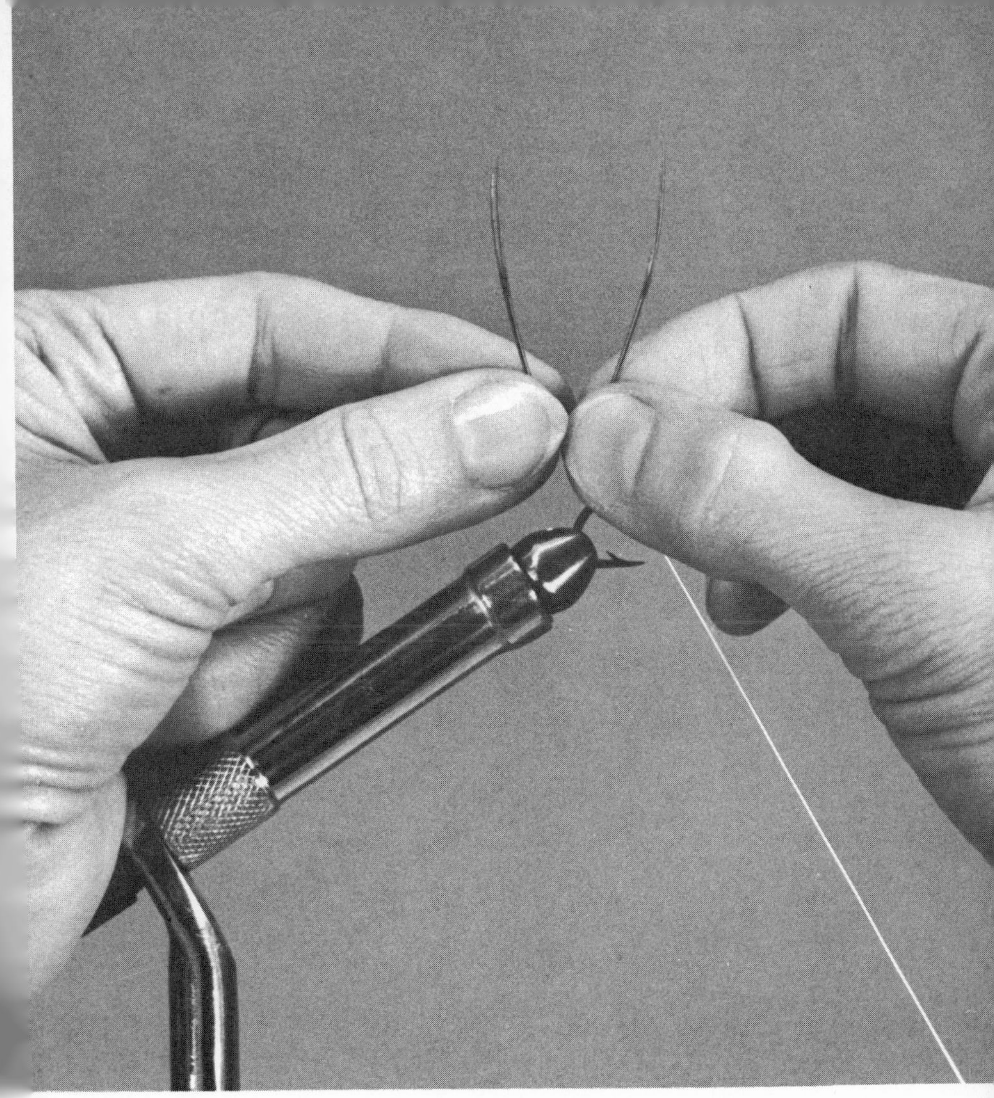

22b. Clip two barbs from each side, matching the markings. If the two barbs are kept in the same relative position on the fly as they were on the feather, the natural curve of each would bring them together, or make the tips cross.

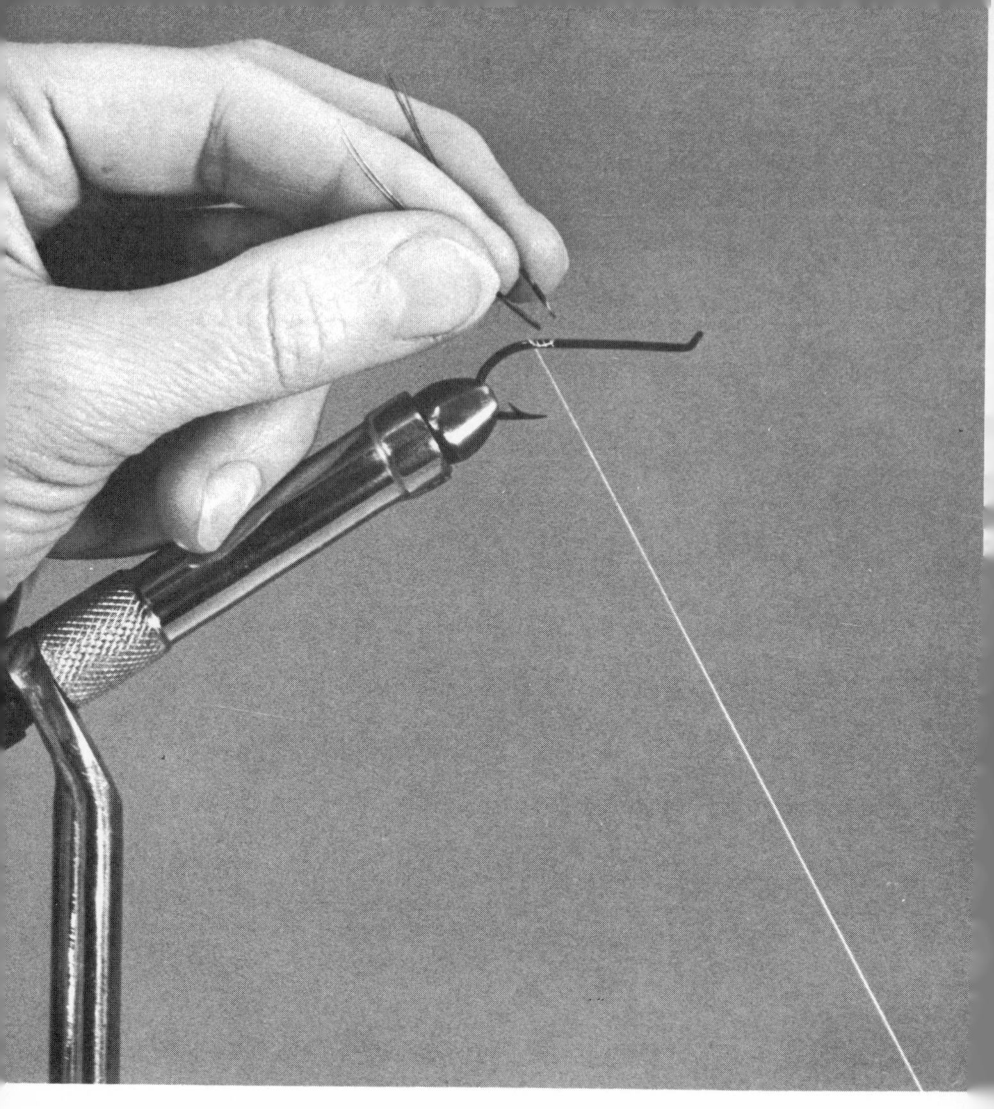

22c. Reverse their positions and hold them with their deepest-colored sides together against the hook. Judge their final length in relation to the hook and with the right hand **bring them together.** Regrip them with the left so that both are between left thumb and forefinger. Bring the tying thread up between thumb and barbs, down between barbs and finger, twice to fasten them to the hook.

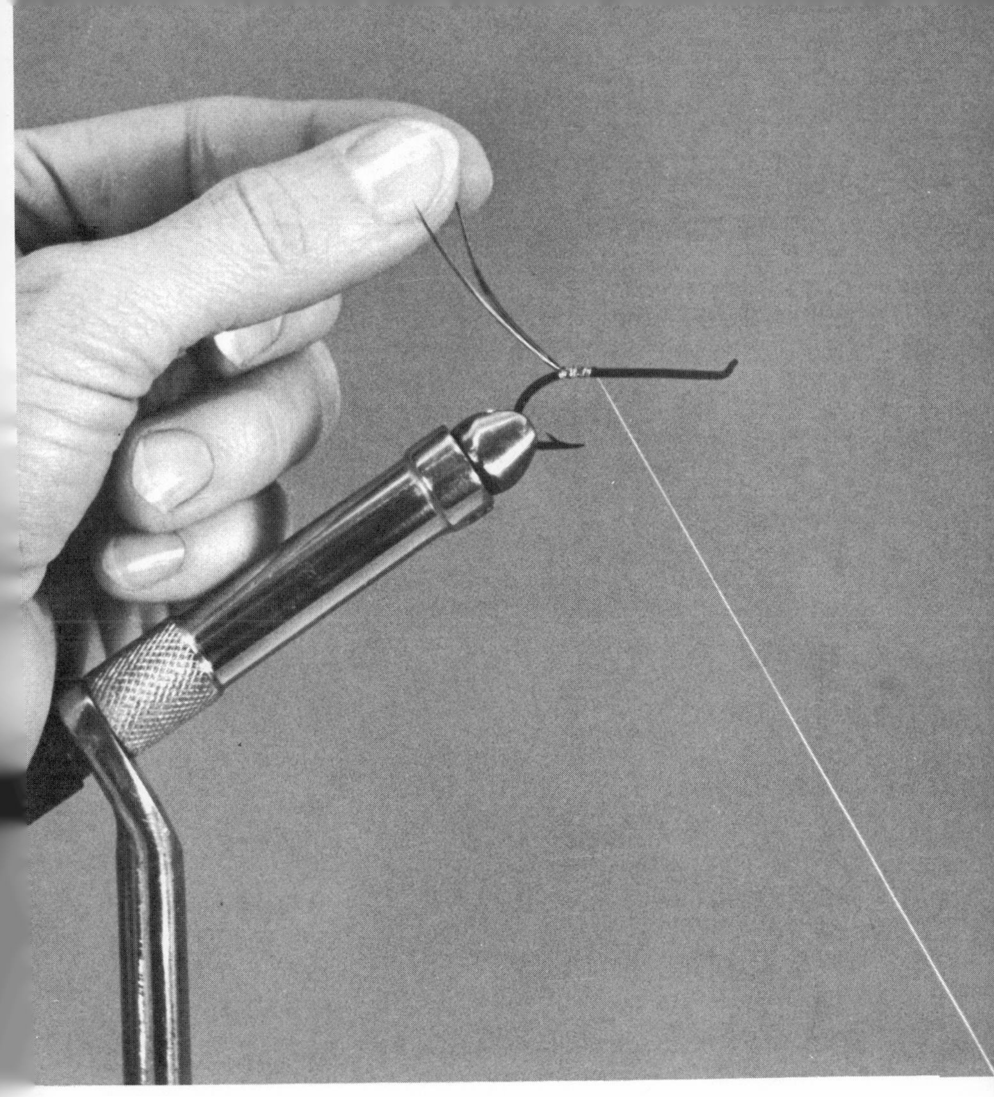

22d. Bind them to the hook with a close spiral of tying thread. Clip off the remaining ends. Barbs from matched wing feathers of goose or duck may be used in the same manner. For streamer flies, a tail no longer than the gape of the hook should be used.

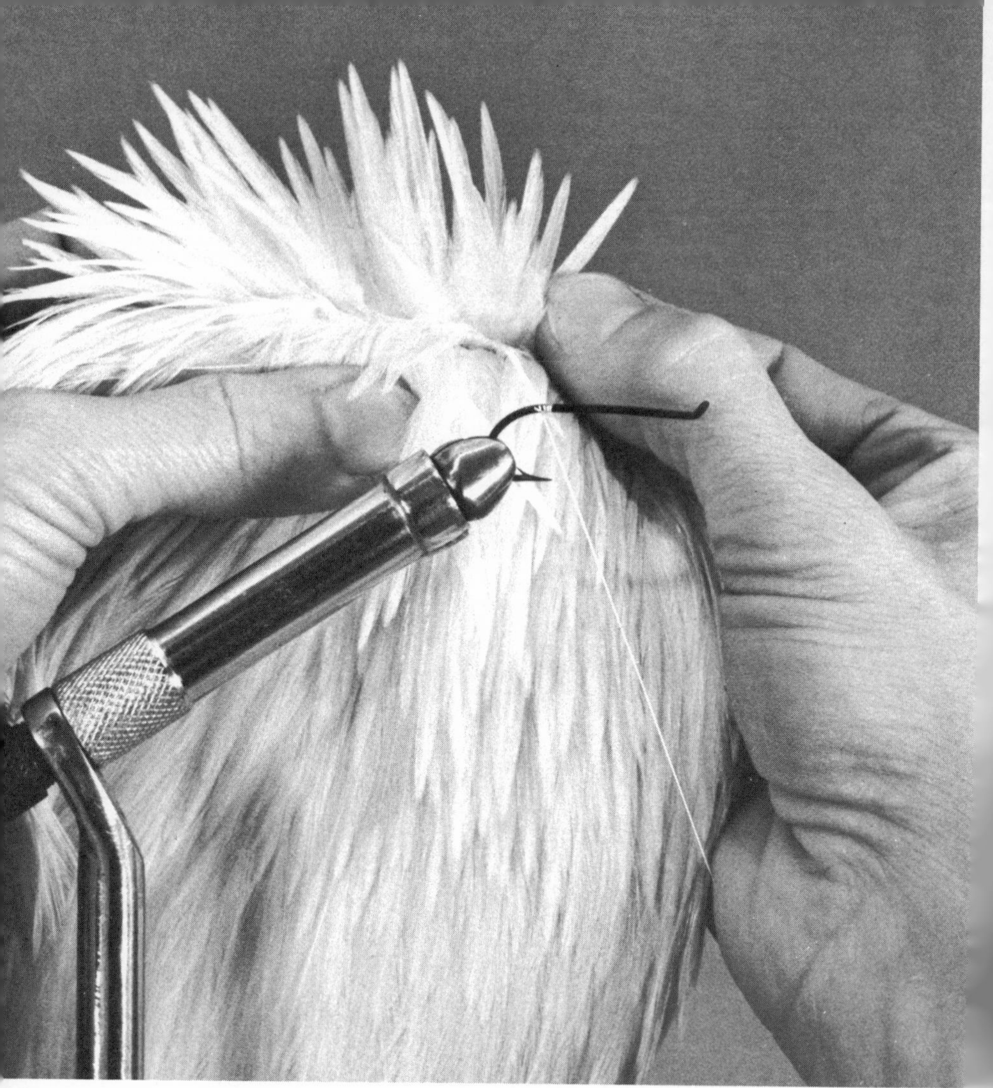

23a. Small neck hackles are excellent for hackle-point tails. Select two matching feathers, one from each side of the neck so that the natural curve of the feather will be equal.

23b. Place the feathers with their glossy sides together, so that the points will be separated and the natural lengthwise curve will be upward at the tips. Measure them against the hook for length and then hold them at "tail position."

Grip them with the left hand and hold them in position for tying. Bring the tying thread up between the fingers and secure the hackles to the hook. The angle of the feathers against the hook can be adjusted with the tying thread. To cock them upward, wind one turn of thread around the hook just behind the base of the feathers. Bind the tems down with a close spiral of our turns of thread. Clip off the nds close to the thread.

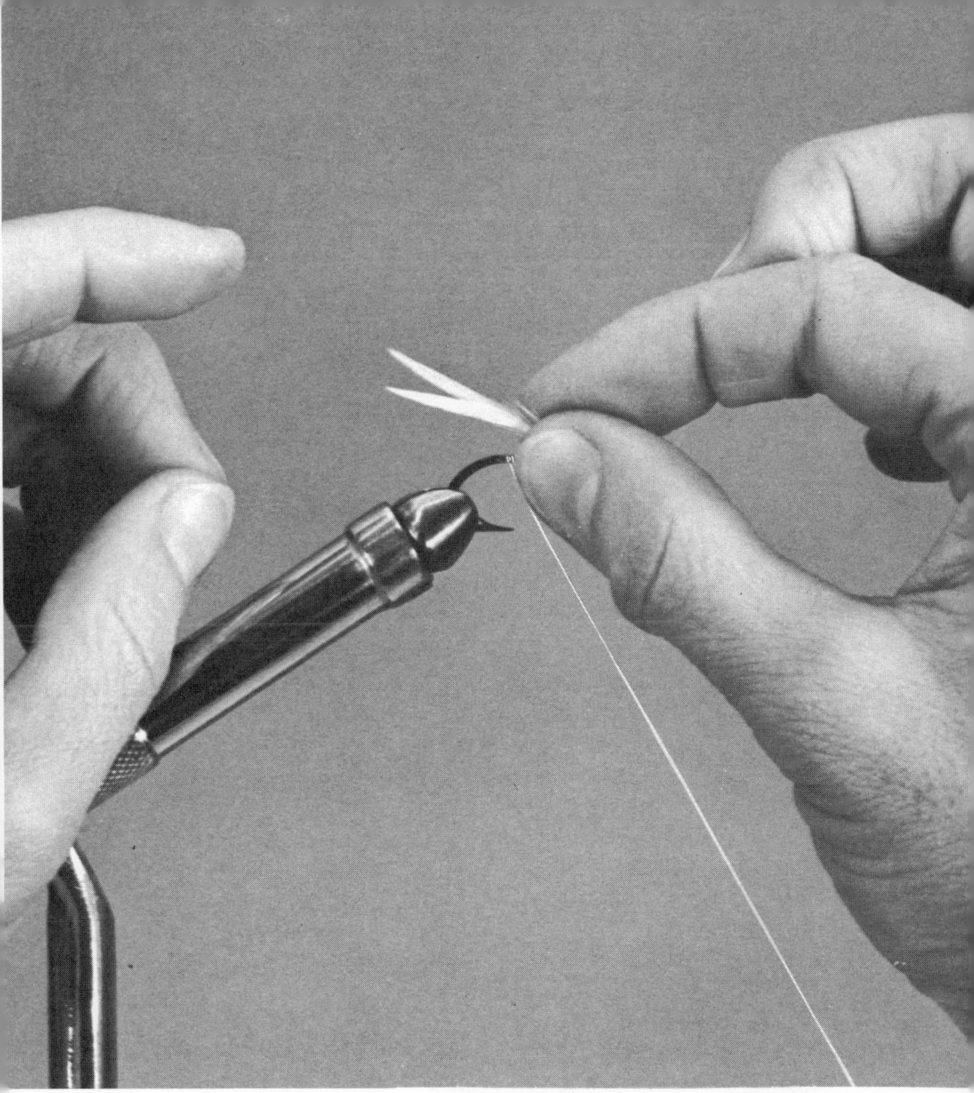

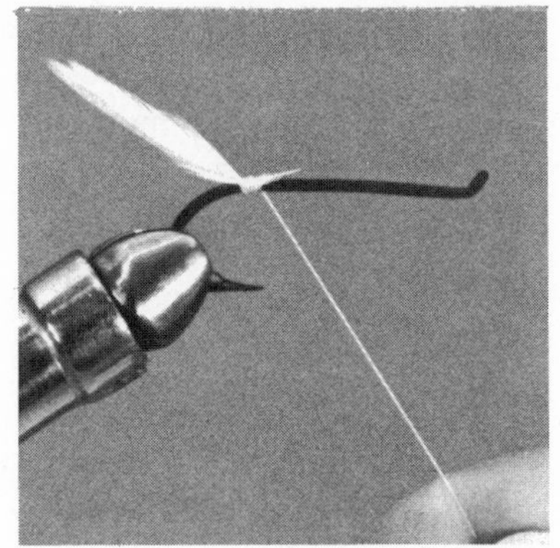

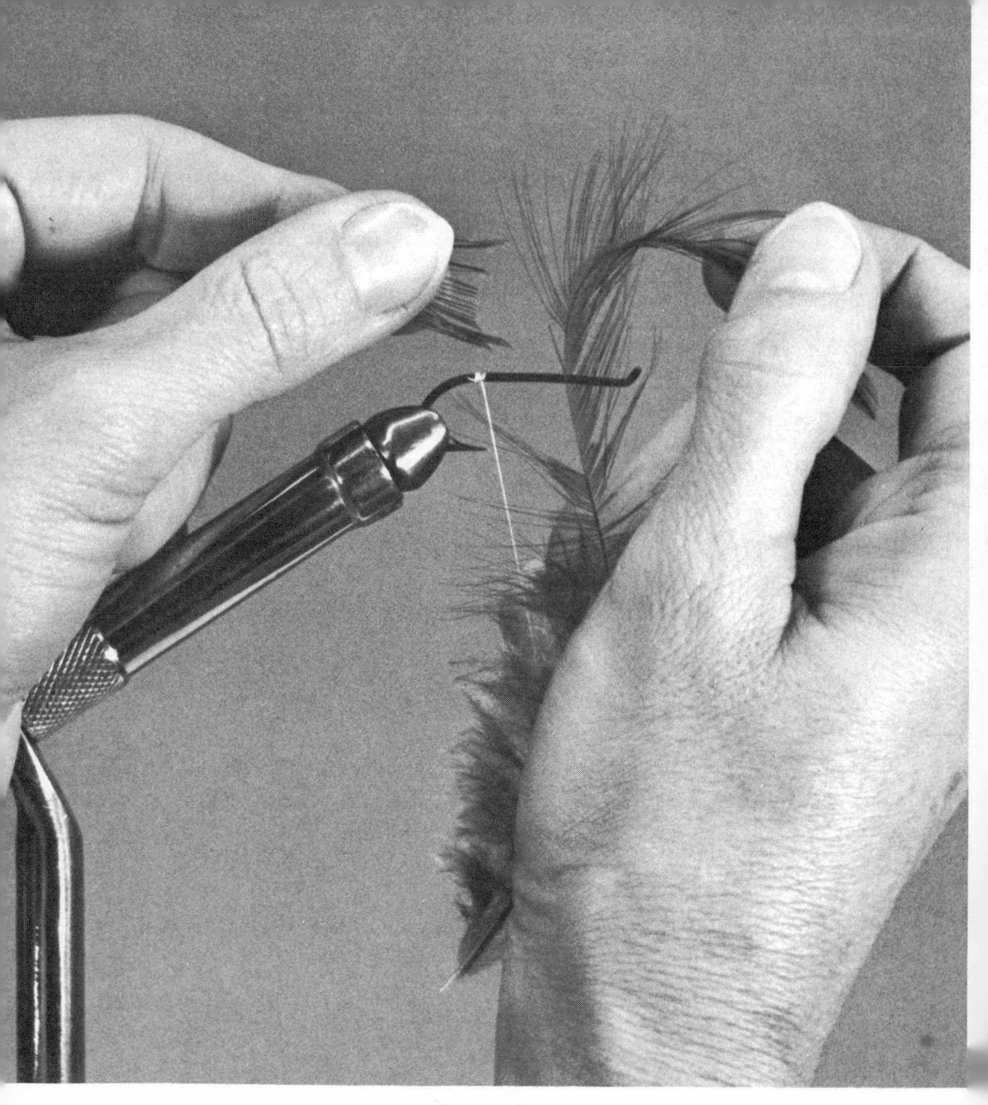

24a. A **wisp tail** made from a few flues or barbs of hackle may be used for a tail less solid in appearance. Grasp several flues between thumb and finger and pull them free from the hackle.

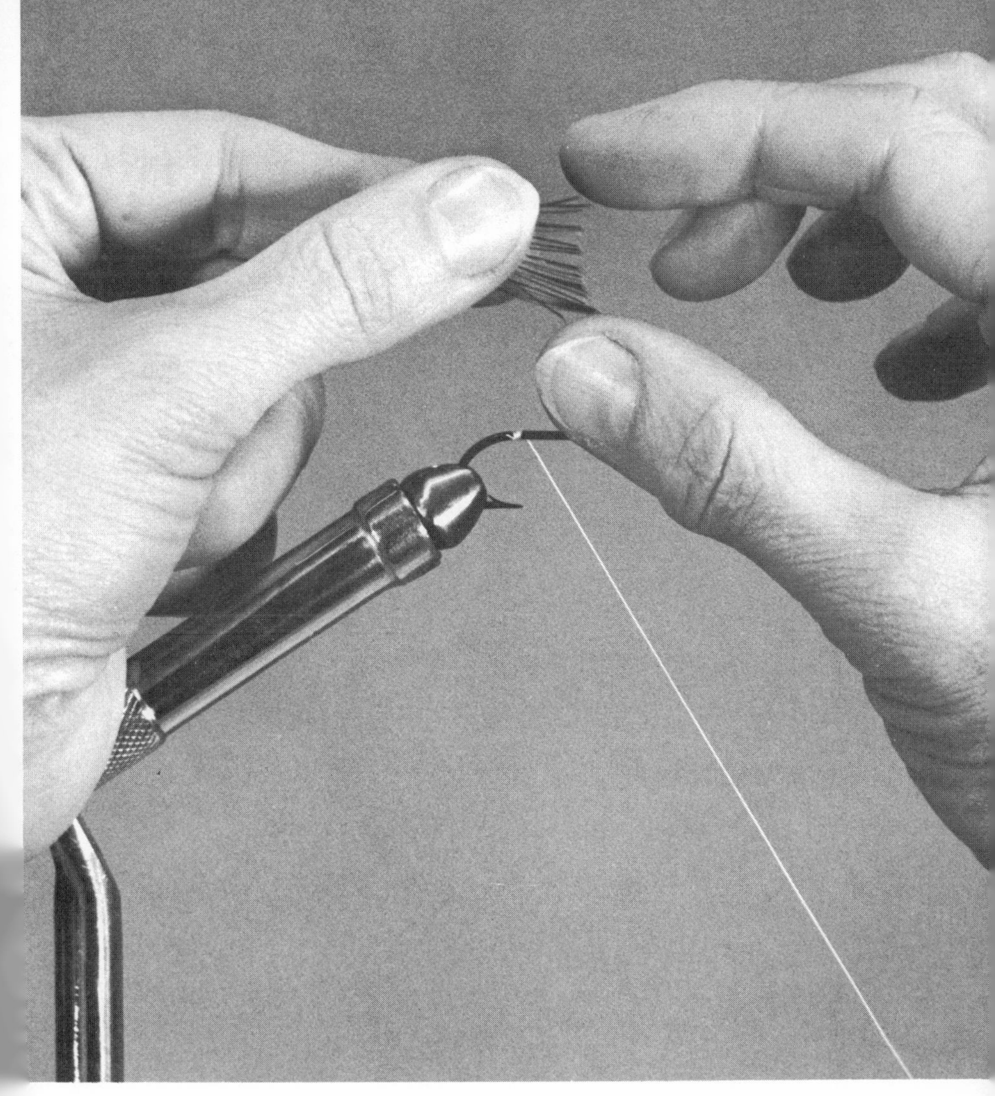

24b. Hold the base ends of the hackle flues with the right hand, to bunch them.

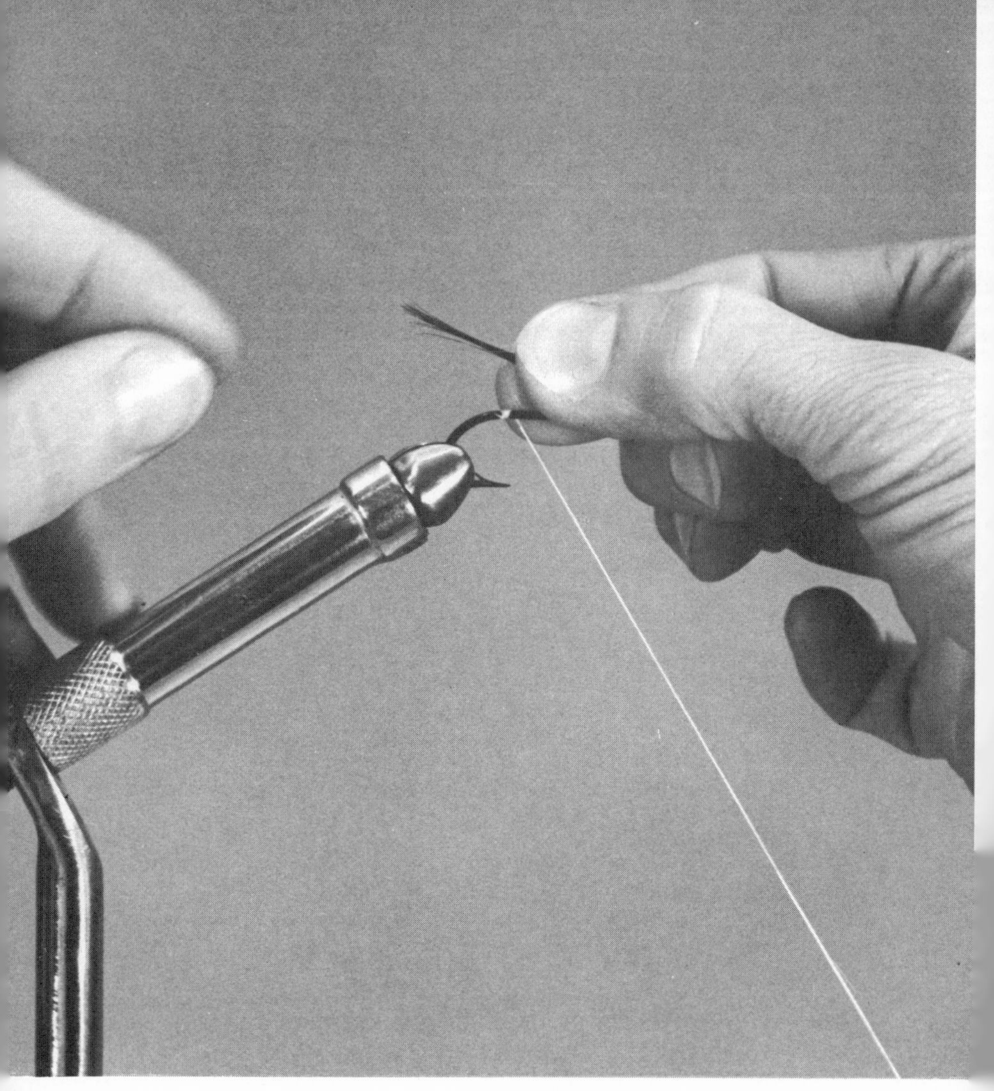

24c. Measure them against the hook for the correct length, approximately that of the hook shank. Regrip them with the left hand and hold them in place at "tail position."

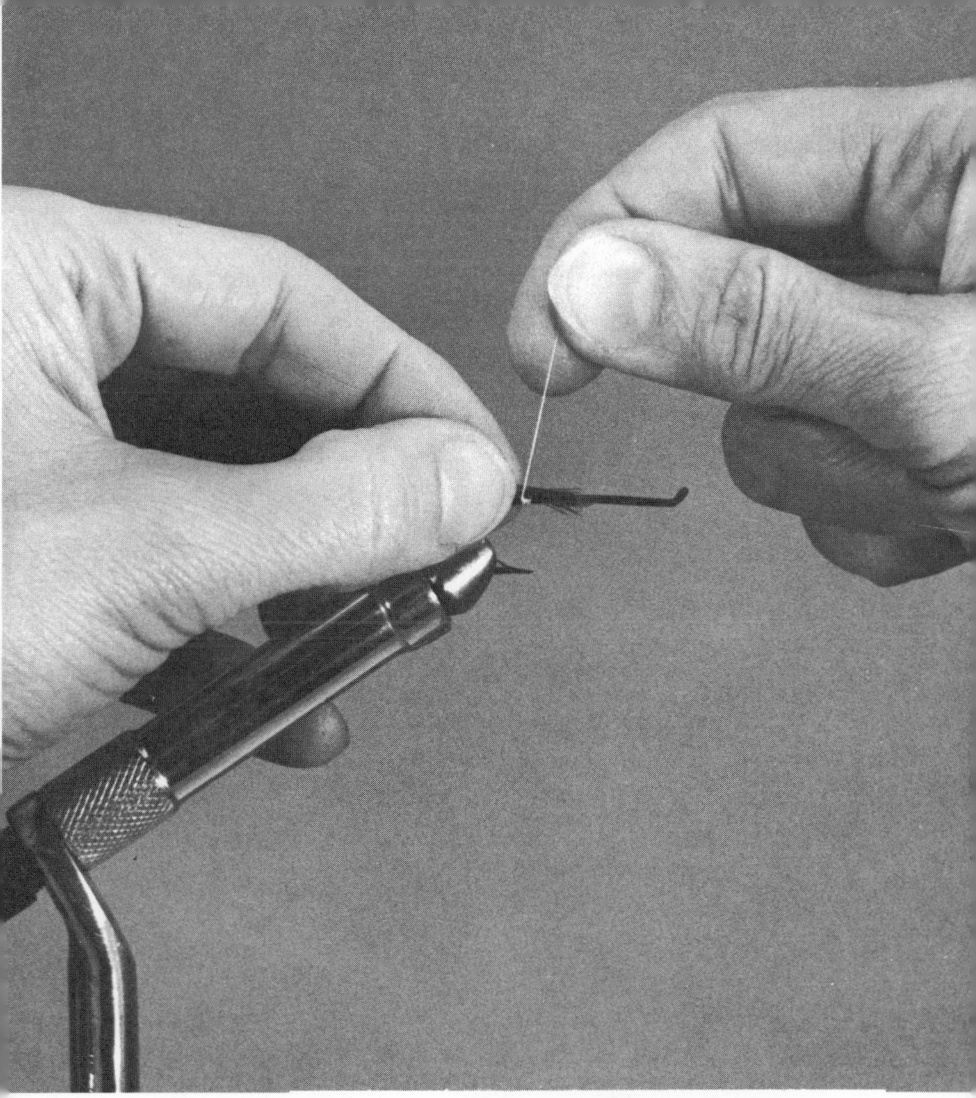

24d. With the right hand, bring ne tying thread up and slip it be-ween the fingers of the left hand, ollowing the method you have earned, and bind the hackle barbs the hook. Make sure all the arbs remain on top of the hook.

Bind down the barbs with a ose spiral of thread and cut off e remaining ends close to the ook.

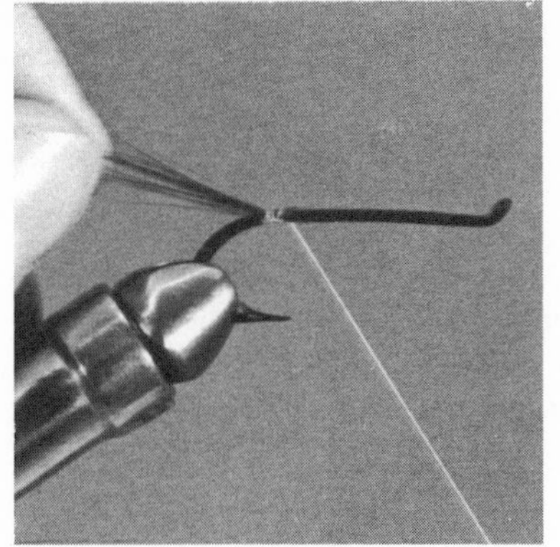

25a. Whole hackles not over 2½ or 3 inches in length with heavily webbed centers are excellent streamer wings. From a string of hackle or a hackle neck pad, select sets of feathers that match in size, color, and marking and that curve in opposite directions. The thread is attached to the hook at "wing position."

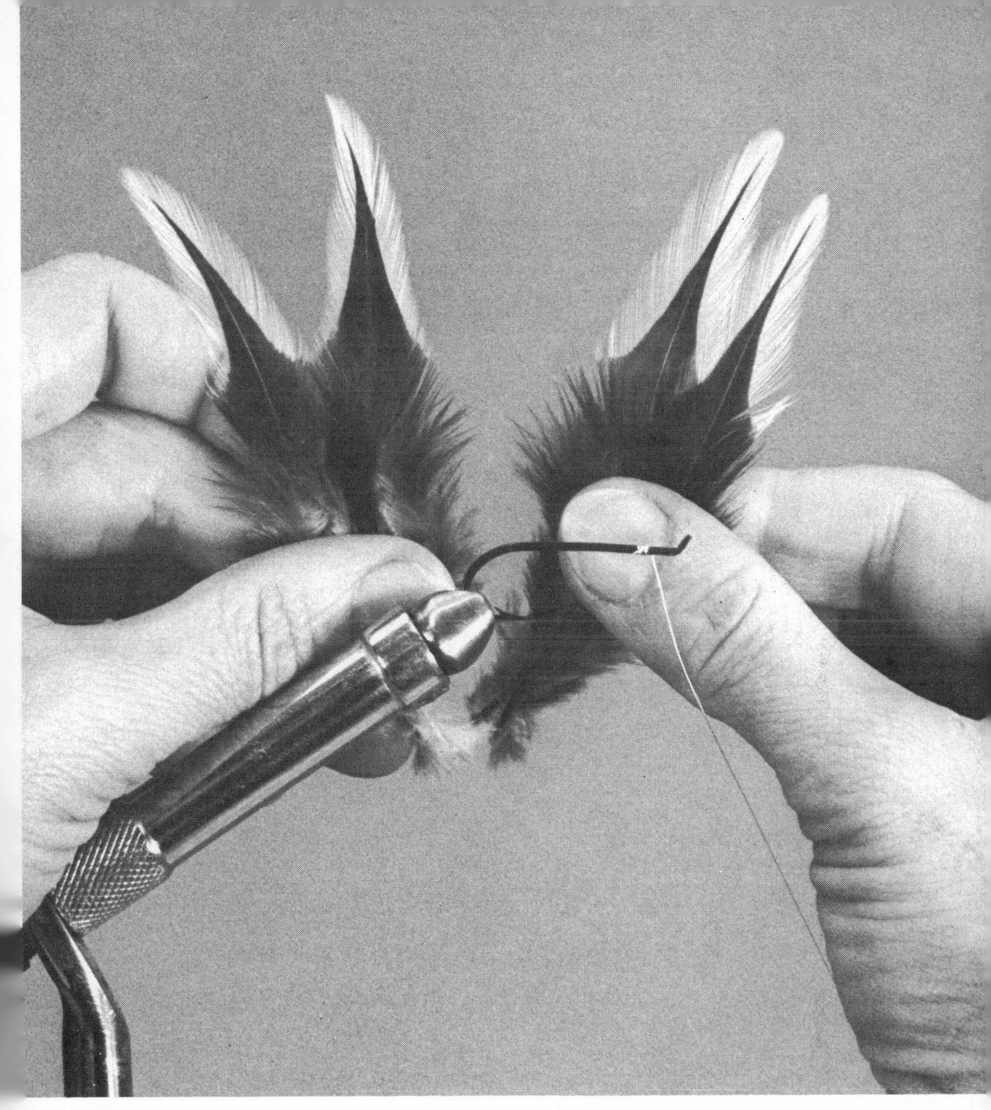

25b. When the feathers are held with their dull sides together, the curves will match.

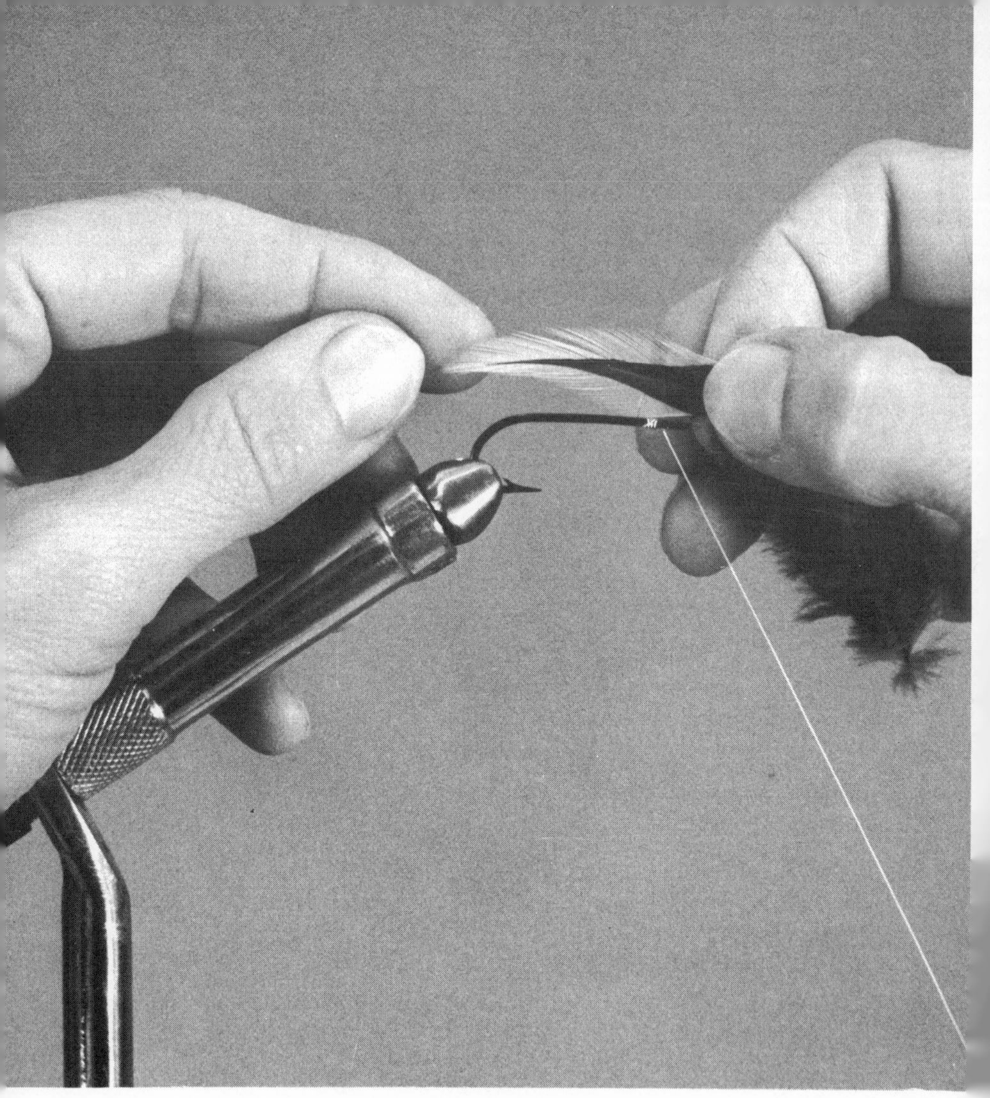

25c. Make sure the glossy sides are outward, the tips even. Hold a pair above the hook to gauge the correct length for the streamer wing, the over-all length of the hook.

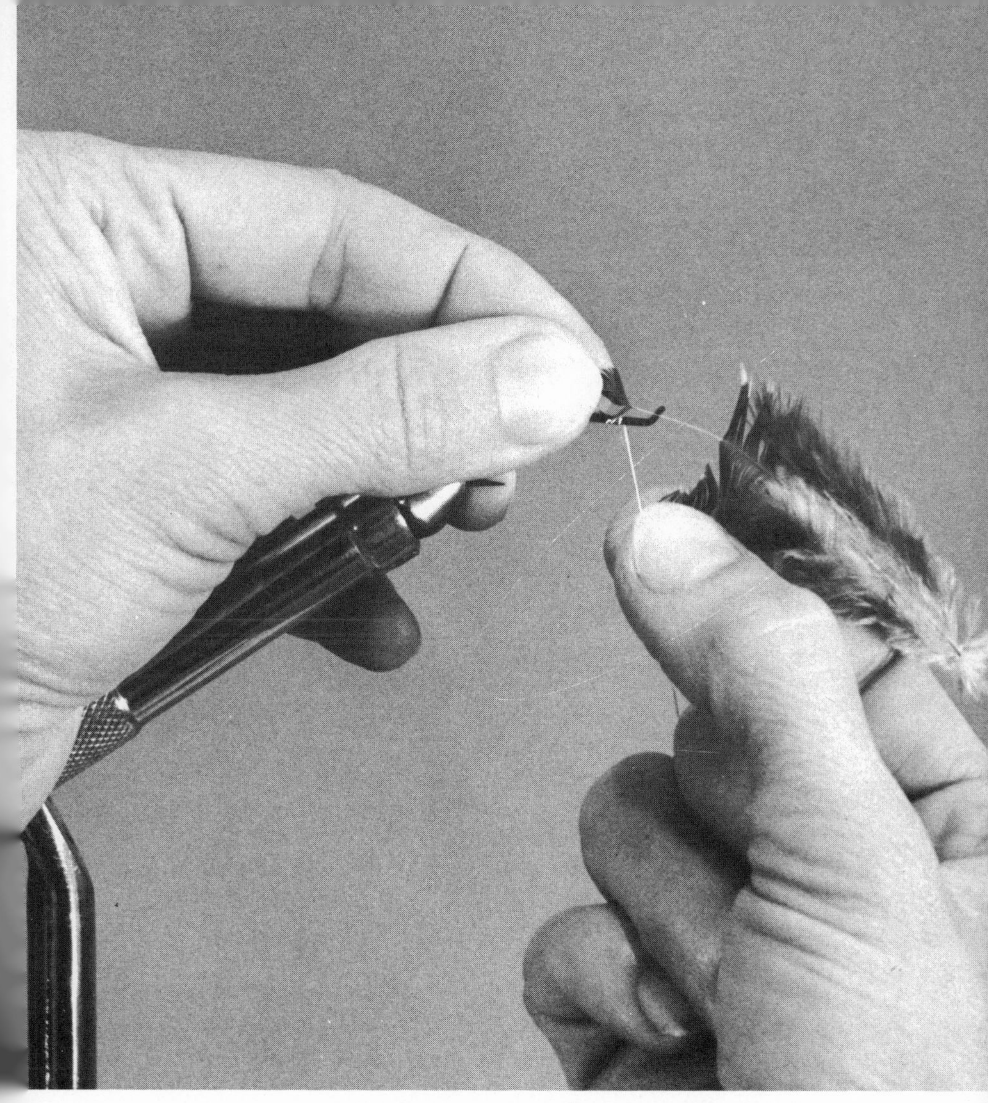

25d. Take the feathers in the left hand, fingertips marking the base of the wing. Strip away all barbs beyond the fingertips.

25e. Leave ½ inch of quill on each feather and clip away the rest. Hold the feathers on top of the hook at "wing position."

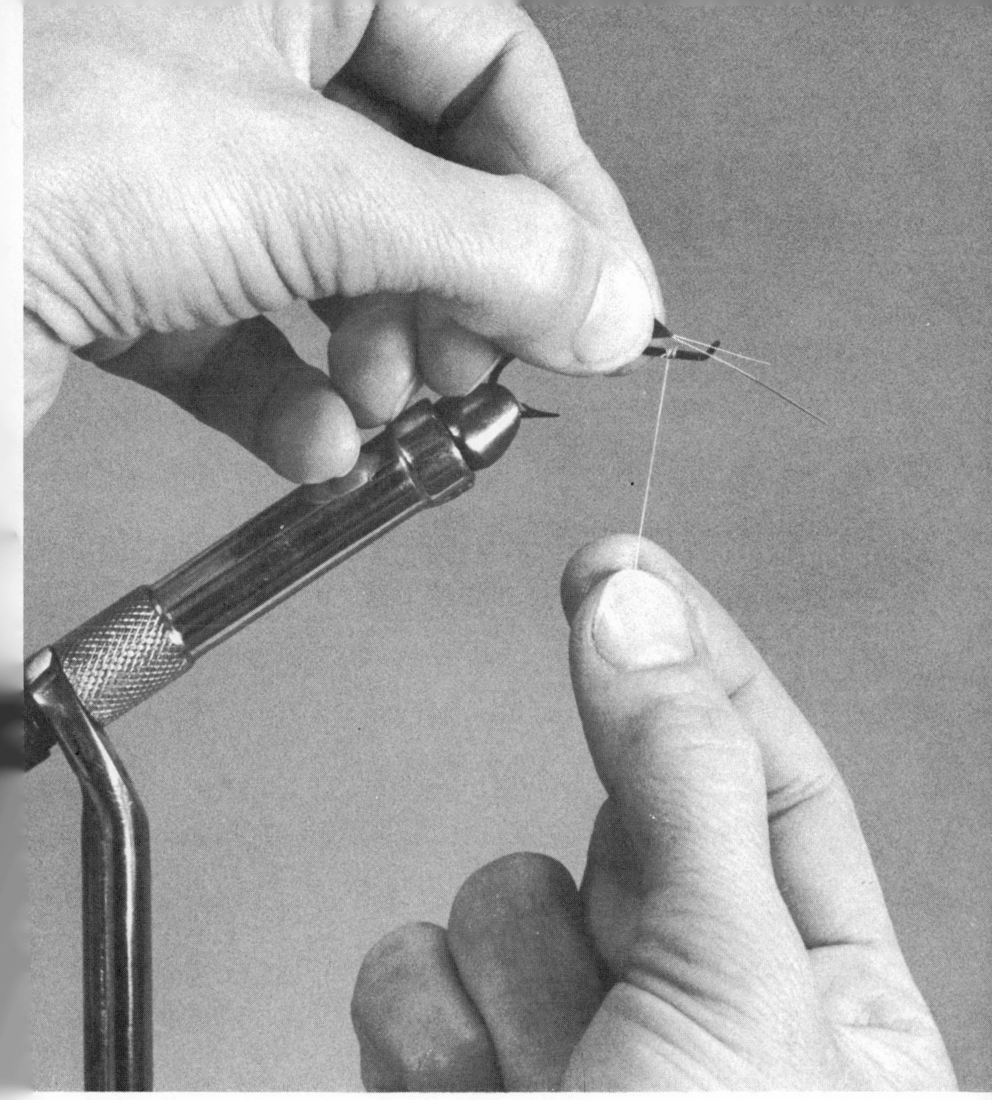

25f. With the base of the feathers now at "wing position," release the tying thread from button. Bind the feathers to the top of the hook.

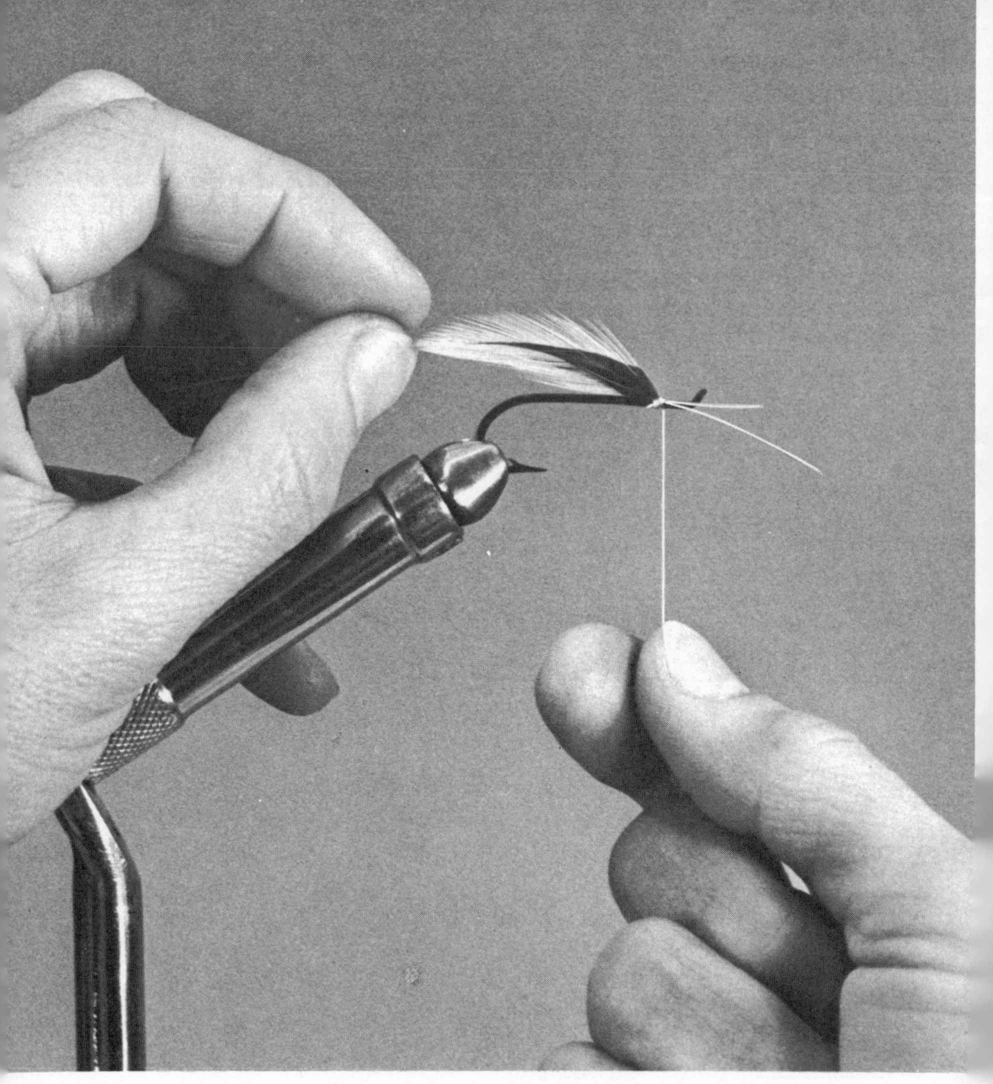

25g. The feathers will extend approximately the width of the gape beyond the hook bend. A wing longer than this in relation to the hook may result in short strikes while fishing.

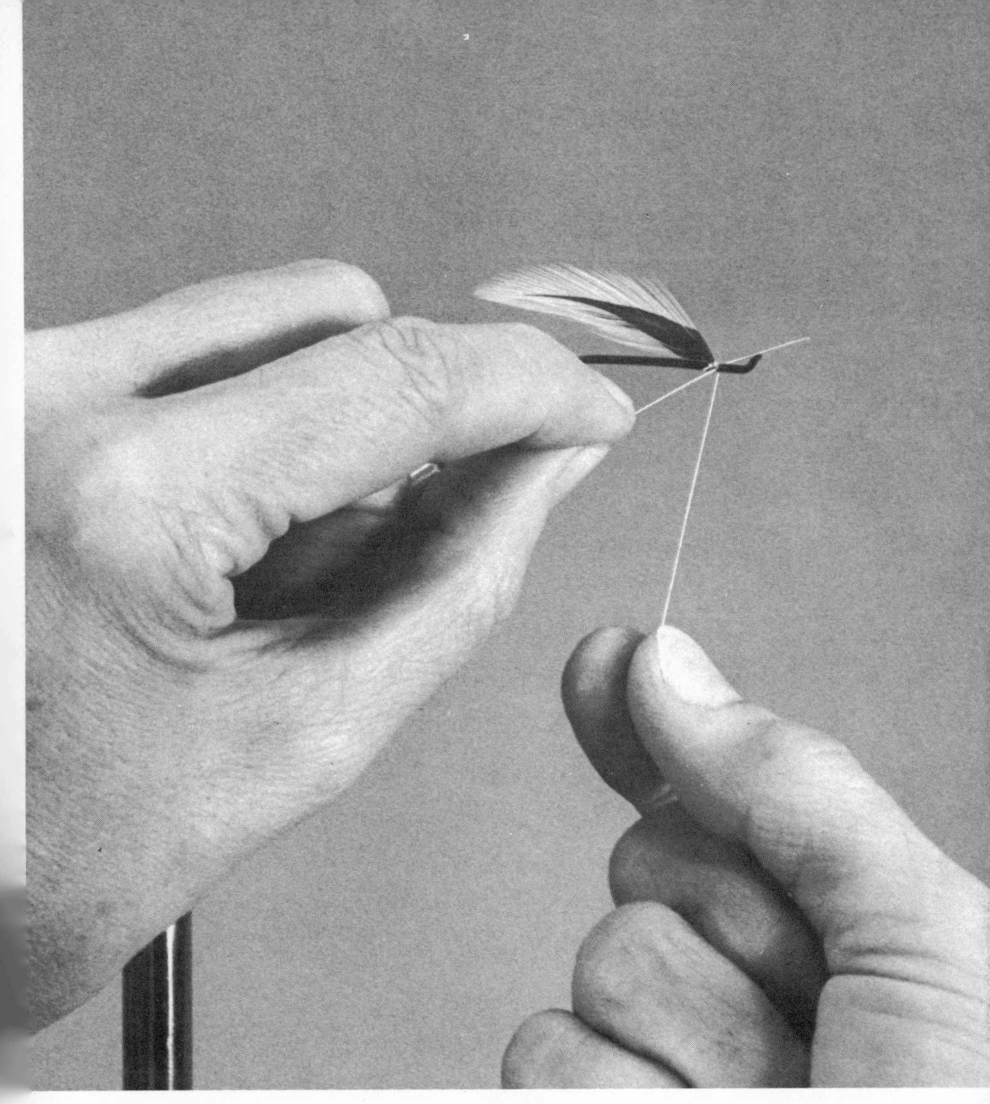

25h. Draw back the nearest quill and bind it to the hook with the tying thread by carrying it upward and over the hook ahead of the base of the wing.

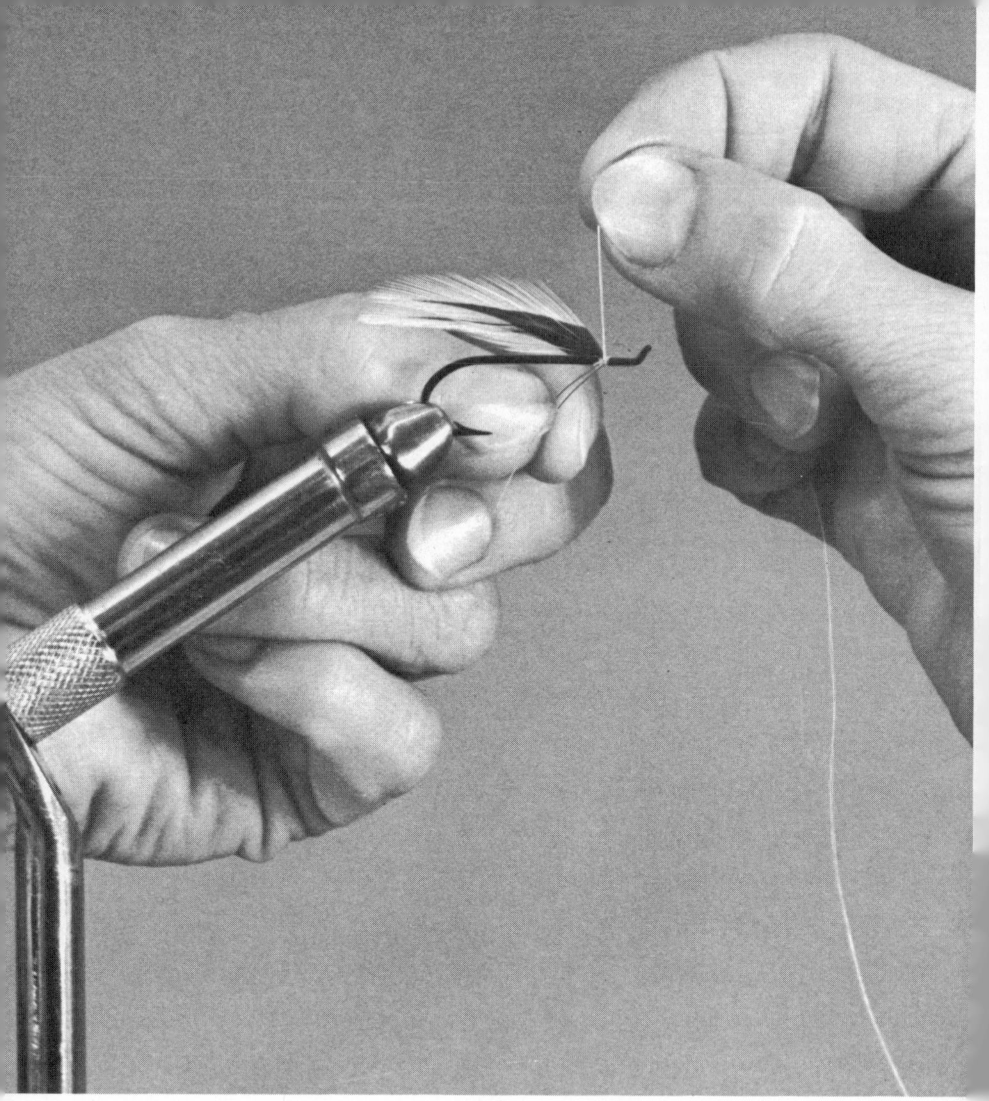

25i. Draw the quill on the far side of the hook back in the same way, and bind it to the hook with the thread as you bring it down on the other side.

25j. As you bring the tying thread up in front of the hook this time, take it in the left hand. Lift the wings with the right hand and carry the thread beneath them, close to the wing base and down on the far side, catching the quills to the hook just back of the wing.

With the thread again in the right hand, hold wings in position with the left and place one more turn of thread as close as possible just ahead of the feathers. Secure the thread to the button and ut off excess quill. Practice tying his wing until the position of the eathers is correct every time. The ving should be in perfect alignnent with the hook.

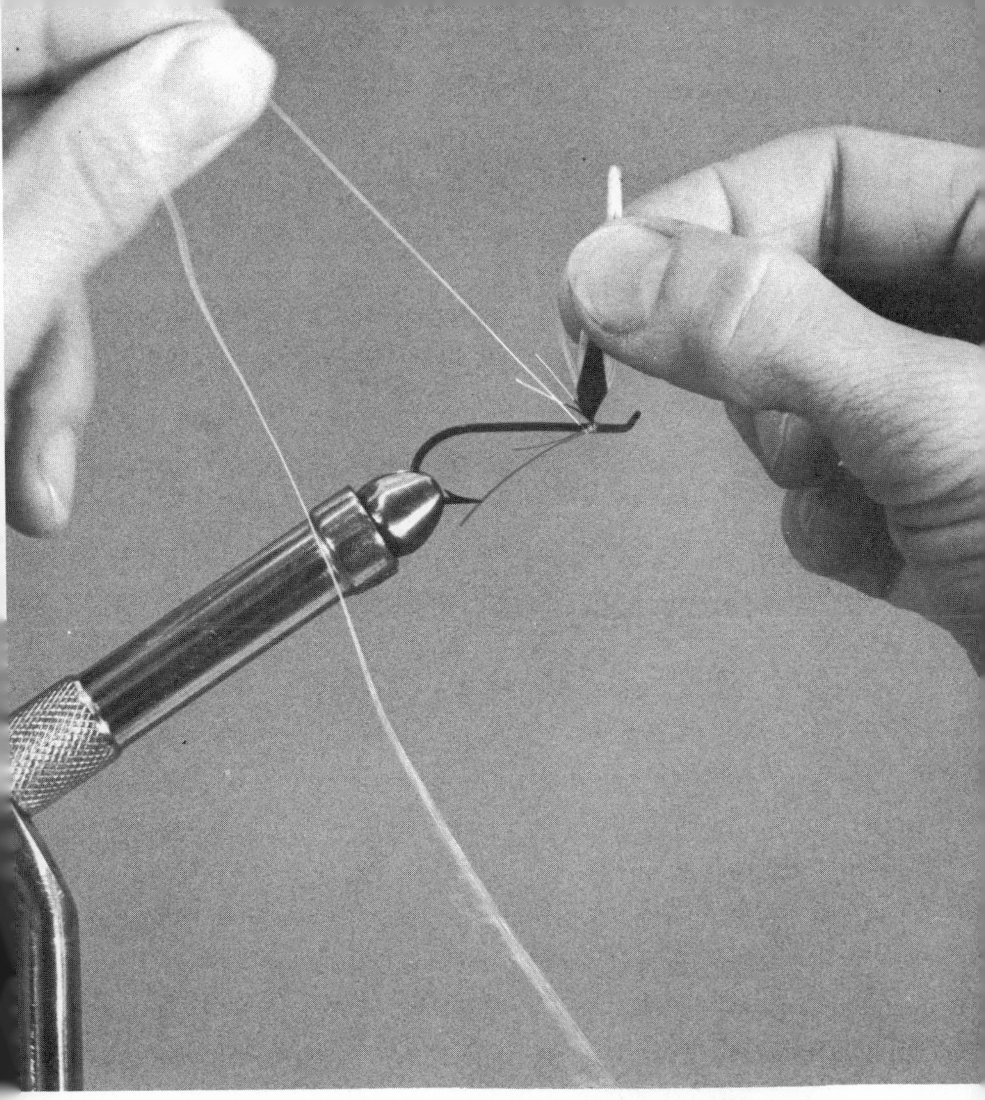

26a. Upright wings are made from very short neck hackles or hackle points. Select two hackles, from a string or from the opposite sides of a neck pad, matching them for width and marking.

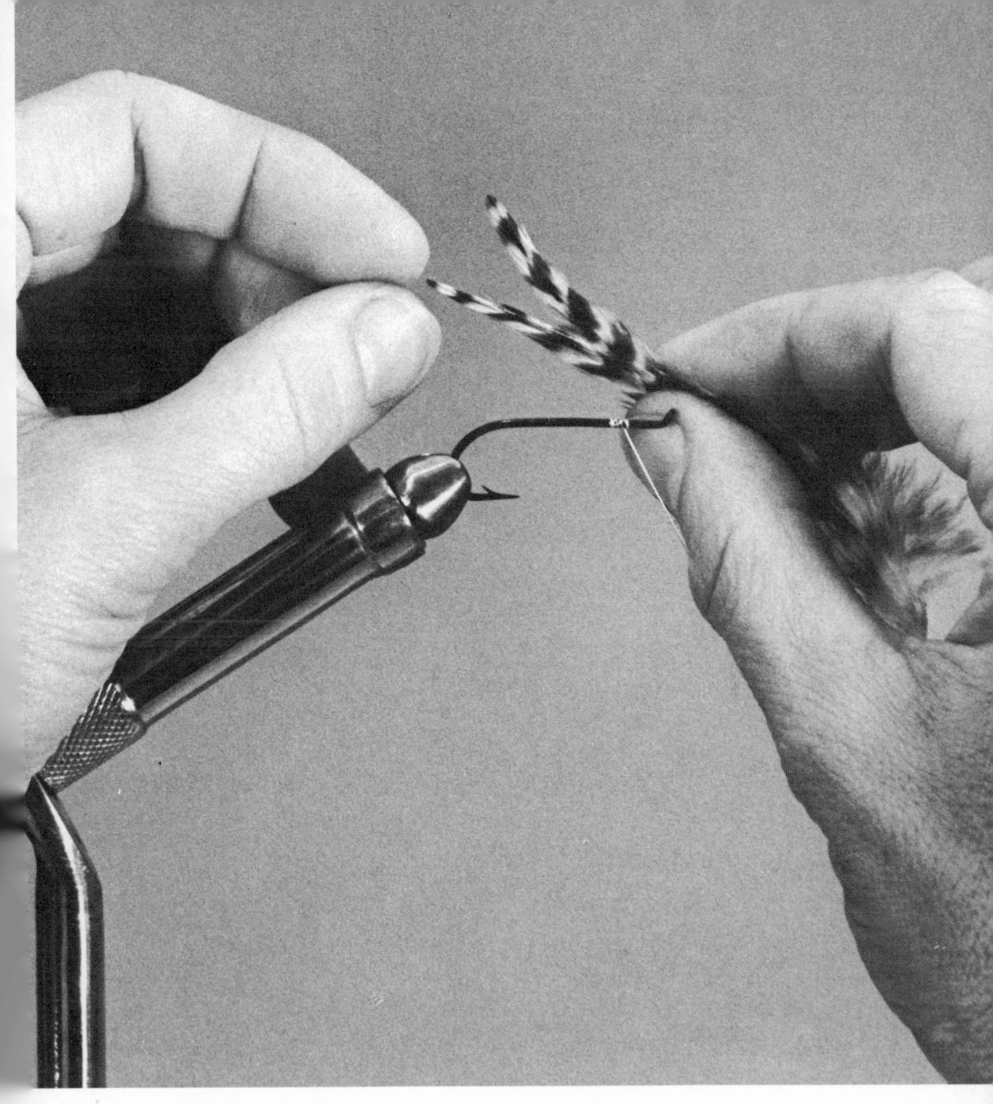

26b. Place their glossy sides together, tips even, and measure for length against the hook. Strip away all fluff below the proper length. Clip away excess quill.

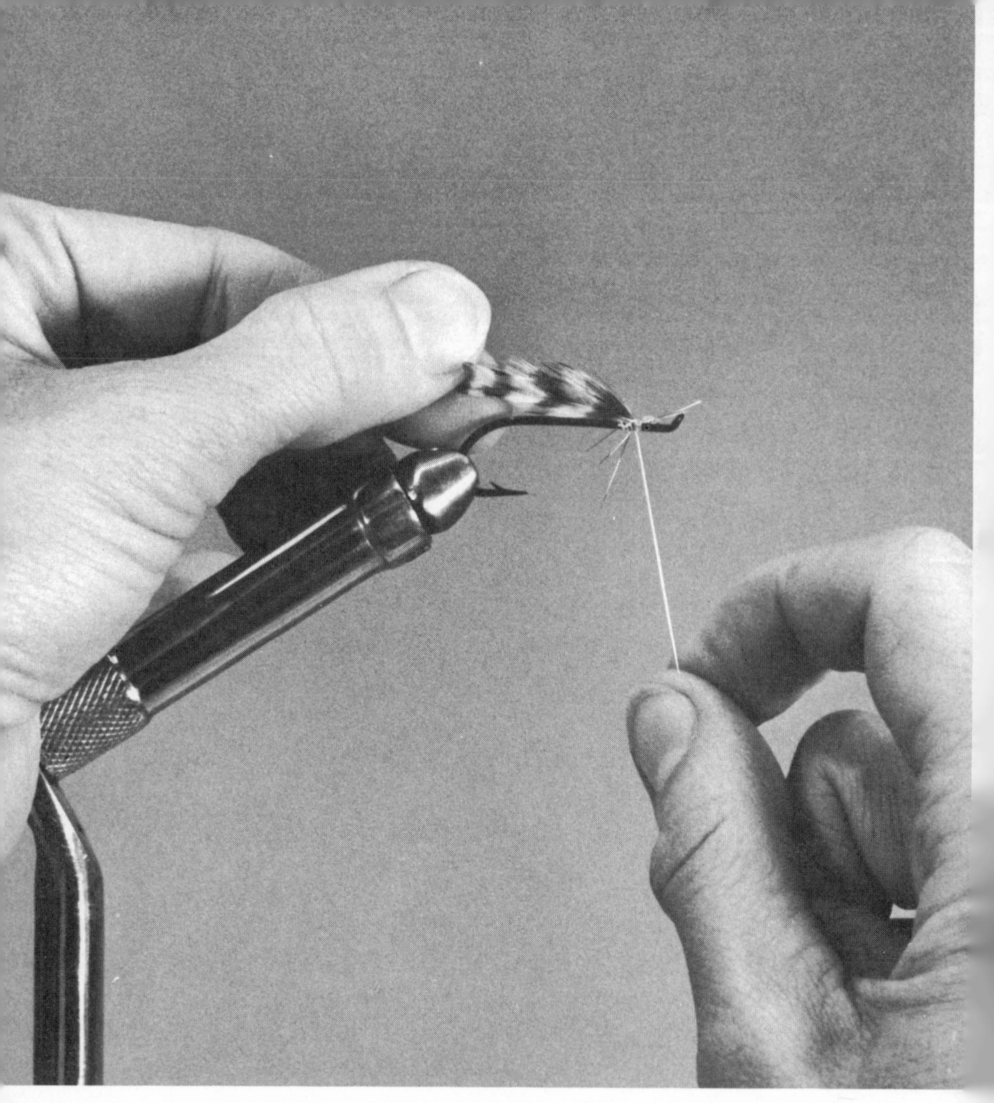

26c. Hold the matched feathers against the hook at "wing position." Secure them to the hook with two or three turns of tying thread.

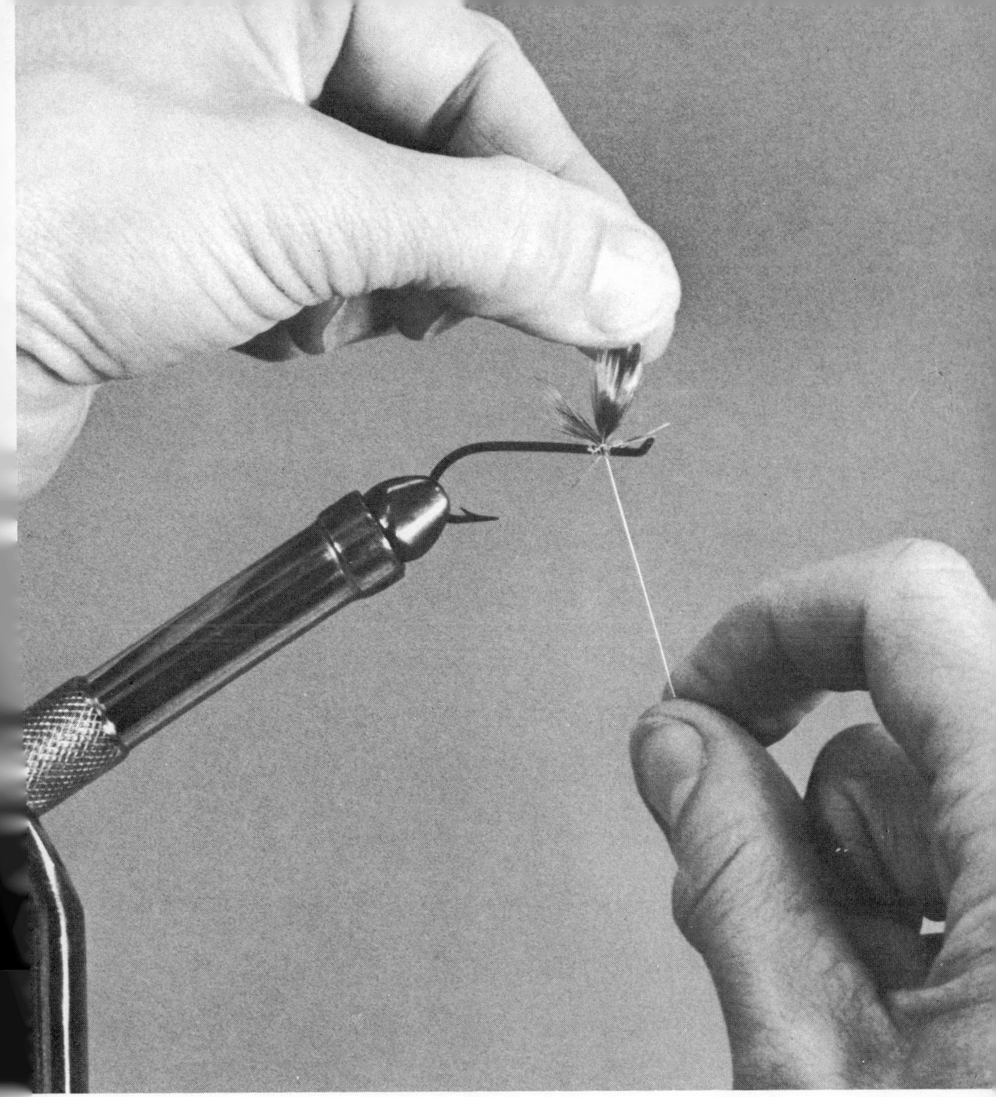

26d. Lift the matched feathers to a vertical position and place a turn of thread around the hook as close behind them as possible.

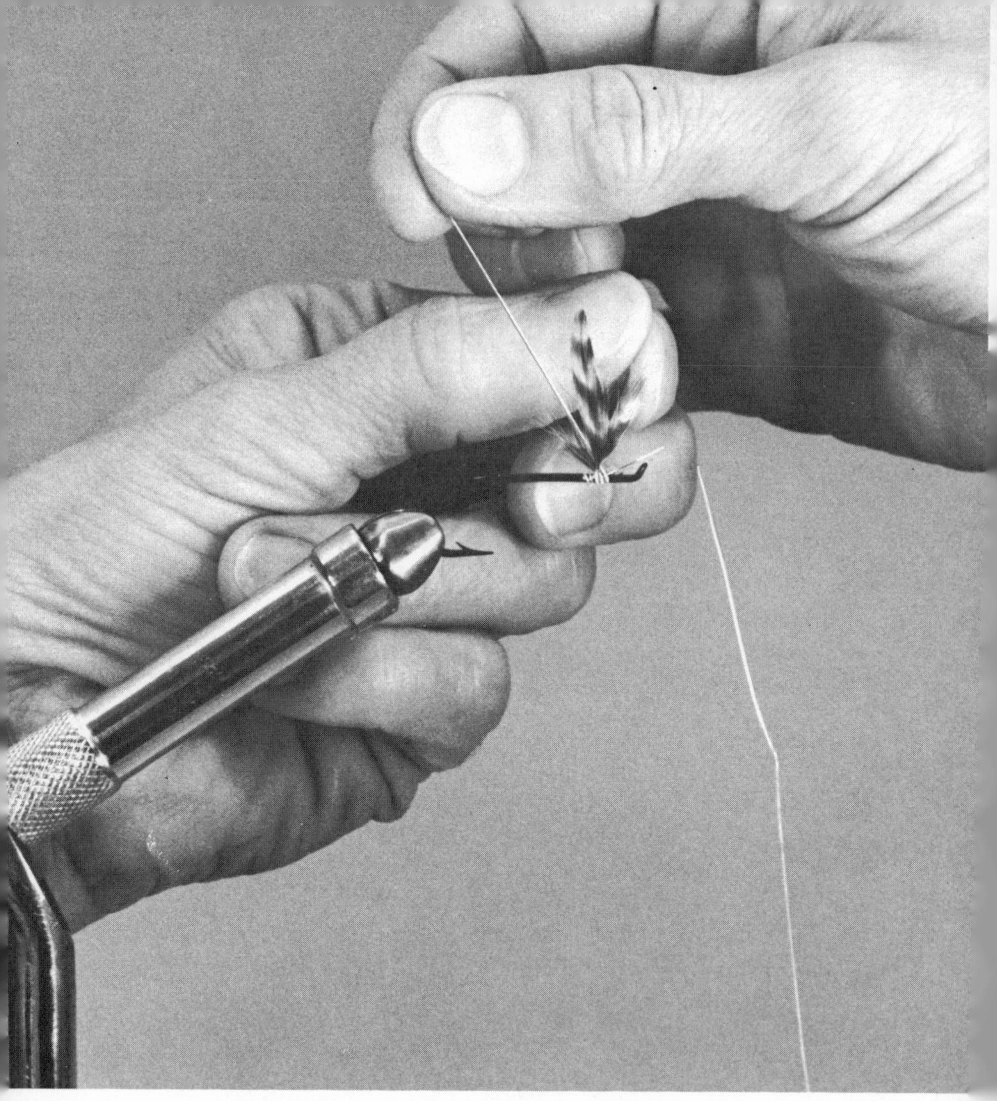

26e. Bring the thread up in front of the hook and carry it through between the hackle points, from right to left, and on down behind the hook. Bring it up in front of the hook, to the left of the wing base, and carry the thread through between the hackle points again, from left to right, continuing down on the far side of the hook.

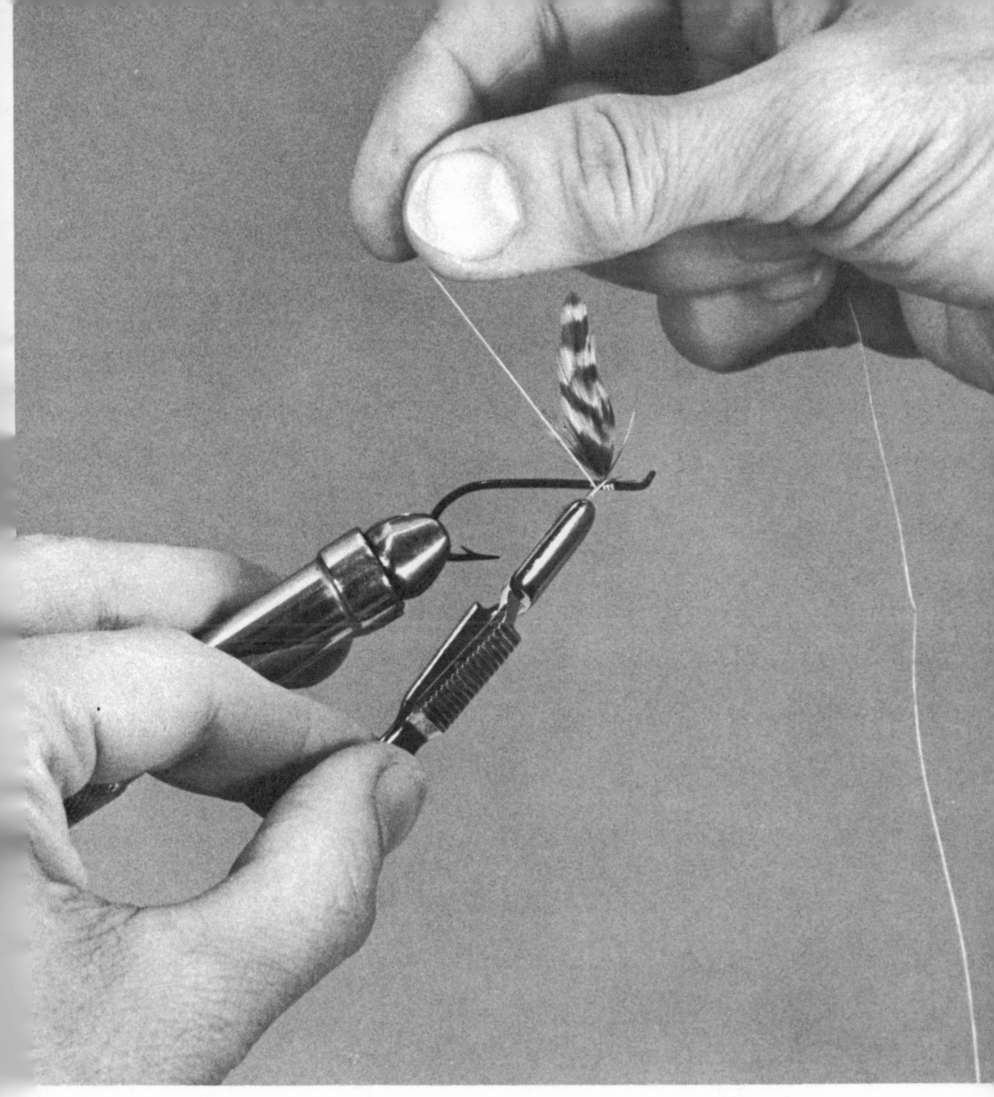

26f. Grip the quill end of the hackle nearest you with the pliers and lay it back along the side of the hook. Bring the thread up and across it, catching it to the hook. Before carrying the thread down on the far side of the hook, hold the remaining quill back in the same manner. Now carry the tying thread down behind the hook, catching the second quill to the hook on the way. One more turn of thread around the hook over the quills will be sufficient to secure them.

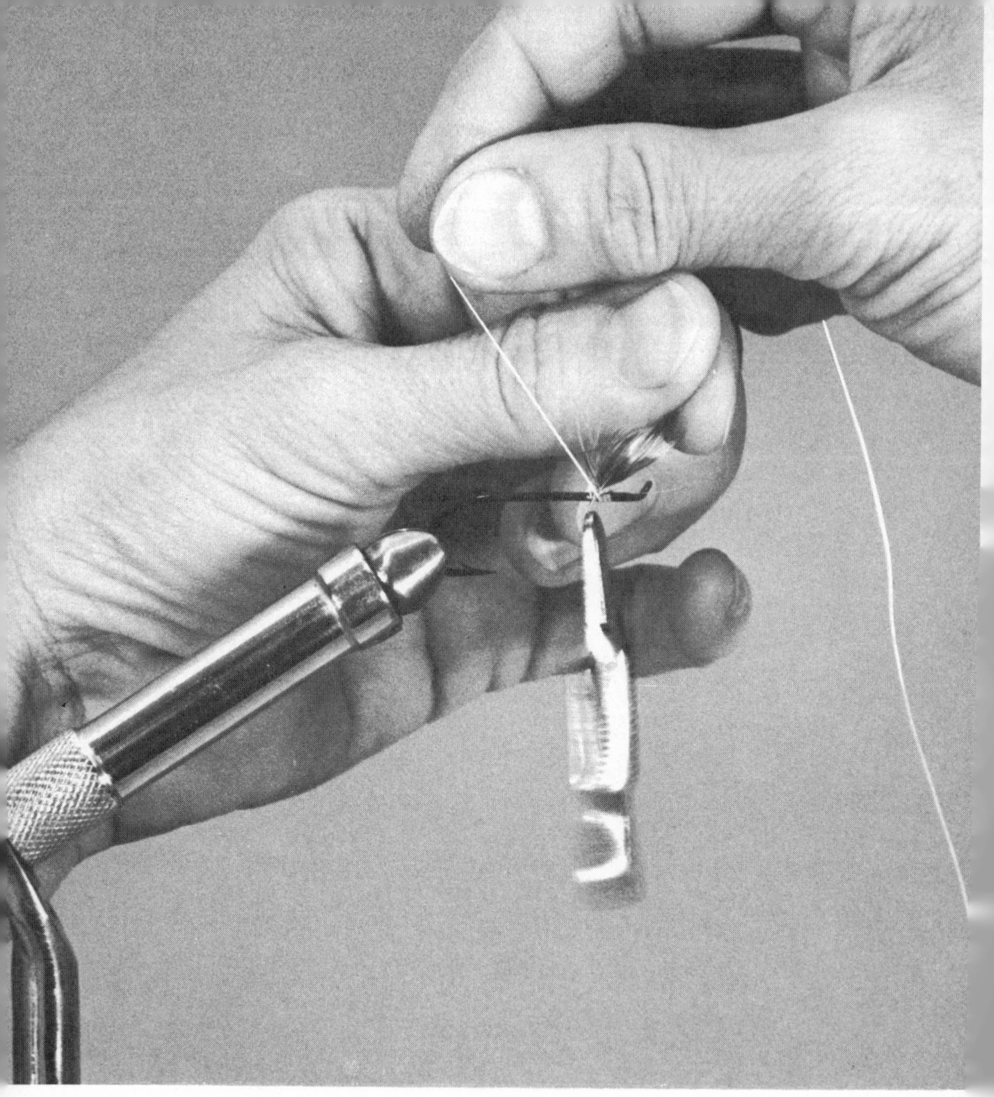

26g. A slight backward tilt of the upright wings can be overcome by holding them forward carefully and placing a turn of thread around the hook behind them, as close as possible to the base of the wing. Keep the thread taut. Bring it up in front of the hook, ahead of the wings, and spiral it forward.

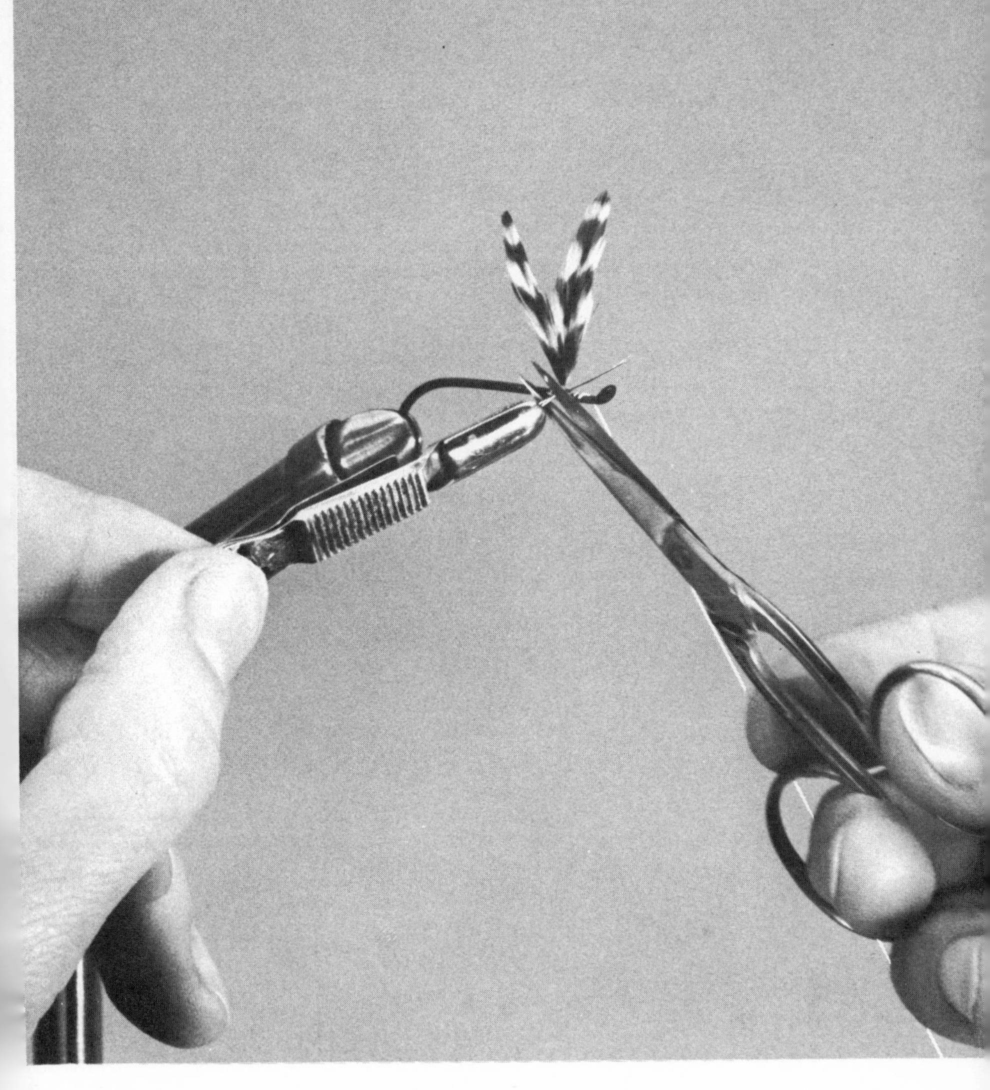

26h. Clip off the quill ends. The erect or upright wings are complete. Practice until you can manage the feathers easily.

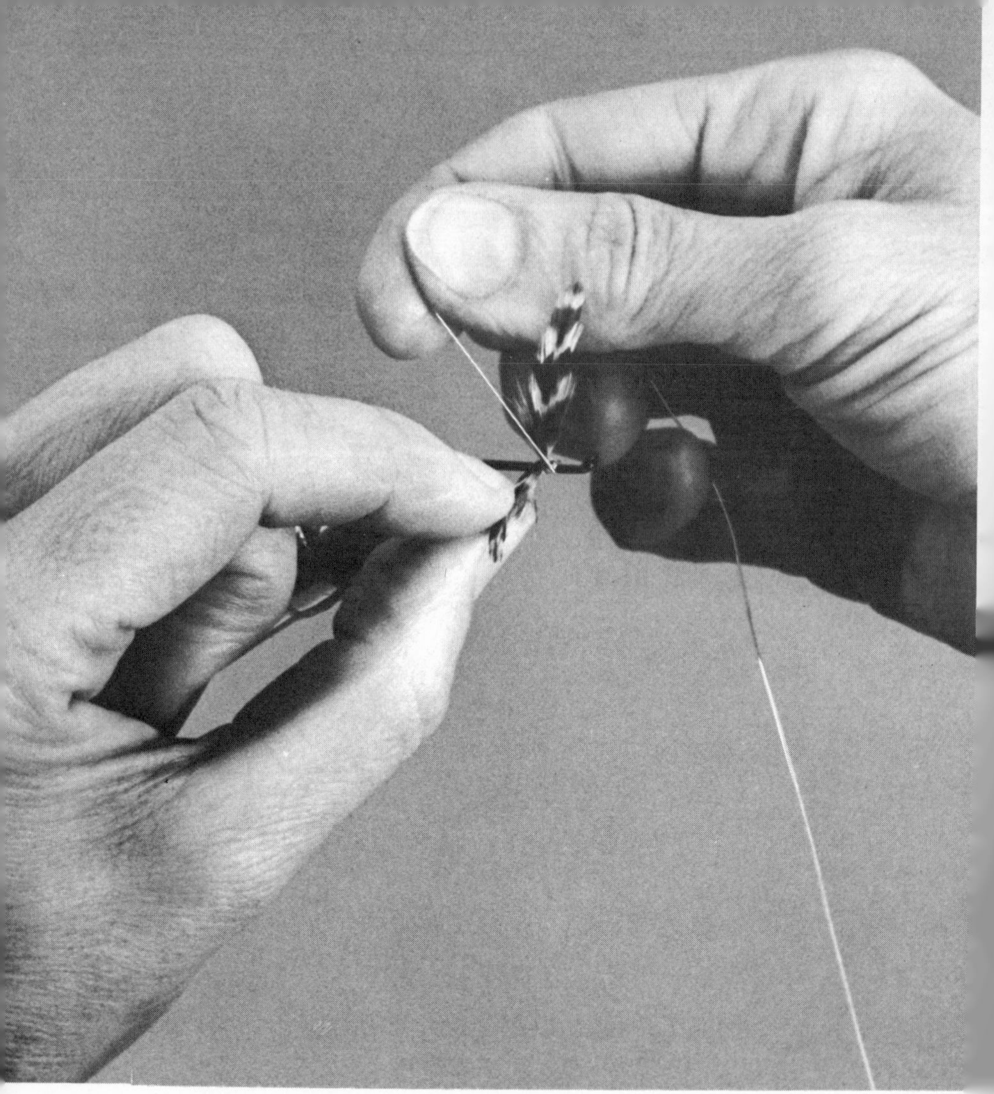

27a. Spent wings can be made from the upright wings by changing their position with the tying thread. Draw the tip of the nearest wing down toward you until the feather is flat, even with the hook, glossy side uppermost, the quill at a right angle to the hook. Carry the tying thread over its base from right to left, keeping the thread gently snug and on the near side of the hook. Release the feather momentarily to permit the hands to pass. Regrip it at once and hold it in place until its new position is maintained by the thread as you carry it under the hook and up on the far side, to the left of the erect wing. Draw the wing tip down and away.

27b. When its position mirrors the first, carry the thread over 's base from left to right and 'own on the far side, then beneath ıe hook and up toward you.

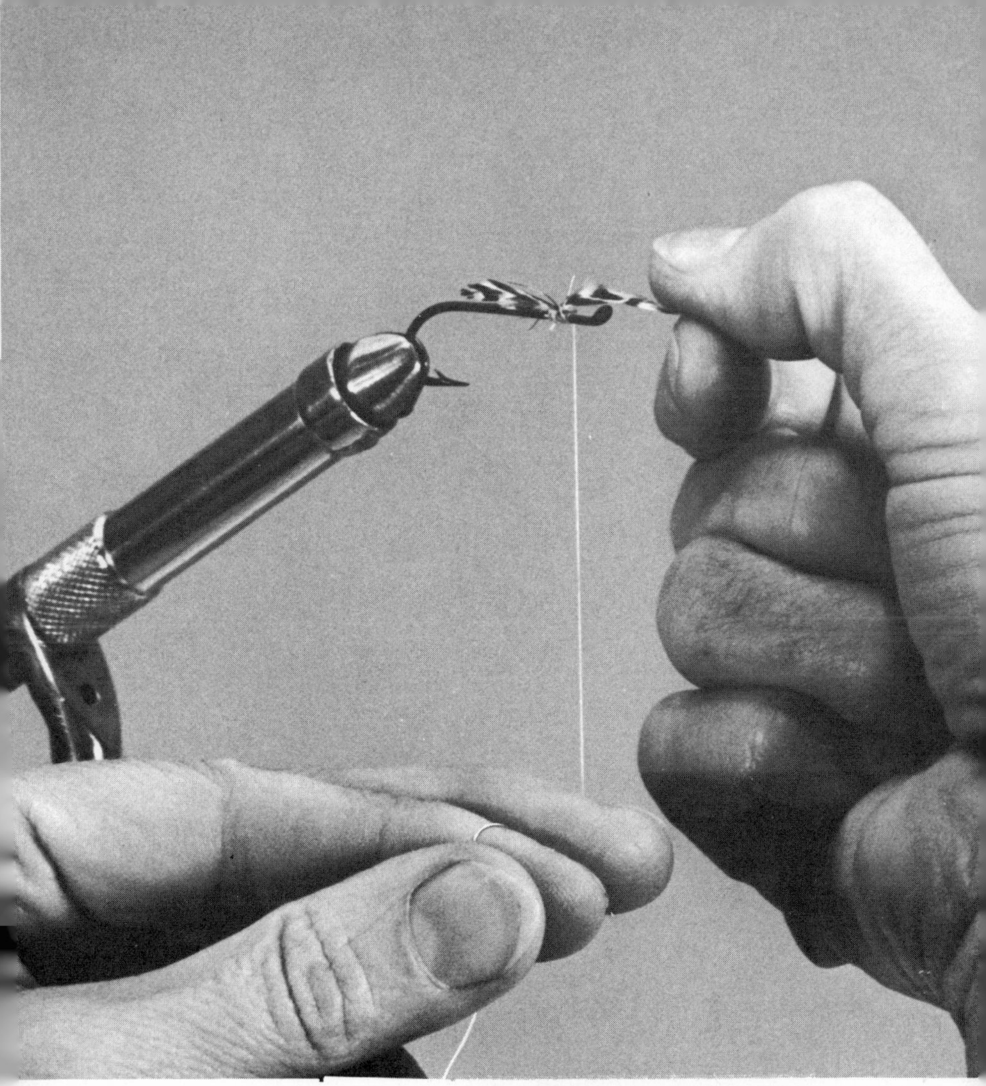

Practice this simple thread patɛrn, one of several that might be sed, until it becomes familiar. 'ind the thread once around the ɔok, close to the horizontal wings. nchor them firmly by crossing the read diagonally between them as r the upright wings.

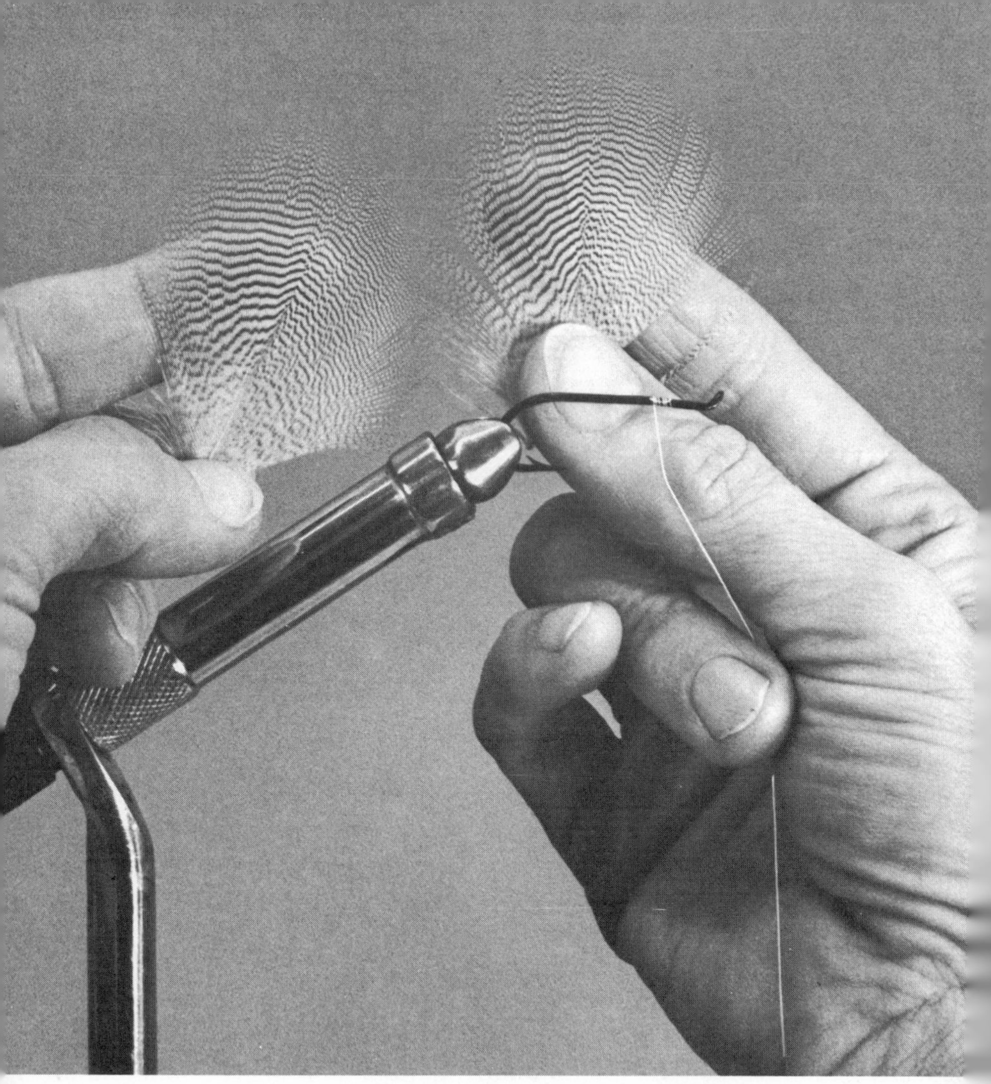

28a. The delicately marked side feathers of teal, mallard, wood, and Mandarin ducks, carefully matched for color and barring, are used for bunched wings and wisp tails, especially on dry flies where the natural buoyancy of the feather aids in keeping the fly afloat. The divided wings may be erect or tilted forward ahead of the hackle on dry flies, or a single one may be made like the single hair wing. One half of the outer surface of a single feather usually has a bolder marking than the other, and matched sections from separate feathers are preferable to an entire feather on a single fly where the difference in barring may be noticeable.

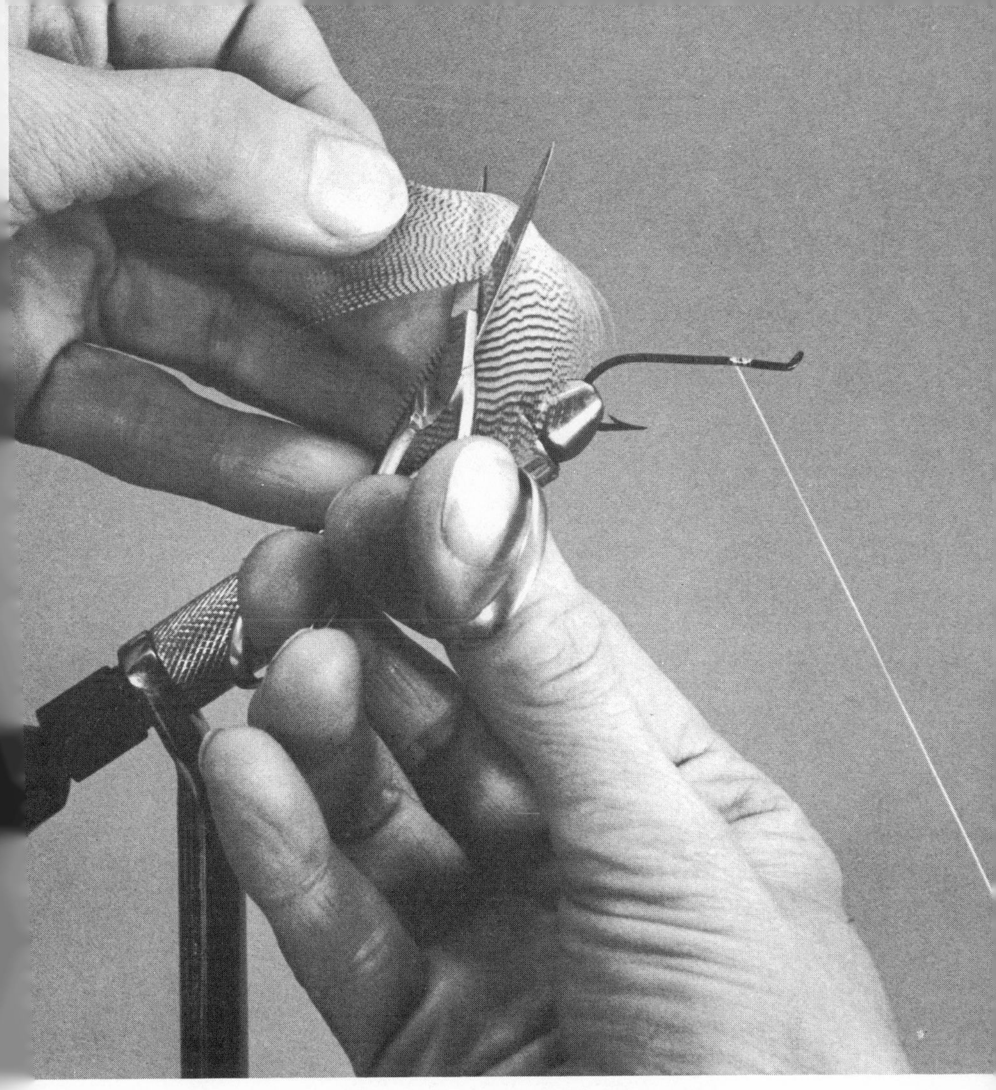

28b. Cut matching sections from two separate feathers. The number of flues depends on the size of hook and the feather being used. Keep the proportion of wing to hook slim rather than heavy.

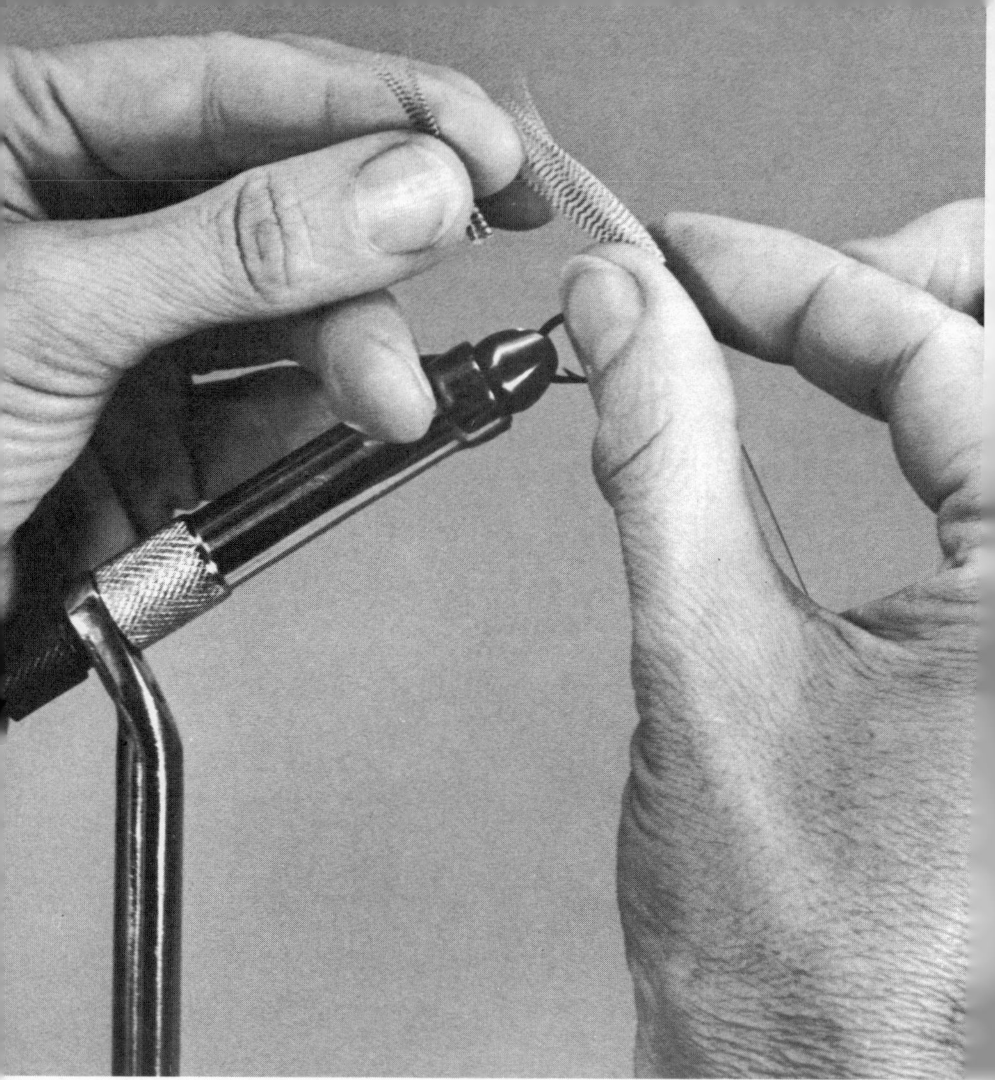

28c. Carefully roll the sections until the barbs (flues) are neatly bunched, their tips even.

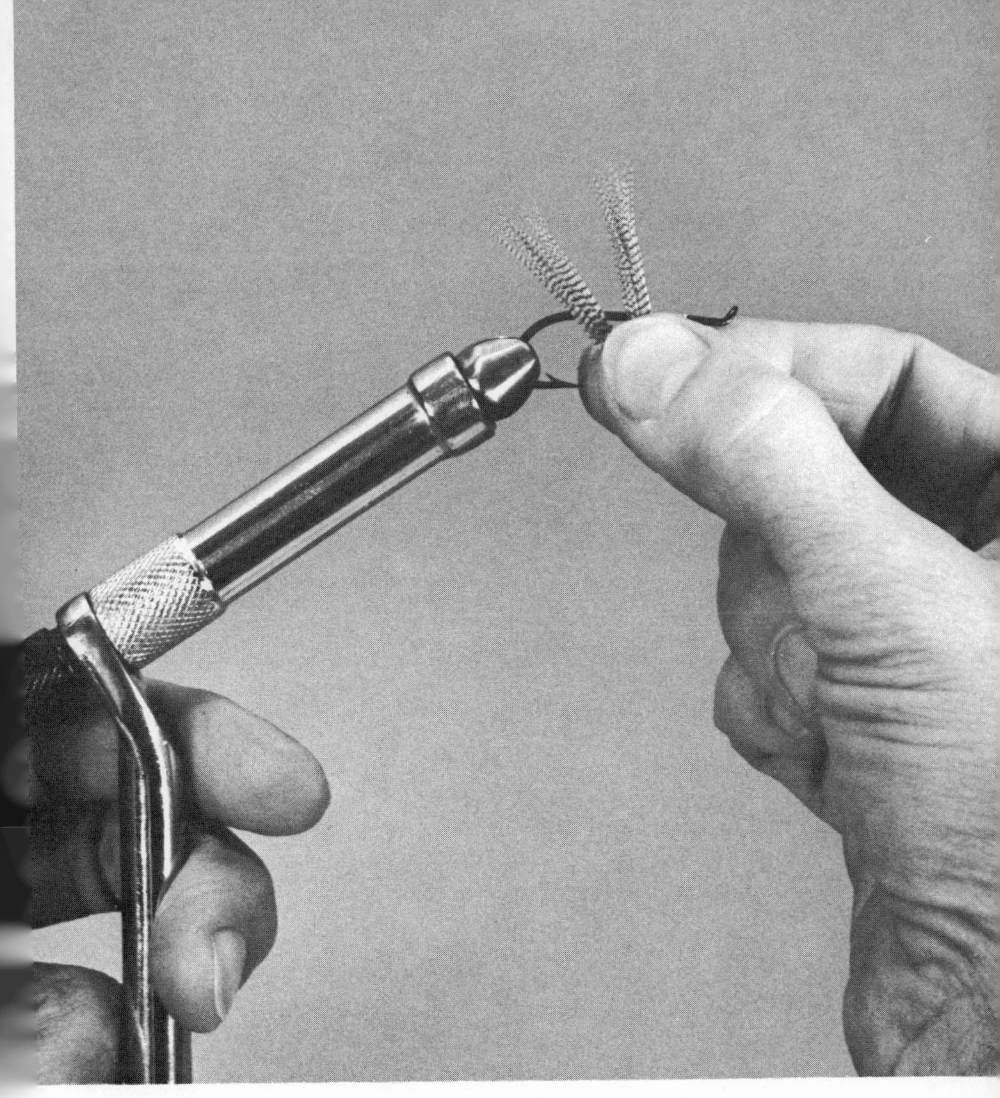

28d. Measure the bunched barbs for length against the hook.

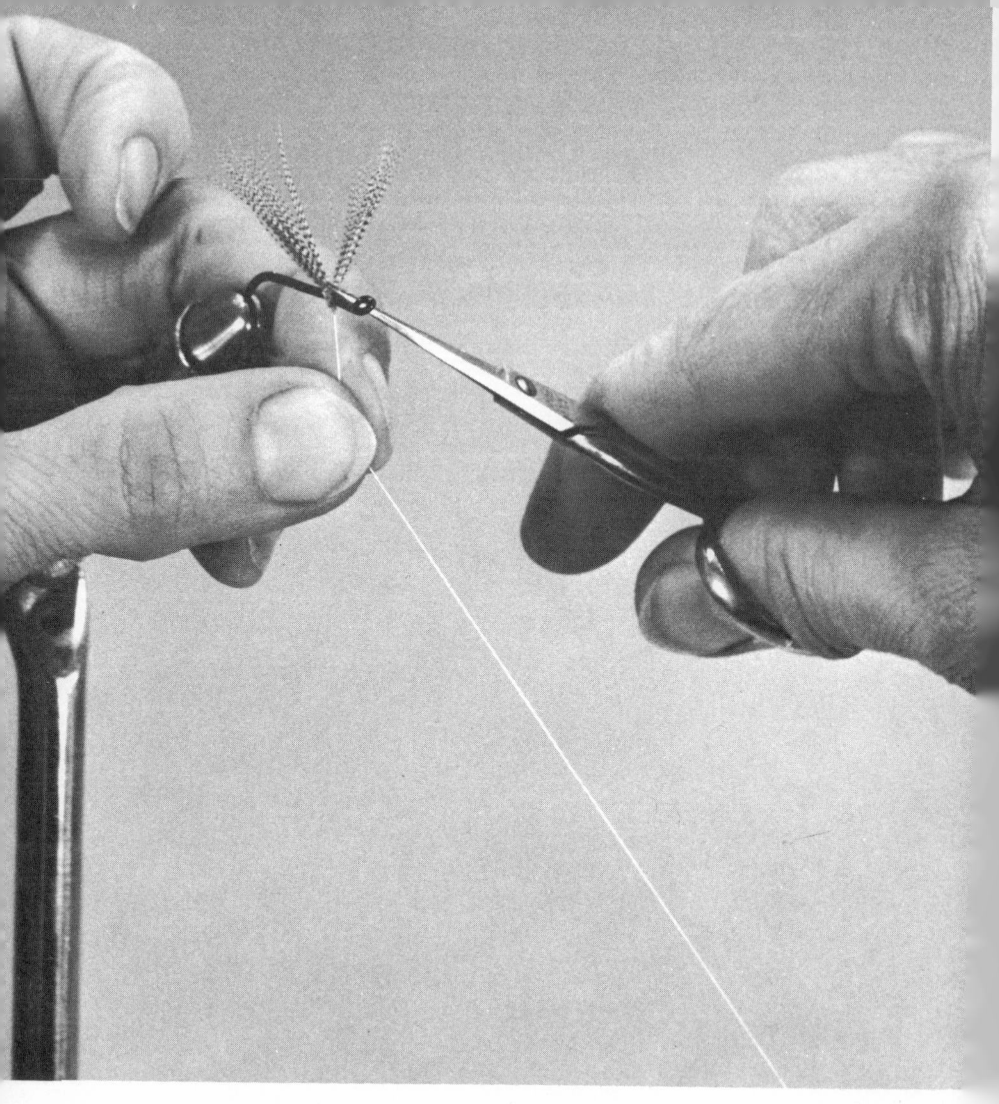

28e. Hold both bunches together, tips even, in the left hand at "wing position." Bring the thread up and through the fingers as you have learned to do and bind the bunched flues side by side to the top of the hook. Divide the wing with the tying thread as you did for the divided hair wing. Clip out any stray barbs to make the two wings even.

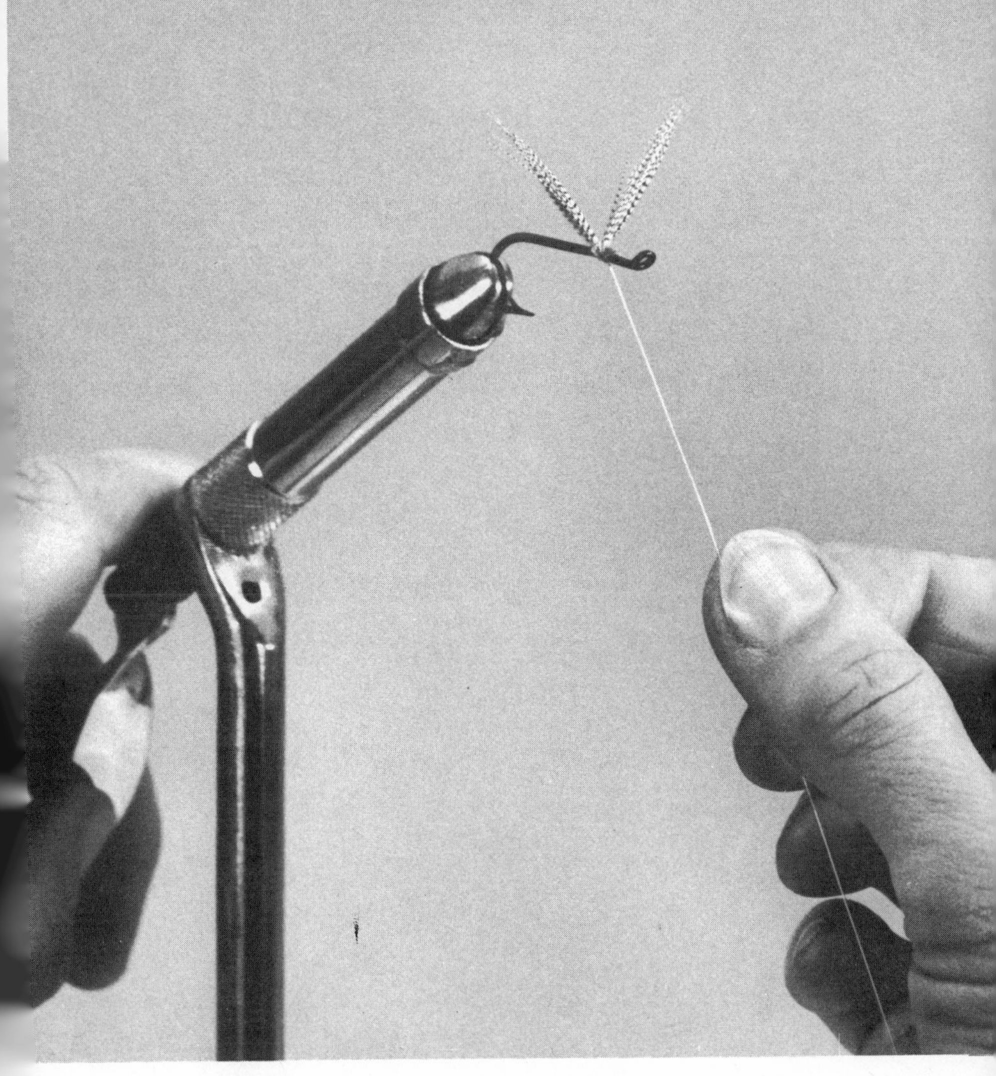

28f. Trim the excess feather ends away close to the hook, at an angle to taper them and create less bulk. In order to tilt this wing forward, hold the *cut ends* in the left hand, with the natural tips extending forward over the hook eye and tie on at "wing position" in the usual way.

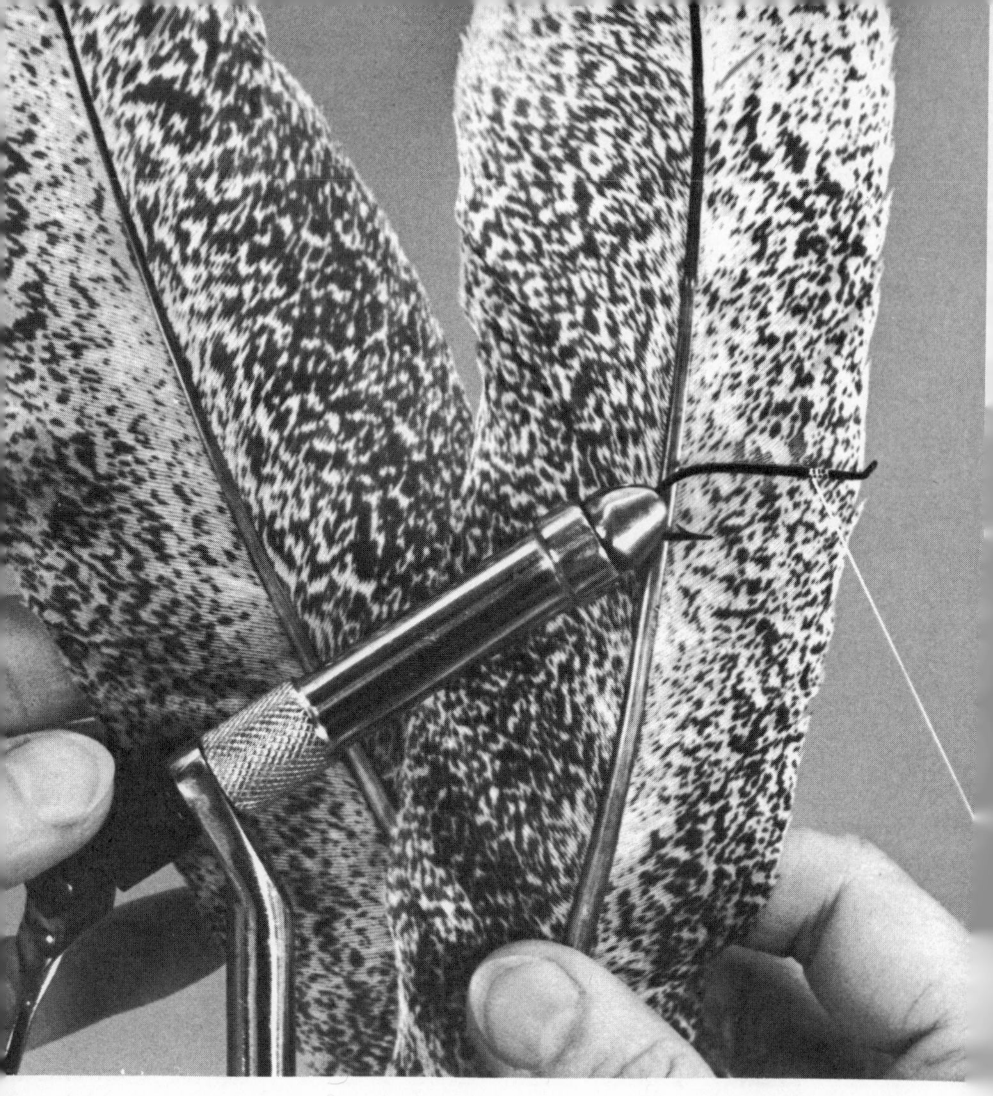

29a. These are turkey wing feathers, matched for length, width, and marking. As the quills are held here, only the material on the outside half of each will be used. The material along the other side is duller, the pattern not quite as distinct and of thinner texture. Along the outer edges, the barbs cling strongly together to their very tips.

29b. Cut a strip from the outer edge of each feather, of a width suitable for the size of hook being used, approximately the width of the hook gape. The natural curve of the barbs sweeps upward tc a point at the tip.

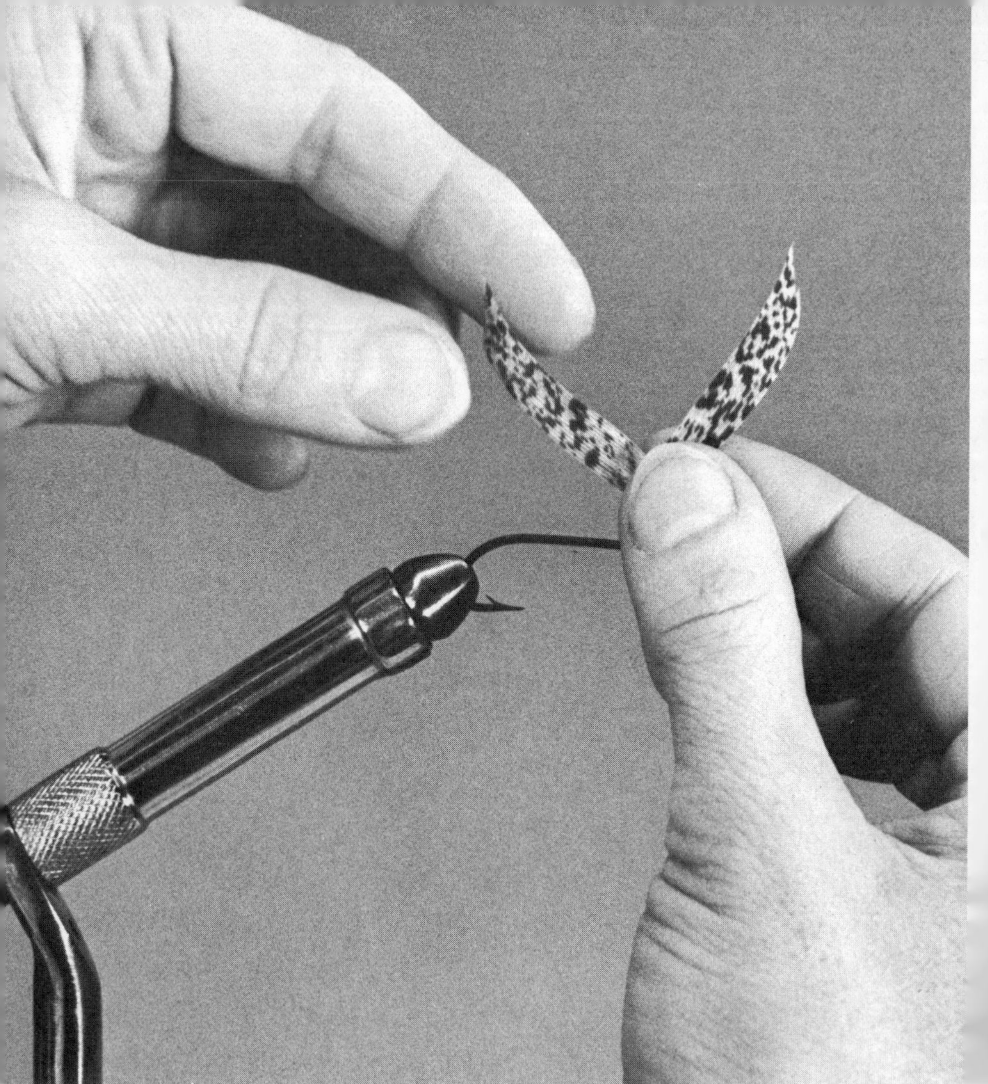

29c. When the strips are cut, keep them in the same relative position as they were on the feathers. The left one will become the wing nearest you on the hook.

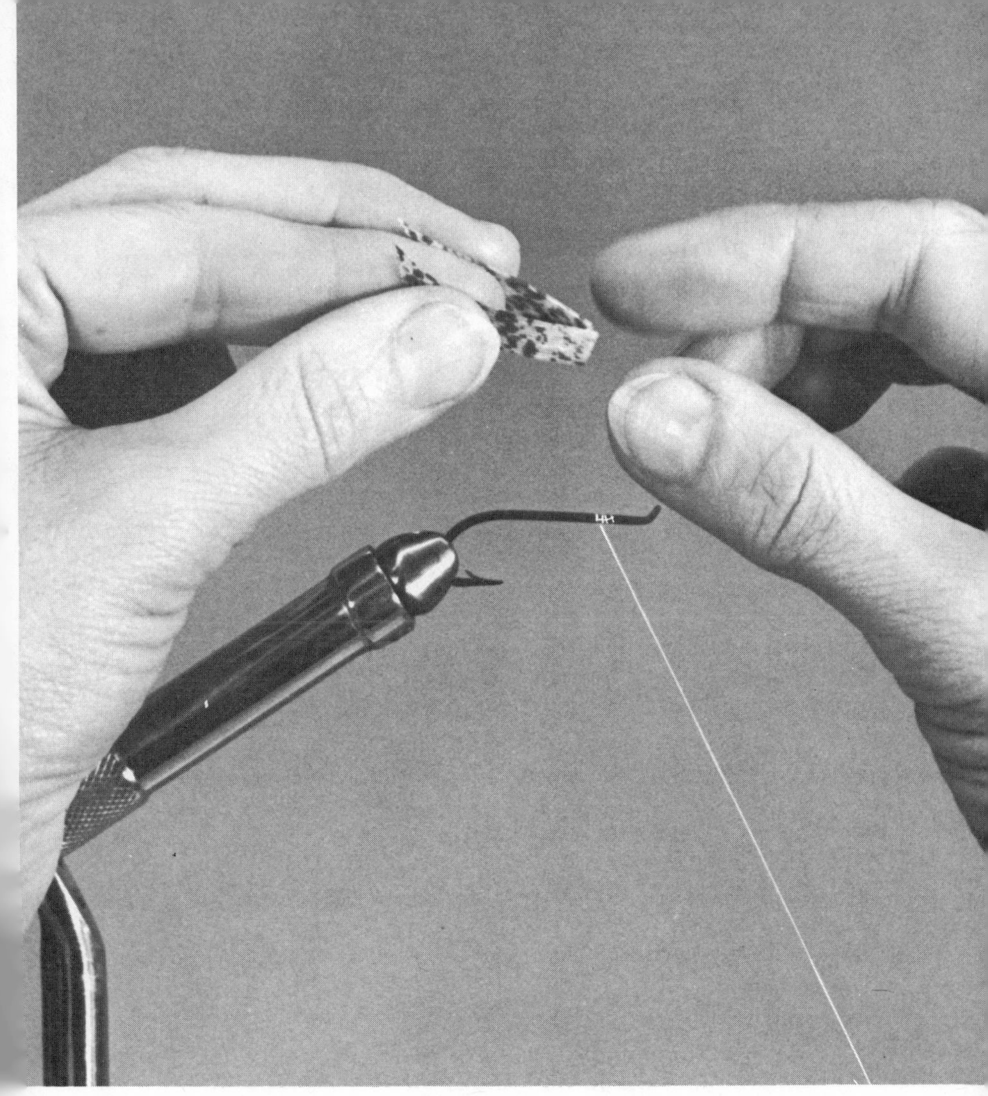

29d. Place the inside of its tip against the index finger and hold it there with the thumb. Place the inside of the other tip against the fingernail of the index finger, holding it there with the middle finger. Make sure the natural tips of the strips are even, with the pointed tips up. By holding them in this way, you can always be sure that you have matched them properly and that they will tie on correctly.

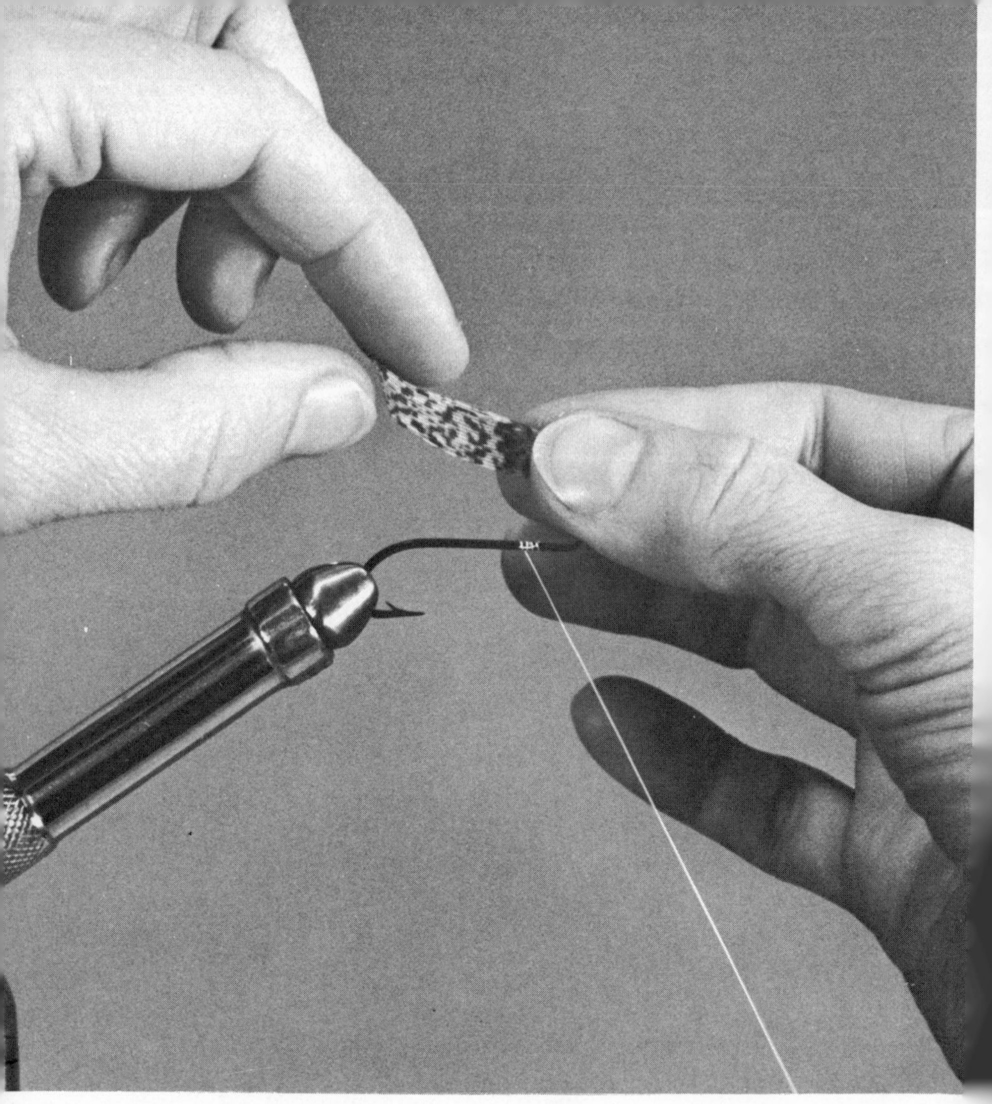

29e. Grip them together with the right hand and measure them against the hook for length. The curve of the feathers at the lower edge is even with the end of the hook; the upper tip extends a bit beyond. Take the strips again with the left hand, fingertips touching the right ones, to keep the proper length of wing.

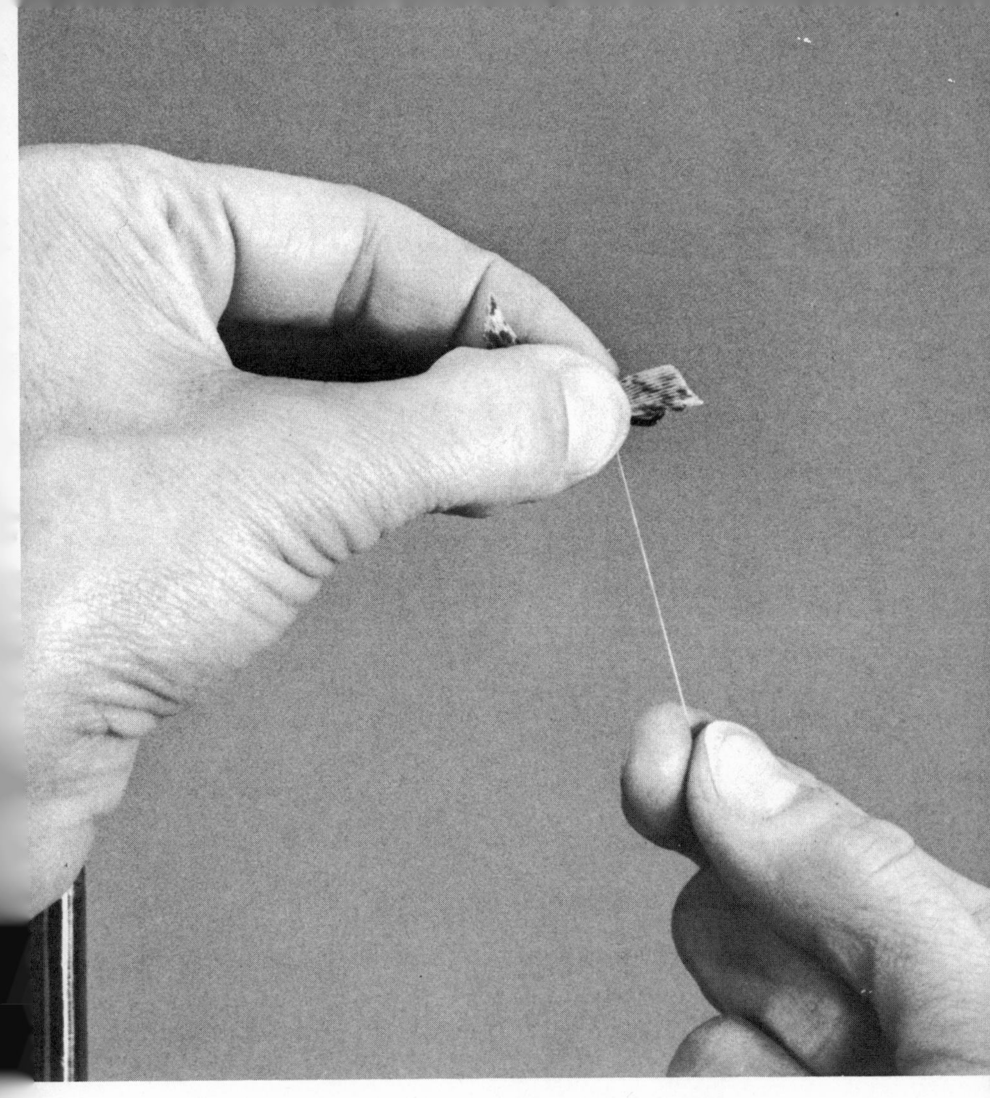

29f. Hold them along the top of the hook, at "wing position." Bring the tying thread up between thumb and feathers, down between feathers and finger, and on down on the far side of the hook. Pull the thread gently downward between the fingers until it is snug. Do this twice more before releasing the feathers. Remember that each flue is like a flat quill, stacked on the one below it. Each one has to be crushed down on the one below it by the tying thread. By holding the flues (barbs) firmly between your fingers, the thread will be guided to pull them down evenly onto the hook.

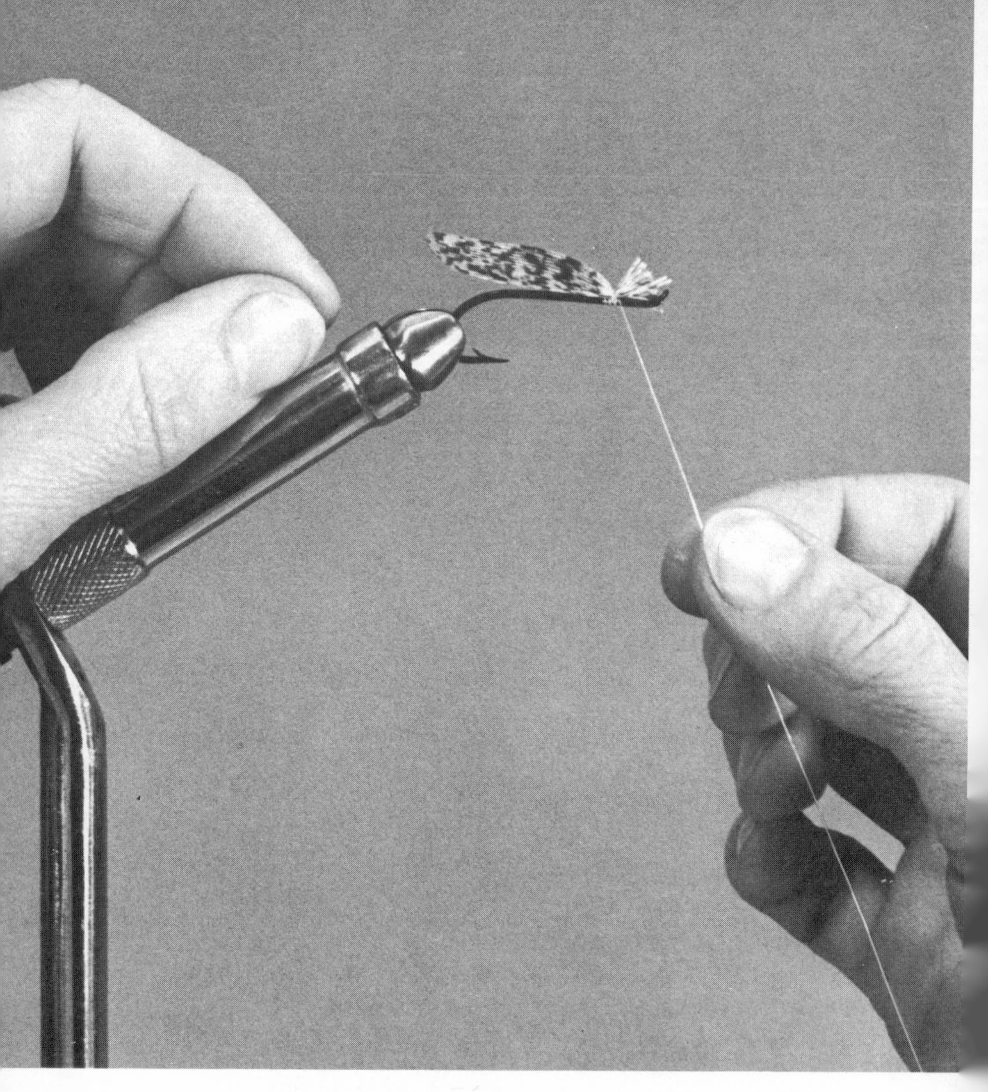

29g. By keeping the tying thread taut at all times, the wings will be securely anchored on top of the hook and in line with it.

29h. The upward sweep of the wing can be adjusted with a stroke of the fingers. It can be left with a slight upward tilt or can be coaxed down in line with the top of the wing.

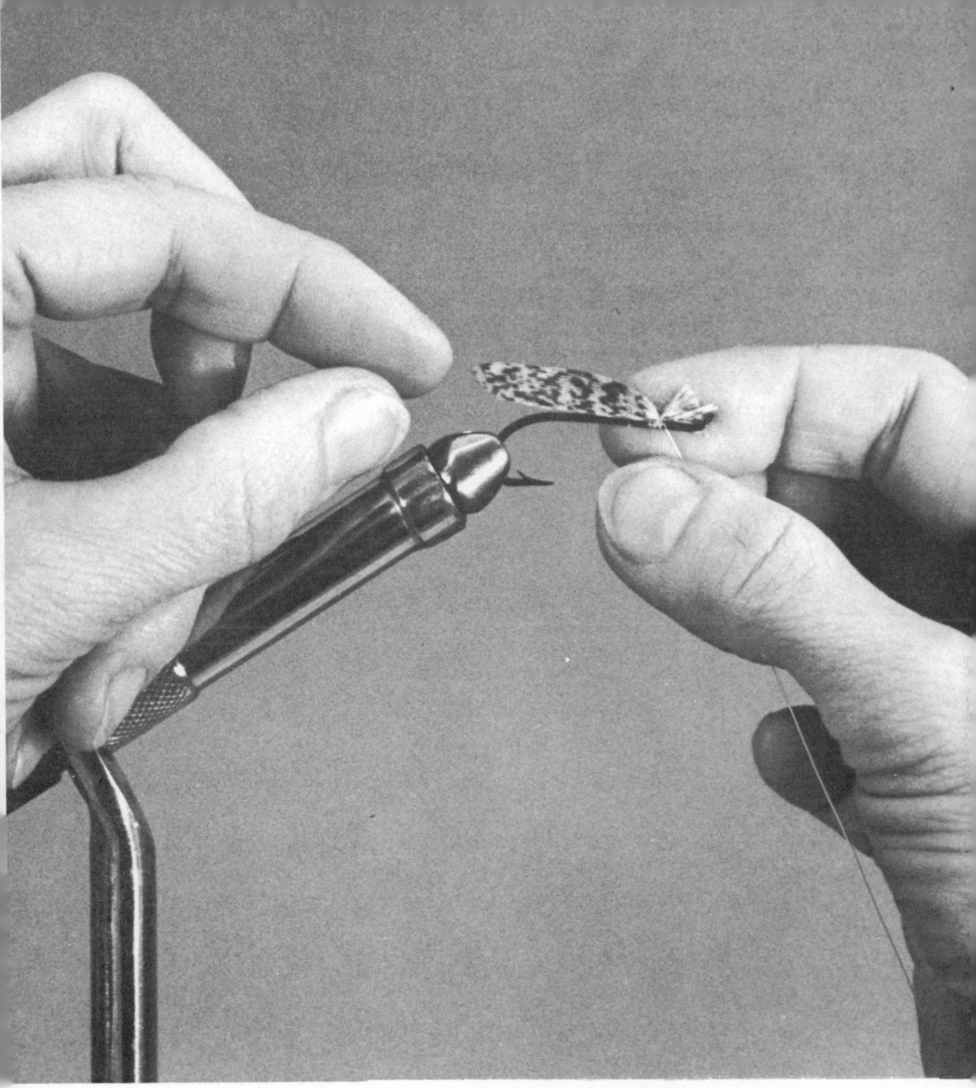

Clip off the excess material at an angle to taper it and bind it flat to the hook with a turn or two of tying thread. Practice until you can keep the feather strips flat between the fingers while the tying thread tightens over them. Use a barb or two less in each strip if the wings have a tendency to buckle under the tying thread. Make sure the tying thread is taut at all times.

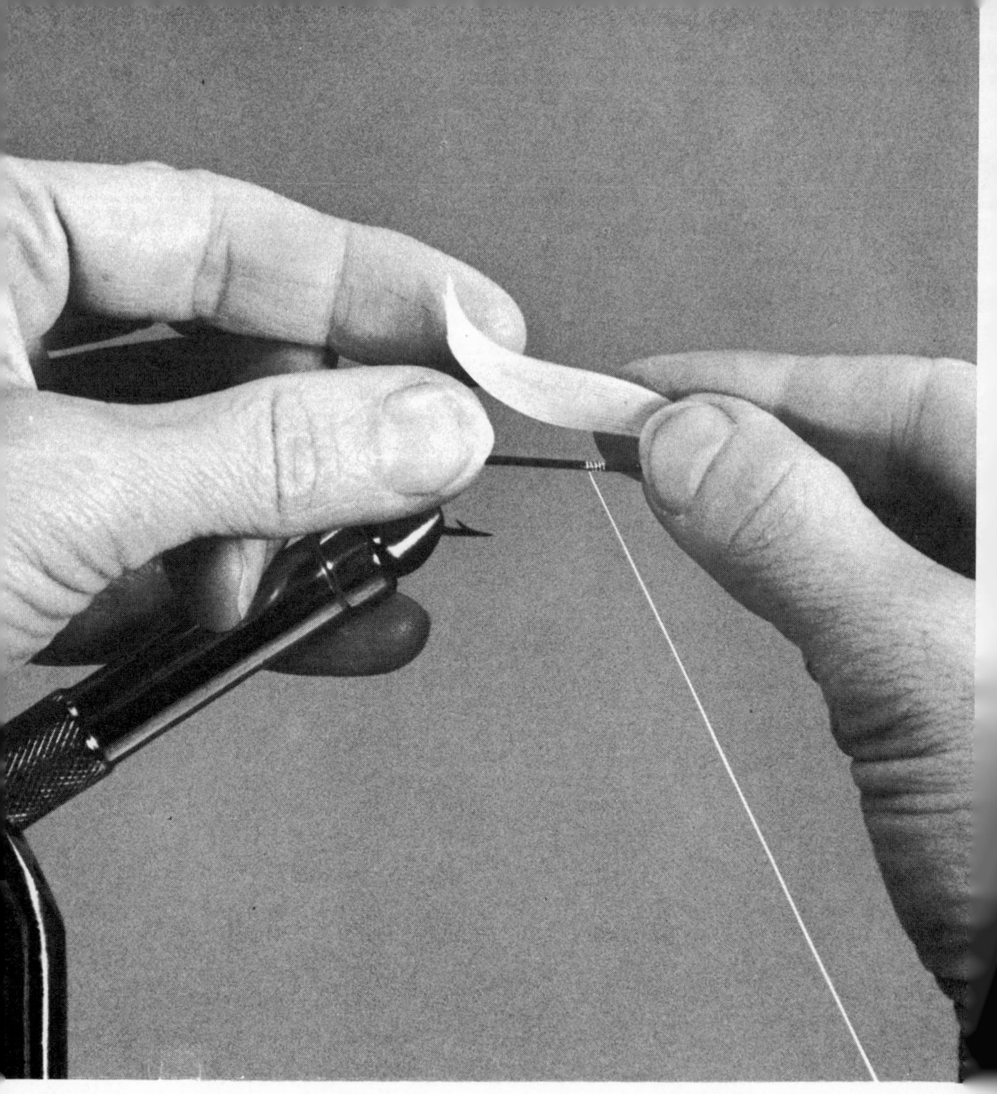

30a. Hold a pair of white- or grey-goose broad quills or "pointers" as you did the turkey feathers. Only the outer material is used here also. Cut matching strips from the outer edge of each feather. As you hold the strip cut from the feather on the left, notice that its naural edge, sweeping up to a point, also curves slightly toward you. This strip will be for the far wing—the strip from the right feather will be the wing nearest you. The curves of the paired wings will be inward.

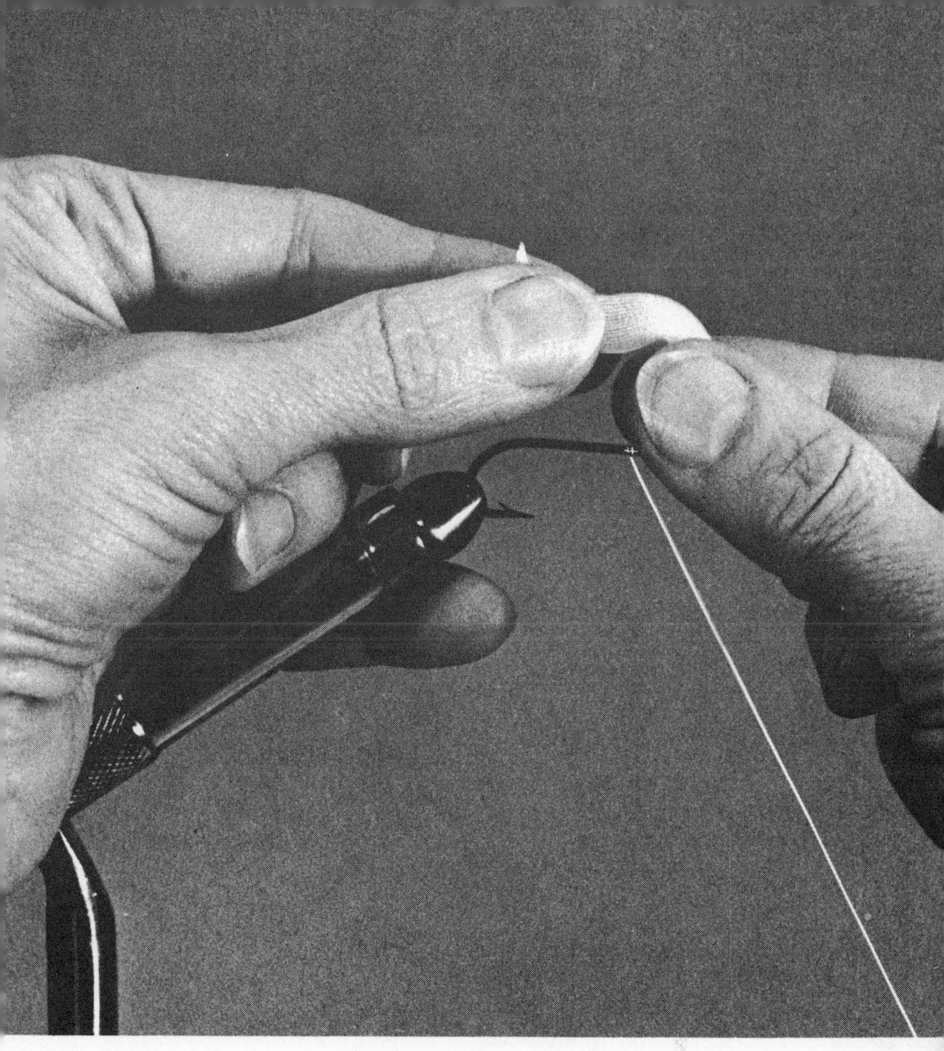

30b. For upright and divided wings on a fly, the ends of the feather strip must be made even so that the finished wings will have rounded tips rather than pointed ones. Hold the tips of the "left" strip between the fingers of the left hand and with the right hand grasp the cut base. Turn the fingers of the right hand upward (or clockwise), gently pulling the barbs of the feather strip through the fingers of the left hand.

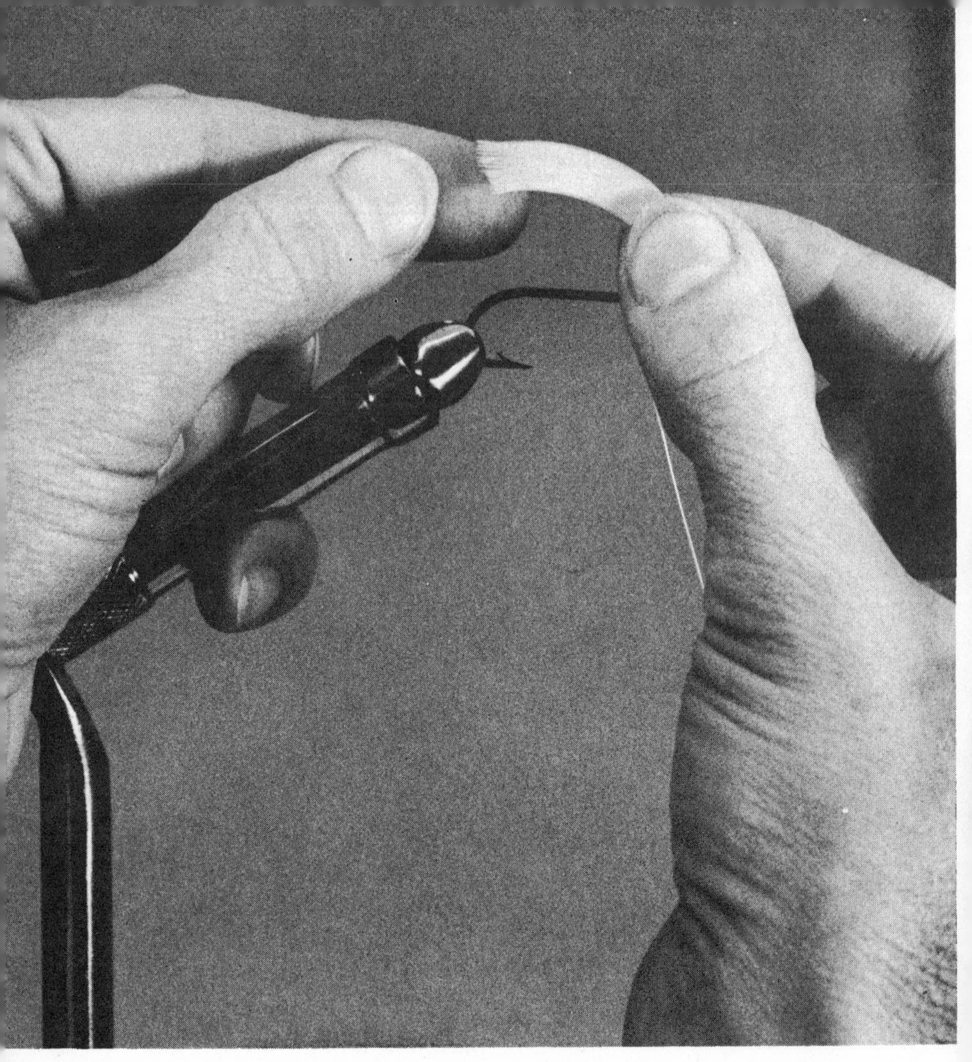

30c. The result will be to pull the tips down out of their natural upward curve. This will be the wing on the far side of the hook. Turn it clockwise until its upper edge becomes the lower one. Lay it carefully aside until you have prepared a matching strip from the "right" feather. Hold the strip as it was cut from the feather and even its end in the same way. Rotate it clockwise also, and this will be your "near" wing.

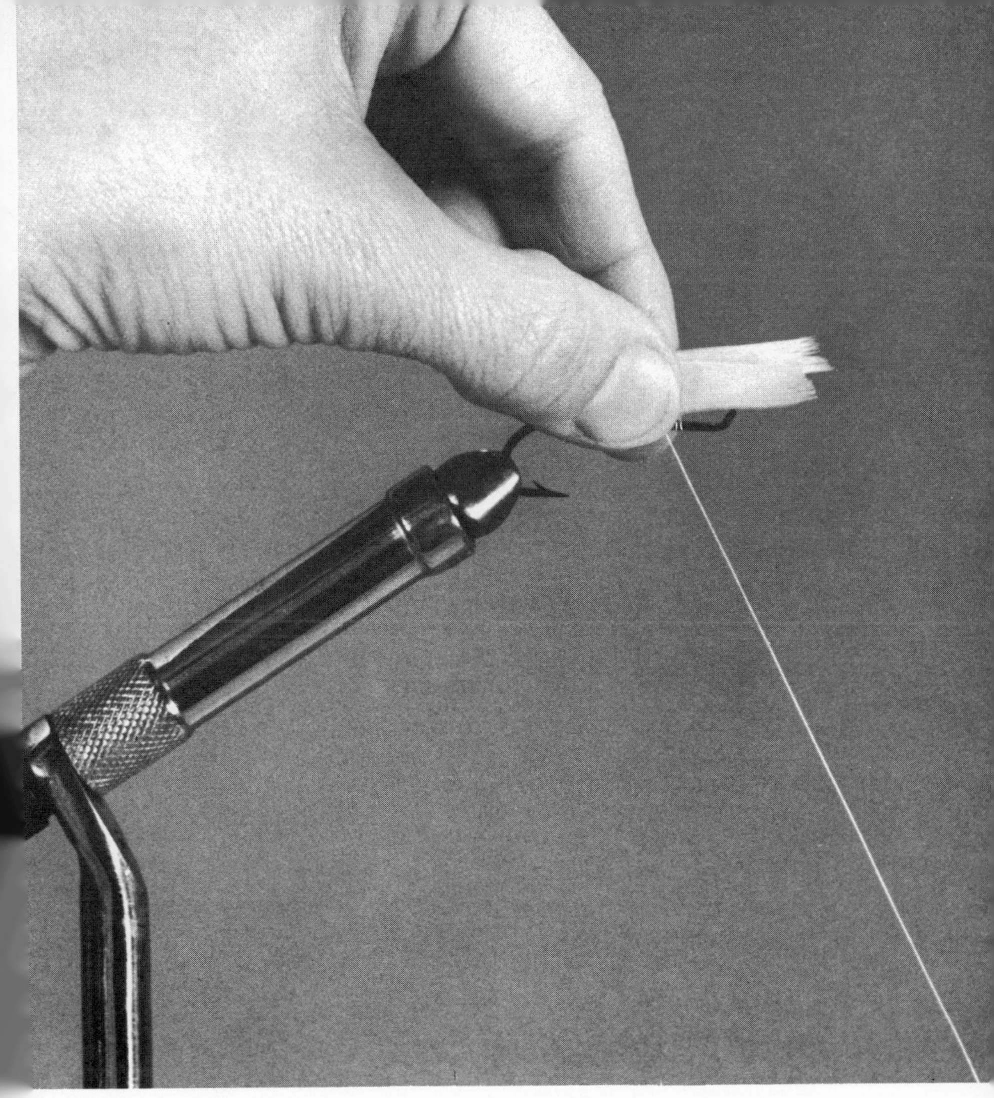

30d. Place the two together now, in their proper relationship to you. Measure them for length against the hook, approximately the length of the hook shank, and hold them against the top of the hook at "wing position" letting the natural ends extend out over the hook eye.

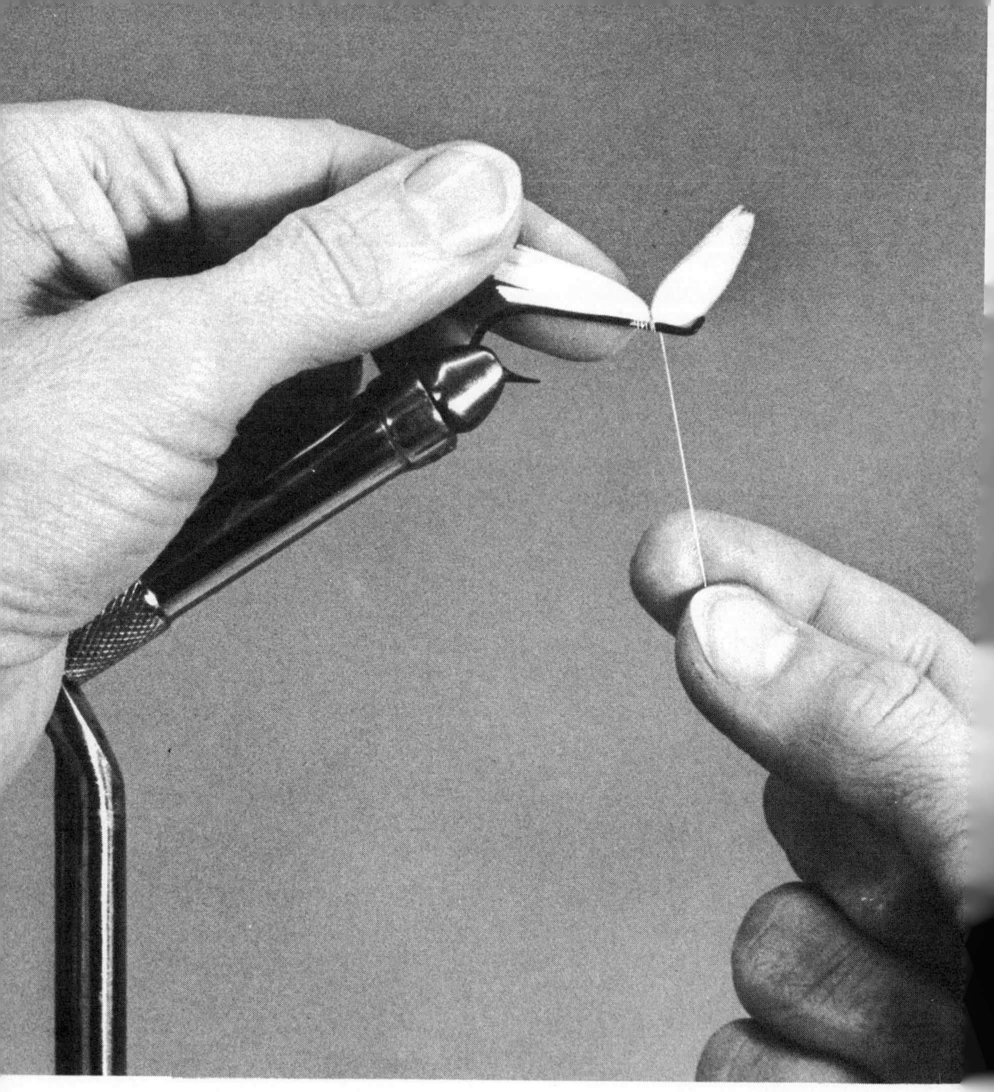

30e. Fasten the strips to the hook as you did with the turkey-feather wing. If you have mastered the turkey feather, this will be easy, for the principal is the same—the flat barbs will be crushed together evenly by the tying thread, compressing them neatly against the top of the hook.

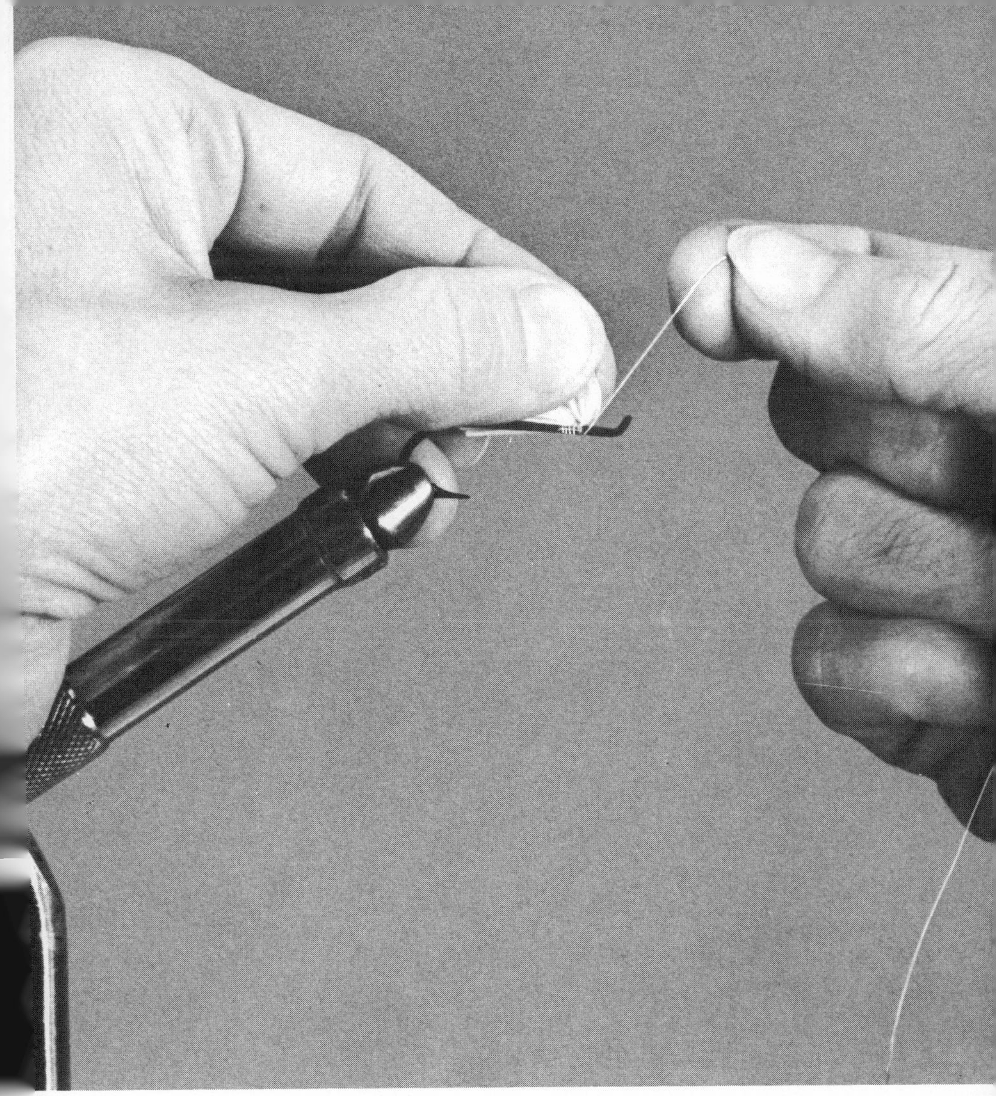

30f. Grip the pair of wings gently but firmly, hold them backward, and wind the tying thread around the hook as close to the base of the wings as possible.

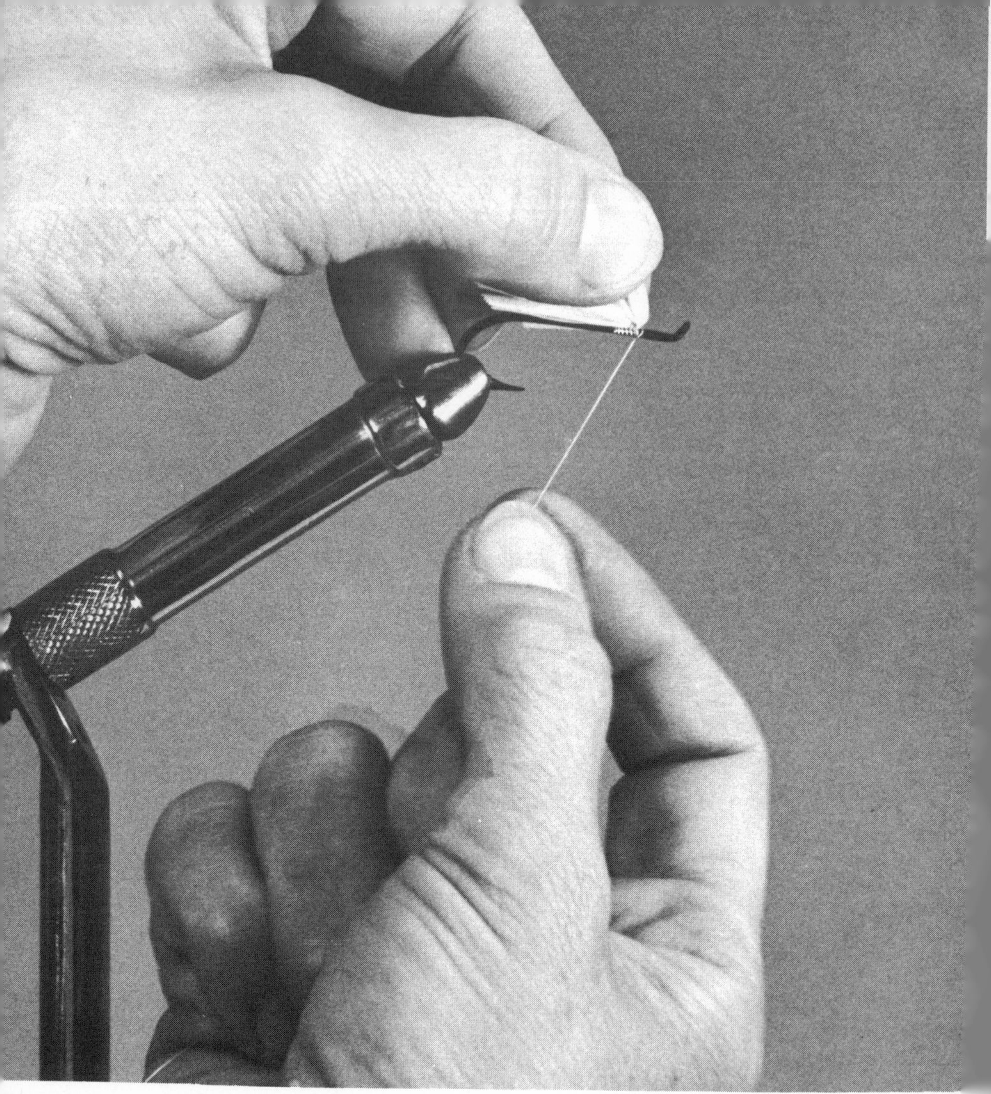

30g. Wind two more turns of thread immediately in front of the wings as you hold them out of the way. Bring the thread up in front of the hook, to the left of the wing base. Carefully separate the wing tips, slipping the thread between them from *left to right.* Carry the thread down the far side of the hook, ahead of the wings. Bring it up in front of the hook and again slip it between the wings, from *right to left,* carrying it down the far side of the hook. Place one more turn of thread as close as possible behind the wings and secure it to the button.

30h. Clip off excess wing material at an angle and bind it down with two or three turns of thread. Secure the thread to the ıtton. Gently stroke the wing tips ıckward to round them nicely.

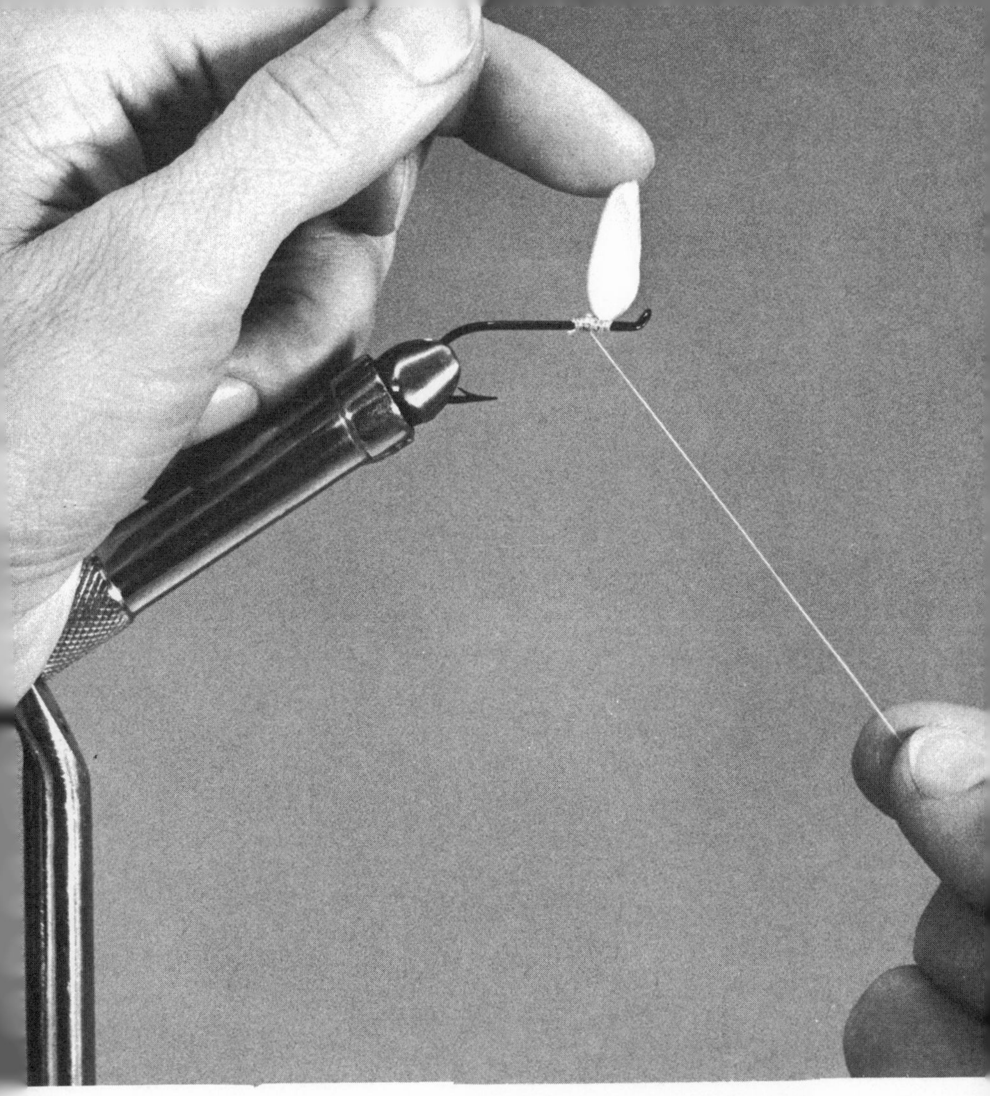

White on white makes the pair wings appear as one, their apes being almost identical. actice until you can tie this type sily. It may be tied on either be-re or after making a body. Be-re, the base will be covered by body material; after, by a ckle. Two strips may be used in ch wing for a sturdier pair.

31a. Tips of maribou feathers are used whole for the wings of streamer flies. Match them for length of flue and for over-all size. Clip away the lower part of the feathers and reserve them for use later whenever strands of maribou are needed.

31b. Make sure the curve of the center shaft of each feather is downward when they are held "back to back" against the hook. If the curve of one is down and one is up, the resulting fly will spin and twist your leader. Hold the center shafts parallel to the top of the hook and bind the feathers there with three turns of tying thread. Make sure the feathers remain on top of the hook. Clip off the extending quills close to the thread.

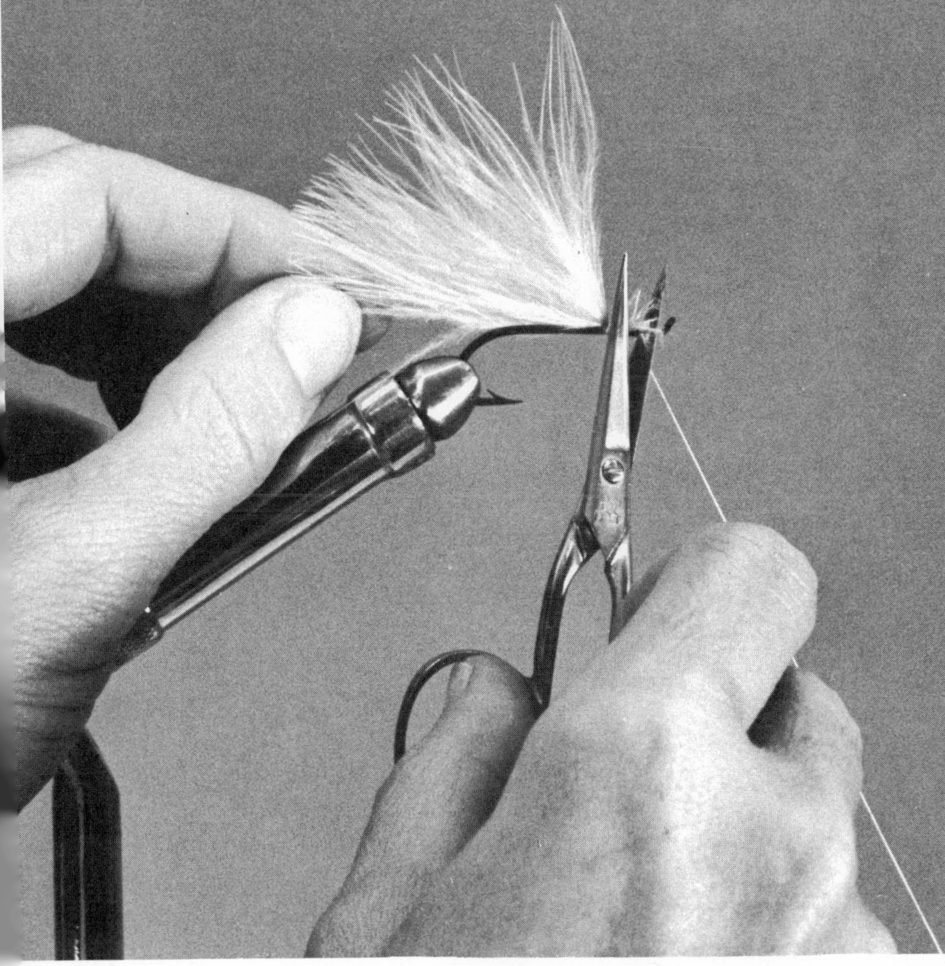

Maribou may extend approxi-
ıately the length of the hook be-
ond the bend of the hook, be-
ıuse when it is wet it becomes so
im at the tip end that it imparts
ıly motion to the wet fly and does
ɔt seem to cause fish to "strike
ıort," which can happen with too
ng a wing.

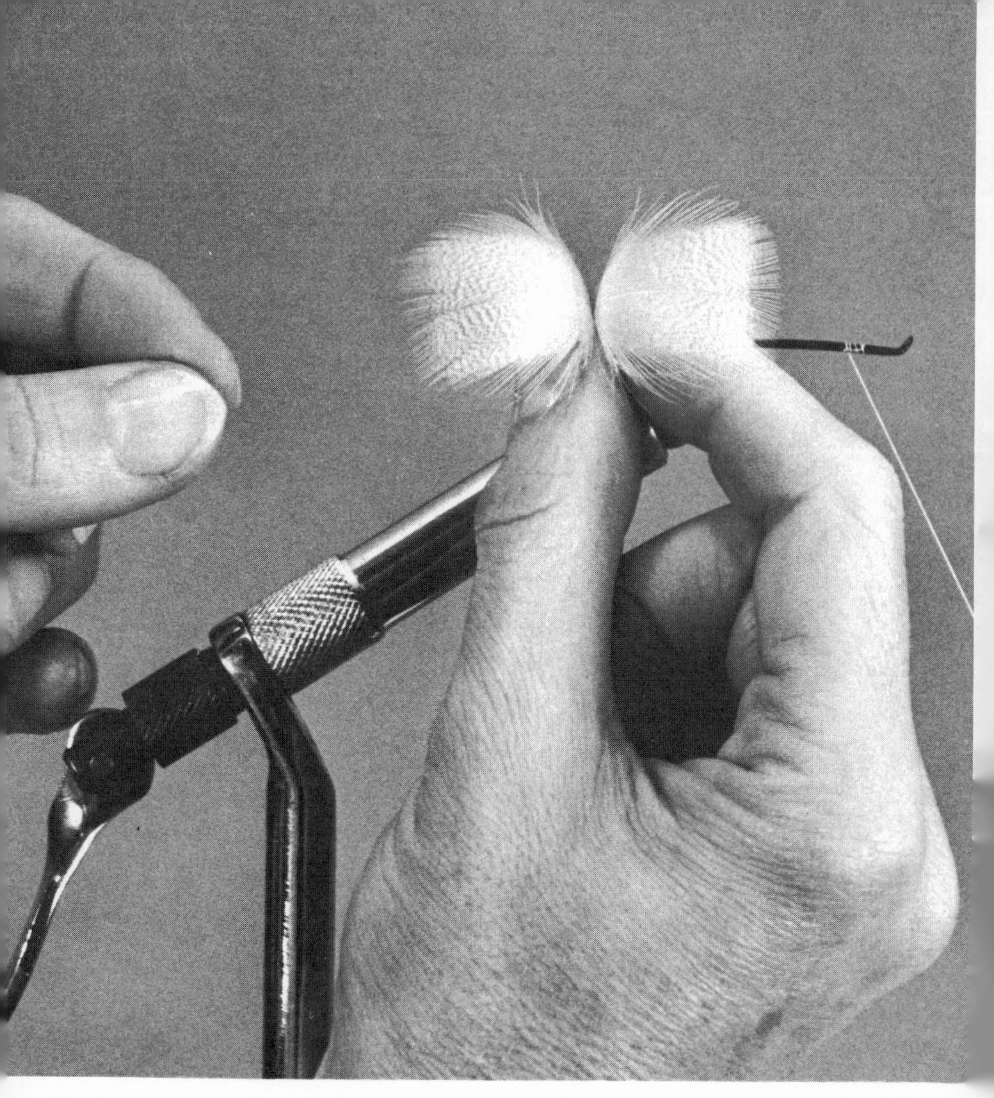

32a. Breast feathers of various ducks may be used for fan wings. The feathers, not much longer than their width, with a naturally curved stem, are perfect for this purpose. Select two that match in size and marking.

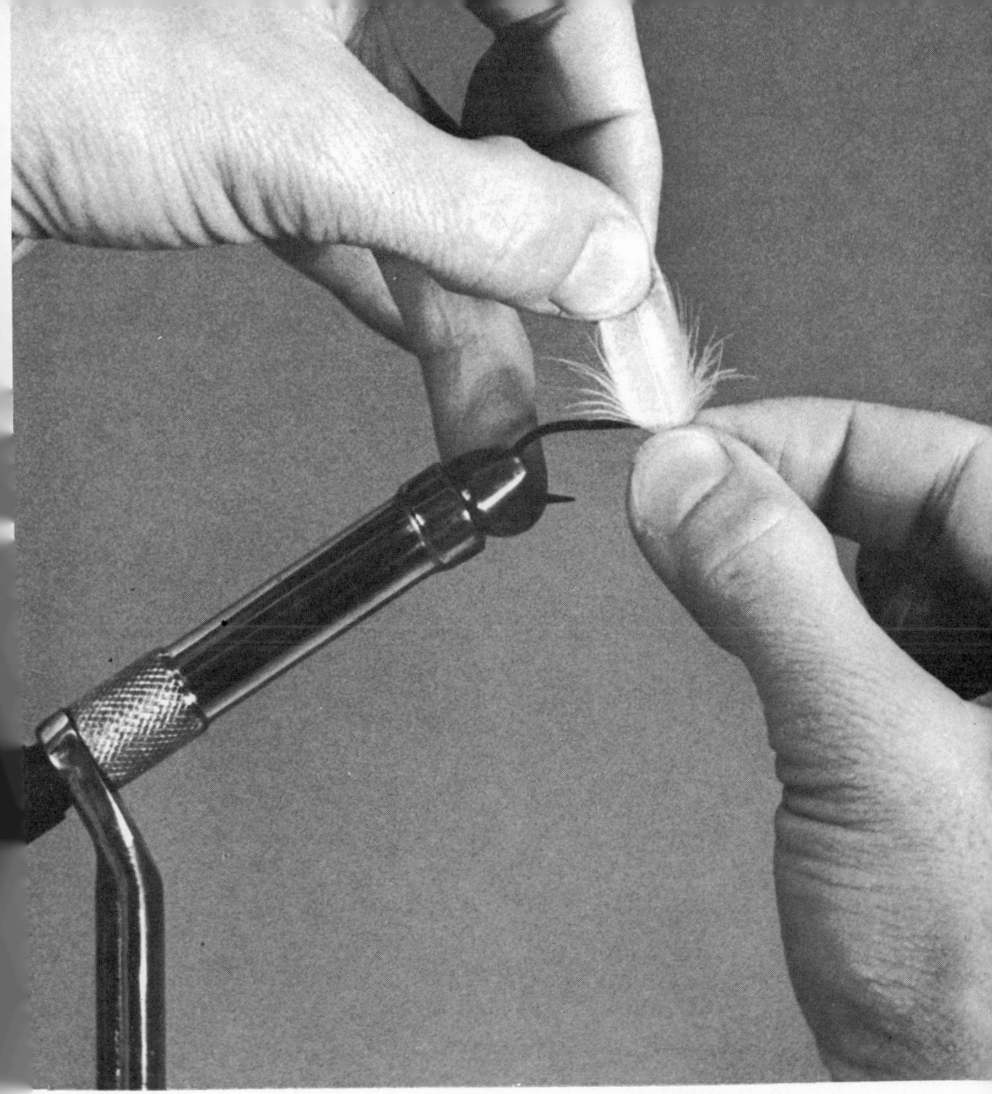

32b. Hold them snugly together, curving away from each other, and measure them against the hook for length.

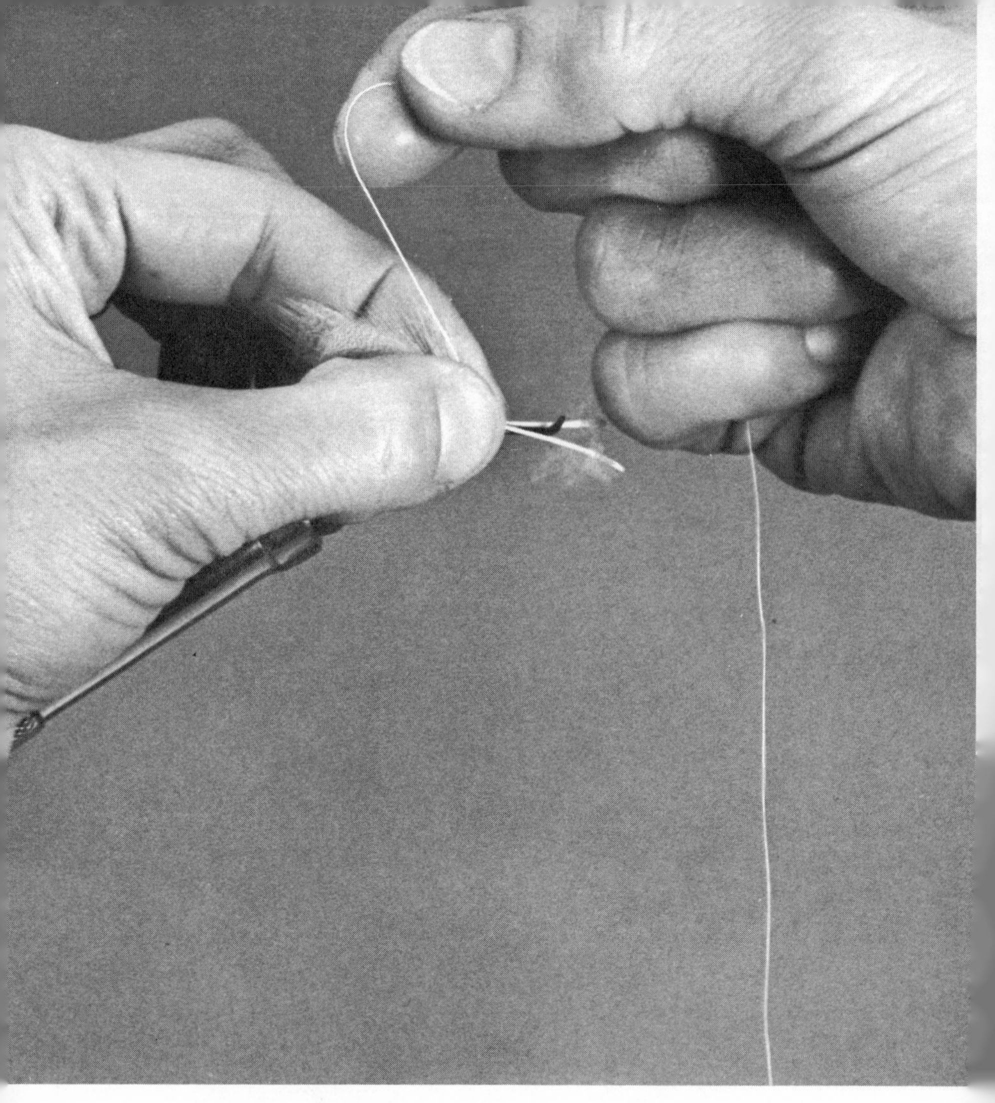

32c. Hold the feathers so that the side of the quill stems will be parallel with the hook shank, on top of the hook at "wing position." Bind them there with three turns of thread. Hold them firmly and bind them tightly so that the quills will not turn.

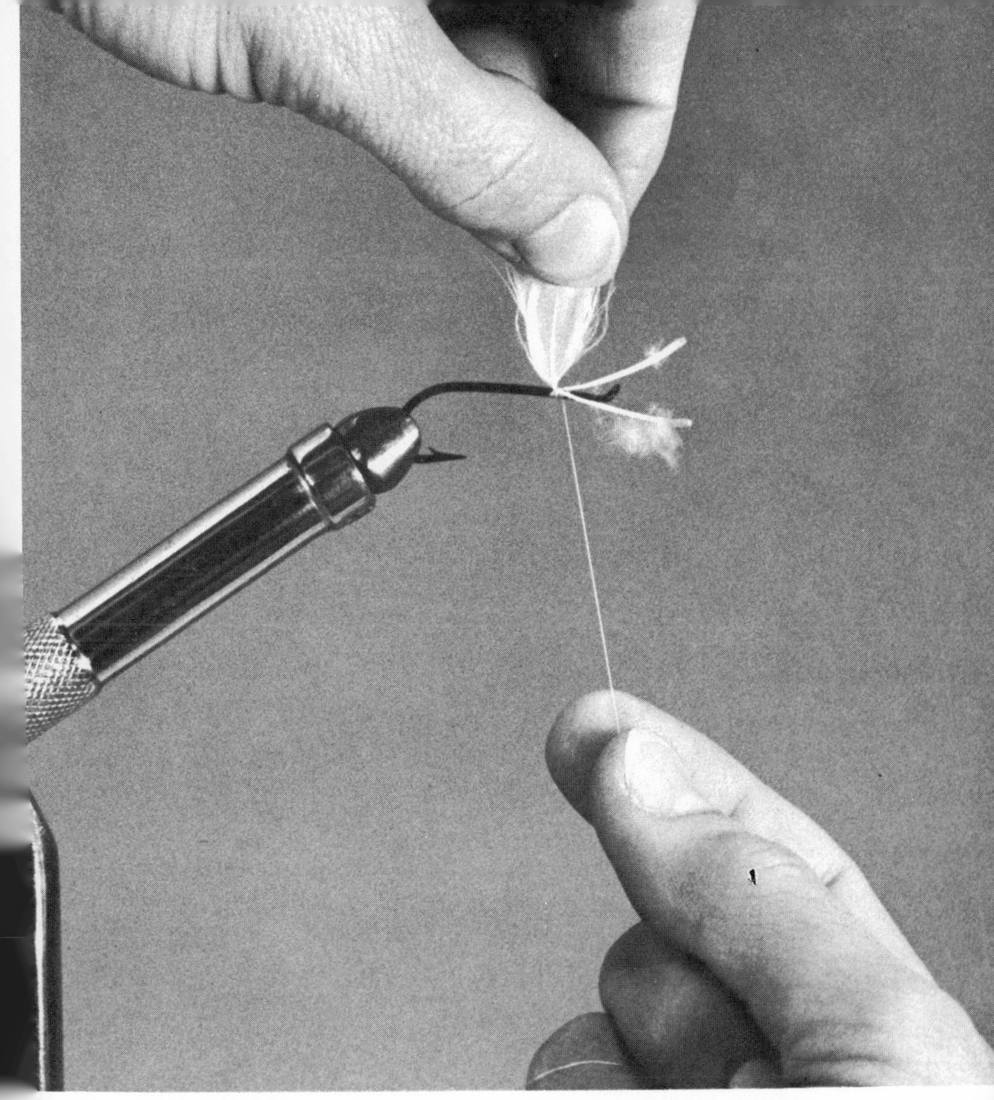

32d. Do not release your grip on the feathers. Raise them together and hold them forward.

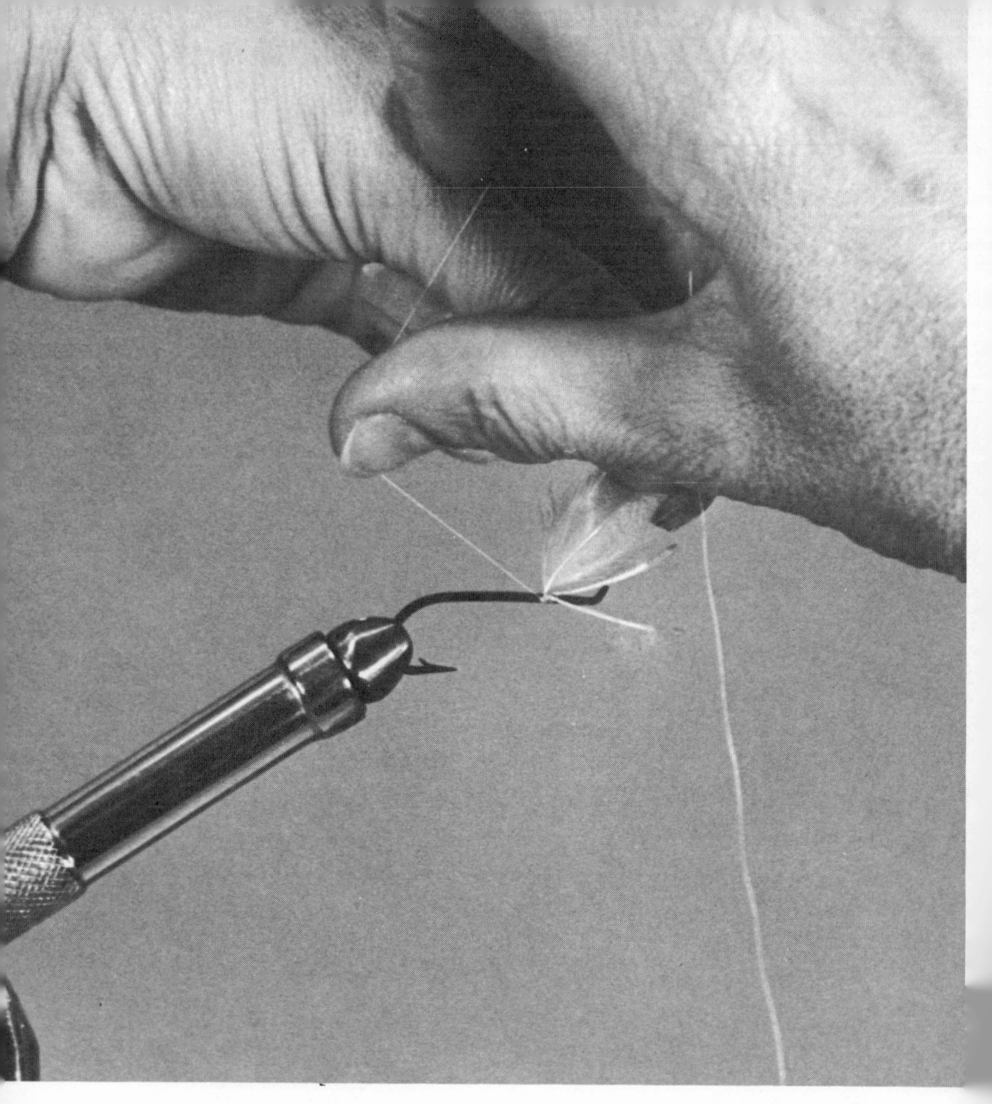

32e. Place a turn of thread behind the quills, carry it forward on the far side of the hook, and bring it toward you above the hook, ahead of the wings. Release the feathers as necessary to permit the hands to pass. Do this twice, binding the feathers together just above the hook.

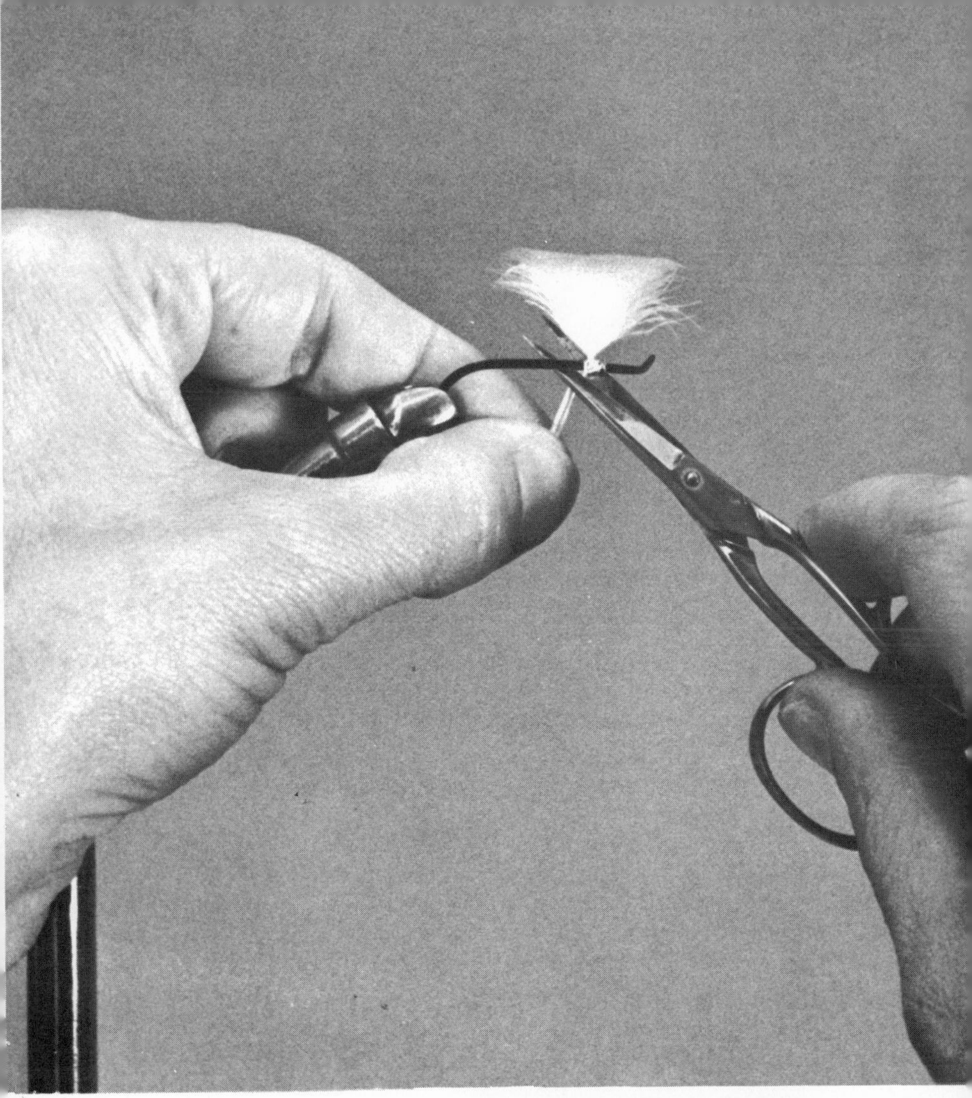

32f. Draw the quills back and bind them to the hook as you did with the hackle streamer wing. Cut off quills close to the hook and bind them down with one more turn of thread. Secure the thread at the button.

Viewed from directly in front of the hook eye, the wings should arch evenly, at the same height. The stems should be at right angles to the hook shank.

33a. On a simple dry fly, the last material to be applied to the hook is the hackle. Select one with a limber stem and stiff barbs of even length.

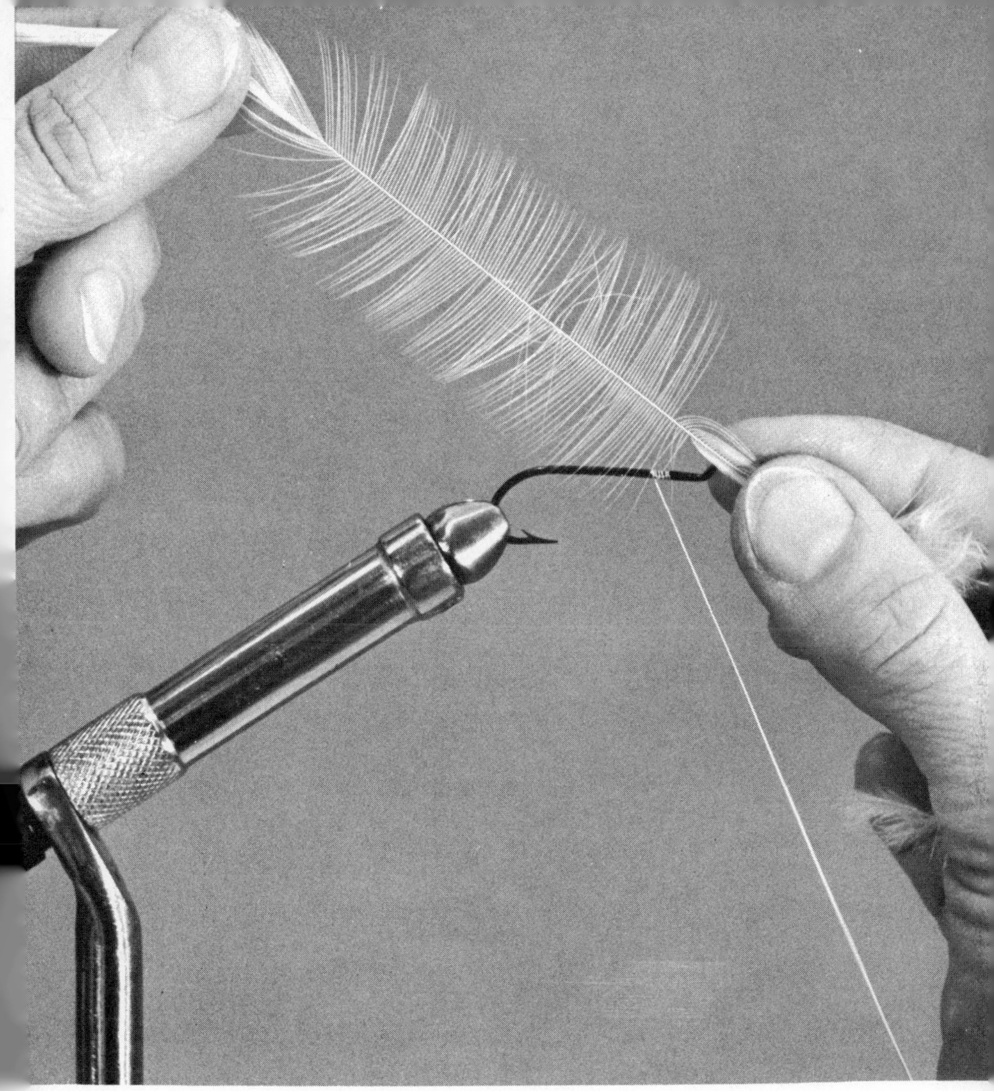

33b. The length of the barbs should be about 1½ times the gape of the hook. And, of course, the longer the hackle itself, the better.

33c. Strip the feather stem below the place where the hackle barbs begin to show too much web. Clip the stem ½ inch below the barbs. A dry-fly hackle, regardless of color, should be applied to the hook with the dull side turned toward the hook eye, so that the natural curve of the feather, however slight, will be against the current when the fly is being fished. It should stand at a right angle to the hook.

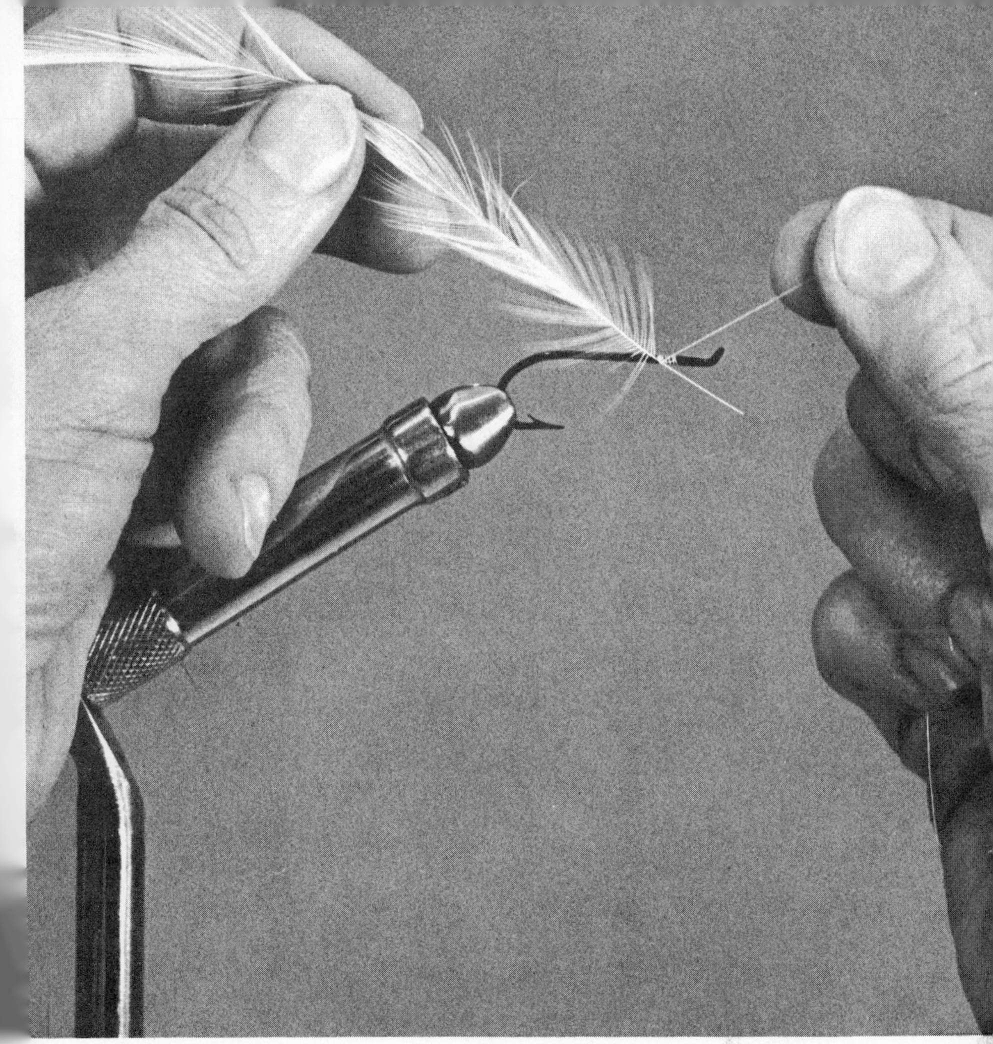

33d. Hold the hackle, dull side toward you, against the hook and bind the stem to the hook at "wing position" with two or three turns of thread in a close spiral toward the hook eye. Secure the thread to the button and clip off excess quill.

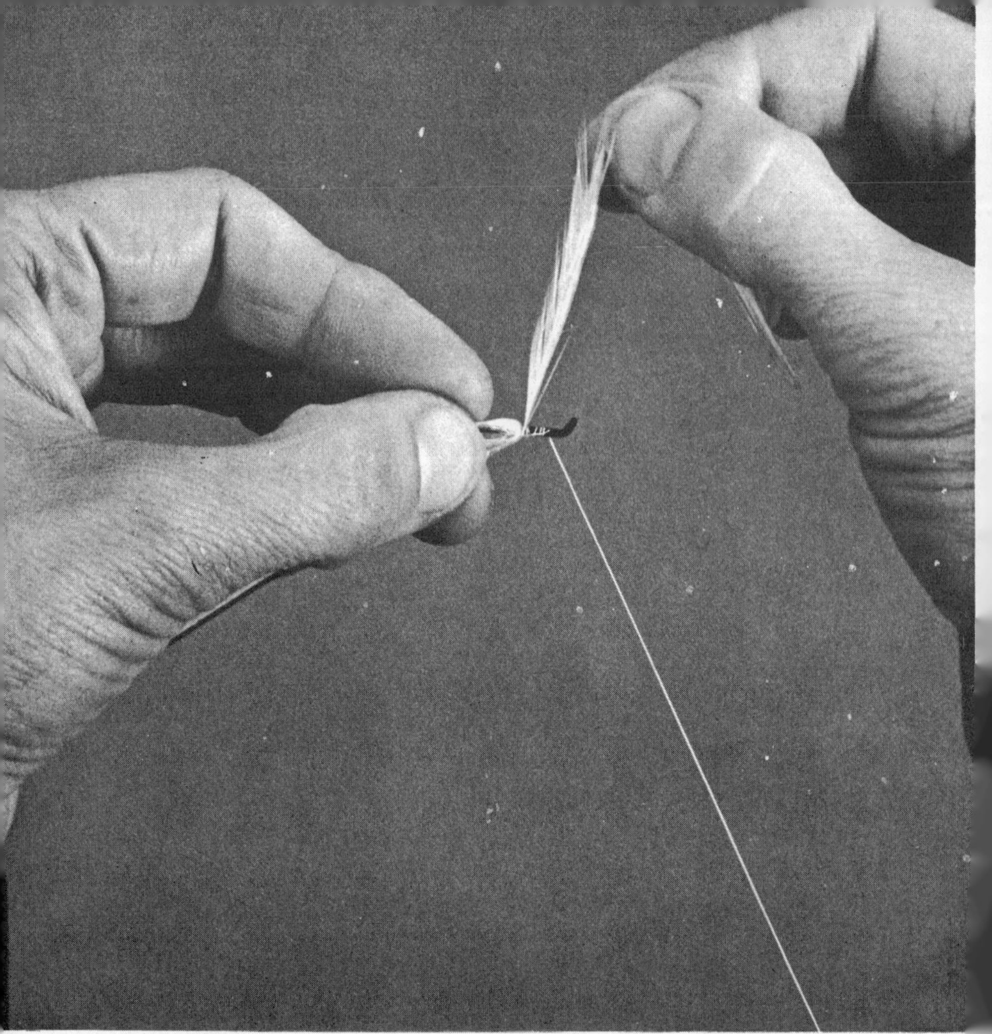

33e. As you begin to wind the hackle, edge on, to the hook, hold the barbs out of the way with the left hand. Wind the hackle in a very close spiral, each turn in front of the preceding one, keeping the dull side toward the hook eye. The barbs will radiate around the hook.

33f. As the hackle is wound on, a space equal to the length of the hook eye must be left for the fly head. To tie the hackle off, extend the third and fourth fingers of the left hand and grasp the hackle tip. Hold it forward over the hook eye and bring the thread up and across the hackle stem twice, as close to the standing hackle as possible. Catch the thread to the button. Clip the ıd of the hackle close to the ıread. Keep the thread taut!

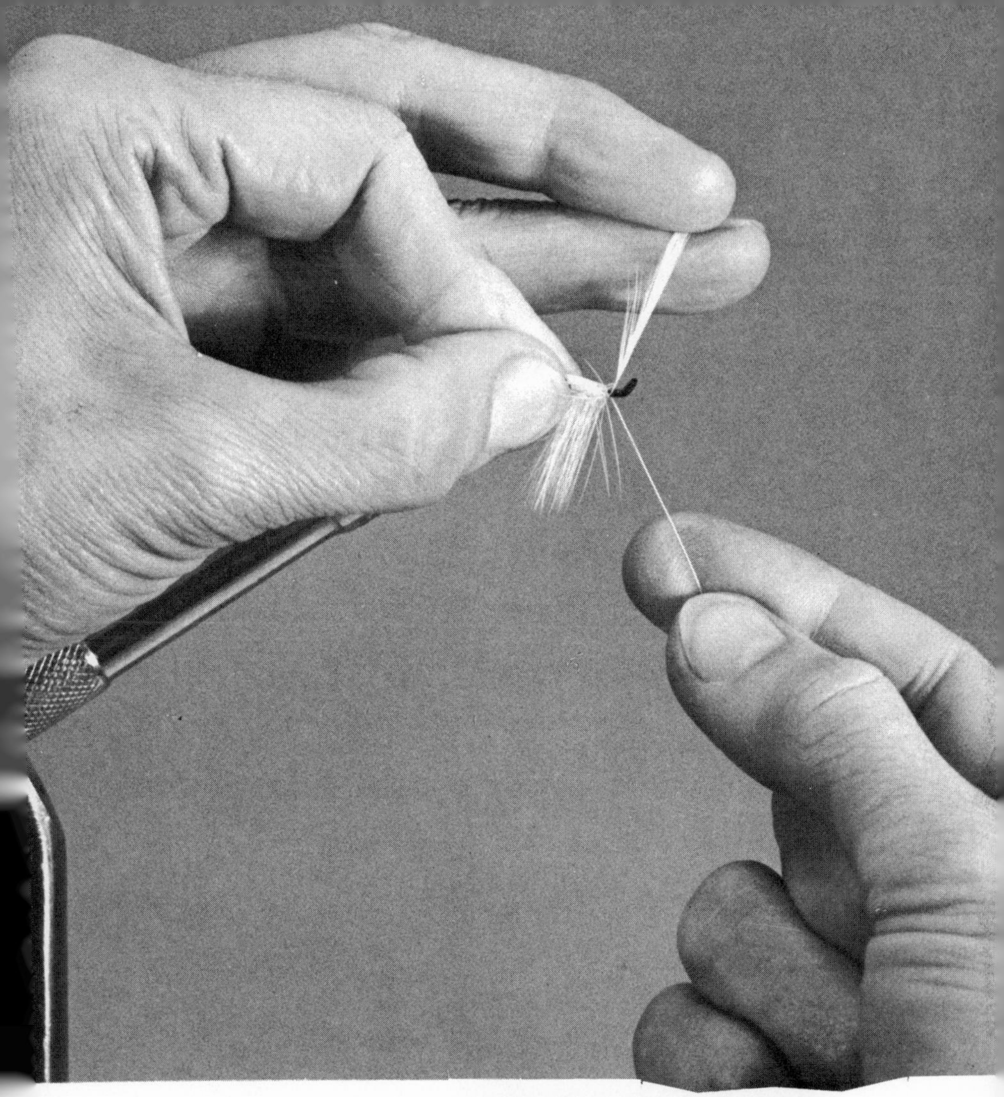

Make a wrap knot of five turns thread, binding the end of the em snugly to the hook, completely vering it and any previous turns thread. The head will be wid- t against the hackle, tapering to single turn of thread at the base the hook eye.

34a. When hackles are short, use more than one, all carefully matched. Tie on the first and wind it as far as it will go.

34b. Tie the second hackle in, tightly against the base of the first with three close turns of thread, and then spiral the thread toward the hook eye. Clip off the extending quill. Wind the first turn of the second hackle *through* the forward face of the standing hackle, with a scalloping or zig-zag motion of the winding hand, so that the two hackles intermingle without binding down any standing barbs. Then wind each turn of hackle closely in front of the preceding one, meanwhile holding the hackle ruff back out of the way.

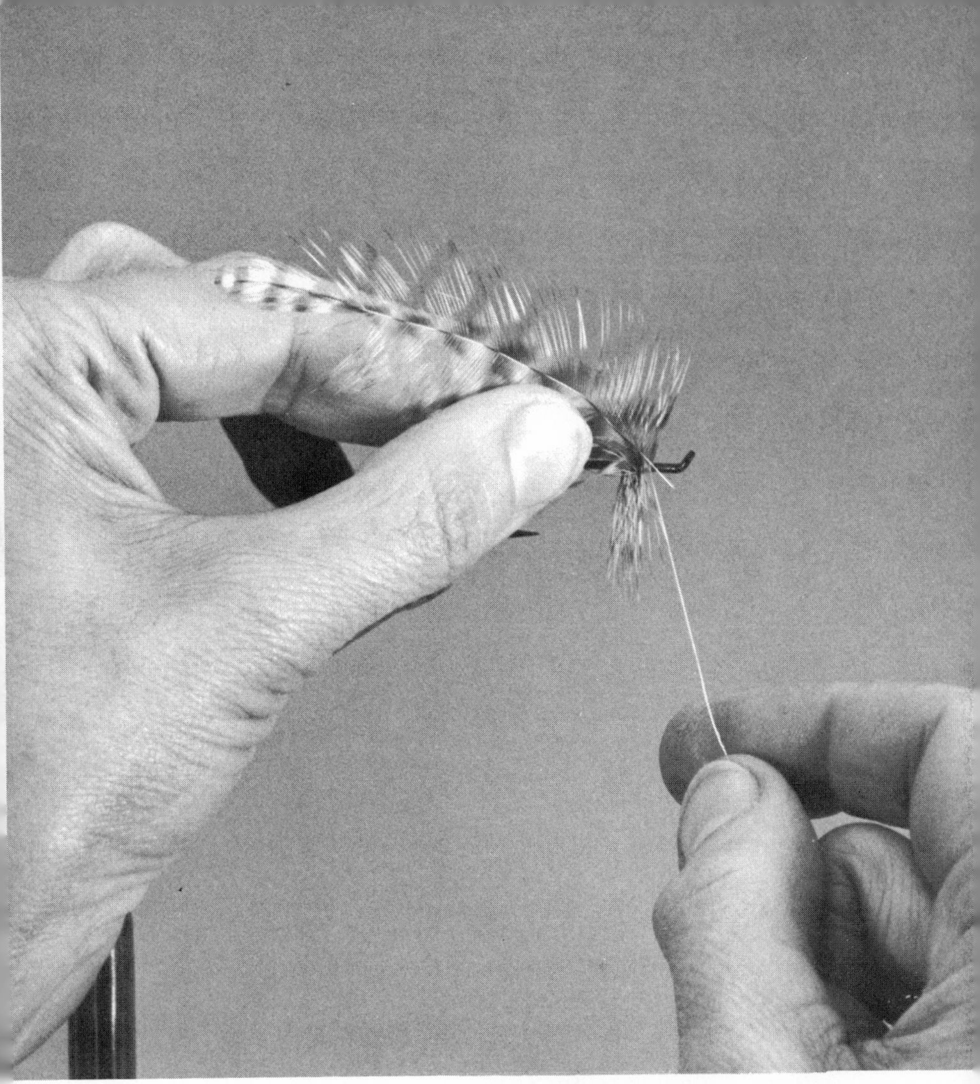

Add a third hackle if necessary. When space for only a head remains, tie off the hackle, clip away excess, and bind down with two turns of thread. Tie the wrap knot, forming the tapered head. Practice applying two hackles so they appear as one. Never wind two at once; the tension on each will be unequal and some barbs will be bound down unnecessarily.

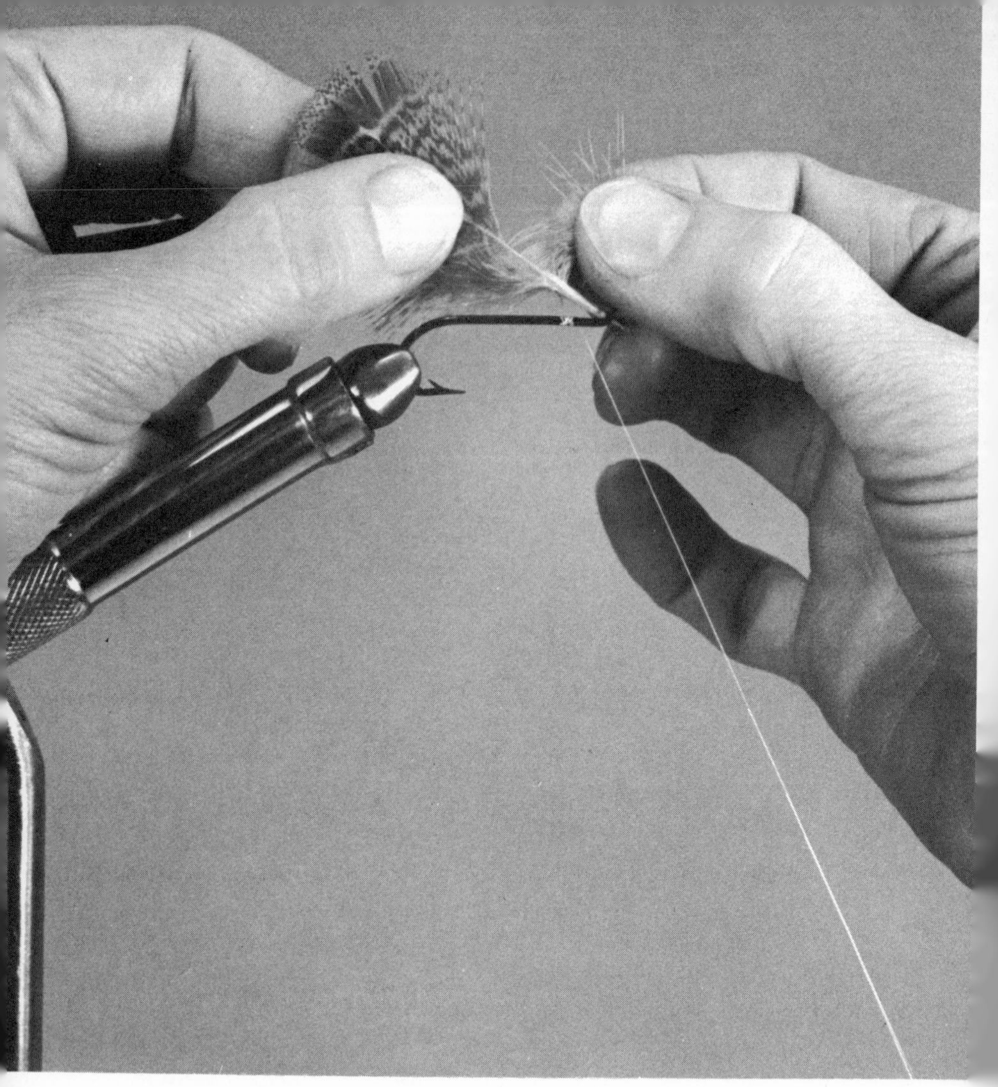

35a. The wet fly hackle may be of grouse, partridge, guinea fowl, or any soft, webby hackle. If no wing is used, the hackle may be slightly longer than for a dry fly of the same size. Remove the fuzz at the base of stem and clip off the thick end. A wet-fly hackle is applied to the hook with the dull side toward the *bend* of the hook. The natural curve of the flues will be backward, around the body of the fly, giving no resistance to water currents when the fly is being fished.

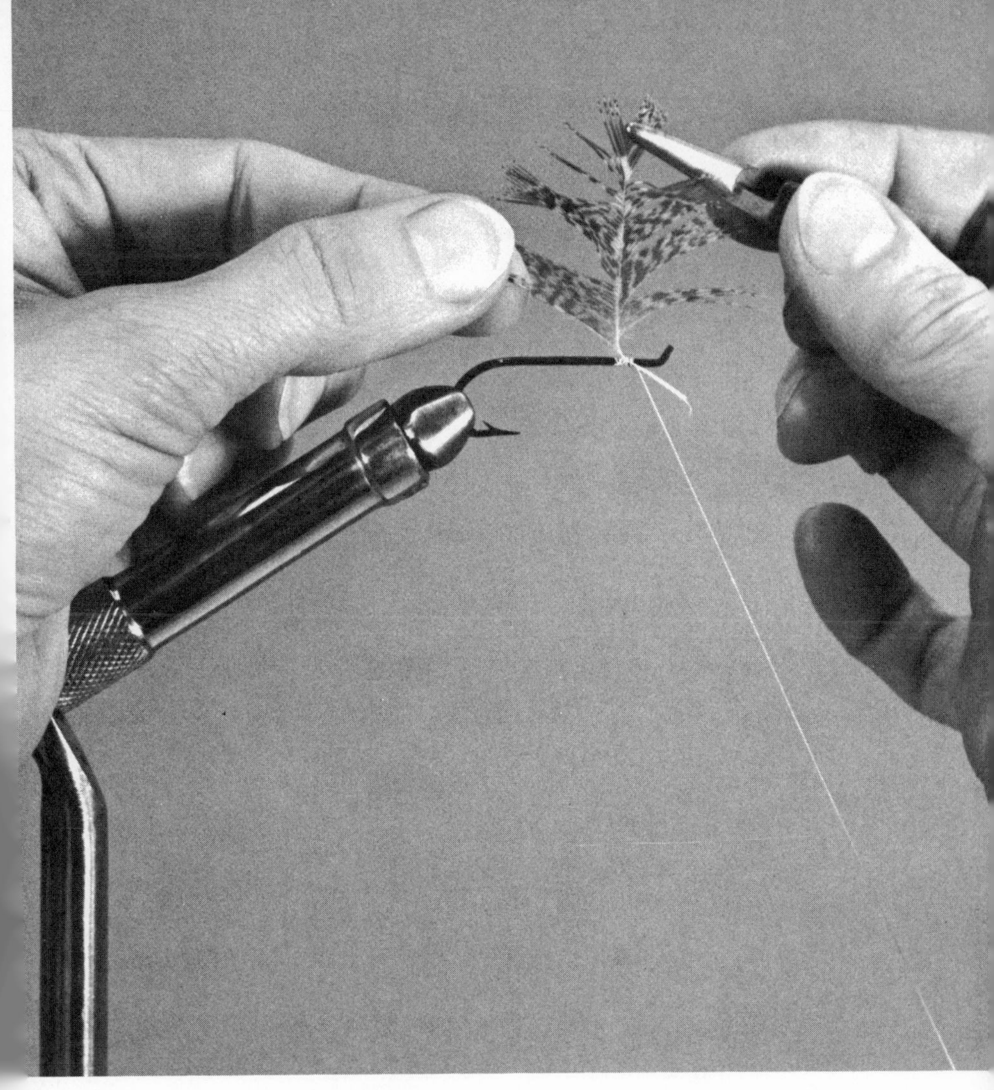

35b. Wind the hackle "edge on" to the hook. If the feather is too short for a comfortable fingerhold, grip the tip of it with a pair of hackle pliers.

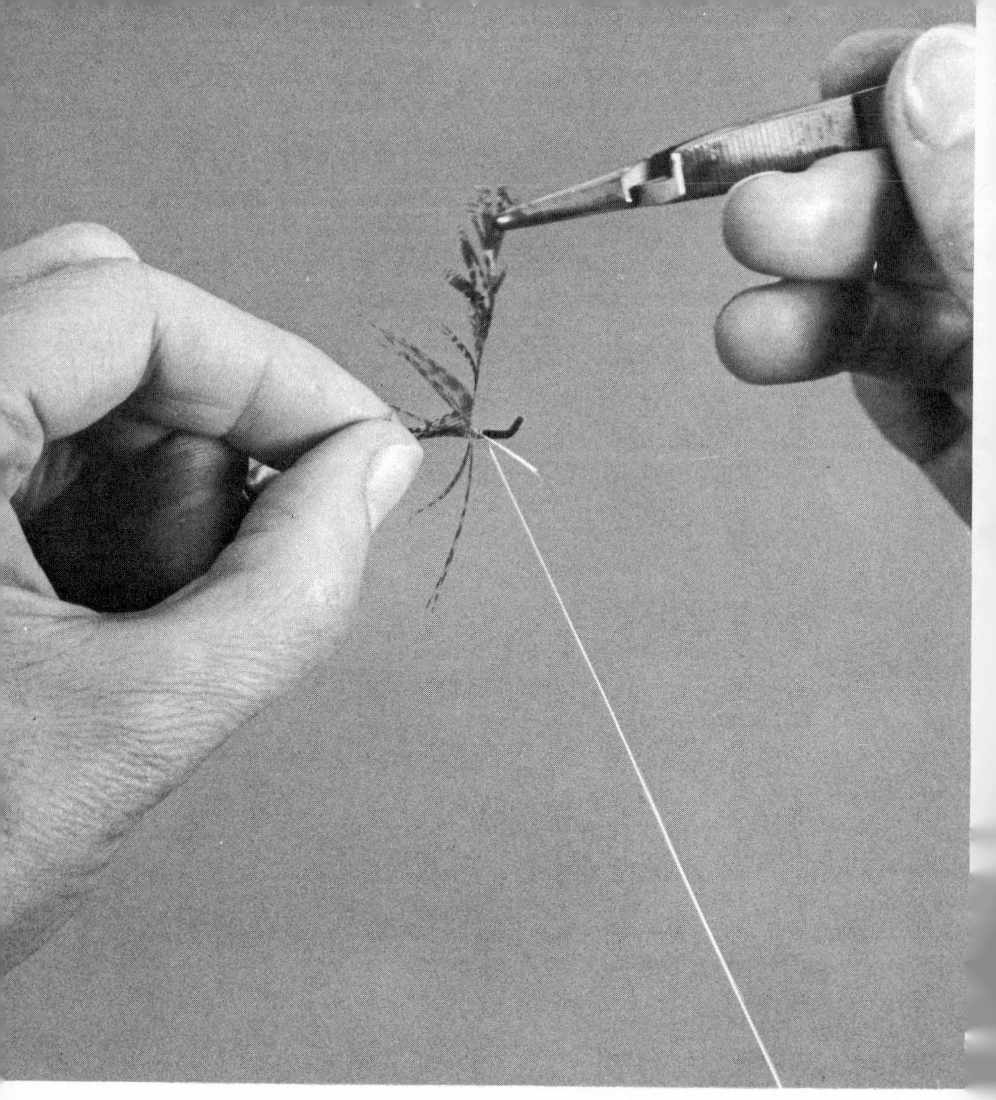

35c. Wind it onto the hook, holding the feather barbs out of your way so that each successive turn of hackle can be placed immediately in front of the preceding one.

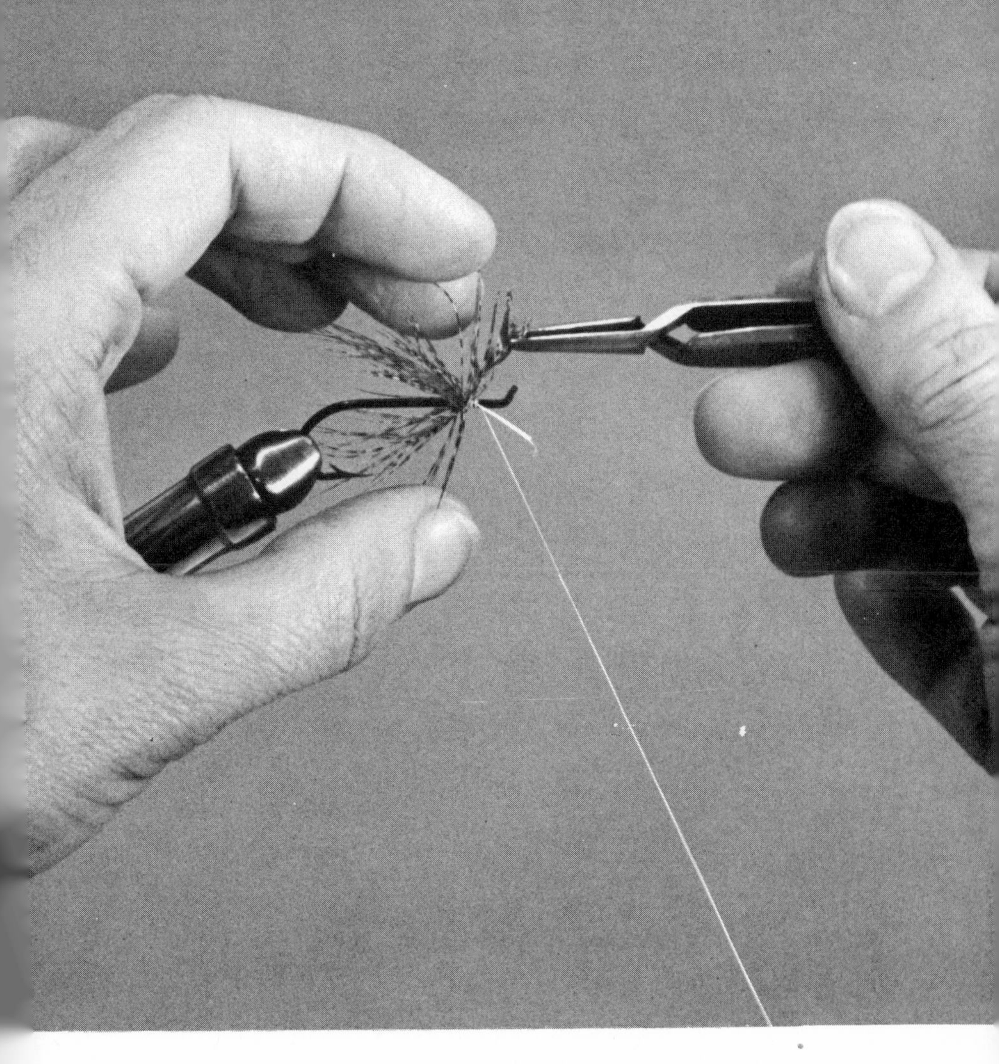

35d. Continue to wind the hackle until the last turn will not go completely around the hook.

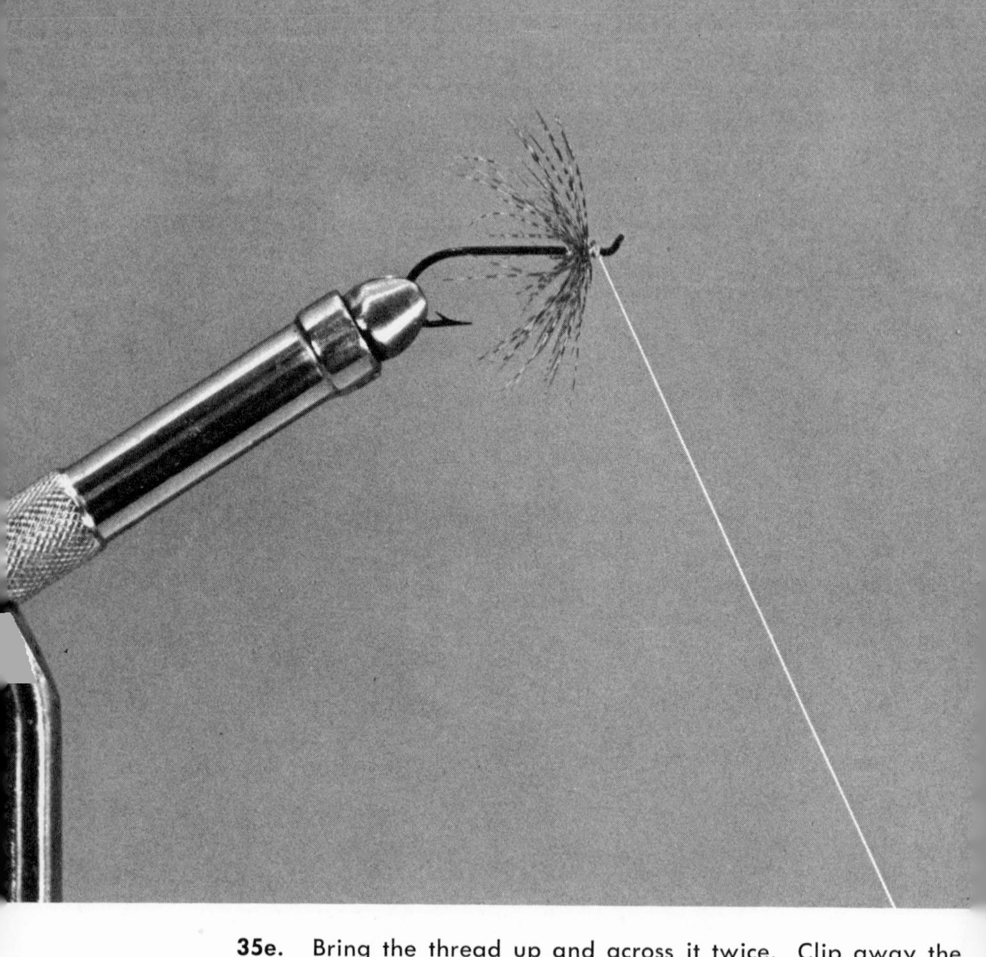

35e. Bring the thread up and across it twice. Clip away the end of the quill and the remaining end of the feather. If it is very small, bind it down to the hook without clipping.

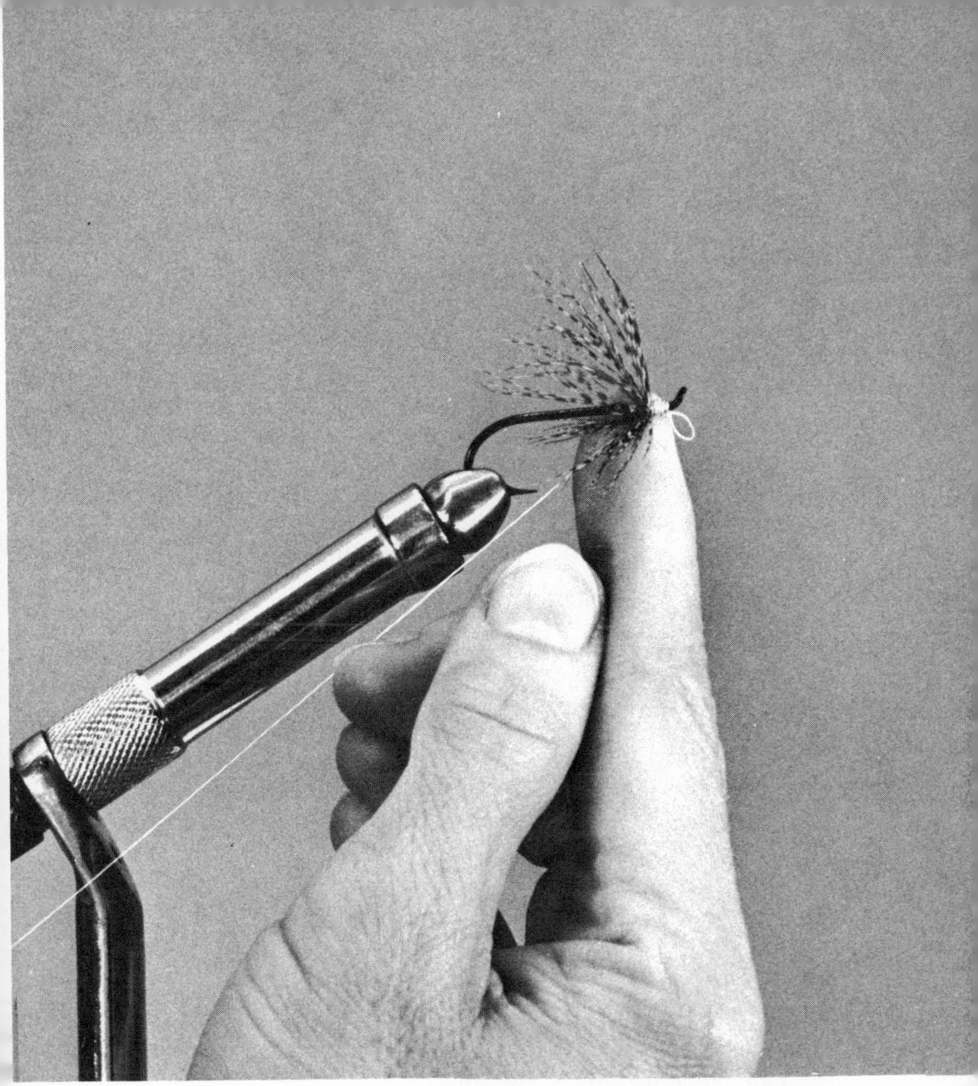

35f. Tie a wrap knot over the binding thread between the hackle and the hook eye, covering it entirely.

Remember that a well-formed head is tapered, cone shaped, and slightly heavier at the hackle base than behind the hook eye. Clip off the tying thread. Hold the hackles out of the way and carefully cover the fly head with a drop of fly lacquer.

OUTLINE TO AID IN SELECTING FEATHERS FOR A SPECIFIC USE

HACKLES

Source 1. Gamecock or rooster neck or saddle feathers

DRY FLY: Main stem must be limber, with glossy, fairly stiff flues of even length with little or no web along stem.

Use as *hackles* and as palmer rib.

Use as *wings*—short hackles or hackle tips for spent or upright wings.

Use as *bodies*—entire body hackled to size as in palmer or bi-visible; or entire body hackled and clipped to desired diameter for caterpillar.

Use as *tails*—short-hackle tips paired; or flues stripped from hackle.

WET FLY: Main stem must be limber, flues soft with web along stem.

Use as *hackles* and as palmer rib.

Use as *wings*—streamer wings of whole feather, flues may taper from short at tip to long at base with center heavily webbed. Hackle points tied flat on back of wet fly.

Use as *tails*—flues stripped from hackle; or short-hackle tips.

Source 2. Guinea fowl, grouse, partridge, etc., breast feathers

Use as wet-fly hackles.

Use on dry flies—sparsely in front of regular dry-fly hackle.

WINGS

Source 1. Duck, goose, or turkey wing feathers, paired

Use in strips as wet- or dry-fly wings.

Source 2. Duck breast feathers, matched

Use whole for dry-fly fan wings.

Source 3. Teal, wood duck, and mandarin duck flank feathers and brown mallard shoulder feathers

Use as bunched feather wings on dry flies.

Use in strips as feather wings on wet flies.

Use in strips with other feathers such as goose, turkey, and duck wing feathers for wet-fly wings.

Source 4. Maribou feathers, paired

Use whole for wet streamer-fly wings.

Use in strands with other feather or hair wings for wet streamer-fly wings.

Source 5. Peacock sword feathers, paired

Use in bunched strands for wet-fly wings, in strands combined with

OUTLINE TO AID IN SELECTING FEATHERS FOR A SPECIFIC USE
(Continued)

other streamer wings; occasionally a strand added decoratively to a dry-fly feather wing.

ource 6. Hackles: see "Dry Fly" and "Wet Fly" under "Hackles"

TAILS

ource 1. Pheasant tail feathers (Golden Pheasant, Lady Amherst, etc.) (Paired, unless using the center feather which has evenly matched flues on both left and right.)
Use in strips as tails for wet or dry flies.

ource 2. Goose, duck, or turkey wing feathers, paired
Use in strips for wet or dry flies.

ɔurce 3. Teal, mallard, wood duck, guinea, etc., flank feathers
Use in strips or bunched flues for wet or dry flies.

ɔurce 4. Hackles: see "Dry Fly" and "Wet Fly" under "Hackles"

BODIES

ɔurce 1. Peacock, eyed tail feathers
Use as herl bodies on wet or dry flies.
Use stripped as quill bodies on wet or dry flies.

urce 2. Ostrich herl
Use as bodies on wet or dry flies.
Use as ribbing or butt joints on wet or dry flies.

urce 3. Duck, goose, and turkey wing feathers
Use in strips for nymph cases, legs, feelers, etc.

urce 4. Hackles: see "Dry Fly" under "Hackles"

Purchase feathers only from reliable dealers whose importing and selling is done with a definite understanding that all feathers from wild birds are sold on condition that they will be used for fishing tackle purposes only.

Notes on the Finished Fly

Now that you have mastered the basic steps in the constructio of a fly—by tying each of the various parts in turn—all that remain in order to make a complete fly is to combine these parts. This ca be done in several ways, depending on whether your fly is to be we or dry.

When a fly is tied completely from beginning to end, no knot interrupt the continuous fly-tying thread until the head is reache and the wrap knot forms the head and finishes the fly.

An exception to the foregoing is the trimmed-hair-body fly wher the wrap knot is vital to secure the body while it is out of the vis being trimmed. With flies of this type, several bodies can be tied trimmed at one time and then all of the wings can be added afte the trimming is done. This procedure will enable the tyer t develop uniform bodies and wings more easily than if he were t finish each individual fly completely from start to finish. He ca set up his own production line, as it were.

Remember that each material as it is added must hide the tyin thread already on the hook and/or the cut ends of any material use before it. Thus, the stub of a tail is covered by the body materia the cut end of the body material is hidden by the wing, and th tapered ends of the wing material may be covered by the hackle o by the tying thread that forms the fly head. The thread formin the head is in turn covered by lacquer, and several coats of this wi hide the individual turns of thread completely, making a durabl fly with a professional, finished appearance.

Probably the most difficult part of fly-tying for a novice is in lea ing enough room for the head of the fly. However, if practice-tyin is done faithfully and the tying thread is carefully attached to th hook at the areas designated as "tail position" or "wing position" i the preceding photographs (proportionately the same on any hook he should have ample room for a neat and uncrowded head.

The simplest fly to make is the tailless and wingless wet fly, consisting only of a body and a hackle. Even this very simple fly can be done in different ways. Made with a dubbing body and a wet-fly hackle, in very small sizes this type of fly is a nymph. An excellent wet fly can be made with a peacock body and a wet-fly hackle, or by adding a grouse or partridge hackle to a wool body.

Ordinarily, the amount of hackle on a wet fly should be fairly sparse, since the fly is intended to sink quickly and a great deal of material, even on an extra-heavy hook, would tend to keep it from doing so; whereas a dry-fly hackle may be quite full to aid in keeping the fly afloat. There is no hard and fast rule for the exact amount of hackle to be used on a dry fly except the preference of the person who is going to fish with it. I like a moderately full hackle on a dry fly.

The hackle of the dry fly usually covers the base of whatever wing material is used. With the single hair wing, the fan wing, or the divided feather wing, the hackle should be distributed fairly equally behind and ahead of the wing. Tie in the hackle behind the wing and wind it forward until the wing is reached. Wind it as close as possible behind the wing, and then begin winding it in front of, and as close as possible to, the wing. Finish it as you did in 33f.

A wet-fly hackle to be used with a wing is tied on after the body is completed and may then be divided on top of the hook and drawn down equally on both sides of the hook until it is all beneath the hook, then bound there with two diagonal turns of thread. A wet-fly wing, whether of hackle or hair (as for a streamer wing) or of goose, turkey, or other similar feathers (as for a regular wet-fly wing), is usually tied on over the hackle. If the hackle is omitted entirely, it is *placed so that the tying is done on the forward edge of "wing position," the trimmed base of it extending into the area immediately behind the hook eye and forming a foundation for the fly head.* Trimming the waste end of the wet-fly wing should be done carefully, and it is important that the tapered end be kept small to prevent crowding it against the hook eye. The wrap knot is made over this tapered base and covers it entirely. The head of a wet fly is beautiful when properly made and covered with several coats of head varnish.

To the trimmed-hair body, add a pair of divided hair wings (18h), but hold the wings back as you set the direction of the wings with the tying thread. This hair body may be made over the hair tail (15j) and the divided wings, lying back, added after the body has been trimmed. Coat the head with lacquer until the threads are not visible.

To the dubbing body, add a grouse partridge hackle or a soft neck hack Finish in the usual way. Or, add pair of spent wings (27b) and a d fly hackle (33f).

To the plain tinsel body, add a pair of maribou wings (31b), and over the stub of the maribou quill, wind on a strand of peacock herl (21g). Finish with a wrap-knot head and cover the head with a drop of lacquer, holding the herl back out of the way.

To the plain wool body add a grouse or partridge hackle (35b-f). Finish with the wrap-knot head and varnish it. Do the same with a floss body.

To the tinsel body with oval-tinsel rib, tie on a small amount of white bucktail hair as for the streamer-type wing (16f), tying in forward of "wing position." Over it tie a few more strands of brown bucktail of the same length. Trim the ends of hair into a small, neat taper. Cover them with the wrap-knot head and lacquer it.

To the peacock-herl body, add a single hair wing (17-d) of Asiatic goat and a dry-fly hackle. Finish it with a wrap-knot head carefully lacquered, holding the hackle back and out of the way.